THE
SPECTRUM OF
CONSCIOUSNESS

THE
SPECTRUM OF
CONSCIOUSNESS

by

KEN WILBER

A QUEST BOOK

*This publication made possible
with the assistance of the Kern Foundation*

THE THEOSOPHICAL PUBLISHING HOUSE
Wheaton, Ill., U.S.A.
Madras, India / London, England

ISBN: 0-8356-0493-4
Library of Congress Catalog Number 76-39690
Printed in the United States of America

It is with warmth and love
that I dedicate
THE SPECTRUM OF CONSCIOUSNESS
to John W. White

CONTENTS

DIAGRAMS AND TABLES

ACKNOWLEDGEMENTS

I wish to extend my appreciation to the authors and publishers whose works are quoted in this book and for which usage of such excerpts they have graciously granted me their permission.

Ken Wilber

Hutchinson Publishing Group Ltd, 3 Fitzroy Square, London, publisher of *The Zen Doctrine of No-Mind* by D. T. Suzuki; *Essays in Zen Buddhism* by D. T. Suzuki; and *The Collected Works of Ramana Maharshi,* ed. Arthur Osborne.

Harper and Row, publishers and J. Krishnamurti, author, of *The First and Last Freedom,* Quest edition, Theosophical Publishing House, Wheaton, 1954.

Geoffrey W. Bonsall, Director, Hong Kong University Press for *Open Secret* and *All Else Is Bondage.*

Works of Erwin Schroedinger published by Cambridge University Press—*What Is Life?* (1967); *Mind and Matter* (1967); and *My View of The World* (1964).

Pantheon Books, Division of Random House, Inc. publisher of the English language edition of *The Supreme Doctrine* by Dr. H. Benoit, (c) 1955.

B. L. Whorf's *Language, Thought and Reality,* 1965, Massachusetts Institute of Technology Press.

Gestalt Therapy Verbatim by F. Perls, Real People Press, 1969.

Harper and Row, Publishers, Inc. from *Zen Buddhism and Psychoanalysis,* 1960, Dr. Erich Fromm; and *The Practice of Zen,* by Garma C. C. Chang, 1959.

R. D. Laing's *The Politics of Experience,* Penguin Books, Ltd., 17 Grosvenor Gardens, London, 1967; Ballantine, N.Y., 1967.

The Zen Teaching of Huang Po by J. Blofeld, published by Grove Press, Inc., N.Y. 1966.

The Central Philosophy of Buddhism, Murti, George Allen and Unwin, Ltd, London.

Routeledge & Kegan Paul Ltd, London, for D. T. Suzuki's *Studies in the Lankavatara Sutra* (c) 1968; *Tractatus Logico Philosophicus,* by L. Wittgenstein, (c) 1961; and to Humanities Press for their edition of the latter.

The Collected Works of C. G. Jung, ed. Herbert Read, Michael Fordham, Gerhard Adler, William McGuire, trans. R.F.C. Hull Bollingen, Series XX, Vol. 8, *The Structure and Dynamics of the Psyche,* 2nd ed. (c) 1969 by Princeton University Press, N.J.

Journal of Transpersonal Psychology, 1975, No. 2, an article "The Psychologia Perennis" by Ken Wilber.

Coward, McCann & Geoghegan, Inc. for the rights to adapt two illustrations from *Depression and The Body,* by Alexander Lowen, M.D., (c) 1972.

Hinduism and Buddhism, A. K. Coomaraswamy, Philosophical Library, Inc, (c) 1943.

PREFACE

"There is no science of the soul without a metaphysical basis to it and without spiritual remedies at its disposal." One might say that the entire aim of this volume is simply to support and document this statement of Frithjof Schuon, a statement that the siddhas, sages and masters of everywhere and everywhen have eloquently embodied. For by-and-large our own present-day science of the soul has been reduced to nothing more significant than the response of rats in learning mazes, the individual *Oedipal* complex, or root-level *ego* development, a reduction that has not only blinded our vision to the depths of the soul, but has also helped to devastate our own traditional spiritual understandings and bring them into a monotonous conformity with a uni-dimensional view of man. The Above has been denied; the Below has been ignored—and we are asked to remain—in the middle—paralyzed. Waiting, perhaps, to see what a rat would do in the same circumstances or, at a bit deeper level, looking for inspiration in the dregs of the *id*.

But, odd as it may sound, I have no quarrel with the particular state of our science of the soul, but only with the monopolization of the soul by that state. The thesis of this volume is, bluntly, that consciousness is pluridimensional, or apparently composed of many levels; that each major school of psychology, psychotherapy, and religion is addressing a different level; that these different schools are therefore not contradictory but complementary, each approach being more-or-less correct and valid when addressing its own level. In this fashion, a true synthesis of the major approaches to consciousness can be effected—a synthesis, not an eclecticism, that values *equally* the insights of Freud, Jung, Maslow, May, Berne, and other prominent psychologists, as well as the great spiritual sages from Buddha to Krishnamurti. This places, as Schoun would have us realize, the *roots* of psychology in the fertile soil of metaphysic but without in any way harming its branches. In the following pages the reader will, I trust, find room for the *ego,* the *super-ego,* and the *id,* but also for the total organism, and for the transpersonal self, and finally for cosmic consciousness—source and support of them all.

I wrote this book in the winter of 1973, at about the time I was finishing graduate studies. Needless to say, in the interim many important and pertinent books and articles have been published, and my own thoughts on spectrum psychology have progressed considerably. I have, therefore, made brief entries in the text,

11

included a fairly detailed Table in Chapter 10, and updated the bibliography to cover some òf these recent advances.

In the three-year interim period between the writing and publication of this volume, it was my good fortune to run into a host of people willing to give time, labor, and moral support to my theretofore solitary efforts. Foremost among these were Jim Fadiman and John White, both of whom I approached with the manuscript in December of 1973. To Jim Fadiman I owe a deeply felt appreciation for his bottomless source of enthusiasm, as well as his constant efforts to find the right publisher for SPECTRUM. As for John White, the man is one massive Heart. Without his persistence, his tireless and always enthusiastic efforts on my behalf, this volume would never have been published. It is with warmth and love that I dedicate THE SPECTRUM OF CONSCIOUSNESS to John, one who has *Heart of Fugen*.

To Don Berquist, Vince LaCoco, and Lou Gilbert—a special thanks for special favors. To Geri Gilbert, a fond acknowledgment to one who followed my thoughts and, for a long time, about the only one who understood them. Thanks also to my parents, Ken and Lucy, for helping in so many ways, and most of all for managing to mute their disbelief in my chosen topic, a magnificent and not to be belittled accomplishment for two people who thought for years that Buddhism was as irritating as a skin rash and an effrontery to their beliefs but are now considering taking up Transcendental Meditation. To Huston Smith, a deep *gassho* for a very helpful and gracious letter. To my wife, Amy, nothing but my love.

To Rosemarie Stewart and Clarence Pedersen of the Theosophical Publishing House, I owe so much. Not only were they kind and generous with their support and encouragement, but they bent over backwards to accommodate my wishes and ideas in the final product. I owe them much and will never forget their efforts.

Obviously, any book that purports to be a "synthesis of psychotherapies East and West" must fail miserably in living up to the claim. I can only say that what follows is but the briefest outline, the barest skeleton, of this incredible spectrum we call consciousness. Shall but some branches of our science of the soul hereby discover again an access to the Above, or an opening to the Below, this work will fulfill its purpose.

K. W.

Lincoln, Nebraska
September, 1976

PART ONE   EVOLUTION

Thus we cannot escape the fact that the world we know is constructed in order to see itself. But in order to do so, evidently it must first cut itself up into at least one state which sees, and at least one other state which is seen.

G. Spencer Brown

Consciousness is in its original nature, quiet, pure, and above the dualism of subject and object. But here appears the principle of particularization, and with the rise of this wind of action, the waves are agitated over the tranquil surface of Mind. It is now differentiated or evolves into eight levels.

D. T. Suzuki

There is thus an incessant multiplication of the inexhaustible One and unification of the indefinitely Many. Such are the beginnings and endings of worlds and of individual beings: expanded from a point without position or dimensions and a now without date or duration.

Ananda K. Coomaraswamy

I. *PROLOGUE*

Willam James, in an oft-quoted remark, has stated that

> Our normal waking consciousness is but one special type of consciousness, while all about it parted from it by the filmiest of screens there lie potential forms of consciousness entirely different. We may go through life without suspecting their existence, but apply the requisite stimulus and at a touch they are there in all their completeness. . . .
>
> No account of the universe in its totality can be final which leaves these other forms of consciousness quite disregarded. How to regard them is the question. . . . At any rate, they forbid our premature closing of accounts with reality.

This volume is an attempt to provide a framework for just such an account of the universe. Now this framework is, above all else, a synthesis of what are generally but nebulously referred to as "Eastern" and "Western" approaches to the understanding of consciousness; and due to the extraordinarily vast and complex nature of both of these approaches, this synthesis is—in at least some aspects—deliberately simplistic. An analogy from physics might prove helpful in explaining this approach.

Our environment is saturated with numerous kinds of radiation—besides the common visible light of various colors, there exist X-rays, gamma rays, infrared heat, ultraviolet light, radio waves, and cosmic rays. Except for that of visible light, the existence of these radiation waves was unknown until around 200 years ago, when William Herschel began the exploration of radiation by demonstrating the existence of "thermal radiation" — now called infrared — using for instruments nothing more than thermometers with blackened bulbs placed in various bands of a solar spectrum. Shortly after Herschel's discovery, Ritter and Wollaston, using photographic instruments, detected ultraviolet radiation, and by the end of the 19th century, the existence of X-rays, gamma rays, and radio waves had been experimentally proven using a variety of techniques and instruments.

All of these radiations are superficially quite different from one another. X-rays and gamma rays, for instance, have very short wavelengths and consequently are very powerful, capable of lethally damaging biological tissues; visible light, on the other hand, has a much longer wavelength, is less powerful, and thus rarely harms living tissue. From this point of view, they are indeed dissimilar. As another example, cosmic rays have a wavelength of less than a millionth of a millionth of an inch, while some radio waves have wavelengths of over a mile! Certainly, at first glance, these phenomena all seem to be radically different.

Oddly enough, however, all of these radiations are now viewed as different forms of an essentially characteristic electromagnetic wave, for all of these apparently different rays share a large set of common properties. In a vacuum they all travel at the speed of light; they are all composed of electric and magnetic vectors which are perpendicular to each other; they are all quantized as photons, and so on. Because these different forms of electromagnetic radiation — on this "simplistic" level — are fundamentally so similar, they are today commonly viewed as composing a single spectrum. That is, X-rays, visible light, radio waves, infrared, and ultraviolet are simply described as being different bands of one spectrum, in the same way that the different color bands of a rainbow form one visible spectrum. So what were once thought to be quite separate events are now seen as variations of one basic phenomenon, and the early scientists — because they were using different instruments — were simply "plugging in" at various different frequencies or vibratory levels of the spectrum, unaware of the fact that they were all studying the same basic process.

Electromagnetic radiation, therefore, consists of a spectrum of energy waves of various wavelengths, frequencies, and energies, ranging from the "finest" and the "most penetrating" cosmic rays to the "densest" and least energetic radio waves. Now compare this with Lama Govinda's description of a Tibetan Buddhistic view of consciousness. Speaking of consciousness as being composed of several shades, bands, or levels, Govinda states that these levels "are not separate layers . . . but rather in the nature of mutually penetrating forms of energy, from the finest 'all-radiating,' all-pervading, luminous consciousness down to the densest form of 'materialized consciousness,' which appears before us as our visible, physical body."[1] Consciousness, in other words, is here described very much like the electromagnetic spectrum, and several Western investigators — taking their cue from just such descriptions — have in fact suggested it might prove fruitful to view consciousness as a spectrum.

If, for the moment, we do consider consciousness as a spectrum, then we might expect that the different investigators of consciousness, especially those commonly termed "Eastern" and "Western", because they are using different instruments of language, methodology, and logic, would "plug in" at different bands or vibratory levels of the spectrum of consciousness, just as the early radiation scientists plugged in at different bands of the electromagnetic spectrum. We might also expect that the "Eastern" and

"Western" investigators of consciousness would not suspect that they were all plugging in at various bands or levels of the very same spectrum, and consequently communication between investigators might be particularly difficult and occasionally hostile. Each investigator would be correct when speaking about his own level, and thus all other investigators—plugged in at different levels—would appear to be completely wrong. The controversy would not be cleared up by having all investigators agree with each other, but rather by realizing that all were talking about one spectrum seen from different levels. It would almost be like M. Curie arguing with William Herschel about the nature of radiation if each didn't understand that radiation is a spectrum. Curie, working only with gamma rays, would claim radiation affects photographic plates, is extremely powerful, and can prove lethal to organisms, while William Herschel, working only with infrared, would claim nothing of the kind! And of course, they would both be right, because each is working with a different band of the spectrum, and when they realized that, the argument would cease, and the phenomenon of radiation would then be understood through a synthesis of all of the information gained on each level, which is exactly the way physicists view it today.

Our expectation that if consciousness is a spectrum, then communication between Eastern and Western investigators would be difficult because each is working on a different vibratory level, is exactly what is happening today. Although there are numerous important exceptions, the general consensus of the Western scientific community is that the "Eastern" mind is regressive, primitive, or at best, just plain feeble, while the Eastern philosopher is apt to reply that Western scientific materialism represents the grossest form of illusion, ignorance, and spiritual deprivation. For example, Franz Alexander, representing a breed of Western investigation called psychoanalysis, states, "The obvious similarities between schizophrenic regressions and the practices of Yoga and Zen merely indicate that the general trend in Oriental cultures is to withdraw into the self from an overbearingly difficult physical and social reality."[2] D. T. Suzuki, representing the Eastern approach, as if to reply, states, "Scientific knowledge of the Self is not real knowledge. . . . Self-knowledge is possible only . . . when scientific studies come to an end, [and the scientists] lay down all their gadgets of experimentation, and confess that they cannot continue their researches any further. . . ."[3]

To continue the analogy, arguments like this abound because each explorer is speaking about and from a different band of the spectrum of consciousness, and should this be realized, the ground of these arguments would evaporate—for an argument can be legitimately sustained only if the participants are speaking about the same level. Argumentation would—for the most part—be replaced with something akin to Bohr's principle of complementarity. Information from and about the different vibratory levels of bands of consciousness—although being superficially as different as X-rays and radio waves—would be integrated and synthesized into one spectrum, one rainbow. That each approach, each level, each band is but one among several other bands should in no way compromise the integrity or the value of the individual levels or of the research done on these levels. On the contrary, each band or level, being a particular manifestation of the spectrum, is what it is only by virtue of the other bands. The color blue is no less beautiful because it exists along side the other colors of a rainbow, and "blueness" itself depends upon the existence of the other colors, for if there were no color but blue, we would never be able to see it. In this type of synthesis, no approach, be it Eastern or Western, has anything to lose—rather, they all gain a universal context.

Throughout this book, whenever consciousness is referred to as a spectrum, or as being composed of numerous bands or vibratory levels, the meaning remains strictly metaphorical. Consciousness is not, properly speaking, a spectrum—but it is useful, for purposes of communication and investigation, to treat it as one. We are creating, in other words, a *model*, in the scientific sense of the word, much like the Michaelis-Menton model of enzyme kinetics, the eight-fold way model of the atomic nucleus, or the model of visual excitation based on the photoisomerization of rhodopsin. To complete this introductory discussion of the spectrum of consciousness, there remains only a brief identification of the basic levels of consciousness that will be treated in this synthesis.

Out of an infinite number of possible levels made available to us through the revelations of psychoanalysis, Yogacara Buddhism, Jungian analysis, Vedanta Hindusism, Gestalt therapy, Vajrayana, Psychosynthesis, and the like, three major bands (and four minor ones to be described later) have been selected on the basis of their simplicity and their ease of identification. These three levels we call: 1) the Ego Level, 2) the Existential Level, and 3) the Level of Mind. (The minor bands being the Transpersonal, the Biosocial, the Philosophic, and the Shadow Levels). The nature of this synthesis will start to become clearer if we realize that numerous investigators of consciousness have studied some of these levels from slightly different viewpoints, and one of our tasks is thus to distill and coordinate their conclusions. For example, Dr. Hubert Benoit refers to these three major levels, respectively, as the level of objectal consciousness, the level of subjectal consciousness, and the level of Absolute Principle. Wei Wu Wei calls them the levels of object, of pseudo-subject, and of Absolute Subject. Yogacara Buddhism has the *mano-vijnana*, the *manas*, and the *alaya*. These levels have also been approached by such other renowned explorers as William James, D. T. Suzuki, Stanislav Grof, Roland Fischer, Carl Jung, Gurdjieff, Shankara, Assagioli, John Lilly, Edward Carpenter, Bucke—to name but a handful. Also of special interest to us is the fact that several psychologists have (albeit unwittingly) confined their investigations to one major level, and their conclusions are of immense importance in clarifying and characterizing each individual level. Foremost among these are the schools of psychoanalysis, existential psychology, Gestalt therapy, behaviorism, rational therapy, social psychology, and transactional analysis.

In other words, what will begin to emerge from our study of the Spectrum of Consciousness is not only a synthesis of Eastern and Western approaches to psychology and psychotherapy, *but also a synthesis and integration of the various major Western approaches to psychology and psychotherapy*. Now at this point, without going into any of the details and "giving the show away", let us only say that the various different schools of Western psychology, such as Freudian, existential, and Jungian, are also by-and-large addressing themselves to various different levels of the Spectrum of Consciousness, so that they, too, can be integrated into a truly encompassing "spectrum psychology". Indeed, the principal reason there exist in the West four or five major but different schools of psychology and psychotherapy is, I contend, that each school has zeroed-in on one major band or level of the Spectrum. It is not, let us say, four different schools forming four different theories about one level of consciousness, but four different schools each predominantly addressing a different level of the Spectrum (e.g., the Shadow, the Ego, the Biosocial, and the Existential Levels). These different schools therefore stand in a complementary relationship to one another, and not, as is generally assumed, in an antagonistic or contradictory one. This, I trust, will become amply apparent as this study proceeds.

Let it be rigorously stated that this synthesis in no way attempts to settle disputes that are now occurring on the same levels, as for instance, if on the Ego Level I have a phobic anxiety of speaking in public, should I go to a psychoanalyst or a behaviorist? Only with time and further experimentation will we be able to delineate the various merits of each approach. This synthesis does, however, attempt to answer a question such as, "I feel generally unhappy about life—should I pursue psychotherapy or Mahayana Buddhism?" with the answer, "You are perfectly free to pursue both, for these approaches refer to different levels, and thus are not fundamentally in conflict."

Now the Ego Level is that band of consciousness that comprises our role, our picture of ourself, our self-image, with both its conscious and unconscious aspects, as well as the analytical and discriminatory nature of the intellect, of our "mind." The second major level, the Existential Level, involves our total organism, our soma as well as our psyche, and thus comprises our basic sense of existence, of being, along with our cultural premises that in many ways mold this basic sensation of existence. Among other things, the Existential Level forms the sensory referent of our self-image: it's what you *feel* when you mentally evoke the *symbol* of your self-image. It forms, in short, the persistent and irreducible source of a separate I-awareness. The third basic level, here called Mind, is commonly termed mystical consciousness, and it entails the sensation that you are fundamentally one with the universe. *So where the Ego Level includes the mind, and the Existential Level includes both the mind and the body, the Level of Mind includes the mind and the body and the rest of the universe*. This sensation of being one with the universe is much more common than one might initially suspect, for—in a certain sense that we will try to explain—it is the very foundation of all other sensations. Briefly, then, the Ego Level is what you feel when you feel yourself to be a father, a mother, a lawyer, a businessman, an American, or any other particular role or image. The Existential Level is what you feel "beneath" your self-image; that is, it is that sensation of total organismic existence, the inner conviction that you exist as the separate subject of all your experiences. The Level of Mind is—as we shall try to demonstrate—exactly what you are feeling right now before you feel anything else—a sensation of being one with the cosmos.

The Ego Level and the Existential Level together constitute our general feeling of being a self-existent and separate individual, and it is to these levels that most Western approaches have addressed themselves. Eastern disciplines, on the other hand, are generally more concerned with the Level of Mind, and thus tend to completely by-pass the levels of egocentricity. In short, Western psychotherapies aim at "patching up" the individual self while Eastern approaches aim at transcending the self.

So while we find ourselves at the Ego Level or the Existential Level, let us avail ourselves of the existing methods—largely "Western"—of creating healthy egos, of integrating projections, of coming to grips with unconscious drives and wishes, of structurally re-aligning our bodily postures, of accepting responsibility for our being-in-the-world, of dealing with neuroses, of living us to our full potentials as individuals. But should we seek to go beyond the confines of the individual self, to find an even richer and fuller level of consciousness, then let us learn from those investigators—largely "Eastern"—of the Level of Mind, of mystical awareness, of cosmic consciousness.

It is certainly obvious that Eastern and Western approaches to consciousness can be used separately, for that is exactly what is happening today; but it should now be clear that they can also be used in a complementary fashion. Many advocates of only the Eastern approaches are apt to scoff at all attempts to create healthy egos, maintaining that the ego is itself the very source of all suffering in the world, and thus a "healthy" ego is at best a contradiction, at worst, a cruel joke. From their level of consciousness, they are right, and—in that context—we totally agree with their pronouncements. But let us not be hasty—even the Hindu views life as a cycle of involution and evolution of the Absolute Self, and concedes that many of us will, in all likelihood, live out this life as *jivatman*, as an isolated (albeit illusory) ego confronting an alien universe. It is precisely in these cases that Western psychotherapies can offer at least a partial release from the suffering entailed in being a *jivatman*, and there is no reason they shouldn't be employed in these situation. Imagine, for instance, a middle-aged businessman, generally happy with his life, father of two children, and successful in his profession, coming to a therapist and complaining of minor symptoms of anxiety and pressure. Should all therapists, following the lead of Eastern teachers, start replying to this type of problem with suggestions like, "My dear Sir, you suffer from basic metaphysical anxiety because you don't realize that you are fundamentally one with God," then patients everywhere would be bolting from psychologists' offices in anxious search of "good doctors." By far the majority of people, especially in Western society, are not ready, or willing, or capable of pursuing mystical experience, nor should they be pushed into this venture. Something like simple counseling aimed at integrating projections on the Ego Level will suffice in many such cases. Thus the Western approaches of ego psychology are perfectly legitimate on these levels.

Should the *jivatman*, however, seek liberation (that is, seek an understanding of the Level of Mind), then Western approaches can be used either as a preliminary preparation or as a concomitant aid, for any methods that help promote a state of relaxation and reduced tension are conducive to mystical experience. To form a very general conclusion, then, we can state that for those pursuing an Eastern approach to the Level of Mind, the Western means of normalizing the Ego Level and the Existential Level can prove immensely helpful, because reducing the tensions inherent in being an ego seems to make it easier to transcend. It is in this spirit, for example, that the late Zen Master Suzuki, of the San Francisco Zen Center, used to sponsor seminars in sensory awareness; and Kent and Nicholls, of the Canadian Institute of Being, are using group encounter and psychoanalysis as aids in reaching mystical awareness.

In the last half century there have appeared numerous books and articles dealing with the various merits of Eastern and Western approaches to consciousness, but with few exceptions, the authors of these works are partisans of one or the other approach, and—despite the enormous contributions of some of these writers—they invariably end up, either subtly or blatantly, denouncing the other approach as inferior, off the mark, or just plain ludicrous. We have suggested that this problem—of deciding which approach is "best"—is a false problem, for each approach is working with a different level of consciousness. Another way of demonstrating this is to point out that Eastern and Western approaches—in practice if not in theory—don't even desire the same goals, and thus to insist on having them compete with one another is to insist on running a race with each contestant given a completely different finish line.

The avowed aim of most Western approaches is variously stated as strengthening the ego, integrating the self, correcting one's self-image, building self confidence, the establishing of realistic goals, and so on. They do not promise a complete release from all of life's sufferings, nor a total annihilation of disturbing symptoms. Instead they offer, and to some extent deliver, a lessening of the "normal neuroses" that are part and parcel of being an ego.

It is true that to some degree the aims of the Eastern and Western approaches coincide, because the bands of any spectrum always overlap the other bands to some extent; but the central aim of most Eastern approaches is not to strengthen the ego but to completely and totally transcend it, to attain *moksha* (liberation), *te* (virtue of the Absolute), *satori* (enlightenment). These approaches claim to tap a level of consciousness that offers total freedom and complete release from the root cause of all suffering, that puts to rest our most puzzling questions about the nature of Reality, and that ends our restless and anxious searchings for an abode of peace. The goals of Eastern and Western approaches are thus startlingly different, but then this shouldn't surprise us: the aims are different because the levels are different.

Having said this much about the nature of the aims of Eastern approaches, many Westerners become either squeamish or condescending, for they have pre-judged all Eastern disciplines as so much mushy-minded rot, lying somewhere between dimly-conscious lunacy and advanced forms of schizophrenia. These Westerners are situated on the Ego Level and view any deviations from it with the utmost suspicion instead of open interest, and many are even viewed as authorities on the nature of the entire realm of consciousness. But surely the only sound, the only believable, the only scientifically reliable authorities are those conscientious explorers who have experienced all the various levels of consciousness, including both that of being an ego and that of transcending the ego. If we seek their advice on the nature of Mind, of mystical awareness, of ego transcendence, their opinions are impressively universal and unanimous; transcending the ego is not a mental aberration or a psychotic hallucination but rather an infinitely richer, more natural, and more satisfying state or level of consciousness than the ego could imagine in its wildest flights of fantasy.

We thus have two options open to us in judging the sanity, or the reality, or the desirability of the Level of Mind, of mystical awareness—we can believe those who have themselves experienced it, or we can endeavor to experience it ourselves, but if we can do neither of these it would be wise to withhold judgement.

Besides, these Eastern disciplines such as Vedanta or Zen are not theories, philosophies, psychologies, or religions—rather, they are primarily *a set of experiments* in the strictly scientific sense of that term. They comprise a series of rules or injunctions which, if carried out properly, will result in the discovery of the Level of Mind. To refuse to examine the results of such scientific experiments because one dislikes the data so obtained is in itself a most unscientific gesture. In the words of Ananda Coomaraswamy:

> It would be unscientific to say that such attainments are impossible, unless one has made experiment in accordance with the prescribed and perfectly intelligible disciplines. . . . That this is so [i.e., that Mind exists, or that mystical awareness is possible] cannot be demonstrated in the classroom, where only quantitative tangibles are dealt with. At the same time, it would be unscientific to deny a presupposition *for which an experimental proof is possible*. In the present case there is a Way [i.e., an experiment] prescribed for those who will consent to follow it. . . . [4]

Just what this Way is, we shall presently see. The point here worth remembering is that when we speak of Mind or the Absolute or mystical awareness, we are not speaking from a purely speculative point of view. Rather, we are simply setting forth experimentally obtained data, and the scientist who guffaws such results, without himself having performed the experiment, is only a dilettante, a scientist in the narrowest and most impoverished sense.

This, of course, in no way invalidates the contributions made by investigators confined to one level, and who have perhaps never heard of the Level of Mind, let alone tried to reach it, for their insights about their own level are of inestimable value. This does suggest, however, that a researcher, aware of only one level and hence denying reality to all other levels, is rather like the tail denying the existence of the dog.

"The whole drift of my education," says Williams James, "goes to persuade me that the world of our present consciousness is only one out of many worlds of consciousness that exist, and that those other worlds must contain experiences which have a meaning for our life also; and that although in the main their experiences and those of this world keep discrete, yet the two become continuous at certain points, and higher energies filter in. By being faithful in my poor measure to this over-belief, I seem to myself to keep more sane and true. I *can*, of course, put myself into the sectarian scientist's attitude, and imagine vividly that the world of sensations and of scientific laws and objects may be all. But whenever I do this, I hear that inward monitor . . . whispering the word 'Bosh!' Humbug is humbug, even though it bear the scientific name, and the total expression of human experience, as I view it objectively, invincibly urges me beyond the narrow 'scientific' bounds."[5]

Shankara, the renowned expounder of Advaita Vedanta (the Hindu approach to the Level of Mind, distilled and systematized from the *Upanishads*, the *Brahma-sutras*, and the *Bhagavad Gita*), created the notion of *subration*, a notion that will be of considerable value in continuing this line of thought. Paraphrasing Eliot Deutsch, subration is the mental process whereby one re-evaluates some previously appraised level of consciousness because of its being cancelled, or at least set in a different context, by the experience of a new level of consciousness.[6] Generally speaking, anyone who experiences the Level of Mind subrates the Ego Level and the Existential Level. That is, he becomes profoundly convinced—often for reasons he cannot fully explain or even articulate—that the Level of Mind is in some way more real, more basic, and more meaningful than the others. So totally and invincibly convincing is this experience, that he may now feel that the other levels of consciousness (such as the Ego and Existential Levels) are completely unreal, illusory, and dream-like. Take, for example, the well-known passage from Tennyson's *Memoirs*:

> A kind of waking trance I have frequently had, quite up from my boyhood, when I have been all alone. This has generally come upon me through repeating my own name two or three times to myself silently, til all at once, as it were out of the

intensity of the consciousness of individuality, the individuality itself seemed to dissolve and fade away into boundless
being; and this is not a confused state, but the clearest of the
clearest, the surest of the surest, the weirdest of the weirdest,
utterly beyond words, where death was an almost laughable
impossibility, the loss of personality (if so it were) seeming no
extinction, but the only true life.[7]

If we are to explore this level, then we have no choice—for reasons
already explained—but to give these types of statements and the
experiences to which they refer due consideration. In the words of
biophysicist Dr. John Lilly:

> In a scientific exploration of any of the inner realities, I follow
> the following metaprogrammatic steps [among which is, upon
> finding a new level of consciousness]: construct a model that
> includes [the old] reality and the new one in a more inclusive
> succinct way. No matter how painful such revisions of the
> models are be sure they include both realities.[8]

This, however, presents another problem for the honestly skep-
tic individual who has never experienced the Level of Mind, for it is
one thing to admit the existence of the mystic awareness of this
Level, but it is quite a different story to hear it claimed that this
Level alone is real, or that it is "the only true life," and that
somehow our cherished ego is a dream. But Shankara and all
others investigating this Level are adamant: what we normally
call our "self" is an illusion.

Now this isn't as alarming as it first may seem. William James
defined a man's self as "the sum total of all that he CAN call his, not
only his body and his psychic powers, but his clothes and his house,
his wife and children, his reputation and works, his lands and
horses, and yacht and bank-account."[9] A biologist would go even
further, and claim that a man's self—his "real" being—is the
entire organism-environment field, for the simple reason that the
biologist can find no independent self apart from an environment.
Even George Mead, the great sociologist, commented that "the
field or locus of any given individual mind must extend as far as
the social activity . . . which constitutes it extends; and hence that
field cannot be bounded by the skin of the individual organism to
which it belongs."[10] Gregory Bateson, creator of the double-bind
theory of schizophrenia, claims that man's only real self is the total
cybernetic network of man plus society plus environment, and
further suggests that we experience it as such.[11] So from these
viewpoints alone, the sensation of being an isolated ego confined to
the body is a half-truth, and to the extent we believe it to be totally
true, that sensation is an illusion.

If we have not personally experienced Mind, but we concede the possibility of its existence, then we must in the same stroke accept the essence of the revelations about this Level given us by its explorers, *including that of the illusory nature of the self and the absolute and only Reality of Mind*. The Level of Mind, by whatever other name it is given, is what there is and all there is—so say its explorers. This, however, introduces a new task for this synthesis, namely, to attempt to describe the apparent (i.e., illusory) creation or evolution of our conventional levels of consciousness "from" or "out of" the Level of Mind, somewhat as a physicist would describe the optics of a prism that creates a rainbow from a single beam of white light. But this is not an actual evolution of Mind *through* time, as we will explain, but a seeming or illusory evolution of Mind *into* time, for Mind itself is intemporal, timeless, eternal. We are approaching consciousness, in other words, from the viewpoint of the absolute Now-moment, and so this synthesis becomes a psychological interpretation of the *philosophia perennis*. It is thus inescapably made prey to the paradoxes, logical contradictions, and baffling assertions that must accompany all such interpretations for the sublimely simple reason that the Level of Mind is ultimately not an idea but an intensely intimate experience which is so close to us that it slips through the net of words; and that is why it was so emphasized that treating consciousness as a spectrum is pure metaphor or analogy—it tells what consciousness is *like*, but not at all what it *is*, for what it is goes behind words and symbols "to the inwardness of one's spiritual experience, which cannot be analyzed intellectually without somehow involving logical contradictions."[12]

Such, then, is a very brief introduction to the Spectrum of Consciousness. Since there exists today a veritable plethora of psychotherapeutic techniques, methods, schools, philosophies, and disciplines, the problem—and it is a very real one, for therapist and layman alike—is to discover a semblance of order, an inner logic, a thread of continuity in this vast complexity of different and frequently contradictory psychological systems. Using the Spectrum of Consciousness as a model, this hidden semblance of order may in fact be demonstrated. For, by means of this model, it becomes possible to integrate, in a fairly comprehensive fashion, not only the major schools of Western psychotherapy, but also what are generally called "Eastern" and "Western" approaches to consciousness.

Indeed, the very existence of a great diversity of psychological systems and disciplines suggests not so much an internal difference in methodology as a real difference in the levels of consciousness to which the various schools have adapted themselves. If there be any truth at all to the Spectrum of Consciousness and to the great metaphysical traditions that subscribe to its major theme,[13] then it immediately becomes obvious that *each of the differing schools of psychotherapy—East and West—are primarily addressing different levels of the spectrum*. We may therefore say that, in a general fashion, the major fields of Eastern and Western psychotherapy are each concerned with a different level of the Spectrum; that these schools need not overly concern themselves as to which is the "correct" approach to human consciousness because each is more-or-less correct when addressing its own level; and that, therefore, a truly integrative and encompassing psychology can and should make use of the complementary insights offered by each school of psychology.

Because of our experimental willingness to investigate all states of consciousness, we are lead into the *philosophia perennis*, because it is not really a philosophy based upon speculation, but an experience based upon one of our levels of consciousness, namely, that of Mind. As a matter of fact, these considerations have lead me recently to suggest the phrase "The Perennial Psychology" be applied to this universal and unanimous insight into the very nature and essence of consciousness.[14] At any rate, following this perennial psychology, we must necessarily view the individual self as—in a certain sense—an illusion and its world as a dream. This does not denigrate Western approaches at all, however, for even if Eastern disciplines can awaken us from this dream, Western ones can, in the meantime, prevent it from becoming a nightmare. Let us avail ourselves of both.

REFERENCES AND NOTES

1. Lama Anagarika, Govinda, *Foundations of Tibetan Mysticism* (New York,:Samuel Weiser, 1973,) p. 148.

2. Franz G. Alexander, and Sheldon T. Selesnich, *The History of Psychiatry* (New York: The New American Library, 1966), p. 457.

3. Erich Fromm, D. T. Suzuki, and Richard DeMartino, *Zen Buddhism and Psychoanalysis (New York:* Harper and Row, 1970), p. 25.

4. Ananda K. Coomaraswamy, *Hinduism and Buddhism* (New York: Philosophical Library), pp. 18, 69. (My italics).

5. William James, *The Varieties of Religious Experience* (New York: Collier Books, 1961), p. 401.

6. Eliot Deutsch, *Advaita Vedanta, A Philosophical Reconstruction* (Honolulu: East-West Center Press, 1969), p. 15.

7. *Memoirs of Alfred Lord Tennyson,* vol. *ii*, p. 473.

8. John C. Lilly, *The Center of the Cyclone, An Autobiography of Inner Space* (New York: The Julian Press, 1972), pp. 218-19.

9. William James, *The Principles of Psychology,* vol. 1 (New York: Dover Publications), p. 291.

10. Anselm Strauss, ed., *George Herbert Mead on Social Psychology* (Chicago: The University of Chicago Press, 1964), p. 243n.

11. Gregory Bateson, *Steps to an Ecology of Mind* (New York: Ballantine Books, 1972).

12. D. T. Suzuki, *Essays in Zen Buddhism,* First Series (London: Rider and Co.,1970), p. 77.

13. Cf. Coomaraswamy, "It is perfectly clear therefore that the *paroksa* and *pratyaka* understandings are not divided by an impassible wall . . . but in their degrees represent a hierarchy of types of consciousness extending from animal to deity, and according to which one and the same individual may function upon different occasions." *The Transformation of Nature in Art.* p. 133.

14. Ken Wilber, "Psychologia Perennis: The Spectrum of Consciousness" *Journal of Transpersonal Psychology,* vol. 7, No. 2 (1975).

II. *TWO MODES OF KNOWING*

When the universe as a whole seeks to know itself, through the medium of the human mind, some aspects of that universe must remain unknown. With the awakening of symbolic knowledge there *seems* to arise a split in the universe between the knower and the known, the thinker and thought, *the subject and the object*; and our innermost consciousness, as knower and investigator of the external world, ultimately escapes its own grasp and remains as the Unknown, Unshown, and Ungraspable, much as your hand can grasp numerous objects but never itself, or your eye can see the world but not itself. In the words of D. T. Suzuki:

> In the beginning, which is really no beginning . . . the will wants to know itself, and consciousness is awakened, and with the awakening of consciousness the will is plit in two. The one will, whole and complete in itself, is now at once actor and observer. Conflict is inevitable; for the actor now wants to be free from the limitations under which he has been obliged to put himself in his desire for consciousness. He has in one sense been enabled to see, but at the same time there is something which he, as observer, cannot see.[1]

The physicist Eddington put it succinctly, "Nature thus provides that knowledge of one-half of the world will ensure ignorance of the other half," and G. Spencer Brown, in a most spectacular passage, explains:

> Let us then consider, for a moment, the world as described by the physicist. It consists of a number of fundamental particles which, if shot through their own space, appear as waves, and are thus of the same laminated structure as pearls or onions, and other wave forms called electromagnetic which it is convenient, by Occam's razor, to consider as travelling through space with a standard velocity. All these appear bound by certain natural laws which indicate the form of their relationship.
>
> Now the physicist himself, who describes all this, is, in his own account, himself constructed of it. He is, in short, made of a conglomeration of the very particulars he describes, no more, no less, bound together by and obeying such general laws as he himself has managed to find and to record.
>
> Thus we cannot escape the fact that the world we know is constructed in order (and thus in such a way as to be able) to see itself.
>
> This is indeed amazing.

Not so much in view of what it sees, although this may appear fantastic enough, but in respect of the fact that it *can* see *at* all.

But *in order* to do so, evidently it must first cut itself up into at least one state which sees, and at least one other state which is seen. In this severed and mutilated condition, whatever it sees is *only partially* itself. We may take it that the world undoubtedly is itself (i.e., is indistinct from itself), but, *in any attempt to see itself as an object, it must, equally undoubtedly, act so as to make itself distinct from, and therefore false to, itself*. In this condition it will always partially elude itself.[2]

So just as a knife cannot cut itself, the universe cannot totally see itself as an object without totally mutilating itself. The attempt to know the universe as an object of knowledge is thus profoundly and inextirpably contradictory; and the more it seems to succeed, the more it actually fails, the more the universe becomes "false to itself." And yet oddly enough this type of dualistic knowledge, wherein the universe is severed into subject vs. object (as well as truth vs. falsity, good vs. evil, etc.) is the very cornerstone of Western philosophy, theology, and science. For Western philosophy is, by and large, Greek philosophy, and Greek philosophy is the philosophy of dualisms. Most of the great philosophical topics still debated today were created and molded by the philosophers of ancient Greece. These include the dualism of truth vs. falsity, whose study is termed "logic;" that of good vs. evil, called "ethics"; and that of appearance vs. reality, named "epistemology." The Greeks also initiated the widescale study of "ontology," the examination of the ultimate nature or being of the universe, and their early inquiries centered around the dualisms of the one vs. the many, chaos vs. order, simplicity vs. complexity. Rutted firmly in these dualisms, Western thought throughout its history has continued to generate those of its own: instinct vs. intellect, wave vs. particle, positivism vs. idealism, matter vs. energy, thesis vs. antithesis, mind vs. body, behaviorism vs. vitalism, fate vs. free-will, space vs. time—the list is endless. Thus did Whitehead state that Western philosophy is an elaborate footnote to Plato.

This is indeed odd, for if dualistic knowledge is at root as contradictory as trying to make your finger touch its own tip or your foot step on itself, why wasn't it abandoned long ago, why did it exert such a pervasive influence throughout the course of European thought, why does it still dominate—in one subtle form or another—the major branches of Western intellection today? Unfortunately, to search the history of *mainstream* Western thought for a credible solution to the problem of dualism is only to come as close as possible to death from boredom.

One of the principal reasons that the dualistic or "divide-and-conquer" approach has been so pernicious is that the error of dualism forms the root of intellection and is therefore next to impossible to uproot by intellection (Catch-22: If I have a fly in my eye, how can I see that I have a fly in my eye?). To detect this demands a rigorous, consistent, and persistent methodology capable of pursuing dualism to its limits, there to discover the contradiction. Imagine, for instance, that you are firmly convinced that the earth is flat, and no matter how much intellectual evidence to the contrary that you might hear, you obstinately retain your belief. The only way your error will become obvious to you is if you start travelling consistently and persistently in one direction. When you don't fall off the edge, your error will become apparent, and you will then more than likely alter your opinion. Because you *persistently* carried your false belief to its ultimate conclusion, you were able to discern the mistake.

Now this type of consistent experimental approach today forms an important part of the methodology of science, and thus it is science that potentially offers the type of rigorous approach capable of rooting out dualisms, principally because of its thorough-going experimentalism and its sophisticated instrumentation that allows it to pursue a dualism to its limits. In this regard, it is true that most branches of science remain today throughly and solidly dualistic, hotly pursuing as they are the "objective facts," but some of the "purer" forms of science, such as physics and mathematics, and some of the emergent sciences, such as system theory and ecology, have dealt lethal blows to several long-cherished dualisms. It is these branches that we have in mind when we refer to "science" as being a potent destroyer of dualisms for the West. Nevertheless, all of these forms of science are relatively recent inventions, being hardly 300 years old, and thus it is only in recent history that we have started to see the elimination of the dualisms that have plagued Western thought for 25 centuries. There is no doubt that all sciences began as pure dualisms—some, however, partly due to chance and partly to their more rigorous nature, pursued their dualisms to the "annihilating edge," and for those scientists involved, there awaited the shock of their lives.

This incredible story has its beginning in 17th century Europe. For 300 years prior to this, European man, slowly breaking down the wall between man and nature imposed by church scholasticism, had begun a passionate although somewhat chaotic exploration of nature and the universe. This was the Age of Discovery, of Rennaisance, of Exploration, of men such as Gutenberg, Petrarch, de Gamma, Columbus, Cortez, daVinci, Michaelangelo, Titian, Marco Polo, Copernicus. Man no longer viewed himself as a passive pawn in the Divine Game, but set out to explore and investigate in a thousand different directions: new ideals, new geographical vistas, new modes of experiencing his personal existence. This collective explorative urge, however, remained rather blind, diffuse, and uncoordinated, until it was concentrated and channeled by the introduction of the single most influential dualistic idea ever conceived by the human mind. This discovery was not just one among numerous other discoveries of this age: it was, in L. L. Whyte's phrase, the "discovery of a method of discovery," or in Whitehead's words, the "invention of a method of invention." It was, in fact, the idea that formed our present age. L. L. Whyte narrates:

> Prior to [1600] the only developed systems of thought had been religious or philosophic organizations of subjective experience, while such objective observations of nature as had been collected had remained relatively unorganized. Medieval rationalism was subjective; there was as yet no rational philosophy of nature of comparable complexity or precision. For 2,000 years man had been observing, comparing, and seeking to classify his observations, but as yet there was no system of thought concerning nature which provided any method which might be systematically used for facilitating the process of discovery. . . .
>
> We have reached a moment of great significance. About 1600 Kepler and Galileo simultaneously and independently formulated the principle that the laws of nature are to be discovered by measurement, and applied this principle in their own work. Where Aristotle had classified, Kepler and Galileo sought to measure.[3]

Within the span of a century, European man had become totally intoxicated with this new idea of measurement, of quantity: it was not just the progressive betterment of mankind or the assurance of human happiness that was promised by the new science of measurement, but a knowledge of Absolute and Ultimate Reality that had escaped the men of all previous ages.

> Nature and nature's laws lay hid in night;
> God said, "Let Newton be," and all was light.

Ultimate Reality was that which could be measured, and European man had begun the frenzied Quest.

Implicit in this search were two other ideas that became welded to that of quantity: Reality was objective, and Reality could be verified. All knowledge was to be reduced to objective dimensions, to the "primary" objective qualities of number, position, and motion, while the subjective aspects, the "secondary" qualities of the emotions, senses, and intuitions were to be completely exterminated, for they were ultimately unreal. "True observation," as Comte would soon declare, "must necessarily be external to the observer." That nagging question of the dualism of subject vs. object was not answered by the new science, it was simply side-stepped: the subject was proclaimed unreal.

The methodology of measurement became the new religion because it allowed, for the first time, a systematic procedure for empirically *verifying* a proposition. No longer would it be sufficient to prove an idea by subjective intellection alone, as had been the case prior to *homo scientificus*. There is the story that Aristotle once gave an elaborate and rigorous demonstration that Mrs. Aristotle had to have exactly 42 teeth in her mouth—it never dawned on him to open her mouth and actually count them, for it was impossible, as his reasoning clearly showed, that she could have any other number of teeth. Philosophy from that time on was by and large a case of grown men, each convinced of the certainty of his position, yelling at one another, "It is so." "No, it is not so." "Yes, it is so." "No, it is not so." "Yes it is." "No it isn't." "Tis!" "Tisn't!" As Bertrand Russell confessed, "This may seem odd, but that is not my fault."[4] At any rate, no longer would this bickering be the accepted case. All propositions were to be confined to that which was objectively measurable and verifiable. In short, if something didn't submit to these criteria, then it just did not exist or plainly was not worth knowing. This is exactly the type of powerful and consistent methodology that is potentially capable of destroying dualisms, and although the scientists of those times didn't realize it, they had started to build upon the Cartesian dualism of subject vs. object a methodology of such persistence that it would eventually crumble the very dualism upon which it rested. Classical science was destined to be self-liquidating.

That this could even happen reflects a positive virtue of the new scientific method, namely, the willingness to pursue a course to its ultimate end, admitting and weighing the evidence as it proceeded. In this respect, it was quite unlike any of the other systems of thought that remained for the most part "closed." For instance, fundamentalistic Christian thought was (and is today) "closed", in the sense that any proper self-criticism is denied, for anyone who questions the dogma is obviously being put up to it by the Devil himself. We know this to be true because the dogma tells us so. "What is the most sacred and authoritative book ever written in the world?" "The Bible." "How do you know?" "It says so in the Bible." This may seem odd, but that is not my fault.

On some levels at least, science was an open-system. Although it flatly rejected the non-measurable, non-objective, and non-verifiable, it nevertheless pursued its own course honestly and rigorously to its ultimate conclusion, which was very soon to arrive. Heisenberg states:

> It had not been possible to see what could be wrong with the fundamental concepts like matter, space, time, and causality that had been so extremely successful in the history of science. Only experimental research itself, carried out with all the refined equipment that technical science could offer . . . provided the basis for a critical analysis—or, one may say, enforced the critical analysis—of the concepts, and finally resulted in the dissolution of the rigid frame.[5]

By 1900, science was convinced that it had nearly reached the end of the Quest for Reality. As a matter of fact, physicists were leaving the field, for as one put it, there was nothing left to do but calculate the next decimal point—every phenomenon in the physical universe had been neatly described in the strictly deterministic terms of cause and effect. In one sense, it was still the old Judaeo-Christian world of a political assembly of finite chunks and bits of matter governed by absolute (i.e., measurable) law—the only item missing was the Monarch Himself, who was looked upon by most scientists as the Great Watchmaker—that Big Mechanic who initially wound the universe up and then, struck by an unexpected case of laziness, sat back to watch it unwind. Yet scientists were now convinced that they had, through objective measurement and verification, discovered the universal and absolute laws of the Monarch. Every phenomenon in nature could be reduced to small lumps of matter and these in turn were rigidly defined by Newtonian mechanics.

There were, however, two major phenomena that utterly eluded explanation by classical mechanics. One was the photoelectric effect; the other is now referred to with a chuckle as the ultraviolet catastrophe. It was indeed a catastrophe, for it marked the first crack in the "rigid frame" of scientific dualism.

The problem concerned the radiation of energy from certain thermal bodies, and the experimental facts in no way correlated with the existing physical theories. To this puzzle came the brilliance of Max Planck, and in a daring and radical leap of genius, he proposed that energy is not continuous, as had been assumed, but that it comes in discrete packets or *quanta*, and with this the "rigid frame" cracked wide open. Albert Einstein took Planck's theory and successfully applied it to the photoelectric effect (the second major phenomenon that had not submitted to classical physics), while Neils Bohr applied it to sub-atomic physics. Louis de Broglie, using these insights, showed that matter as well as energy produced waves, and this led Erwin Schroedinger to formulate the monumental quantum mechanics. And all of this in the brief span of hardly a generation.

All of these formidable insights culminated in an inescapable yet devastating conclusion, formulated as the Heisenberg Uncertainty Principle, whose implications were (and still are) enormous. Recall that science had been proceeding on the dualism of subject vs. object, of observer vs. event, with Reality allegedly being that which could be objectively measured and verified. This dualistic investigation eventually extended into the world of sub-atomic physics, and scientists naturally wanted to pinpoint and measure the "particles", such as electrons, comprising the atom, for these were supposedly the realities of realities, the ultimate and irreducible things composing all of nature.

Exactly here was the problem. To measure anything requires some sort of tool or instrument, yet the electron weighs so little that any conceivable device, even one as "light" as a photon, would cause the electron to change position in the very act of trying to measure it! This was not a technical problem but, so to speak, a problem sewn into the very fabric of the universe. These physicists had reached the annihilating edge, and the assumption that had brought them there, the assumption that the observer was separate from the event, the assumption that one could dualistically tinker with the universe without affecting it, was found untenable. In some mysterious fashion, the subject and the object were intimately united, and the myriad of theories that had assumed otherwise were now in shambles. As the physicist Eddington exclaimed:

> *Something unknown is doing we don't know what*—that is what our theory amounts to. It does not sound a particularly illuminating theory. I have read something like it elsewhere—
>
> ... The slithy toves
> Did gyre and gimble in the wabe.[6]

And Haldane muttered that "the universe is not only queerer than we suppose, it is queerer than we can suppose." This inability to totally pinpoint the "ultimate realities" of the universe was mathematically stated as the Heisenberg Uncertainty Principle,[7] and it marked the end of the classical and purely dualistic approach to reality. Declared Whitehead:

> The progress of science has now reached a turning point. The stable foundations of physics have broken up. ... The old foundations of scientific thought are becoming unintelligible. Time, space, matter, material, ether, electricity, mechanism, organism, configuration, structure, pattern, function, all require reinterpretation. What is the sense of talking about a mechanical explanation when you do not know what you mean by mechanics?[8]

Louis de Broglie, who had himself played a prominent role in the "quantum revolution", expressed its profoundly cataclysmic nature by noting that "on the day when quanta, surreptitiously, were introduced the vast and grandiose edifice of classical physics found itself shaken to its very foundations. In the history of the intellectual world there have been few upheavals comparable to this."[9]

The quantum revolution was so cataclysmic because it attacked not one or two conclusions of classical physics but its very cornerstone, the foundation upon which the whole edifice was erected, and that was the subject-object dualism. That which was Real was supposed to be that which could be objectively observed and measured, yet these "ultimate realities" could not themselves be totally observed or measured under any circumstances, and that is, to say the least, a sloppy form of Reality. Every time you try to measure these ultimate realities they move—it was almost like calling an apple absolute truth and then trying to bob for it. As Sullivan put it, "We cannot observe the course of nature without disturbing it,"[10] or Andrade, "Observation means interference with what we are observing . . . observation disturbs reality."[11] It was abundantly clear to these physicists that *objective measurement and verification could no longer be the mark of absolute reality, because the measured object could never be completely separated from the measuring subject—the measured and the measurer, the verified and the verifier, at this level, are one and the same*. The subject cannot tinker with the object, because subject and object are ultimately one and the same thing.

Now at about the same time that the "rigid frame" of scientific dualism was collapsing in physics, a young mathematician named Kurt Gödel (then only 25 years old) was authoring what is surely the most incredible treatise of its kind. In essence, it is a type of logical analogue to the physical Heisenberg Uncertainty Principle. Known today as the "Incompleteness Theorem," it embodies a rigorous mathematical demonstration that every encompassing system of logic must have at least one premise that cannot be proven or verified without contradicting itself. Thus, "it is impossible to establish the logical consistency of any complex deductive system except by assuming principles of reasoning whose own internal consistency is as open to question as that of the system itself."[12] Thus logically as well as physically, "objective" verification is not a mark of reality (expect in consensual pretense). If all is to be verified, how do you verify the verifier, since he is surely part of the all?

In other words, when the universe is severed into a subject vs. an object, into one state which sees vs. one state which is seen, *something always gets left out*. In this condition, the universe "will always partially elude itself." No observing system can observe itself observing. The seer cannot see itself seeing. Every eye has a blind spot. And it is for precisely this reason that at the basis of all such dualistic attempts we find only: Uncertainty, Incompleteness!

At the bottom of the physical world, an Uncertainty Principle; at the bottom of the mental world, an Incompleteness Theorem—the same gap, the same universe eluding itself, the same "something-gets-left-outness." (And we will find the same principle operating *psychologically* in the generation of the "unconscious.") When science had started with the dualism between subject and object, it had started badly, and by the first decades of the 20th century, it had run its course to that annihilating edge.

Figuring in the epistemological dualism of subject vs. object was the parallel but ontological dualism of spirit vs. matter, or mental vs. material. This dualistic problem revolved around trying to decide of what basic "stuff" the universe was composed: was it all nothing but material atoms, arranged in such a way that consciousness was just an illusion, being in reality reducible to the interplay of physical particles so that "mind" is really just a conglomeration of matter? But what of the argument that all sensations of "matter" exist nowhere but in somebody's mind—doesn't that demonstrate that matter is really nothing but an idea? Ever since Plato separated ideas from experience, the argument as to which is "really" real has continued, with no side clearly winning.

Is consciousness really matter, or is matter really consciousness? The idealists, or mentalists, just could not stomach the thought that consciousness was not much more than a fancy lump of clay, differing not at heart from rocks, tables, and dirt; thus, they were always on hand with the question, "But where does the impression of matter have its existence?" The answer, of course, is that material impressions exist only in consciousness, and so the conclusion is obvious: all matter is but a mental idea. This, however, was too much for the materialists, who would reply, "Well, then, where does consciousness come from?" The answer here being, "From nothing but physical processes in the human brain," and so the opposite conclusion is equally obvious: all ideas are just material. Emotions were high, for both sides of the argument could be put with equal persuasion, and so the final decision usually rested upon individual inclination, as is shown in the following story told by Eddington:

> When Dr. Johnson felt himself getting tied up in argument over "Bishop Berkeley's ingenious sophistry to prove the non-existence of matter, and that everything in the universe is merely ideal," he answered, "striking his foot with mighty

force against a large stone, till he rebounded from it, — 'I refute it *thus*.' " Just what that action assured him of is not very obvious; but apparently he found it comforting. And to-day the matter-of-fact scientist feels the same impulse to recoil from these flights of thought back to something kickable, although he ought to be aware by this time that what Rutherford has left us of the large stone is scarcely worth kicking.[13]

As this story hints, the old science had allied itself with the materialists, for lumps of matter could be "kicked," that is, measured and verified, whereas no scientist had come up with any sort of instrument capable of recording spirituality. The new quantum physicists didn't argue with this—they certainly couldn't find any spiritual stuff either—but, and here is the point, *neither could they find any material stuff*. As one physicist put it:

> Our conception of substance is only vivid so long as we do not face it. It begins to fade when we analyze it . . . the solid substance of things is another illusion. . . . We have chased the solid substance from the continuous liquid to the atom, from the atom to the electron, and there we have lost it.[14]

And Bertrand Russell summed it up succinctly—"The world may be called physical or mental or both or neither as we please; in fact the words serve no purpose."[15] In short, quantum physics had taken another dualism, that of mental vs. material, to the annihilating edge, and there it had vanished.

But the crucial issue was that the core dualism of subject vs. object, of observer vs. event, was found untenable, and found untenable not because of the arbitrary opinion of a particular group of philosophers, but by no less than the authority of physics. Bronowski sums up the essential aspects of relativity by asserting that "Relativity derives essentially from the philosophical analysis which insists that there is not a fact and an observer, but a *joining of the two in an observation . . . that event and observer are not separable.*"[16] And Erwin Schroedinger, founder of quantum mechanics, put it bluntly:

> Subject and object are only one. The barrier between them cannot be said to have broken down as a result of recent experience in the physical sciences, *for this barrier does not exist.*[17]

Now the conclusions that can be drawn from the insights of the quantum revolution are numerous; so numerous, in fact, that most modern philosophers take Heisenberg's Uncertainty Principle and Schroedinger's Quantum Mechanics as veritable proof of whatever theory they happen to believe in. The only conclusion, therefore, with which we will deal is the one put forth by these two physicists themselves. Werner Heisenberg's conclusion is clear:

> From the very start we are involved in the argument between nature and man in which science plays only a part, so that the common division of the world into subject and object, inner world and outer world, body and soul, is no longer adequate and leads us into difficulties.[18]

Erwin Schroedinger heartily concurs, and states simply, "These shortcomings can hardly be avoided except by abandoning dualism."[19]

"Abandoning dualism" is exactly what the new physics had done. Besides relinquishing the illusory division between subject and object, wave and particle, mind and body, mental and material, the new physics—with the brilliant help of Albert Einstein—abandoned the dualism of space and time, energy and matter, and even space and objects. The universe is so constructed that, as Niels Bohr remarked, the opposite of a true statement is a false statement, but the opposite of a profound truth is usually another profound truth.

As we shall see, in relinquishing the core dualism of subject vs. object, these physicists had in principle relinquished *all* dualisms. For them, at least, the dualistic war of the opposites was over. This 2500-year-old war had been almost as if man were given two pictures of his body—one taken from the front, and the other taken from the back. In trying to decide which of these views was "really real", man divided into two camps: the "Frontists," who firmly believed that only the picture taken from the front was real; and the "Backists," who steadfastly insisted just the opposite. The problem was a tricky one, for each camp had to devise a theory to explain the existence of the other, and so the Frontists had just as much trouble explaining the existence of the back as the Backists had in explaining the existence of the front. To avoid the contradiction, the Frontists spent their time running away from their backs, and the Backists were just as ingenious in devising ways to run away from their fronts. Occasionally the two would cross paths, yell obscenities at one another, and this was called philosophy.

It was not that this problem of front vs. back was extremely difficult, or even that it was a false problem. It was instead a nonsensical problem. In the words of Wittgenstein:

> Most of the propositions and questions to be found in philosophical works are not false but nonsensical. Consequently we cannot give any answer to questions of this kind,

but can only establish that they are nonsensical. . . . And it is
not surprising that the deepest problems are in fact *not* problems at all.[20]

Recall Schroedinger's remark that the barrier between subject and
object (or in this analogy, back and front) cannot be destroyed
because it doesn't exist in the first place. So just as front and back
are simply two different ways of viewing one body, so subject and
object, psyche and soma, energy and matter are but two ways of
approaching one reality. Not to realize this, and to set the "opposites" *against* one another while trying to figure out which is
"really" real—*this* is to condemn oneself to the perpetual and
chronic frustration of trying to solve a nonsensical problem (and
then getting furious or confused for not finding the non-existent
answer). Explains the biophysicist L. L. Whyte:

> Thus the immature mind, unable to escape its own prejudice
> in favor of permanence even in approaching the neglected
> process aspect of experience, fails to recognize the actual form
> of the process of development and is condemned to struggle in
> the strait jacket of its dualisms: subject/object, time/space,
> spirit/matter, freedom/necessity, free will/law. The truth,
> which must be single, is ridden with contradiction. Man can-
> not think where he is, *for he has created two worlds from
> one*.[21]

It is precisely in the dualism of "creating two worlds from one"
that the universe becomes severed, mutilated, and consequently
"false to itself," as G. Spencer Brown pointed out. And the very
basis of this "creating two worlds from one" is the dualistic illusion
that the subject is fundamentally separate and distinct from the
object. As we have seen, this is exactly the insight that these
physicists had stumbled upon, the culminating insight of 300
years of persistent and consistent scientific research. Now this is of
the utmost importance, for these scientists could realize the inadequacy of dualistic knowledge only by recognizing (however
dimly) the possibility of *another mode of knowing* Reality, a mode
of knowing that does not operate by separating the knower and the
known, the subject and the object. Eddington explains this second
mode of knowing:

> We have two kinds of knowledge which I call symbolic knowl-
> edge and intimate knowledge. . . . [The] more customary
> forms of reasoning have been developed for symbolic knowl-
> edge only. The intimate knowledge will not submit to codifica-
> tion and analysis; or, rather, when we attempt to analyze it
> the *intimacy is lost and it is replaced by symbolism*.[22]

Eddington calls the second mode of knowing "intimate" because the subject and object are intimately united in its operation. As soon as the dualism of subject-object arises, however, this "intimacy is lost" and is "replaced by symbolism," and we fall instantly back into the all-too-common world of analytical and dualistic knowledge. Thus—and we will presently elaborate upon this at great length—*symbolic knowledge is dualistic knowledge*. And since the separation of the subject from the object is illusory, the symbolic knowledge that follows from it is, in a certain sense, just as illusory. In Eddington's graphic metaphor:

> In the world of physics we watch a shadowgraph performance of familiar life. The shadow of my elbow rests on the shadow table as the shadow ink flows over the shadow paper. . . . The frank realization that physical science is concerned with a world of shadows is one of the most significant of recent advances.[23]

Commenting on this passage Erwin Schroedinger elaborates: "Please note that the very recent advance does not lie in the world of physics itself having acquired this shadowy character; it had ever since Democritus of Abdera and even before, *but we were not aware of it; we thought we were dealing with the world itself*."[24]

Physics and, for that matter, most Western intellectual disciplines were not dealing with "the world itself" because they were operating through the dualistic mode of knowing and hence were working with *symbolic representations* of that world. This dualistic and symbolic knowledge is at once the brilliance and the blind-spot of science and philosophy, for it allows a highly sophisticated and analytical picture of the world itself, but however illuminating and detailed these pictures may be, they remain just that—*pictures*. They therefore stand to reality just as a picture of the moon stands to the real moon. Korzybski, father of modern semantics, lucidly explained this insight by describing what he called the "map-territory" relationship. The "territory" is the world process in its actuality, while a "map" is any symbolic notation that represents or signifies some aspect of the territory. The obvious point is that the map is not the territory. This is easily seen in the common road-map, for although it may be a highly accurate representation of the country-side itself, it nevertheless is not the actual territory, and no one would dream of taking a vacation to Miami by looking through a book of road-maps. There are, however, much more subtle forms of maps, as for instance our everyday language. Words themselves are not the things to which they refer (if indeed the word has a real referent at all — many words refer to nothing but other words). Thus the word s-k-y is not itself blue, the word w-a-t-e-r will not quench your thirst, the word s-t-e-a-k will not satisfy your hunger, and so on. Korzybski summed this up bluntly—"whatever you say a thing is, it isn't." Our words, then, our ideas, our concepts, our theories, even our everyday language, are all *maps* of the actual world, of the "territory," and just as a map of America is not the real territory, so our scientific and philosophical *ideas about* reality are not reality itself.

Now in itself, there is nothing particularly damaging or misleading about symbolic maps—they are of immense practical value and are quite indispensible to a civilized society. As Schroedinger pointed out, however, the problem comes as soon as we forget that the map is not the territory, as soon as we confuse our symbols of reality with reality itself. Reality, so to speak, lies "beyond" or "behind" the shadowy symbols that are, at best, a second-hand facsimile. Not realizing this, man becomes lost in a world of arrid abstractions, thinking only of symbols about symbols about symbols about nothing, and the reality never gets in at all. The physicist Sir James Jeans explains:

> As the new physics has shown, all earlier systems of physics, from the Newtonian mechanics down to the old quantum theory, fell into the error of identifying appearance with reality; they confined their attention to the walls of the cave, without even being conscious of a deeper reality beyond.[25]

To approach the "deeper reality beyond" is nothing more than to discover the actuality of the territory from which all of our maps are drawn. Precisely here, however, is the difficulty, for the problem is not to elaborate a more detailed, more "scientific," more authentic, or more accurate symbolic map, but rather to discover an approach to the territory that *dispenses*, temporarily at least, *with all maps whatsoever*. After all, if the only knowledge that is academically respectable is symbolic-map knowledge, we will very shortly have nothing but maps about maps about maps, and we will have long forgotten the territory that was the original object of our investigation. Thus dualistic-symbolic knowledge will not do here, for what is demanded is instead a non-symbolic, non-dualistic, or in Eddington's phrase, an "*intimate knowledge of the reality behind the symbols of science.*"[26]

Recall the essential insight of the work of Heisenberg, Schroedinger, and Einstein that the texture of reality is one in which the observer and the event, the subject and the object, the knower and the known, *are not separable*. To deeply comprehend this therefore requires a comparable mode of knowing,[27] a mode of knowing whose nature it is to be undivided from what it knows. It is this non-dual mode of knowing that Schroedinger had in mind when he stated, "The world is given but once. Nothing is reflected. The original and the mirror-image are identical,"[28] and elsewhere when he stated, "All of this [i.e., Western philosophy] was said from the point of view that we accept the time-hallowed discrimination between subject and object. Though we have to accept it in everyday life 'for practical reference,' we ought, so I believe, to abandon it in philosophical thought."[29]

We have, then, available to us *two basic modes of knowing*, as these physicists discovered: one that has been variously termed symbolic, or map, or inferential, or dualistic knowledge; while the other has been called intimate, or direct, or non-dual knowledge.[30] As we have seen, science in general started exclusively with symbolic and dualistic map knowledge, focusing its attention on the "shadows," but as a result of recent advances in the physical sciences, this mode of knowing—in some aspects at least—was found to be inadequate for that "knowledge of the Real" that it had so deceptively promised. This inadequacy led many physicists to draw on the second or intimate mode of knowing, or at least to envisage the necessity of this type of knowledge.

But now we must pass out of the strictly physical scientific realm, for these two modes of knowing are universal, that is to say, they have been recognized in one form or another at various times and places throughout mankind's history, from Taoism to William James, from Vedanta to Alfred North Whitehead, from Zen to Christian theology—as the following examples will illustrate. We could easily produce numerous examples from the various schools and traditions of philosophy, psychology, religion, and science, but the following very brief ones will have to suffice.

The way of liberation called Taoism recognizes these two general forms of knowing as *conventional knowledge* and *natural knowledge*, that is, knowledge of the universe as it is conventionally named and defined as opposed to a knowledge of the way (tao) the universe is in its actuality.

> For us, almost all knowledge is what a Taoist would call *conventional* knowledge, because we do not feel that we really know anything unless we can represent it to ourselves in words, or in some other system of conventional signs such as the notations of mathematics or music. Such knowledge is called conventional because it is a matter of social agreement as to the codes of communication.[31]

This, in other words, is the first or symbolic mode of knowing, while the second mode, for Taoism, is "unconventional knowledge, [aimed at] the understanding of life directly, instead of in the abstract, linear terms of representational thinking."[32]

These two forms of knowing are also clearly distinguished in

Hinduism, as it states in the *Mundaka Upanishad* (1.1.4), "There are two modes of knowing to be attained—as the knowers of Brahman say: a higher and a lower." The lower mode, termed *aparavidya*, corresponds to what we have called symbolic-map knowledge: it is inferential, conceptual, and comparative knowledge, and is based on the distinction between the knower (*pramatr*) and the known (*visaya*). The higher mode, called *paravidya*, "is reached not through a progressive movement through the lower orders of knowledge, as if it were the final term of a series, but all at once, as it were, intuitively, immediately."[33] This corresponds to our second or non-dual mode of knowing, for it is a "unique, self-certifying *intuitive vision of non-duality*."[34]

Christian theology is also well acquainted with these two modes of knowing, as the following from theologian Nicholas Berdyaev will demonstrate:

> We cannot dispense with symbolism in language and thought, but we can do without it in the primary consciousness. In describing spiritual and mystical experience men will always have recourse to spatial symbols such as height and depth, to symbols of this or another world [first mode of knowing]. But in real spiritual experience these symbols disappear. . . . The primal creative act is realistic and non-symbolic [second mode of knowing]; *it is free from conceptual elaboration.*[35]

Insights similar to these abound in Christian theology—Meister Eckhart, for example, called symbolic-map knowledge "twilight knowledge in which creation is perceived by clearly distinguished ideas;" while the second or non-dual mode he called "daybreak knowledge," for with this mode "creatures are perceived without distinctions, all ideas being rejected, all comparisons done away in that One that God himself is."[36] Christian theology in general recognizes this second mode as the "divine manner of knowing, not by means of any objects external to the knower," pointing out very clearly its non-dual nature.

In Mahayana Buddhism, the symbolic mode and the non-dual mode of knowing are termed *vijnana* and *prajna*, respectively. The Sanskrit root *jna* is similar to our roots cna and gno, from which derive such words as "know" and "gnosis," while the Sanskrit prefix *vi-* means essentially "to divide," so the word *vijnana* signifies that knowledge which is at heart dualistic. Contrasted with *vijnana* is *prajna* ("pro-gnosis"), that mode of knowing which is non-conceptual, non-symbolic, and non-dual. D. T. Suzuki elaborates:

> Prajna goes beyond vijnana. We make use of vijnana in our world of the senses and intellect, which is characterized by

dualism in the sense that there is one who sees and there is the other that is seen—the two standing in opposition. In prajna this differentiation does not take place; *what is seen and the one who sees are identical; the seer is the seen and the seen is the seer*.[37]

Perhaps no modern philosopher has so stressed the fundamental importance of distinguishing these two modes of knowing as has Alfred North Whitehead. Whitehead pointed out most forcefully that the core characteristics of the symbolic form of knowing are *abstraction* and *bifurcation* (i.e., duality). According to Whitehead, the process of abstraction, useful as it may be in everyday discourse, is ultimately "false," in the sense that it operates by noting the salient features of an object and ignoring all else, and therefore "*abstraction is nothing else than omission of part of the truth.*" The symbolic mode of knowing also operates by bifurcation, by "*dividing the seamless coat of the universe,*" and hence does violence to the very universe it seeks to understand. Whitehead further pointed out that these errors have usually been compounded because "we have mistaken our abstractions for concrete realities," a mistake that Whitehead termed the Fallacy of Misplaced Concreteness (which we earlier referred to as confusing the map with the territory). Opposed to this mode of knowing is what Whitehead called Prehension, which is an intimate, direct, non-abstract, and non-dual "feel" of reality.[38]

In this respect, Whitehead is in close agreement with his "spiritual predecessor," William James. In James' words:

> There are two ways of knowing things, knowing them immediately or intuitively, and knowing them conceptually or representatively. Although such things as the white paper before your eyes can be known intuitively, most of the things we know, the tigers now in India, for example, or the scholastic system of philosophy, are known only representatively or symbolically.[39]

Symbolic or representational thought is a mode of knowing with which we are all familiar: the subject is taken as "separate" from the object, and "knowing" consists in establishing "an outer chain of physical or mental intermediaries connecting thought and thing." The second mode of knowing, however, contains no such duplicity, for, as James explains, "*To know immediately, then, or intuitively, is for mental content and object to be identical.*"[40]

The recognition of the symbolic mode and the non-dual mode of knowing also figures prominently in the work of Henri Bergson (intellect vs. intuition), Abraham Maslow (intellectual vs. fusion knowledge), Trigant Burrow (ditention vs. cotention), Norman O.

Brown (dualistic vs. carnal knowledge—"carnal" because subject and object become one in the act of knowing), Andrew Weil (straight vs. stoned), Krishnamurti (thought vs. awareness), Wei Wu Wei (outseeing vs. inseeing), Spinoza (intellect vs. intuition), not to mention the seminal work of Dewey on transactionalism— and these to name but a very, very few.

Now if it is by the severance of the universe into a subject and an object, into a knower and a known, if it is by the "creating of two worlds from one," if it is by the "dividing of the seamless coat of the universe," if, in short, it is by this primal act of dualism that the universe becomes mutilated, torn and estranged from itself, and thus rendered "false to itself," then our only hope of contacting Reality—if indeed there be such—will necessarily lie in the utter abandonment of the dualistic mode of knowing that repeats this primal act of mutilation in every move it makes. If we are to know Reality in its fullness and wholeness, if we are to stop eluding and escaping ourselves in the very act of trying to find ourselves, if we are to enter the concrete actuality of the territory and cease being confused by the maps that invariably own their owners, then we will have to relinquish the dualistic-symbolic mode of knowing that rends the fabric of Reality in the very attempt to grasp it. In a word, we will have to move from the dimness of twilight knowledge to the brilliance of daybreak knowledge—*if we are to know Reality, it is to the second mode of knowing that we must eventually turn.* Enough is it now to know that we possess this daybreak knowledge; more than enough it will be when at last we succeed in fully awakening it.

REFERENCES AND NOTES

1. D. T. Suzuki, *Essays in Zen Buddhism,* First Series (London: Rider and Co., 1970), p. 131.

2. Brown, B. Spencer, *Laws of Form* (New York: Julian Press), pp. 104-5.

3. L. L. Whyte, *The Next Development in Man* (New York: New American Library, 1950), p. 106.

4. A statement made in regard to Nietzsche but which serves nicely here. I am indebted to A. Watts for the analogy.

5. Werner Heisenberg, *Physics and Philosophy: the Revolution in Modern Science* (Harper, 1958), p. 198.

6. Saxe Commins, and Robert N. Linscott, ed., *Man and the Universe, the Philosophers of Science* (New York: Washington Square Press, 1969), p. 428.

7. Mathematically, $\Delta x \Delta p \geq h/4\pi$, where Δx is the uncertainty of a coordinate, Δp the uncertainty of the corresponding component of momentum, and h Planck's constant.

8. Alfred North Whitehead, *Science and the Modern World* (New York: The Free Press, 1967), p. 16.

9. Louis De Broglie, *The Revolution in Physics* (New York: Noonday Press, 1953), p. 14.

10. J. W. N. Sullivan, *The Limitations of Science* (New York: Mentor Books, 1949), p. 140.

11. E. N. da C. Andrade, *An Approach to Modern Physics* (New York: Doubleday Anchor Books, 1957), p. 255.

12. "Gödel's Proof," *Scientific American*, CXCVI.6 (June, 1965), pp. 71-86. Thus logically as well as physically, verification is not an absolute mark of reality. If all is to be verified, how do you verify the verifier, since he is part of the all?

13. Commins and Linscott, *Man and the Universe*, p. 457.

14. Ibid., p. 450.

15. Ibid., p. 390.

16. J. Bronowski, *The Common Sense of Science* (Cambridge: Harvard University Press, 1955), p. 77. (My italics).

17. Erwin Schroedinger, *What is Life? and Mind and Matter* (London: Cambridge University Press, 1969), p. 137. (My italics).

18. Werner Heisenberg, *The Physicist's Conception of Nature* (Harcourt, Brace, 1958), p. 24.

19. Erwin Schroedinger, *My View of the World* (London: Cambridge University Press, 1964), p. 62.

20. Ludwig Wittgenstein, *Tractatus Logico-Philosophicus* (London: Routledge and Kegan Paul, 1969), p. 37.

21. Whyte, *Next Development in Man*, p. 42.

22. Commins and Linscott, *Man and the Universe*, p. 453. (My italics).

23. From his *The Nature of the Physical World* (London: Cambridge University Press, 1928). Quoted in Schroedinger's *What is Life?* (see note 17, p. 130.

24. Ibid., p. 130. (My italics).

25. Commins and Linscott, *Man and the Universe*, p. 384.

26. Ibid., p. 468. (My italics).

27. Cf. Alan W. Watts, *Psychotherapy East and West* (New York: Ballantine Books, 1969).

28. Schroedinger, *What is Life? p. 146.*

29. Ibid., p. 137.

30. We must emphasize that this second mode of knowing, which is variously called insight, intuition, prajna, etc., is by no means to be confused with what is ordinarily termed "hunch" or "intuition." This "hunch" knowledge has historically fared very poorly in Western thought, and philosophers and scientists today recoil in horror when this type of knowledge is mentioned, and understandably so, for many of the "self-evident" truths revealed by this "intuition" have turned out to be most false. Rather, this second mode of knowing of which we speak is a transparent knowing, devoid of content, dimensionless, wherein knower and known are one process.

31. Alan W. Watts, *The Ways of Zen* (New York: Vintage Books, 1957), p. 4.

32. Ibid., p. 10.

33. Eliot Deutsch, *Advaita Vendanta, A Philosophical Reconstruction* (Honolulu: East-West Center Press, 1969), p. 82.

34. Ibid., p. 83.

35. Nicholas Berdyaev, *Spirit and Reality* (New York: 1939).

36. Raymond B. Blakney, trans., *Meister Eckhart* (New York: Harper Torchbooks, 1941), p. 79.

37. D. T. Suzuki, *Studies in Zen* (Dell Publishings, 1955), p. 85.

38. For Whitehead's views, see *The Concept of Nature, Science and the Modern World, Process and Reality, Nature and Life,* and *Adventures of Ideas.*

39. John J. McDermott, *The Writings of William James* (New York: Modern Library, Random House, 1968), p. 155.

40. Ibid., p. 157.

III. *REALITY AS CONSCIOUSNESS*

We have seen that man has available to him two basic modes of knowing. Now it is of the utmost significance that, of the vast number of scientists, philosophers, psychologists, and theologians that have fully and deeply understood these two modes of knowing, their unmistakable and unanimous conclusion is that the non-dual mode alone is capable of giving that "knowledge of Reality." They have reached, in other words, the same conclusion as that of the modern quantum physicists whose work we have discussed at length. Yet most Westerners find this extremely difficult to comprehend, for our civilization, our personal identities, our philosophies, and our life goals are so thoroughly based upon the dualistic mode of knowing that any suggestion that this dualistic mode gives illusion and not reality initiates in most of us a frantic flight from insight. Yet we have pointed out the difficulties inherent in symbolic-map knowledge. It is dualistic, dividing the universe into a "seer" and a "seen," thus "creating two worlds from one," and thereby making the universe "false to itself." This process of knowing becomes doubly corrupt when the universe so abstracted and so symbolized becomes confused with the universe in its actuality, when we confuse the map with the territory and commit the Fallacy of Misplaced Concreteness. Thus bumfuzzled, and with this equipment and only this equipment, we approach Reality, only to find our theories and world-pictures fall apart as fast as we can manage to construct them, to find at the basis of the physical world not a promise of certainty but an Uncertainty Principle, to find at the basis of the mental world an Incompleteness Theorem, to find, in short, that all "observation disturbs reality." Such is the nature of dualistic knowledge, and yet we seem not so much to want to examine the adequacy of this knowledge itself as we want to find "innovative" and "ingenious" means—principally through technology (for techno-logic is a natural extension of duo-logic)—to increase our use of it. We are, in other words, fighting tooth and nail to defend the source of our illusions. As Eddington exclaimed, ". . . we who have to solve the problem are ourselves part of the problem," and the problem is that, in the strictest sense of the word, we are addicted to dualistic knowledge. "Thus," states Alan Watts, "we are hardly aware of the extreme peculiarity of our own position, and find it difficult to recognize the plain fact that there has otherwise been a single philosophical consensus of universal extent. It has been held by men who report the same insights and teach the same essential doctrine whether living today or six thousand years ago, whether from New Mexico in the Far West or from Japan in the Far East."[1]

The great majority of us probably find this type of statement to be a gross exaggeration, for most of us can hardly agree on politics, let alone Absolute Reality. Surely the ancient Chinese Ch'an Buddhists had a view of reality that differed sharply from that of a modern and well-educated biochemist, and this view in turn must certainly differ from one held by a 14th century European theologian? The answer, however, isn't quite that simple, for this question must be approached from two different levels, because—as we have seen—there are two different modes of knowing Reality. Approaching the problem thus, it is demonstrably true that the world-pictures presented by symbolic-map knowledge have always differed greatly from culture to culture and usually from person to person within single cultures throughout history. Furthermore, our symbolic world-picture of reality will continue to change as we update and revise our scientific, economic, and historical ideas *about* reality. But the non-dual mode of knowing does not take as its "contents" *any* ideas or symbols, but rather Reality itself, a Reality that is everywhere and everywhen *identical*, so that this mode of knowing itself results in "a single philosophical consensus of universal extent," an understanding of Reality that "has been held by men who report the same insights and teach the same essential doctrine whether living today or six thousand year ago." The Reality experienced by the Ch'an Buddhist, the European theologian, and the modern biochemist—using this mode—is one and the same.[2]

Thus symbolic-map knowledge can generate numerous and different pictures of the world, while non-dual and non-symbolic knowledge presents but one picture (or rather, one *understanding*, since this mode of knowing is non-verbal and therefore non-pictoral.) As a rather crude example, imagine an ordinary, commonplace banana split: it can be described, via symbolic-map knowledge, in several different ways. Chemically, it can be viewed as a composite of carbon, nitrogen, hydrogen, oxygen, sulfur, phosphorus, and certain trace elements. Economically, it can be described in terms of the market-fluctuations governing the cost of its constituents. Ordinarily, it is simply described as an ice-cream goodie made with bananas, nuts, ice-cream, and chocolate sauce. These are three different descriptions of a single banana split, but do we then conclude that there exist three different banana splits? We do not, for we know that underlying the three different symbolic descriptions there is but one banana split, and we finally know that banana split not by describing it but by tasting it, by

non-verbally experiencing it. Similarly, there is but one reality—
so claims this universal tradition—yet it can be described in many
different ways using various symbolic maps. Throughout history,
then, men have understood this one reality by temporarily abandoning symbolic-map knowledge and by directly experiencing this
underlying reality, the single territory upon which all of our maps
are based. In other words, they quit talking about it and experienced it instead, and it is the "content" of this non-dual experiencing that is universally claimed to be absolute Reality.

As we pointed out, the final "proof" of this consists not in logical
demonstration but in experimental fact, and it is only in taking up
the Experiment to awaken the second mode of knowing that we
will know for ourselves whether this be true or not. We will presently describe this Experiment, but in the meantime we will have
to be content with showing only the *plausibility* that the second
mode of knowing reveals Reality. And plausible it is indeed, for it
*directly by-passes the mutilations associated with the dualistic
mode of knowing*. It does not bifurcate the universe, nor tear into
its seamless coat so as to render it ragged and false to itself, nor
strain it through the wire mesh of logic and then puzzle at the
mush that results. In the words of Teilhard de Chardin:

> Up to now we have been looking at matter as such, that is to
> say according to its qualities and in any given volume—as
> though it were permissible for us to break off a fragment and
> study this sample apart from the rest. It is time to point out
> that this procedure is merely an intellectual dodge. Con-
> sidered in its physical, concrete reality . . . the universe can-
> not divide itself but, as a kind of gigantic "atom," it forms in its
> totality . . . the only real indivisible. . . . The farther and more
> deeply we penetrate into matter, by means of increasingly
> powerful methods, the more we are confounded by the inter-
> dependence of its parts. Each element of the cosmos is posi-
> tively woven from all the others. . . . *It is impossible to cut into
> this network, to isolate a portion without it becoming frayed
> and unravelled at all its edges*. All around us, as far as the eye
> can see, the universe holds together, and only one way of
> considering it is really possible, that is, to take it as a whole, in
> one piece.[3]

And that is precisely what the non-dual mode of knowing does—
it "takes" the universe "as a whole, in one piece," without the
divisions and fragmentations characteristic of the symbolic-map
mode. Now as to the more specific "characteristics" of the non-dual
mode, we will be pointing them out as we proceed throughout this
volume. It is obviously nothing that can be fully described symbolically, for that would be symbolic-map knowledge! As Eddington

pointed out, this "intimate knowledge" will not submit to analysis or codification—but by approaching it from several different angles the reader will hopefully, by the time he finishes this book, have a "feel" for it. Right now we must only point out that in speaking of it as "whole" or "in one piece," as Chardin does, we do not mean the Hegelian sleight-of-hand that reaches "the whole universe" by a type of supernuminous addition process. For Hegel, the reality of each separate "thing" consists in its being an aspect of the whole, so that a thing has "reality" only as a part of the whole, and thus it is by an everlasting addition of fragments that we finally reach the Absolute. Doubtless there is some merit to this, but ultimately to "add up fragments" is just as much an "intellectual dodge" as to "divide up fragments"—the non-dual mode of knowing operates where there are as yet no fragments, no divisions, and no dualities to add or divide.[4] Besides, as we shall try to explain, each "separate thing" is not so much an *aspect* of the whole as it *is* itself the whole. Hence, neither is the "whole" to be confused with Spinoza's pantheism.

We can shift this epistemological discussion to a more psychological basis by noting that *different modes of knowing correspond to different levels of consciousness*, to distinct and easily recognized bands of the spectrum of consciousness. Moreover, our personal identity is intimately related to the level of consciousness from and on which we operate. Therefore, a shift in our mode of knowing results in a shift in our basic sense of identity. Thus, while we are only utilizing the symbolic and dualistic mode of knowing, which separates the knowing subject from the known object, and then signifies the known object with an appropriate symbol or name, we likewise feel ourselves to be fundamentally distinct and alien from the universe, an identity that is signified by our role and our self-image, that is to say, the symbol-picture that we have formed of ourselves by dualistically becoming an object to ourselves. Non-dual knowledge, however, does not so operate, for—as we have pointed out—it is the nature of the non-dual mode of knowing to be one with what it knows, and this obviously entails a shift in one's sense of identity.

But before pursuing this any further, we must pause to clarify an extremely important point. Figuratively, we have stated that the "content" of the non-dual mode of knowing is absolute Reality, because it reveals the universe as it absolutely is and not as it conventionally is divided and symbolized. Speaking more strictly, however, there is not one thing called Reality and another thing called knowledge of Reality, for this is most dualistic. Rather, *the non-dual knowing is Reality*, it takes as its "content" itself. If we continue to speak of non-dual knowledge *of* Reality, as if the two were somehow separate, it is only because our language is so dualistic that it is positively awkward to state it in any other fashion. But we must always remember that knowing and the Real coalesce in the Primal Experience.

We therefore reach a startling conclusion. Since modes of knowing correspond with levels of consciousness, and since Reality *is* a particular mode of knowing, it follows that *Reality is a level of consciousness*. This, however, does not mean that the "stuff" of reality is "consciousness-stuff," or that "material objects" are really made of consciousness, or that consciousness is some nebulous cloud of undifferentiated goo. It means only—and here we must temporarily lapse back into dualistic language—*that Reality is what is revealed from the non-dual level of consciousness that we have termed Mind. That* it is revealed is a matter of experimental fact; *what* is revealed, however, cannot be accurately described without reverting to the symbolic mode of knowing. Thus do we maintain that reality is not ideal, it is not material, it is not spiritual, it is not concrete, it is not mechanistic, it is not vitalistic—*Reality is a level of consciousness, and this level alone is Real*.

By stating that the level of Mind, or simply Mind, alone is absolute Reality, this emphatically is not the philosophical doctrine of subjective idealism, although it may superficially be so interpreted. For subjective idealism is the view that the universe can be accounted for solely as the contents of consciousness, that the subject (or the ideal) alone is real while all objects are fundamentally epiphemonena. This, however, is just a sophisticated and subtle form of the Front vs. Back game, a side-stepping of the problem of dualism by proclaiming one-half of the dualism unreal, in this case, all objects. Furthermore, when we say Mind is Reality, this is not so much a logical conclusion as it is a certain experience—as we pointed out, Reality is "what" is understood and felt from the non-dual and non-symbolic level of Mind. Although a type of philosophy usually hangs itself onto this fundamental experience, the experience itself is not at all a philosophy—it is rather the temporary suspension of all philosophy; it is not one view among many, but the absence of all views whatsoever. It is what the Hindu calls *nirvikalpa samadhi*, "imageless awareness," or the Tibetan Buddhist terms *hzin-dan-bral-pahi sems*, "mind freed from all thought-concepts," or the Ch'an Buddhist names *wu-nien*, the Mind in a state of "no-thought." Dualistic thought, which negates reality, must itself be negated.

So by stating that Reality is a level of consciousness, or that Reality is Mind-only, we mean nothing more, nothing less, than a state of awareness wherein the observer *is* the observed, wherein the universe is *not* severed into one state which sees and another state which is seen. For if it is by this mutilating severance that the universe becomes false to itself, Reality can only be that state of affairs prior to this severance. Very simply, it is this level of non-dual awareness that we are calling Mind-only, for this state alone is Real.

We mentioned that a shift in one's mode of knowing corresponds with a shift in one's level of consciousness, and this in turn corresponds with a shift in one's sense of identity. We will presently elaborate on these correspondences at length, but now we must at least touch upon the last factor—that of one's shift in identity. The dualistic mode of knowing confines one's identity to the *knower*, while all else, the *known*, seems substantially alien and foreign. With the shift to the non-dual mode of knowing, however, the knower is felt to be one with all that is known, so that one's identity similarly shifts from the isolated individual to the whole, for again, to know Reality is to be identical to and thus identified with Reality. In the words of Erwin Schroedinger:

> Inconceivable as it seems to ordinary reason [i.e., the first or dualistic mode], you—and all other conscious beings as such—are all in all. Hence this life of yours which you are living is not merely a piece of the entire existence, but is in a certain sense the *whole*. . . . Thus you can throw yourself flat on the ground, stretched out upon Mother Earth, with the certain conviction that you are one with her and she with you. You are as firmly established, as invulnerable as she, indeed a thousand times firmer and more invulnerable. As surely as she will engulf you tomorrow, so surely will she bring you forth anew to new striving and suffering. And not merely "some day":
>
> Now, today, every day she is bringing you forth, not *once* but thousands upon thousands of times, just as every day she engulfs you a thousand times over.[5]

And this, not from a confused "mystic," but from the clarity of the mind that founded quantum mechanics!

To demonstrate that this experience of "Mind-only," as we have described it—that is, the experience "of" Absolute Reality "reached" by the non-dual mode of knowing—is in fact universal, we now propose to set forth a very brief but more-or-less comprehensive survey of the major traditions that have subscribed to this experience. But in order to do so, we must first explain the tools of communication that we will use, and this is instantly problematic. Verbal or linguistic communication is generally understood as the transfer of information or restraint via images, symbols, or ideas. But Reality isn't an image—it is not a map, but the territory, and although we could include a map of Louisiana in this volume, we could never include the actual territory of Louisiana itself. Reality cannot be verbally communicated. Thus the Taoists insist that "Those who know do not speak; those who speak do not know." Because words themselves are "part" of reality, if we attempt to fully and completely describe reality in words, we must also describe the words that we use, and then describe the words we use to describe our words. . . , and reality is lost in a vicious circle. As one philosopher put it, "In the strictest sense, we cannot actually think about life and reality at all, because this would have to include thinking about thinking, thinking about thinking about thinking, and so *ad infinitum*."[6] The move to do so is simply another example of futile attempts to split the universe into a seer and a seen, a describer and a described, thus mutilating it and rendering it false to itself. Linguistic communication, which in its broadest sense is simply the transmission of word-patterns, is ultimately nothing more than the "reflection of reality in the mirror of illusion."

Nevertheless, words can be useful, if for no other reason than to constantly remind us of what we are—that is, to re-Mind us, to center us once again in Mind. In order to do this as accurately as the linguistic medium allows, we will have to carefully point out the basic ways in which language can be used to *point* or to *hint* at reality. We maintain that, generally speaking, *there are two basic types of symbolic elaborations that can be used* (either singly or together) *in three major ways* to talk "about and about" Reality. We will first describe the two basic types of symbolic elaborations, and then explain the three ways in which they are used.

The first type of symbolic elaboration is linear, one-dimensional, analytical, and usually logical. It is the type of symbolic elaboration that one can find in scientific journals, in law treatises, and in most philosophical works, wherein sets of accurately defined symbols are strung together, one after the other in a "line" according to the peculiar syntax of the system. This sentence is an example of such, and its linearity is most obvious because it is actually strung-out across the page to form "lines of print." It is a most accurate form of symbolic elaboration, but it is also most clumsy, for it must break down the vast "complexity" of the universe into simple lines, and digest reality bit by clumsy bit, which is much like exploring the inside of a dark cave with only a flashlight. Now this class of symbolic elaboration could be sub-divided into deductive, inductive, alogical, analogical, binary, metalogical, etc., but these general characteristics will serve our purposes.

The second basic type of symbolic elaboration is what we generally know as "imaginative." That is, it is a pictoral and multi-dimensional symbolic elaboration, and it lies at the heart of artistic expression, of myth, of poetry, of the imagination, of dreams. It is not logical—at least in the strict sense of the word "logic"—but it frequently carries a meaning, and can be usually surveyed in a glance, such as a painting or icon; in these senses it is quite unlike the first or linear type of elaboration.

Now both of these types of symbolic elaboration can be used to partially express reality, but neither can be used to totally grasp it. As Zen would say, they are like the finger pointing to the moon. The problem, as always, is not to confuse the finger with the moon itself.

These two types of symbolic elaboration can be used (singly or together) in three basically different ways to point to Mind. These three ways are the analogical, the negative, and the injunctive ways. The first way, the analogical, describes Reality in terms of *what it is like*. It uses positive and finite qualities that are so overpowering that they can effectively hint at or point to the Absolute. These qualities are usually ones such as omnipotence, omnipresence, omniscience, infinite being, supreme bliss, unexcelled wisdom and love, infinite consciousness, and so on. In Vedanta, for example, the Absolute so characterized is called *saguna Brahman*. "*Sa-*" means "with," while "*guna*" means "qualities," so that *saguna Brahman* means the Absolute analogically given qualities to help direct our finite intellect, and the qualities usually attributed to *saguna Brahman* are those of absolute being, consciousness, and bliss. St. Dionysius (pseudo-Areopagite) referred to this analogical way of pointing to the Absolute as *kataphatic*—positive and finite descriptions used to suggest the nature of reality. Generally speaking, these analogical descriptions are of the linear type of symbolic elaboration, but they are almost invariably accompanied by the imaginative type of elaboration evidenced in religious icons, paintings, crosses, mandalas, mythological imagery and narratives, etc. This analogical way is very noticeable in almost all popular forms of religion, but especially in Christianity, certain forms of Tantra, such as Vajrayana, and Hinduism.

The second way, the negative, describes reality in a thoroughly negative way, since as St. Thomas pointed out, "we must proceed by the way of remotion, since God by his immensity exceeds every conception which our intellect can form." St. Thomas thus called it the *via negativa*; and this way is what St. Dionysius termed *apophatic*, which he likened to sculpture, for the "finished product" is arrived at only by chipping away all obstructions. This in no way represents a rank nihilism, but is simply the recognition that we must, sooner or later, give up looking at only our maps if we desire to see the territory directly. In Vedanta, this is expressed by the phrase "neti, neti," the Absolute is "not this, not that," not any particular idea or thing but the "underlying reality." Brahman is thus referred to in this context as *nirguna Brahman*—"*nir-*" meaning "without". Brahman in essence is without any describable qualities, for every quality ascribed to Brahman necessarily excludes its opposite quality (e.g., if he is "good" he cannot be "bad"), and this places a *limitation* on Brahman, but the Absolute has no such limitations: it is "neti, neti." In Mahayana Buddhism, especially in the Madhyamika and its descendents, Reality is called *sunyata*, "void," and this does not mean a blank and featureless nothingness, but the realization that one cannot make a direct statement about the absolute without involving oneself in that vicious circle of having to make statements about statements about statements about . . . what? Reality is Void because it is void of conceptual elaboration.

These two ways—the analogical and negative—useful as they may be, nevertheless remain as so much gossip, as futile attempts to define or discuss reality which will "not submit to analysis or codification." "And what will you find?" asks Zen Master Rinzai. "Nothing but words and names, however excellent. You will never reach [Reality]. Make no mistake." The third way is therefore an invitation, in the form of a set of experimental rules, to discover Reality for oneself. It is what G. Spencer Brown calls *injunction*, which he states

> is comparable with practical art forms like cookery, in which the taste of a cake, although literally indescribable, can be conveyed to a reader in the form of a set of injunctions called a recipe. Music is a similar art form, the composer does not even attempt to describe the set of sounds he has in mind, much less the set of feelings occasioned through them, but writes down a set of commands, which if they are obeyed by the reader, can result in a reproduction to the reader, of the composer's original experience.[7]

Thus Reality, just like all insights and experiences, is literally indescribable, but it can nevertheless be indirectly pointed to by setting down a group of rules, an experiment, which, if it be followed faithfully and wholly, will result in the experience-reality. It is especially in this sense that we state Mind or Consciousness is Reality: *that is not a description but an instruction*.

This third and injunctive way forms the core of Hinduism, Buddhism, and Taoism, and can be found in the mystical aspects of Islam, Christianity, and Judaism. Thus in Hinduism and Buddhism alike, the word for absolute truth, *dharma*, also means "way," so that when reality is called the Buddha's *Dharma*, it means the Buddha's Way, his instructions for reaching reality, or—which amounts to the same thing—for reaching the non-dual mode of knowing. The Truth, insofar as it can be stated in words, must always be a set of instructions on how to awaken the non-dual mode of knowing, therein to experience Reality directly. Here again we can see how the verbal elaborations of reality can differ greatly from culture to culture and individual to individual, for each investigator—besides using a different set of analogical or negative symbols—will have his own peculiar set of instructions, but wherever the instructions lead to the non-dual mode of knowing, the Reality experienced will universally be one and the same.

Notice that these three ways, the analogical, negative, and injunctive, suggest respectively what Reality *is like*, what it *is not*, and what one can do *to reach it*. None say what *it is*, however, for a direct and positive statement about reality as a whole must either be meaningless or self-contradictory. Meaningless, because to predicate something about everything is to predicate it about nothing. Self-contradictory, because the statement itself is part of reality, and thus it would be referring to itself as well, and any statement that tries to say something about itself will usually contradict itself (e.g. "This statement is false").

Using these three ways of "pointing to the moon," we can now begin a brief survey of the major universal traditions concerned, in one way or another, with the Absolute, bearing in mind always, however, that whatever we may say is necessarily somewhat of a distortion, and that what we are putting forward is not an argument to be proven but a Reality to be intimately experienced.

> Were language adequate, it would take but a day fully to set forth Tao. Not being adequate, it takes that time to explain material existences. Tao is something beyond material existences. It cannot be conveyed either by words or by silence.[8]

We will not always point out which of the three ways we are using, but hopefully the reader will recognize when we are speaking analogically, negatively, or injunctively. Since we began our study of the two modes of knowing with the quantum physicists, we will start this survey with them.

Sir James Jeans, who was keenly aware of what he called "a deeper reality beyond," and always insisted "that we must probe the deeper substratum of reality before we can understand the world of appearance," finally came to the following conclusion:

> When we view ourselves in space and time, our consciousnesses are obviously the separate individuals of a particle-picture, but when we pass beyond space and time, they may perhaps form ingredients of a single continuous stream of life.

As it is with light and electricity, so it may be with life; the phenomena may be individuals carrying on separate existences in space and time, while in the deeper reality beyond space and time we may all be members of one body.[9]

As for this "one body," this single Reality beyond space and time, Erwin Schroedinger stated that it is "essentially eternal and unchangeable and numerically *one* in all men, nay in all sensitive beings. . . . Inconceivable as it seems to ordinary reason, you—and all other conscious beings as such—are all in all. Hence this life of yours which you are living is not merely a piece of the entire existence, but is in a certain sense the *whole*. . . ."[10]

These physicists frequently refer to Reality as Mind or Consciousness (as we have), as when Schroedinger states "all consciousness is essentially *one*," but again this does not imply subjective idealism, which holds the external and objective world to be illusory, while the subjective world is real. Rather, *both* are illusory: there is but one Reality, and *it can be approached subjectively or objectively*; there is but one Body, and it can be viewed from the front or the back. Thus Schroedinger maintains that "*The external world and consciousness are one and the same thing*."[11] And it is that "thing," that Reality, which is conveniently labeled "Mind," with a capital "M" to distinguish it from individual "minds," as when Schroedinger states, "Their multiplicity [i.e., the multiplicity of individual minds] is only apparent, in truth there is only one Mind,"[12] and elsewhere that "physical theory in its present stage strongly suggests the indestructibility of Mind by Time."[13] Of this one Mind, which alone exists, Schroedinger further states:

> The only possible alternative is simply to keep to the immediate experience that consciousness [i.e., Mind] is a *singular of which the plural is unknown*; that there *is* only one thing and that what seems to be a plurality is merely a series of different aspects of this one thing, produced by a deception; the same illusion is produced in a gallery of mirrors, and in the same way Gaurisankar and Mt. Everest turned out to be the same peak seen from different valleys.[14]

Let us pause here a moment to note that Schroedinger uses a common analogy—that of a mirror's reflection—to explain illusion, that is, to explain how the One Mind *appears* as a subject vs. an object, to explain, in other words, the "creation of *two* worlds from *one*," for that is what *seems* to happen when you place an object in front of a mirror—you get "two" objects where there is in fact but one. Similarly, when the bifurcating intellect *reflects* upon the world, we get "two" images—a seer and a seen, a subject and an object, where there is actually but one Mind.

It is this one Mind that Sir Arthur Eddington refers to when he claims that "We have only one approach, namely, through our direct [i.e., non-dual] knowledge of mind. The supposed approach [dualistic] through the physical world leads only into the cycle of physics, where we run round and round like a kitten chasing its tail...."[15]

Like these physicists, Mahayana Buddhism frequently refers to this one reality with such terms as Mind-Only (*cittamatra*), or one Mind (*ekacitta*), or various similar names. Thus throughout the *Lankavatara Sutra* we find statements such as the following:

> Language, Mahamati, is not the Ultimate Truth; what is attainable by language is not the ultimate truth. Why? By means of speech one can enter into the truth, but words themselves are not the truth. Truth is the self-realization inwardly experienced by the wise through their non-dual insight, and does not belong to the domain of words, duality, or intellect.... The world is nothing but Mind.... All is Mind.[16]

The *Hua Yen* (*Avatamsaka*) *Sutra* puts it more poetically:

> Just as a painter mixes and blends the various Colors, so by the delusory Projections of Mind are made the various forms of all phenomena.[17]

The *Awakening of Faith*, a profound compendium of the essence of Mahayana "doctrine," insofar as it can be stated in words, lucidly explains:

> The Mind in terms of the Absolute is itself the Realm of Reality (*dharmadhatu*) and the essence of all phases of existence in their totality.
>
> That which is called the "essential nature of Mind" is unborn and imperishable [i.e. beyond time and space, as Jeans put it]. It is only through illusions that all things come to be differentiated [as in Front vs. Back].... All things from the beginning transcend all forms of verbalization, description, and conceptualization and are, in the final analysis, undifferentiated. All explanations by words are provisional and ultimately without validity. Reality has no attributes, and the word is rather the limit of verbalization wherein a word is used to put an end to words. All things are only of the One Mind.[18]

Of course, Mind-only is not so much a theory as it is a vivid and living experience, and the sect of Mahayana Buddhism that most directly and straightforwardly dives to the heart of Mind-only is the Ch'an sect (Japanese: Zen). States the great Master Huang Po:

> All the Buddhas and all sentient beings are nothing but the

One Mind, beside which nothing exists. This Mind, which is without beginning, is unborn and indestructible. It is not green or yellow, and has neither form nor appearance. It does not belong to the categories of things which exist or do not exist, nor can it be thought of in terms of new or old. It is neither long nor short, big nor small, for it transcends all limits, measures, names, traces, and comparisons. Only awake to the One Mind.[19]

Thus Zen has taken its stand not on doctrine, dogma, or idle talk, but on "direct pointing to Mind," and whenever words are used at all, they are almost always injunctive, for "the Buddha does but point the way." Thus does Chang-ching, who tried to reach Mind through the screen of thought, proclaim upon seeing it directly:

How mistaken was I! How mistaken!
Raise the screen and see the world!
If anybody asks me what philosophy I have,
I'll straightway hit him across the mouth
with my staff.

Understandably, not all traditions refer to this One Reality as Mind, preferring instead Absolute Being, or Absolute Way, or the Void or Abyss, or—in more familiar terms—God, the Godhead, or the one Spirit, but nevertheless "they call him many who is really one." Thus, in Christianity, we find such statements as the following from I Corinthians:

Know ye not that your bodies are the members of Christ? Whoever is joined unto the Lord is One Spirit. (6:16-17)

Or the words of Jesus recorded in the Gospel of St. John:

That they all may be One; as thou, Father, art in me, and I in thee, that they also may be One in us. (17:21)

Therefore does Plotinus speak of the "reduction of all souls to One," and Meister Eckhart proclaims that "Everything in the Godhead is One, and of that there is nothing to be said," and he therefore exhorts us to "be therefore that One so you may find God."

And to "be that One" we must abandon dualism, as is suggested in the *Gospel of St. Thomas*:

They said to Him: Shall we then, being children, enter the Kingdom? Jesus said to them: *When you make the two one*, and when you make the inner as the outer and the outer as the inner and the above as the below, and when you make the male and female into a single one . . . then shall you enter [the Kingdom].[20]

And again from this Gospel:

> Jesus said: I am the Light that is above them all, I am the All,
> the All came forth from Me and the All
> attained to Me. Cleave a piece of wood, I am there; lift up the
> stone and you will find Me there.[21]

Christ is everywhere, because, as the apocryphal *Acts of Peter* explains:

> Thou art perceived of the spirit only, thou art unto me father,
> thou my mother, thou my brother, thou my friend, thou my
> bondsman, thou my steward: thou art the All and All is in
> thee: and thou ART, and there is nought else that IS save thee
> only.[22]

This type of "Christ-only" experience is formally indistinguishable from that of "Mind-only" of the Buddhists or physicists, and moving on to Hinduism, these are both formally indistinguishable from the core "doctrine" of Vedanta that Reality is Brahman-only. Thus is it proclaimed in the *Katha Upanishad*:

> As the wind, though one, takes on new forms in whatever it
> enters; the Spirit, though One, takes new forms in whatever
> that lives. He is within all, and is also outside. . . . There is one
> Ruler, the Spirit that is in all things, who transforms His one
> form into many. Only the wise who see Him in their souls
> attain the joy eternal.

And in the *Mundaka Upanishad*:

> From Him comes all life and mind and the senses of all life.
> From Him comes space and light, air and fire and water, and
> this earth that holds us all . . . and thus an infinity of beings
> comes from the Spirit supreme.

And thus throughout the Upanishads we find it declared that there is a Single Reality, that it can be called Prajapati, Vishnu, or Brahma, but that the Lord under many different names is nevertheless the sole Reality, that "All this universe is in truth Brahman". (*Chandogya Upanishad* 3.14.1)

> Above time all is Brahman, One and Infinite. He is beyond
> north and south, east and west, above or below. To the unity of
> the One goes he who knows this. (*Maitri Upanishad*, 6.17)

Yet this One is not one among many, but "One without a second," *completely beyond dualism but not excluding dualism, containing all relativities but bound by none*. Moving to Taoism, Chung Tzu speaks of this "One without a second," that is completely beyond dualism and the opposites, in the following way:

There is nothing which is not *this*; there is nothing which is not *that*. . . . Hence I say *this* emanates from *that*; *that* also derives from *this*. This is the theory of the interdependence of *this* and *that*.

Nevertheless, life arises from death, and *vice versa*. Possibility arises from impossibility, and *vice versa*. Affirmation is based upon denial, and *vice versa*. Which being the case, the true sage rejects all distinctions [and dualisms] and takes his refuge in Heaven. For one may base it on *this*, yet *this* is also *that* and *that* is also *this*. *This* also has its "right" and "wrong," and *that* also has its "right" and "wrong". Does then the distinction between *this* and *that* really exist or not? When *this* (subjective) and *that* (objective) are both without their correlates, that is the very "Axis of Tao." And when that Axis passes through the center at which all Infinities converge, afffirmations and denials alike blend into the infinite one.[23]

Lao Tzu, therefore, announces that "The Sage thus clasps the Primal Unity." We will eventually elaborate on just what "clasping the Primal Unity" means—here we are but surveying the ways in which these universal traditions treat of the Infinite and Sole Reality, and yet here we run smack into a formidable problem. For we have been speaking of Reality as the One—as Mind-only, as Christ-only, as Brahman-only, as Spirit-only, as Tao-only. This is undoubtedly helpful, for it *metaphorically* points to reality as that "single" and absolute ground of all phenomena—it is helpful *provided* we remember that it is metaphor. But most people do not remember this, and speaking of reality as the "One" can thus prove ultimately confusing, because we are apt to start thinking of the absolute as actually being One Thing—a great big all-powerful and all-knowing Absolute Thing, standing above the universe and omnipotently ruling over it. We imagine the One Thing as existing against the universe of Many Things—but this is just a glorified version of Back vs. Front—and *that* is not the Absolute, that is absolute dualism, for we have separated the absolute one from the relative many. We are then forced into a featureless pantheism or an insipid monism. So wherever these traditions speak of the "one," they always point out emphatically that they mean not literally "one," but what could better be expressed as the "Nondual." This is not a theory of monism or pantheism, but an experience of non-duality, and the *literal* theory of an absolute One is most dualistic. In the words of Seng-tsan:

All forms of dualism
Are ignorantly contrived by the mind itself.
They are like unto visions and flowers in the air:
Why should we trouble ourselves to take hold of them?
When dualism does no more obtain,

Even Oneness itself remains not as such.
The True Mind is not divided—
When a direct identification is asked for,
We can only say, *"Not two* [non-dual]."[24]

But this "Not two!" does not imply One—for, as Seng-tsan points out, in pure non-duality there is neither two nor one! Says Silpabhijna in the *Avatamsaka Sutra*, "The truth of Self-realization [and Reality itself] are *neither one nor two*.[25] And Tao-wu of Tien huang proclaims that "Even Oneness when held onto is wide of the mark!"[26] The point is that when we, as Christ commands, "make the two one," *then the two no longer exist, but then neither does the one!*

These traditions therefore speak of the "One" only as a concession to popular imagination. They are utilizing, in other words, the analogical way of pointing to reality, but when pressed to make a definite statement about Reality, they move instantly to the negative way, pointing out that Reality is actually neither one nor many, singular nor plural, transcendent nor immanent—it is a non-dual experience "about which nothing can be said," that "nameless nothingness" of Eckhart, which nevertheless, in the words of Behmen," to the World *appears Nothing*, but to the Children of Wisdom *is* All Things." Thus does St. Dionysius state:

> Going yet higher, we say that He is neither a soul, nor a mind, nor an object of knowledge; neither has He opinion, nor reason, nor intellect; neither is He reason, nor thought, nor is He utterable or knowable; neither is He number, order, greatness, littleness, equality, inequality, likeness, nor unlikeness; neither does He stand nor move, nor is He quiescent; neither has He power, nor is power, nor light; neither does He live, nor is life; neither is He being, nor everlastingless, nor time, nor is His touch knowable; neither is He knowledge, nor truth, nor kingship, nor wisdom, nor one, nor one-ness, nor divinity, nor goodness; neither is He Spirit, as we can understand it, nor Sonship, nor Fatherhood, nor any other thing known to us or to any other creature...; neither is He darkness, nor light; nor falsehood, nor truth; neither is there any entire affirmation or negation that may be made concerning Him. (*Theologia Mystica*, V)

Compare this with the following from the *Mandukya Upanishad* (7), which speaks of the highest reality as

> That which is not conscious of the subjective, nor that which is conscious of the objective, nor that which is conscious of both, nor that which is a mass all-conscious, nor simple consciousness, nor unconsciousness. It is invisible, uncontrollable, ungraspable, without distinction, beyond thought, indescrib-

able, the situation of the Self, the end of development, tranquil, benign, without duality.

And all of this "neti, neti" because to assign a characteristic to Reality is to deny reality to that characteristic's opposite, thus rending the fabric of reality right down the middle, mutilating it, delivering it up false to itself. And typically we compound this murder by confusing these "characteristics" such as Truth or Goodness with the Absolute itself, and then worship these *images of reality*, hardly aware that we are committing the most subtle and insidious form of idol-worship. "Anyone content with what can be expressed in words—God is a word, Heaven is a word—is aptly styled an unbeliever." In the words of Coomaraswamy:

> Idolatry is the misuse of symbols, a definition needing no further qualifications. The traditional philosophy has nothing to say against the use of symbols and rites; though there is much that the most orthodox can have to say against their misuse. It may be emphasized that the danger of treating verbal formulae as absolutes is generally greater than of misusing plastic images.[27]

Thus, as Coomaraswamy suggests, no Christian in his right mind would confuse a plastic statue or image of Christ with Christ himself, but many usually confuse their mental images of Christ as Great, Glorious, Loving, or whatever, with Christ himself, yet these are every bit as much graven images as are the Golden Calf and the icon of Baal.

> Thou shalt not make unto thee any graven image, or any likeness of any thing that is in heaven above, or that is in the earth beneath, or that is in the water under the earth. (Exodus 20:4)

To better comprehend why graven images so mutilate Reality, let us move on to the Madhyamika school of Mahayana. The Madhyamika represents the purest form of the negative way, of "neti, neti," of the *via negativa*, and what we say of it may be taken as representative of the *via negativa* in general, of the attempt to deliver us from the idols of symbolic-map knowledge to the direct and intimate knowledge of Reality itself.

The Madhyamika was founded around the second century A.D. by Nagarjuna, considered by many to be the greatest philosopher who ever lived. In one sense this is untrue, for Nagarjuna was not a philosopher, if by that term is meant someone who establishes or holds a sophisticated philosophy, for Nagarjuna subscribed to no logical philosophy whatsoever. Instead, he only turned logic back upon itself to uncover the contradictory nature of that very logic.

He held no philosophy about reality, but confined himself to the
task of demonstrating that all philosophies claiming to embrace
reality must be self-contradictory. In doing this, Nagarjuna and
the Madhyamika do not put forth a counter-thesis; they do not
demolish a philosophy in order to erect one of their own, but rather,
by systematically and thoroughly following any philosophy to its
logical conclusion, they demonstrate that that philosophy is self-
contradictory. There is a reason for this, as we shall see—it is no
mere skepticism or nihilism, for these latter views are attacked as
vigorously as any other. In the meantime, T. R. V. Murti explains
the Madhyamika operation:

> How does the Madhyamika reject any and all views? He uses
> only one weapon. By drawing out the implications of any view
> he shows its self-contradictory character. The dialectic is a
> series of *reductio ad absurdum* arguments. Every thesis is
> turned against itself. The Madhyamika is a prasangika or
> vaitandika, a dialectician or free-lance debater. The
> Madhyamika *disproves* the opponent's thesis, and does *not*
> prove any thesis of his own. . . . The *reductio ad absurdum* is
> for the sole benefit of the holder of the thesis; and it is done
> with his own logic, on principles and procedure fully accept-
> able to him.[28]

The Madhyamika can do this with any and all philosophical
views

> because language is dualistic or relational, [and thus] any
> affirmation or denial whatsoever can have meaning only in
> relation to its own opposite. Every statement, every defini-
> tion, sets up a boundary or limit; it classifies something, and
> thus it can always be shown that what is inside the boundary
> must coexist with what is outside. Even the idea of the bound-
> less is meaningless without the contrast of the bounded. The
> Madhyamika dialectic uses this as an infallible method for
> pointing out the relativity of any metaphysical premise, and
> thus to engage such a dialectician in argument is inevitably to
> play a losing game.[29]

The Madhyamika accomplishes this by first demonstrating that
any proposition about Reality must fall into one of the following
four categories:

    1. Being (or simply X)
    2. Non-being (not-X)
    3. Both Being and Non-Being (both X and not-X)
    4. Neither Being nor Non-Being (neither X nor not-X)

It then proceeds to show that any proposition, insofar as it claims
to embrace Reality, must contradict itself. For example, suppose I

state that Reality is Absolute Being, that it is Infinite and Unlimited (a statement that falls into category 1). Absolute and
Unlimited Being, however, positively excludes non-being and
relativity, and exclusion is a mark of limitation, because to exclude
is to place a boundary or limit between what is to be excluded and
what is not. Thus my "Unlimited Being" is limited, and I have
contradicted myself. If I change my statement to Absolute Non-
being (category 2), I fare no better, for non-being excludes being
and is therefore just as limited. I might now get clever and claim
that Reality includes both being and non-being, that it is immanent in both being and non-being (category 3), but that *excludes* it
from having neither being nor non-being, from transcending being
and non-being. And if I claim that Reality is neither being nor
non-being, that it transcends them both (category 4), that excludes
it from immanence, from having both being and non-being. In
short, because any statement makes sense only in terms of its
opposite, then any statement can be shown to be purely relative,
and if that statement is made to embrace Reality, it will turn on
itself as a contradiction.

The Madhyamika, however, is most emphatically not maintaining that there is no Absolute Reality; it is simply pointing out that
no idea is applicable to Reality itself. The rejection by the
Madhyamika of all the logical alternatives, of all four logical
categories, is simultaneously the rejection of the competence of
dualistic reason to comprehend Reality. Reason generates illusion,
never Reality. Reality is thus *Void* of reason!

But by now, the fact that whatever we can think about is not
Reality, should come as no surprise; that, in the words of the
Lankavatara Sutra, the "highest Reality is the eternally unthinkable."[30] An idea—any idea that one can possibly conceive—has
meaning only in relation to its opposite: up makes no sense without
down, left makes no sense without right, being makes no sense
without non-being, boundless without bounded, truth without falsity, good without evil, dark without light. . . . Yet, as John Scotus
(Erigena) pointed out, Reality as a whole *has no opposite and thus
it can never be thought about*. Suzuki put it simply. "As [Reality] is
beyond all forms of dualism, in it there are no contrasts, [and so] no
characterization is possible of it."[31] It is in this spirit that Nicholas
de Cusa called God the "coincidence of opposites." Actually, this is
today the way the astro-physicists view the universe—it curves
back in on itself like a Mobius strip, and thus has no outside, and
having no outside neither does it have an inside, or, one can say *its
inside is its outside*: the coincidence of opposites, the universe as
non-dual. Our everyday logic balks at such statements, for it
operates on the basis of pure dualism, and it therefore cannot see

that an inside *is* an outside, an up *is* a down, a good *is* an evil. Thus, for example, logic traces out on a flat surface a distinction, such as a circle, and maintains that the inside of that circle is clearly and evidently distinct and separate from the outside, as follows,

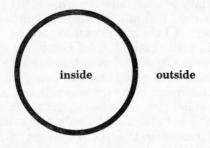

Now this is true on a *flat* surface—the universe, however, is not flat. It seems to more clearly resemble a torus, that is, it has a donut-like curvature, and if we draw a circle on a torus, its inside *is* its outside, as follows:

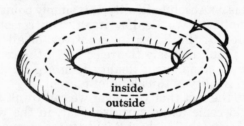

We can separate the inside from the outside only because we *agree to*, or *pretend to*, but it is only pretend. Thus proclaims the *Lankavatara Sutra*:

> Again, Mahamati, what is meant by non-duality? It means that light and shade, long and short, black and white, are relative terms, Mahamati, and not independent of each other; as Nirvana [absolute] and Samsara [relative] are, *all things are not-two*. There is no Nirvana except where is Samsara; there is no Samsara except where is Nirvana; for the condition of existence is not of mutually-exclusive character. Therefore it is said that all things are non-dual.[32]

Duality and the opposites are, in short, terms of relation or of thought, but not of reality. Most of us, however, thoroughly obscure reality with the terms in which we represent it, and thus the Madhyamika's purpose is to demonstrate to us the utter inapplicability of dualistic reason to Reality. T. R. V. Murti explains:

> The implication of the Madhyamika method is that the real is overlaid with the undergrowth of our notions and views. Most of them are *a priori*; this is avidya [illusion, which is] ideal construction screening the real. The Real is known by uncovering it, by the removal of the opacity of ideas. . . . The Madhyamika method is to *de*conceptualize the mind and to disburden it of all notions, empirical as well as *a priori*. The dialectic is not an avenue for the acquisition of information, but a catharsis; it is primarily a path of purification of the intellect. . . . Reason works through differentia and distinction. It cannot dispense with the duality of the opposites without losing its nature as Reason. The standpoint of Reason is that of a particular special viewpoint; it is not universal or disinterested knowledge. Non-dual knowledge is the abolition of all particular view points which restrict and distort reality.[33]

The Madhyamika is thus designed to root out and abolish these "ideal constructions screening the Real," and hence is not a particular philosophy but a criticism of all philosophies. In this respect, it is not unlike Kant's critique and the criticisms of logical positivism, for all agree that statements about Reality do not give the information that they claim. But unlike Kant and the positivists, the Madhyamika does not stop here. Its sole reason for demolishing all dualistic conceptions is to break us of the habit of relying exlusively on the symbolic-map form of knowing, and thus to open us to the non-dual mode of knowing, which alone touches Reality. The total negation of thought is not nihilism, but the opening of *prajna*, of non-dual insight.

> Negation is thus the despair of thought; but it is at once the opening of a new avenue—the path of intuition. Negation is the threshold of intellectual intuition. Sunyata [Void] is not only the negation of drsti (view, judgement), but is Prajna. . . . Sunyata is negative only for thought; but in itself it is the non-relational knowledge of the absolute. . . . The dialectic as Sunyata is the removal of the constrictions which our concepts, with their practical or sentimental bias, have put on reality. It is the *freeing* of reality of the artificial and accidental restrictions, and *not the denial* of reality. Sunyata is negation of negations; it is thus a reaffirmation of the infinite and inexpressibly positive character of the Real.[34]

That Reality is Void (Sunyata) of conceptual elaboration (drsti) has some startling consequences. It is perhaps easy enough to see that no symbolic representation or idea is applicable to Reality, but it is much less obvious that many of our ideas *about* reality operate on unconscious levels. Thus our perception of Reality can be—and almost universally is—distorted by unconscious conceptions, in ways of which we are hardly aware. Benjamin Whorf, pioneer in the science of linguistics, put it thus:

> We say "see that wave"—the same pattern as "see that house." *But with outthe projection of language no one ever saw a single wave.* We see a surface in everchanging undulating motions. Some languages cannot say "a wave;" they are closer to reality in this respect. Hopi say walalata, "plural waving occurs," and can call attention to one place in the waving just as we can. But, since actually a wave cannot exist by itself, the form that corresponds to our singular, wala, is not the equivalent of English "a wave," but means "a slosh occurs," as when a vessel of liquid is suddenly jarred. . . . [This is one example of the fact that] scientists as well as [the rest of us] all unknowingly project the linguistic patterns of a particular type of language upon the universe, and SEE them there, rendered visible on the very face of nature.[35]

As a simple but enlightening example, try looking at the difference between your fingers. We are all aware that our fingers are different from each other, but can you point to that difference, can you actually *see* it? It doesn't exist *in* your fingers, and neither does it exist *between* them—in fact, it isn't there! You cannot *see* the difference because it is nothing but a concept, a map that we have constructed of reality to facilitate discussion and communication. We never actually *see* that concept, for we are using it as something *with which* to see, and thus *interpret*, reality.

Now take this one step further: try looking at a "thing"—any thing, a chair, a tree, a book, a word on this page. What you are actually *seeing* however, is not a single "thing," just as you never see *a* wave, because what your eye really takes in is an entire visual field or continuum or gestalt, as for instance when you are reading the word "COW," your eye takes in not just that word but actually the entire page and some of the surrounding area. As we read, however, we usually attend to the words and ignore the surrounding background. That is, from the entire visual continuum we intellectually and unconsciously abstract—and therefore *create*—"things" by selectively attending to one aspect of the field and ignoring all else. In the words of William James:

> Out of what is in itself an undistinguishable, swarming continuum, *devoid of distinction* [sunyata] or emphasis, our senses *make* for us, by *attending* to this motion and *ignoring* that, a world full of contrasts, of sharp accents, of abrupt changes, of picturesque light and shade.

Helmholtz says that we notice only those sensations which are signs to us of *things*. But what are things? Nothing, as we shall abundantly see, but special groups of sensible qualities, which happen practically or aesthetically to interest us, to which we therefore give substantive names, and which we exalt to this exclusive status of independence and dignity.[36]

Bergson was also aware of the spurious reality of "things," because—as he himself pointed out—thought creates things by slicing up reality into small bits that it can easily grasp. Thus, when you are think-ing you are thing-ing. Thought does not *report* things, it *distorts* reality to *create* things, and, as Bergson noted, "in so doing it allows what is the very essence of the real to escape." Thus to the extent we actually imagine a world of discrete and separate things, *conceptions* have become *perceptions*, and we have in this manner populated our universe with nothing but ghosts. Therefore the Madhyamika declares that Reality, besides being Void of conceptual elaboration, is likewise Void of separate things (*dharmas*).

In sum, the Madhyamika calls the Absolute: Sunyata, Void! Void of things and Void of thoughts. But again, the Void is not mere nothingness, it is not nihilism, it is simply Reality before we slice it up with conceptualism—pure territory beyond any descriptive maps. This is why Buddhism also refers to Reality as *tathata*, which means "suchness" or "thusness"—the real world *as it is*, not as it is classified or described. Now we will be discussing *tathata*, Suchness, in a later chapter, and so won't dwell on it here. We need only note that there is obviously no way to describe that which is beyond description, and hence the real world of Suchness is referred to as the Void. Even to say that it is "pure territory" misses the point! Thus the Void is not to be mistaken as an idea itself, or as an object of thought. You can't think about the Void, but you are looking at it right now! Dualistically stated, Sunyata is not the object of thought but the "object" of Prajna, non-dual awareness (more correctly, Sunyata is Prajna: knowledge and the Real being not-two). And if Sunyata is conceived as an idea, then that idea is also to be voided —

It cannot be called void or not void,
Or both or neither;
But in order to point it out,
It is called "the Void."[37]

If Reality is "devoid of distinction," as James and the Madhyamika contend, then what we ordinarily call "distinct things" must, in some sense, actually be identical to all other "distinct things," since the distinctions "separating" them are only conventional. Now to say that all "things" are identical is only another way of saying that separate "things" don't exist, but the Hua-yen (Kegon) school of Mahayana Buddhism has chosen the former approach to the Void and has elaborated it into the profound doctrine of the *Dharmadhatu,* or Realm of Reality. The Hua-yen declares that when we see through the illusion that separate things exist, we reach a level of experience wherein each "thing"—because it is in itself unreal—contains or is penetrated by all other things, an experience called *hu-ju,* "mutual interpenetration." Hence the universe is likened to a net of glittering gems, wherein each jewel contains the reflections of all other jewels, and its reflection in turn exists in all the other gems: "one in all, all in one," or "unity in diversity, diversity in unity." This realm of mutual interpenetration is called the *Dharmadhatu,* the Universal Field or Universal System, and it is actually but a different approach to the Void.

> In the infinite Dharmadhatu, each and every thing simultaneously includes all [other things] in perfect completion, without the slightest deficiency or omission, at all times. To see one object is, therefore, to see all objects, and vice versa. This is to say a tiny individual particle within the minute cosmos of an atom actually contains the infinite objects and principles in the infinite universes of the future and of the remote past in the perfect completeness without omission.[38]

or, as Blake expressed it:

> To see a World in a grain of sand,
> And a Heaven in a wild flower,
> Hold Infinity in the palm of your hand,
> And Eternity in an hour.

Yet it must be re-emphasized that the Dharmadhatu, although forming the basis of Hua-yen "philosophy," is ultimately not a philosophy but an experience based on *prajna,* on the non-dual mode of knowing; and *prajna* reveals Reality as *cittamatra,* "Mind-only," or Brahman, "one without a second," or Jehovah, "there is none beside me." Thus the reality or the ground of all separate "things" is Mind, and hence each thing, because it is really nothing but Mind, is identical to all other things, for they, too, are nothing but Mind. Every inside *is* an outside, the World *is* a grain of sand, and Heaven *is* a wild flower.

> When water is scooped up in the hands,
> The moon is reflected in them;
> When flowers are handled,
> The scent permeates the robe.

The doctrine of mutual interpenetration and mutual identification of the Dharmadhatu represents man's highest attempt to put into words that non-dual experience of Reality which itself remains wordless, ineffable, unspeakable, that nameless nothingness.

The Dharmadhatu is not entirely foreign to Western thought, for something very *similar* to it is seen emerging in modern System Theory, in Gestalt psychology, and in the organismic philosophy of Whitehead. As a matter of fact, Western science as a whole is moving very rapidly towards a Dharmadhatu view of the cosmos. As biophysicist Ludwing von Bertalanffy states:

> We may state as a characteristic of modern science that [the] scheme of isolable units acting in one-way-causality has proved to be insufficient. Hence the appearance, in all fields of science, of notions like wholeness, holistic, organismic, gestalt, etc., which all signify that in the last resort, we must think in terms of systems of elements in mutual interaction.[39]

Likewise Scott declares that the only meaningful approach for modern science is the study of "organization as a system of mutually dependent variables." "Mutual interaction" and "mutual dependence" are precisely the Hua-yen doctrine of mutual interpenetration, for to say that two variables or two things are mutually dependent is only to say that fundamentally they are inseparable, not-two, or non-dual, and that is mutual interpenetration. Recall the example of the word "COW" and this page, which is actually an example of what gestalt psychologists call a figure ("COW") and the background (the "page"). In one sense the figure is different from the ground, but at the same time, without the background of the page, one would never be able to see the figure, the word "COW." Figure and ground are therefore "different" but not separable, just as subject and object, event and observer, good and evil, and, in fact, all opposites are *"different" but not separable*, expressing unity in diversity and diversity in unity, or what Eckhart called *"fusion without confusion."* Whitehead, the philosopher of modern science, describes what amounts to mutual interpenetration this way:

> We have to construe the world in terms of the general functionings of the world. Thus as disclosed in the fundamental essence of our experience, the togetherness of things involves some doctrine of mutual immanence. In some sense or other, this community of the actualities of the world means each happening is a factor in the nature of every other happening. . . . We are in the world and the world is in us. . . . This fact of observation, vague but imperative, is the foundation of the connexity of the world. . . .[40]

The "connexity of the world" is mutual interdependence and interpenetration. The final word on the return of modern science and philosophy to the wisdom of the Dharmadhatu belongs to the incredible Joseph Needham:

> The Chinese world-view depended upon a totally different line of thought [than the West's view of a mechanical universe externally ruled by a political Monarch and Creator]. The harmonious cooperation of all beings arose, not from the orders of a superior authority external to themselves ["God"], but from the fact that they were all parts in a hierarchy of wholes forming a cosmic pattern, and what they obeyed were the internal dictates of their own natures. Modern science and the philosophy of organism, with its integrative levels, have come back to this wisdom, fortified by new understanding of cosmic, biological, and social evolution.[41]

The final tradition that we will touch upon in this survey is that of Yogacara Buddhism, developed in the fourth century A.D. by the brothers Asanga and Vasubandhu. The only point we want to bring out in connection with the Yogacara is the emphasis it places upon the role of the subject vs. object dualism in creating illusion, in rendering the universe false to itself. All of these traditions, of course, maintain that the subject vs. object dualism is indeed a major, if not the major, source of "creating two worlds from one," but the Yogacara has made it the basis of a profound and consistent psychology, and for this reason is worth mentioning. The core insight of the Yogacara might be stated thus: all objectification is illusion, or simply all objects are illusory; and all *objects* are *mental* objects.

Let us give an example—I am reading the words on this page, and the page itself certainly seems separate and different from I who is reading it. It appears, in other words, as an *object* "out there," the *object* of my sight, or my touch, or whatever. But the Yogacara claims that this separation between myself as subject "in here" [i.e., "in my head"] and this page as object "out there" is a blatant illusion. Perhaps we can understand this by starting with another insight of Whitehead, namely, that "my present experience is what I now am." That is, my "present experience" and my "self" are two words for the same thing. To most of us, however, this seems rather odd, because dualistic knowledge persuades me not to feel that I *am* my present experience but that I *have* my present experience. If, however, this were really the case, then I should never be able to experience anything at all! For if all sensations are something that I *have*, then what happens when I am aware of myself? For myself is a conglomerate of various sensations, and if all sensations are something I *have*, then I am forced to say not that I *am* a self but that "I" *have* a self. Now just who is this "I" that *has* a self? Another self—a *second* self? And who *has* this sensation of a second self? A third self? How many selves must I postulate?

Yogacara declares this ring-around-the-rosie to be so much dualistic nonsense. As I read this page, there is actually but *one* sensation, namely the *single* sensation of the entire visual field as it exists in my nervous system. But when I abstract the "page" from the visual field by forming a mental concept of it, that concept *appears* separate from me as an object in my consciousness, because all images seem to parade by in front of me as objects in my mind, almost as if there were a miniature motion-picture projector in my head projecting mental images upon the screen of my consciousness. I sit, as it were, in the back seat of the theater and watch in fascination as these pictures flash by. Although in one sense I feel these ideas are mine, I—and nearly all other individuals—nevertheless feel separate from them—I am *watching them as objects*. Thus, when I abstract the "page" from the visual field by forming a mental concept of it, because that concept *appears* separate from me as an object, then the "page" likewise must *appear* separate from me as an object. This subject-object dualism besets us all, with very few exceptions, but the Yogacara declares it illusory. There is not one sensation called myself that senses another sensation called the page! Rather, there is but one sensation, and approached objectively we call it "the page," while approached subjectively we term it "the self." The inside *is* the outside, and to the extent we actually feel them to be separate, we are caught in an illusion—thus, all objects are illusory, and all objects are mental objects.

Should the fact that the sensation called "yourself" is, at this moment, *the very same* sensation called "page"—should this fact seem somewhat odd, or should it appear the product of a deluded and primitive Eastern mind, we will let William James say the same thing for us:

> If our own private vision of the paper [or this "page"] be considered in abstraction from every other event, as if it constituted by itself the universe (and it might perfectly well do so, for aught we can understand to the contrary), *then the paper seen and the seeing of it are only two names for one indivisible fact which,* properly named, is *the datum, the phenomenon, or the experience*. The paper is in the mind and the mind is around the paper, because paper and mind are only two names that are given later to the one experience. . . .[42]

Now according to the Yogacara, when we deeply realize that subject and object are not two, then *prajna*, the non-dual mode of knowing, is awakened, and it is in this fashion and this fashion alone that the reality of Mind-only is revealed. For, as we have stated, if it is by the severance of the universe into a subject and an object that reality is lost, paradise can only be regained in the state prior to that severance.

In concluding this brief survey of some of the major "branches" of this universal tradition, we should mention a few general points. In outlining the different expressions that the experience of Mind-only has taken throughout mankind's history, we have dwelled almost exclusively upon the analogical and the negative ways—at a later time we will elaborate considerably upon the injunctive way. In doing so, we have presented some of these traditions as if they utilized exclusively either the analogical, or the negative, or the injunctive way, and this is rarely the case. Most traditions, athough they might emphasize one approach over the others, usually use all three. Frequently, when a teacher of one of these traditions is initiating a student, he will begin with the analogical and positive approach, explaining that there is an absolute reality that is all-powerful and all-knowing, the discovery of which will confer an invincible peace upon the student. This helps the initiate to orient himself, and he begins his search for the ultimate. More than likely, however, the pupil will get nowhere, for he is clinging, consciously or unconsciously, to his ideas and analogies *about* Reality, and he is therefore confusing the map with the territory. At this point, the Master might begin to emphasize the negative approach, explaining that although ideas about reality are useful, nevertheless reality itself is not an idea, and so the student—who by now has had his *faith* in the absolute awakened by the analogical approach—must now proceed by negating *all* of his ideas about reality, for they are ultimately hindrances. In the words of Coomaraswamy:

> There always remains a last step, in which the ritual is abandoned and the relative truths of theology denied. As it was by the knowledge of good and evil that man fell from his first high estate, so it must be from the knowledge of good and evil, from the moral law, that he must be delivered at last. However far one may have gone, there remains a last step to be taken, involving a dissolution of all former values.[43]

Sri Ramana Maharshi put it curtly: "There will come a time when one will have to forget all that one has learned." Perhaps this is part of the meaning behind the rich Biblical symbolism of "Verily, verily, I say unto you, except a corn of wheat fall into the ground and die, it abideth alone: but if it die, it bringeth forth much fruit;" and "It is expedient for you that I go away;" as well as the *Cloud of*

Unknowing's "forgetting, forgetting, forgetting." So also does Lao Tzu announce that "Learning consists in adding to one's stock day by day; the practice of Tao consists in subtracting day by day (XLVIII)," and the whole essence of Buddhism has been summed up as "empty oneself!" To assist in this "dissolution," in this "emptying," the injunctive approach is usually then applied, wherein the student is given a set of experiments, which if followed correctly will result in his directly experiencing Reality as it *is*, not as it is named.

Hence, in most traditions, all three approaches—analogical, negative, and injunctive—are utilized, with only the emphasis given to each varying somewhat from tradition to tradition. Thus the Christian mystics have the analogical God, which is omniscient and omnipotent, as well as the Godhead, "of which nothing can be said." The Hindus have the analogical *saguna* Brahman, which is Being-Consciousness-Bliss, and the negative *nirguna* Brahman, which is "neti, neti." Similarly the Buddhists have the analogical Dharmadhatu (as well as the Dharmakaya, "Universal Organism," Citta, "Absolute Mind," etc.) as well as the negative Sunyata. And naturally, all of these traditions have developed sets of injunctive experiments, so-called spiritual exercises, where all ideas—analogical or negative—are temporarily set aside so as to experience reality directly.

In sum: our ordinary conception of the world as a complex of things extended in space and succeeding one another in time is only a conventional map of the universe—it is not real. It is not real because this picture painted by symbolic-map knowledge depends upon the splitting of the universe into separate things seen in space-time, on the one hand, and the seer of these things on the other. In order for this to occur, the universe necessarily has to split itself into observer vs. observed, or, in Brown's words, the universe must become distinct from, and therefore false to, itself. Thus our conventional, dualistic, symbolic pictures are subtle falsifications of the very reality they seek to explain.

But the split is not so much false as illusory, and the philosophies, psychologies, and sciences that depend on it are therefore not wrong but nonsensical. Man can no more separate himself from the universe and extract "knowledge" from it than a hand can grab itself or an eye can see itself. But man, relying as he does on dualistic knowledge, attempts the nonsensical and imagines he has succeeded. The result is a picture-image of the universe as composed of fragments called "things" disjointed in space and time, all alien and foreign to the isolated island of awareness man now imagines himself to be.

Thus lost in his own shadow, confined to this purely abstract and dualistic picture-map of the cosmos, man forgets entirely what the real world is in its actuality. Yet inescapably, *if* it is by the splitting of the universe into seer and seen, knower and known, subject and object, that the universe becomes distinct from and false to itself, *then* clearly it is only by understanding that, as Schroedinger put it, "subject and object are only one," that there emerges a realization of the actual world. If this be true, then this realization alone can claim the title of "absolute truth."

Now this is all these traditions are trying to tell us.[44] See through the illusions that dualistic-symbolic knowledge has given us, and thus awaken to the real world. Because this real world as whole has no opposite, it is clearly not something that can be defined or grasped, for all symbols have meaning only in terms of their opposites, while the real world has none. Thus it is called Void, *Sunyata*, Empty, *Agnosia*—which means only that all thoughts and propositions about reality are void and invalid. At the same time, this is to say that the real world is also void of "separate" things, since things are products of thought, not reality. Thus the real world is also called the Dharmadhatu, the realm wherein supposedly separate things have no real existence except as inseparably inter-woven into the "seamless coat" of the entire universe. And just because of this, just because reality is a seamless coat not split into subject vs. object, not abstracted into separate objects extended in space-time, then the discovery of the real world will make it plainly obvious that what was once thought to be the subject alienated from its objects, that what was once thought to be a multi-verse of independent things hanging in space and time—all are in fact "members of one Body." Or, if you prefer, the universe is actually indistinct from itself. Thus the real world is also called Brahman-only, Christ-only, Suchness-only, Tao-only, Consciousness-only, itself-only, one without a second, the universe *not* separate from *nor* false to itself.

If reality is inexpressible, it is nevertheless experienceable. But since this experience of the real world is obscured by our concepts *about* it, and since these concepts rest on the split between the subject that knows vs. the concepts that are known, all of these traditions emphatically announce that Reality can only be experienced non-dually, without the gap between the knower and the known, for in this manner alone is the universe not delivered up to illusion. This means that Reality and your perception of it are one and the same, which R. H. Blyth called "the experience by the universe of the universe." Now this awareness we have called the non-dual mode of knowing, the universe knowing itself as itself. And further, since we have suggested that this mode of knowing corresponds with a function, state, or level of consciousness which we term "Mind," and since to *know* Reality is to *be* Reality, then we can distill the entire essence of these traditions into the phrase "Reality as a level of consciousness," or simply "Reality as Mind-only."

Whether Reality is called Brahman, God, Tao, Dharmakaya, Void, or whatever is of no great concern, for all alike point to that state of non-dual Mind wherein the universe is not split into seer and seen. But that level of consciousness is not a difficult one to discover, nor is it buried deep within your psyche. Rather, it is very close, very near, and ever-present. For Mind is in no way different from you who now hold this book in your hands. In a very special sense, in fact, Mind is that which at this moment is reading this page. Let us now see if we can unravel the special sense in which this is so.

REFERENCES AND NOTES

1. Alan W. Watts, *Myth and Ritual in Christianity* (Boston: Beacon Press, 1970), pp. 14-15.

2. Only because it is what St. Augustine called a "Wisdom that was not made, but is now what it always was and ever shall be."

3. Teilhard de Chardin, *The Phenomenon of Man* (New York: Harper Torchbooks, 1965), pp. 43-44.

4. Cf. Chuang Tzu, "Three in the Morning"—
   "To wear out your brain trying to make things into One without realizing that they are already One—this is called 'three in the morning.' What do I mean by 'three in the morning'? When a monkey trainer was handing out acorns, he said, 'You get three in the morning and four at night.' This made the monkeys furious. 'Well, then,' he said, 'you get four in the morning and three at night.' This delighted all the monkeys. There was no change in the reality behind the words, and yet the monkeys responded with either anger or joy. Well, let them if they so want. The Sage harmonizes with both right and wrong and rests in the Harmony of Heaven."
   In short the "fragments" never existed, and so they can hardly be "joined" to give a "whole One." In the words of Suzuki:
   "We often speak of identification in our Zen discipline, but this word is not exact. Identification presupposes original opposition of two terms, subject and object, but the truth is that from the very first there are no two opposing terms whose identification is to be achieved by Zen. It is better to say that there has never been any separation between subject and object . . . Followers of identity and tranquillity are to be given the warning: they are ridden by concepts; let them rise to facts and live in and with them" *Zen and Japanese Culture.* p. 359.

5. Erwin Schroedinger, *My View of the World* (London: Cambridge University Press, 1964), p. 21.

6. Allan W. Watts, *The Wisdom of Insecurity* (New York: Vintage Books 1968), p. 114.

7. G. S. Brown, *Laws of Form* (New York: Julian Press), p. 77.

8. H. A. Giles, *Chuang Tzu* (Shanghai: Kelly and Walsh, 1926), p. 351.

9. Saxe Commins, and Robert N. Linscott, ed., *Man and the Universe, the Philosophers of Science* (New York: Washington Square Press, New York, 1969), p. 395.

10. Shroedinger, *My View of the World,* p. 21.

11. Ibid., p. 37. (My italics).

12. Erwin Schroedinger, *What is Life? and Mind and Matter* (London: Cambridge University Press, 1969), p. 139.

13. Ibid., p. 165.

14. Ibid., p. 95. (My italics).

15. Commins and Linscott, *Man and the Universe,* p. 419.

16. D. T. Suzuki, *Studies in the Lankavatara Sutra* (London: Routledge and Kegan Paul, 1968), pp. 243-245.

17. Garma C. C. Chang, *The Buddhist Teaching of Totality* (University Park: Pennsylvania State University Press, 1971), p. 173.

18. Distilled from the *Awakening of Faith,* Part 3, chapter 1. An authoritative translation is that of Yoshito S. Hakeda, (New York: Columbia University Press, 1968).

19. John Blofeld, trans., *The Zen Teaching of Huang Po* (New York: Grove Press, 1958), pp. 29-30.

20. Puech Guillaumont, Till Quispel, and 'Abd al Masih, trans., *The Gospel According to Thomas* (New York: Harper, 1959), pp. 17-19.

21. Ibid., p. 43.

22. M. R. James, *The Apocryphal New Testament* (Oxford: 1924), p. 335.

23. Lin Yutang, ed., *The Wisdom of China and India* (New York: The Modern Library), p. 636.

24. D. T. Suzuki, *Essays in Zen Buddhism, First Series* (London: Rider and Co., 1970), p. 199.

25. Ibid., Second Series, p. 21.

26. Ibid., First Series, p. 87.

27. Ananda K. Coomaraswamy, *Christian and Oriental Philosophy of Art* (New York: Dover, 1956), p. 50.

28. T. R. V. Murti, *The Central Philosophy of Buddhism* (London: George Allen and Unwin, 1960), pp. 131-132.

29. Alan W. Watts, *Psychotherapy East and West* (New York: Ballantine, 1969), p. 160.

30. Cf. Nietzsche, "whatever can be thought, cannot but be a fiction." And "Logic rests on presuppositions to which nothing in the actual world corresponds."

31. Suzuki, *Essays in Zen Buddhism,* Third Series, p. 266.

32. Suzuki, *The Lankavatara Sutra,* pp. 67-68.

33. Murti, *Central Philosophy of Buddhism,* pp. 212-214.

34. Ibid., 160.

35. Benjamin Lee Whorf, *Language, Thought, and Reality,* ed. John B. Carroll, (Cambridge: M. I. T. Press, 1956), pp. 262-263.

36. William James, *The Principles of Psychology,* vol. 1 (New York: Dover Publications), pp. 284-285.

37. *Madhyamika Shastra,* XV. 3. Cf. Suzuki, "Reality is differentiated and Emptiness vanishes into an emptiness."

38. Chang, *Buddhist Teaching of Totality,* p. 156.

39. Ludwig von Bertalanffy, *General System Theory* (New York: George Braziller, 1968), pp. 45, 49.

40. Alfred North Whitehead, *Modes of Thought* (New York: Free Press, Macmillan, 1968).

41. Joseph Needham, *Science and Civilization in China, vol. 2,* (London: Cambridge University Press, 1956), p. 582.

42. John J. McDermott, *The Writings of William James* (New York: Modern Library Random House, 1968), p. 157.

43. A. K. Coomaraswamy, *Hinduism and Buddhism* (New York: Philosophical Library), p. 28.

44. Cf. Coomaraswamy, "But what is proved by the analogies is not the influence of one system of thought upon another, but the coherence of the metaphysical tradition in the world and at all times." *Transformation of Nature in Art.* p. 202.

IV. *TIME/ETERNITY, SPACE/INFINITY*

Reality is a level of consciousness, that of non-dual Mind, containing concepts yet never grasped by them. Because it is free from conceptual elaboration, it can be partially described in any number of analogical or negative ways, but fully described in no way whatsoever. Thus the Dharmadhatu, the Tao, the Godhead, Brahman, the Void—all are attempts to convey Reality as it *is*, *yathabhutam*, in its "is-ness," its suchness (*tathata*), and not as it is labeled; as it is experienced in its purity after the "doors of perception have been cleansed" of all intellectual fabrications, and not as it is reported-distorted by symbolic thought processes.

Now in speaking of Reality as non-dual consciousness, most of us conjure up ideas of consciousness as somehow being connected with subjectivity. That is, we feel consciousness belongs not to "objects" such as this page but rather to myself as the subject who is supposedly "conscious" of this page. This is, of course, dualistic to the core. But since consciousness *is* Reality, and Reality is actually non-dual, it would be much more accurate to view consciousness not as relative subject *confronting* objects but as Absolute Subjectivity above the dualism of subject vs. object. Consciousness, as Absolute Subjectivity, belongs exclusively to neither subject nor object, but embraces both. In this sense, Absolute Reality is Absolute Subjectivity. The theologian Berdyaev explains:

> Spirit is never an object; nor is spiritual reality an objective one. In the so-called objective world there is no such nature, thing, or objective reality as spirit. Hence it is easy to deny the reality of spirit. God is spirit because he is not object, because he is subject. . . . In objectification there are no primal realities, but only symbols. The objective spirit is merely a symbolism of spirit. Spirit [Absolute Subject] is realistic while culture and social life are symbolical. In the object there is never any reality, but only the symbol of reality. The subject alone has reality.[1]

This Absolute Subjectivity is not the ego subject, as in the dualism subject vs. object. It is called Subject only because it hints that Reality lies *in what now appears to be the direction that we call inward*, subjective, towards the very center of our being, a center so deep and profound that it is God's center as well. But once we reach that center, we realize that it contains no dualisms at all, either that of subject vs. object or inward vs. outward. Here is the marriage of heaven and hell, and dualistic language fails us— "whereof one cannot speak, thereof one must remain silent."

> On the threshold of the most profound and ultimate depths we are faced with the revelation that our experience is contained within the depths of Divine life itself. But at this point silence reigns, for no human language or concept can express this experience. That is the *apophatic* sphere of irreconcilable contradictions baffling human thought. That is the ultimate realm of free and purified spirituality, which no monistic system is capable of defining. On *this side* there remain dualism, tragedy, conflict, man's dialogue with God, the plural world confronted with the One. It is not by discarding the principle of personality that the absolutely Divine One can be attained, but rather by exploring the spiritual depths of the personality which is antinomically united to the One.[2]

It is for this reason that Tillich suggested we take the word God to mean "depth," and this "depth" is exactly that Absolute Subjectivity or Witness within each of us, identified with neither subject nor object, but paradoxically including both. Sri Ramana Maharshi puts it thus:

> Since the Self, which is pure Consciousness, cognizes everything, it is the Ultimate Seer [Absolute Subjectivity]. All the rest: ego, mind, body, etc. are merely its objects; so each one of them except the Self or pure Consciousness is a merely externalized object and cannot be the true Seer. Since the Self cannot be objectified, not being cognized by anything else, and since the Self is the Seer seeing all else, the subject-object relation and the *apparent subjectivity of the Self* exist only on the plane of relativity and vanish in the Absolute. There is in truth no other than the Self, which is neither the seer nor the seen, and is not involved as subject or object.[3]

This is an extremely important point, a point we will return to again and again, for it forms a most critical link in our perpetual generation of dualism whereby "man stands in his own shadow and wonders why it is dark." Every individual habitually feels that his ego, his self, is the subject of his experiences, feelings, and thoughts, that his subjective self in some way *perceives* the external world, that his subjective self is now reading the words on this page. And this he expresses by saying "I am aware of my self reading." But the fact that something in me can look at my subjective self, that is, the fact that there exists in me right now an awareness of my "self" reading this page, should show me clearly that my supposedly subjective self is really an *object* of awareness! It is not a real subject at all, for it can be perceived objectively. Now just what is it "in" me that is aware of my self reading this page? We have seen, in connection with the Yogacara, that it cannot be simply another "subjective" self, for what is then aware of that self—another self? No—but "what" is it in me that is doing the looking, the seeing, the reading, the hearing, the thinking? It cannot be my subjective ego-self that is doing the looking, for that can be *looked at*, and as Huang Po stated, "Let me remind you that the *perceived* cannot *perceive*," that, in other words, my "self," since it can be perceived, cannot be that which is perceiving. But what is that in me which *is* perceiving? "There is within oneself *that which knows* . . ." says Hui-Heng, but what is it? Zen Master Bassui asks:

> My body is like a phantom, like bubbles on a stream. My mind, looking into itself, is as formless as empty-space, yet somewhere within sounds are perceived. Who is hearing?

He then proceeds to suggest an answer:

> To know this subject you must right here and now probe deeply into yourself, inquiring: "What is it that thinks in terms of good and bad, that sees, that hears?" If you question yourself profoundly in this wise, you will surely enlighten yourself. If you enlighten yourself, you are instantly a Buddha. The Mind which the Buddhas realized in their enlightenment is the Mind of all sentient beings. . . . This Mind, like space, is all-embracing. It does not come into existence with the creation of our body, nor does it perish with its disintegration. Though invisible, it suffuses our body, and every single act of seeing, hearing, smelling, speaking, or moving the hands and legs is simply the activity of this Mind.[4]

Shankara elaborates upon this Absolute Subjectivity:

> Now I shall tell you the nature of this Absolute Witness. If you recognize it, you will be freed from the bonds of ignorance, and attain liberation.
>
> There is a self-existent Reality, which is the basis of our consciousness of ego. That Reality is the Witness of the states of ego consciousness and the bodily coverings. That Reality is the Knower in all states of consciousness—waking, dreaming, and dreamless sleep. It is aware of the presence or absence of the mind and its functions. It is your real Self. That Reality pervades the universe, but no one penetrates it. It alone shines. The universe shines with its reflected light. Because of its presence, the body, senses, mind and intellect apply themselves to their respective functions, as though obeying its command.
>
> Its nature is eternal Mind. It knows all things, from the ego to the body. It is the Knower of pleasure and pain and of the sense-objects. This is your real Self, the Supreme Being, the

Ancient. It never ceases to experience infinite joy. It is always the same. It is Mind itself.[5]

Because it is that in us which witnesses our ego, or our individual "I", Ramana Maharshi called the absolute the "I-I", which is Plotinus' "what the mind thinks before it thinks itself." This "I-I" is just that Absolute Subjectivity that we have elsewhere called non-dual consciousness or Mind. So again we must emphasize that although for the sake of convenience we speak of Mind as the Absolute Subjectivity or Witness, it really is neither subjective nor objective—it remains non-dual awareness, *witnessing everything without separation from anything*, so that "the apparent subjectivity of the Self exists only on the plane of relativity and vanishes in the absolute."

Absolute Subjectivity, then, is non-dual consciousness, whose nature it is to be one with its "objects" of knowledge. We however, mistakenly take our ego-self as the real Subject, thereby separating this "self" from "external" objects and ushering in the dualistic mode of symbolic and "objective" knowledge. This is the psychological prototype of all dualisms—and, as we shall see, *this* is the root of all illusions.

It should be obvious that the Absolute Subjectivity is just another name for the Dharmadhatu, or Sunyata, or Tao, or Brahman, or Godhead. We have seen, in connection with each of these, that Reality cannot be intellectually grasped in any definite and final fashion whatever, and naturally the same holds for Absolute Subjectivity. It cannot be thought about because it is doing the thinking; it cannot be looked at because it is doing the looking; it cannot be known because it is doing the knowing. To quote Shankara once more:

> Now a distinct and definite knowledge is possible in respect of everything capable of becoming an object of knowledge: but it is not possible in the case of that which cannot become such an object. That is Brahman, for it is the Knower, and the Knower can know other things, but cannot make Itself the object of Its own knowledge, in the same way that fire can burn other things but cannot burn itself. Neither can it be said that Brahman is able to become an object of knowledge for anything other than Itself, since outside Itself there is nothing which can possess knowledge.[6]

And Lao Tzu has this:

> Because the eye gazes but can catch no glimpse of it,
> It is called elusive.
> Because the ear listens but cannot hear it,
> It is called the rarefied.

Because the hand feels for it but cannot find it,
It is called the infinitesimal.
These three, because they cannot be further scrutinized,
Blend into one.
Its rising brings no light;
Its sinking, no darkness.
Endless the series of things without name
On the way back to where there is Nothing.[7]

In a similar vein, because Absolute Subjectivity is pure consciousness not conscious of itself as an object, Zen refers to it as the Unconscious (*wu-hsin*), and the *Lankavatara Sutra* explains it simply: "As a sword cannot cut itself, as a finger cannot touch its own tip, Mind cannot see itself." Hence we are back to the point where if the attempt is made to know Reality as an object-concept, then Reality *apparently*, but not actually, becomes severed into a knower vs. a known. Recall the words of G. Spencer Brown:

> We may take it that the world undoubtedly is itself (i.e., is indistinct from itself [which we have called non-dual]), but, in any attempt to see itself as an object, it must . . . act so as to make itself distinct from, and therefore false to, itself.[8]

Thus—as we began to suggest in connection with the Yogacara—the apparent source of our dualistic illusions is the process of *objectification*, of trying to know Reality *as* an object *through* a subject—a project that must inevitably fail since Absolute Subjectivity cannot become an object without ceasing to be itself (i.e., "indistinct from itself"). Previously, however, we have argued that the process whereby we generate dualisms depends upon our misguided use of symbolic-map knowledge, or *conceptualization*. In fact, however, whether speaking of *conceptualization* or whether speaking of *objectification*, we are essentially referring to the same process, because at the precise moment that we form *concepts* about the universe we are (apparently) making that universe *objective*. This is exactly the conclusion reached in discussing the Yogacara and the Madhyamika, namely, that concepts and objects are, in a certain sense, synonymous. Hence, when we no longer confuse concepts with the universe, that universe no longer appears as an object, and vice versa.

It is the identity of objectification and conceptualization, as we have explained it, that lead Berdyaev to state, "In *objectification* there are no primal realities, but only *symbols*. . . . In the *object* there is never any reality, but only the *symbol* of reality." Likewise did Eddington maintain that the "loss of intimacy," that is, the loss of non-duality, is connected with the rise of symbolism. Similarly, Huang Po declares that "our original Buddha-nature is, in highest truth, devoid of any atom of *objectivity*," and then announces that this will become evident "if you can only rid yourselves of *conceptualization*."[9] Thus also does the *Awakening of Faith* maintain that ignorance and illusion occur when "suddenly *conceptualization* arises," but ignorance is also defined as "hindrance originating from the conception of *objects*."[10] In this sense, then, conceptualization and objectification are but two names for that one primal act of duality whereby Absolute Subjectivity mitotically becomes false to itself.

This, of course, does not imply that if we are to "see the world aright" that we must abandon forever our symbolic constructions and grunt and mumble incoherently where once a scholarly discourse prevailed. It implies only that once we understand fully that subject and object are not two, *then* we may return to conceptualization, for we will no longer be deceived by its reports. And unless we can do this, unless we can realize the territory that these object-concepts deceptively represent, we are merely barking at shadows. And as a Chinese proverb says, "One dog barks at a shadow, and a thousand dogs take it for reality."

Just as the non-dual mode of knowing is universally recognized, so is the metaphor of Absolute Subjectivity. Asked where the Kingdom of Heaven is to be found, Christ answered "within." The "within" is precisely the Source, the Witness, that in Hinduism is called *Atman*, the Supreme Knower in each and every one of us that is none other than Brahman, the sole and basic Reality of the universe, so that in realizing this "within," this Atman, this Absolute Subjectivity, each of us can say "I and my Father are one," or, as the *Chandogya Upanishad* words it, "That which is the finest essence—this whole universe has as its Self. That is Reality. That is Atman. *That art thou.*"[11]

In Mahayana Buddhism, this "within which is beyond" is called the *Tathagatagarbha*, or Matrix of Reality. The word "matrix" suggests the universal field-like nature of reality, and thus is reminiscent of the Dharmadhatu or Universal Field. In fact, the Tathagatagarbha is actually identical to the Dharmadhatu as centered on the individual, just as in Hinduism the Atman is identical to Brahman as centered on the individual. But the Tathagatagarbha (as well as the Atman) has a more psychological and "personal" ring, as evidenced by the fact that it also means the Womb of Reality, the womb in which we are reborn, as when Hermes says:

> I see that by God's mercy there has come to be in me a form which is not fashioned out of matter. . . . I am not now the man I was; I have been born again in Mind, and the bodily shape

> which was mine before has been put away from me. I am no longer an object colored and tangible; a thing of spatial dimensions; I am now alien to all this, and to all that you perceive when you gaze with bodily eyesight. To such eyes as yours, my son, I am not now visible.

"Not now visible" because Absolute Subjectivity, Mind, no one can see—it does not suffer itself to become an object, except in illusion.

In Ch'an Buddhism, the "position" of Absolute Subjectivity, that is, the "state" of knowing Reality non-dually, is called the "Host" position, as opposed to the "Guest" position of knowing reality through objective concepts. The man centered in the Host position is what in Taoism is called the "Superior Man," and Rinzai calls it "The True Man of no Rank (*wu-i*)." But this is not man, as in Mr. John Doe, but Man (*jen*), the Divine Son, the second person of the Trinity, *al-insan al-Kamil*, Pneuma, *ruarch adonai*, Nous, the Absolute Knower common in and to us all, the Atman, Purusa, Adam-Kadmon, Divine Man, Universal Man, Nietzche's Superman, of no rank because nothing can be predicated of it, as when Shelley sings in *Prometheus Unbound*:

> The painted veil, by those who were, called life,
> Which mimicked, as with colours idly spread,
> All men believed and hoped, is torn aside;
> The loathsome mask has fallen, the man remains
> Sceptreless, free, uncircumscribed. . . .

Let us here state a fact that has been implicit in this entire discussion of Absolute Subjectivity but which can now be explicitly stated: man, as the Knower, the Witness, the Atman, the Absolute Subjectivity, the Host, the Tathagatagarbha, the THAT in you which is reading this page, is the Godhead, Brahman, Dharmadhatu, Universal man of no rank, Mind, Reality itself; while man, as an object of knowledge, as a perceived phenomenon, as Guest, as clothed in "the painted veil, the loathsome mask," is the ego, the individual person (from the Greek *persona*, "*mask*"), the separate and alienated self.

Now Absolute Subjectivity or Mind is generally described as being Infinite and Eternal, but again these are just two concepts representing Reality as it is revealed with the non-dual mode of knowing. The problem, as always, is that when we attempt to speak of reality, we have no recourse but to utilize concepts, and as all concepts are dualistic we miss the point as soon as we open our mouths. It is like the four monks who took a vow of silence, and after a considerable length of time, one of the monks inadvertently said, "I have decided to remain silent for the rest of my life." Hearing this, the second monk commented, "But you've just broken the vow by saying something!" The third monk then exclaimed to the second, "But so have you just now!" The fourth monk began laughing, for all three had broken the vow of silence, and so he blurted out, "Well, it looks as if I'll be the only one to remain silent." Huang Po thus stated, "Begin to reason about it, and you at once fall into error," and St. Augustine would finally have it that "All scripture is in vain."

This difficulty is particularly acute when we are dealing with Infinity and Eternity. For example, when we think of the realm of the infinite, we usually understand it as somehow standing above or apart from the finite realm, and this at once deprives the infinite of its absolute nature, for the infinite, being "all-inclusive," has no opposite and stands apart from nothing, being (metaphorically) without any boundaries whatsoever. "The *finite is not the opposite of the infinite*, but only, so to speak, an excerpt from it."[12] If we are to think of it at all, then, the negative concepts of sizeless, space- less, extensionless, or dimensionless are the closest that ideation can come. Thus the "spaceless" Infinite, in its entirety, is present at every single point of space, and therefore, *to the Infinite*, every single point of space is absolutely HERE. A very crude and even somewhat misleading analogy might be that of the color "blue," for "blueness" itself is without form or space, but it does not exclude form, for one can take a blue pen and draw a variety of forms, shapes, and figures, and the "same blueness" is equally and en- tirely present "in" all of the forms so created. The infinite is thus not the opposite of finite being, but rather its "ground," and so between the infinite and the finite there is absolutely no bound- ary.[13]

The brightest of theologians and metaphysicians have always understood this. In the Hua-yen, for instance, this insight is ex- pressed as *shih li wu ai*, "between the Infinite and the finite there is no obstruction." The Soto Zen (Ch'an) Master Tung-shan ex- pressed this as *pien chung chih*, which roughly translates as "the Infinite understood through finite particulars," which is Blake's "seeing the world in a grain of sand." The great Ch'an Master Yun-men was more direct, and one day drew a line in the dirt with his staff and announced, "All the Buddhas, numberless as grains of sand, are gathered right here in endless dispute!"—this being roughly the Buddhist analog of the (perfectly reasonable) Chris- tian question, "How many angels can fit on the head of a pin?"

An analogy frequently used to convey the "non-idea" of the Infinite is that of a mirror and its reflected objects, for a mirror can reflect apples and horses, men and trees, chairs and birds—the mirror itself is none of these reflections, yet neither is it separate from them, which Clement of Alexandria expresses as "the Spirit of God indivisibly divided to all." Huang Po explains it thus:

> The essential Buddha-nature is a perfect whole, without
> superfluity or lack . . . It permeates the finite realms of exis-
> tence and yet remains everywhere completely whole. Thus,
> every single one of the myriads of phenomena in the universe
> *is* the absolute.[14]

Likewise, Nagarjuna was adamant on this point, as Murti so
expertly explains:

> The absolute is not one reality set against another, the em-
> pirical [and finite]. The absolute looked at through thought-
> forms is phenomenon. The latter, freed of the superimposed
> thought-forms, is the absolute. The difference is epistemic,
> and not ontological. Nagarjuna therefore declares that there
> is not the least difference between the world and the abso-
> lutely real.[15]

Despite the seeming likeness, this is most definitely not the
philosophical system called pantheism, which maintains that all
things are God.[16] First, things don't exist. Second, this is not a
philosophy but a level of consciousness. Third, *shih li wu ai*, "between the Infinite and the finite there is no obstruction," simply
maintains that the infinite and the finite cannot be opposed or set
against one another, for that drags the infinite down to the level of
finiteness, making it nothing more than one being beside other
beings, for that which is set apart from finite beings must itself be
finite. Paul Tillich spent much of his life trying to demonstrate
this, and one of his students, Rollo May, summed it up this way:

> God cannot be a being beside other beings. To insist that he is a
> being "above" or "below" all others still makes him a being
> apart from other beings, some "greatest being" we posit in the
> universe existing among the stars. If he is a thing, some other
> things in the universe must be outside his control, and he must
> be subject to the structure as a whole. A whole hornet's nest of
> absurd problems is opened up, such as the question, "How did
> God spend his time before he created the earth?" Paulus [Til-
> lich] told us once the answer for that given by his students in
> Germany: "Thinking up punishments for those who ask such
> questions."[17]

Let us now point out that in speaking of Infinity as sizeless,
dimensionless, or spaceless, the *space* which is *absent* in Infinity
is primarily the *space* between subject and object—or, if you will,
the *space* between you and this page, you and your objects of
perception. It is this space which seems to set you as "subject in
here" apart from the rest of the universe as "object out there." Now
this space seems real because you are convinced that your sub-

jective self is real, and further, that it is actually separate from your objects of perception.

Yet both of these assumptions are demonstrably false. In fact, your "separate and subjective" self is not a real subject at all, not a real perceiver or real observer, for it can easily be perceived and observed, and to repeat the words of Huang Po, "Let me remind you that the perceived cannot perceive." This separate "subject," in other words, is simply a complex of perceivable objects with which, for some strange reason, I have identified. In short, it is not a true subject at all, but a pseudo-subject! Now what happens if we go "behind" this pseudo-subject, in the direction that appears inward, in order to find the real Perceiver, the real Self, the Absolute Subjectivity? What do we find? Listen to David Hume, from his *Treatise of Human Nature*:

> For my part, when I enter most intimately into what I call *myself*, I always stumble on some particular perception or other, of heat or cold, light or shade, love or hatred, pain or pleasure. I never catch *myself* at any time without a perception, and never can observe any thing but the perception.

In other words, whenever I look for my true Self, all I find is objects of perception, which is the surest demonstration that the *space* between subject and object is absent in Absolute Subjectivity. Hence Ramana Maharshi could proclaim that "The notion that the Seer is different from the seen abides in the mind [i.e., in thought.] For those that ever abide in [Absolute Subjectivity] the Seer is the same as the seen." In short, Absolute Subjectivity is one with its universe of knowledge, so that you, in fact, *are* what you observe.

Thus the split, the *space*, between the "subject in here" and the "object out there" is a subtle illusion. The real Self does not know the universe from a distance, it knows the universe by being it, without the least trace of *space* intervening. And that which is spaceless is and must be infinite.

Now Eternity is to time what Infinity is to space. That is, just as all of Infinity is completely present at every point of space, so also all of eternity is completely present at every point of time. Thus, from the viewpoint of Eternity, absolutely all time is NOW, just as to the Infinite, all space is HERE. Since all time is NOW, it follows that the past and future are very much illusions, and that "the only Reality is present Reality."

> The Now-moment in which God made the first man and the Now-moment in which the last man will disappear, and the Now-moment in which I am speaking are all one in God, in whom there is only one Now. Look! The person who lives in the

light of God is conscious neither of time past nor of time to come but only of one eternity.

This is why the Bible speaks variously of the soul's day in time and of God's day in Eternity, and this prompted St. Dionysius to state, "need there is, methinks, to understand the sense in which the Scripture speaketh of Time and Eternity."[18] Meister Eckhart explains:

> There are more days than one. There is the soul's day and God's day. A day, whether six or seven ago, or more than six thousand years ago, is just as near to the present as yesterday. Why? Because all time is contained in the present Now-moment. . . . The soul's day falls within this time and consists of the natural light in which things are seen. God's day, however, is the complete day, comprising both day and night. It is the real Now-moment. . . . The past and future are both far from God and alien to his way.[19]

Because in the light of Eternity, past, present, and future are simultaneously contained in this Now-moment, Christ could claim that "Before Abraham *was*, I *am*," and Plotinus states simply, "There is all one day, series has no place; no yesterday, no tomorrow." St. Augustine elaborates: "Examine the changes of things, and thou wilt everywhere find 'has been' and 'will be.' Think on God and thou wilt find 'is' where 'has been' and 'will be' cannot be."[20] Even St. Thomas himself understood well that Reality is eternal, as he clearly states in the *Summa Contra Gentiles* (1.14, 15):

> God does not move at all, and so cannot be measured by time; neither does He exist "before or after" or no longer exist after having existed, nor can any succession be found in Him . . . but has the whole of His existence simultaneously; and that is the nature of eternity.

Similarly, Nicolas de Cusa announces that "all temporal succession coincides in one and the same Eternal Now. So there is nothing past or future. . . ."[21]

The insight that Reality is Eternal is by no means confined to Christian theology. Because it is part and parcel of that "philosophical consensus of universal extent," it is found everywhere from Hinduism to modern physics. For instance, the Vedantist Ramana Maharshi states:

> Apart from us where is time and where is space? If we are bodies, we are involved in time and space, but are we? We are one and identical Now, then, forever, here, there, and everywhere. Therefore we, timeless and spaceless Beings, alone

are.... What I say is that the Self is here and now, and alone.[22]

And as for Buddhism, one might say in general that the primary aim of all forms of Buddhist practice is simply to awaken ("Buddha" means "the Awakened One") to the Eternal Present. Thus Huang Po counsels: "Beginningless time and the present moment are the same.... You have only to understand that time has no real existence."[23] And Chao-chou states that "Even before the world was, this Reality *is*." D. T. Suzuki, explaining the *Gandavyuha Sutra* proclaims that "In this spiritual world there are no time-divisions such as the past, present, and future; for they have contracted themselves into a single moment of the present where life quivers in its true sense;"[24] and in the sutra itself Sudhana declares Reality to be "the abode of those who ... are able to perceive billions of years (kalpas) existing in one moment (ksana)..., perceiving in one moment all the past, present, and future." And the *Awakening of Faith* authoritatively states that *"The realization that Mind is Eternal is called Final enlightenment."*[25]

Thus the Ch'an (Zen) Masters utilize every conceivable means (*upaya*) to awaken their students to the Eternal Now, as Chang Chung-Yuan states, "This is the gist of the teaching of Chan. The ultimate reality lies right at the heart of daily existence, if one but knows how to grasp the absolute moment."[26] Even the Buddha himself declared, "Get yourselves across the sticky-mire, and let not the Moment pass, for they shall mourn those whose Moment is past."[27] To seize this Moment Ch'an resorts to direct and immediate action, for this spontaneous activity alone knows neither past nor future. One day, while Ch'an Master Ma-tsu was walking with one of his students, Po-chang, a flock of wild geese flew overhead, whereupon Ma-tsu asked, "What is that?" "Wild geese." "Where are they at this moment?" "Why, they have already flown away." At this, Ma-tsu seized Po-chang's nose and gave it a violent twist, so that Po-chang screamed out. "How can you say they have flown away?" demanded Ma-tsu. "They have been here from the very beginning!"

Representing Islam, Jalalu'd Rumi declares, in speaking of God, that "His existence in time past or future is only in relation to you; both are the same to Him, but *you think them two*." Thus a true Sufi [follower of esoteric Islam] is called a "son of the Moment; he is ... not of time ... the past and future and time without beginning and time without end do not exist, [therefore] it is not the Way to speak of 'tomorrow,' "[28] which is very similar to Christ's "take no thought of the morrow."

Even the modern quantum physicists have destroyed forever the old Newtonian notion of serial time, and have replaced it with the absolute Here-Now for a given individual. Schroedinger, who understood deeply that Reality is Mind-only, speaks of it as follows:

> I venture to call it [Mind] indestructible since it has a peculiar time-table, namely Mind is always Now. There is really no before and after for Mind. . . . The *present* is the only thing that has no end. . . . We may, or so I believe, assert that physical theory in its present stage strongly suggests the indestructibility of Mind by time.[29]

Mind is indestructible by time because, as Parmenides put it, "Nor *was* it ever, nor *will* it be, for Now it *is*, all at once." And that Now, in the words of Dante, is "the Moment to which all times are present."

Equally important, however, is that quantum mechanics and relativity theory have brought forth another insight, namely, that space, time, and objects are in some sense *continuous*. In a rough and non-mathematical fashion, we may approach this in the following manner: space is properly thought of as a surrounding function; that is, space is not a blank and featureless nothing, but rather is that which surrounds or encloses objects, which is why physicists speak of space as having certain properties such as curvature. Space, in other words, cannot exist apart from objects, since by definition it is that which surrounds them. Objects, on the other hand, must be enclosed by space, that is, they must have a boundary or else they would simply explode. Space and objects—in this sense—are therefore one. Furthermore, objects, in order to exist, must endure; that is, duration or time is necessary for the existence of objects, for without duration there could be nothing to endure. Conversely, the existence of duration depends upon objects, for without objects to endure, there could be no duration; and in this sense, time and objects are one. It follows that space and time are also one. Hence space, time, and objects are mutually dependant and inseparable, and therefore the unreality of any one of these three implies the unreality of the other two! The point is that since space and time are illusory, we have simply demonstrated—in a slightly different fashion—the Madhyamika "doctrine" of the voidness of "things," as well as the Hua-yen doctrine of *shih shih wu ai*, "mutual interpenetration of all things." In the words of Aristotle:

> If the before and after are both in one and the same Now, then what happened ten thousand years ago would be simultaneous with what is happening today, and nothing would be

before or after anything else. . . . Then everything would be in anything, and the universe in a grain of millet, only because the grain of millet and the universe are both existent at the same time.[30]

Coomarswamy, in commenting on this passage, explains:

> There is a sense in which the universe is "in a grain of millet;" for if the grain and the universe and considered not in their extension but as regards their common and immutable essence that insists in the absolute Now, then it can be said that the universe is "in" the grain at the same time that the grain is in the universe. . . .[31]

And all of this simply because the unreality of time implies the unreality of individual objects!

Now the insight that the real world "has the whole of its existence simultaneously, and that is the nature of eternity"—that insight leads directly to what is perhaps the most serious indictment of reason's competence to comprehend reality. Put bluntly, thought proceeds in a line, while the real world does not. This inescapable limitation, built into the very structure of thought, was first pointed out, I believe, by Lancelot L. Whyte, and later elaborated upon by such scholars as McCluhan, Bateson, Lilly, Watts, and Weil. Thought is sequential, successive, one-dimensional, while the real world presents itself as a multi-dimensional, non-successive, simultaneous pattern of infinite richness and variety; and trying to make the one grasp the other is like trying to appreciate a beautiful landscape by looking through a narrow slit in a fence or trying to take in a Renoir painting by microscope alone.

Recall that "things" are simply products of thought and not actual entities composing the universe. That is to say, a "thing" is nothing but a narrowed bit of selective attention, the "figure," sliced from the total sensory gestalt by ignoring its inseparable "background." In the words of William James, a "thing" is a product of "attending to this and ignoring that." These narrowed bits of attention, as James further noted, are then signified by words, names, or some other symbols, and thus exalted to the imaginary status of real, live, independent "things." And since all words except proper names are dualistic, this process merely aggravates the illusion that "things" are separate and self-existent entities just lying around awaiting perception. At the point we completely confuse these symbols with reality itself, the illusion is vouchsafed.

The fact remains, however, that figure and ground constitute an inseparable relationship of unity-in-diversity and diversity-in-unity, for the express reason that the one could never be manifest without the other, just as there is no such thing as a convex without a concave, an inline without an outline, a buyer without a seller, an up without a down, an inside without an outside. Again, to say that "things" don't exist is not to say that the world is really a uniform mush—as R. H. Blyth pointed out, *the "Void" means "seamless," not "featureless."* At any rate, it is only by habitually narrowing attention to only particular facets of the seamless field of awareness that thought presents us with the convincing illusion that the world is a multiple of separate and independent "things" existing "out there."

Now the only way that thought can handle these small bits of narrowed attention is to arrange them in a linear order. Obviously, once the world is sliced into a vast number of small chunks, these chunks cannot be swallowed all at once—they must be taken in successively, bit by bit by bit, just as you must now read this material word by word by word. As everybody knows, you can't think of even two or three "things" at once without being thrown into paralyzing confusion; and so, to introduce some measure of coherence and order, the thought process, with the help of memory, strings out these separate bits of attention along a line which it creates for that very purpose, in almost the same manner that these words are arranged into "lines of print."

This "line" of successive bits of narrowed attention, this "line" upon which thought strings out its objects-concepts, this "line" which thought itself conjures up, is nothing other than *time*. In other words, time is nothing more, nothing less, than thought's successive way of viewing the world. But by habitually viewing nature in this linear, successive, temporal fashion, we soon arrive at the "obvious" conclusion that nature herself proceeds in a line, from the past to the future, from cause to effect, from before to after, from yesterday to tomorrow—completely ignoring the fact that this supposed linearity of nature is entirely a product of the way we view it. But then, to a hammer, the whole world looks like a nail.

Nature, however, does not proceed in a line—it happens simultaneously—everywhere-at-once. And the evidence of this simultaneity is right at hand—simply stop reading and look up, where you will discover an infinite number of processes all happening at once: sun shining, heart beating, birds singing, kids playing, lungs breathing, dogs barking, wind blowing, crickets chirping, eyes seeing, ears hearing—need we continue? These phenomena do not proceed one another nor follow one another in time—they are all happening everywhere at once, no before, no after. In other words, to say that nature does not proceed in a *line* is to say that nature does not proceed in *time*: it has the whole of its existence simultaneously, and that is the nature of Eternity.

Actually, the whole notion of succession, of one "thing" succeeding another "thing" in time, depends directly upon our processes of *memory*, for it is quite obvious that without memory we would have absolutely no idea of time, either of the past or of the future. The question, then, is whether memory *reports* a real phenomenon which we call "time," or whether memory *creates* an illusion of "time."

At first sight, it certainly seems that memory reports a very real picture of a very real past. For we feel unequivocally that not only can we know present bits of attention, but also past bits stored in memory. From these memory bits we naturally infer that there must have been a real past, and in so doing we generate a most vivid sense of time and imagine that we are somehow moving through it towards the future. The whole idea of time thus depends directly upon the notion that we can, through memory, know the actual past.

Yet a subtle illusion has entered into this picture, an illusion first spotted and clearly announced by St. Augustine, and recently confirmed by the likes of Schroedinger and Watts. For, strictly speaking, we are never directly aware of a real past at all—rather, we are only aware of a memory-picture of the past, and further, that memory exists only in and as the *present*! In the words of Watts:

> But what about memories? Surely by remembering I can also know what is past? Very well, remember something. Remember the incident of seeing a friend walking down the street. What are you aware of? You are not actually watching the veritable event of your friend walking the street. You can't go up and shake hands with him, or get an answer to a question you forgot to ask him at the past time you are remembering. In other words, you are not looking at the real past at all. You are looking at a present trace of the past. . . . From memories you infer that there have been past events. But you are not aware of any past events. You know the past only in the present and as part of the present.[32]

Thus, in remembering any "past event," we are not really aware of the actual past at all. If you remember, for example, what you had for dinner last night, can this memory allow you to really see that meal? Touch it? Eat some of it? Surely, you are *never* aware of any actual past at all, but rather only dim pictures of the past, and those pictures exist only as a *present* experience.

The same holds for the "future" as well, for any thought of tomorrow is nevertheless a *present* thought. Inescapably, we know the past and future "only in the present and as part of the present." Thus, the only time we are ever aware of is *Now*! Hence did Schroedinger state that "Mind is always *now*. There is really no before and after for Mind. There is only a *now* that includes memories and expectations."[33] St. Augustine was of the same opinion, for, as Bertrand Russell summarized his viewpoint, the "past and future can only be thought of as present: 'past' must be identified with memory, and 'future' with expectation, memory and expectation being both present facts."[34] Hence, it is only in confusing present memory with past knowledge that we conjure up, out of this present moment, the vast illusion called "time."

This is the *how* of time's genesis—we will eventually see that the *why* of time's genesis is man's avoidance of death. But leaving this aside until the proper point, it should presently be obvious that when memory is no longer imagined to be a real knowledge of the "past," but is instead understood to be a *present* experience, then the support of the time-illusion instantly collapses. Past and future collapse into now, before and after collapse into present, linearity collapses into simultaneity, and time vanishes into Eternity. Thus all of the above quotes on time and eternity (which you now might wish to re-read) point to the same insight: this present moment contains all time and is therefore itself timeless, and hence *this timeless present is Eternity itself*—a moment without date or duration, extension or succession, past or future, before or after, "having the whole of its existence simultaneously, which is the nature of Eternity." Thus we can state with René Guénon that:

> He who cannot escape from the standpoint of temporal succession so as to see all things in their simultaneity is incapable of the least conception of the metaphysical order.[35]

Or with Coomaraswamy, "His [Godhead's] timeless nature is that of the 'now' without duration, of which we, who can only think in terms of past and future, have not and cannot have experience."[36] Or with Wittgenstein, "If we take eternity to mean not infinite temporal duration but timelessness, then eternal life belongs to those who live in the present. Our life has no end in just the same way in which our visual field has no limits."[37]

Wittgenstein's point that eternity is not everlasting temporal duration but timelessness is worth repeating. Just as infinity as not big nor small, but sizeless and spaceless, so eternity is not everlasting time nor a split fraction of a second—rather, it is timeless, a moment without date or duration, existing in its *entirety* right now. *This* present moment, since it knows neither past nor future, is itself timeless, and that which is timeless is Eternal.

Thus "the eternal life belongs to those who live in the present."

The incredible confusion of everlasting time with Eternity in popular Christianity, and hence in the imagination of most Westerners, might be called a major philosophical catastrophe, spawning such wild questions as, "How does God know the future?" If, on the other hand, we understand Eternity, the answer becomes obvious. As Boethius pointed out, God's knowledge of the future, or "foreknowledge," should be understood as "the knowledge of a never fading instant rather than a foreknowledge, as if of the future. Wherefore it is not called a *pre*-vision or *fore*-sight but rather an *on*-sight, because, placed far from lower things, it overlooketh all things, as it were, from the highest summit of things."[38] What Boethius called "onsight" we might today call *insight*—and insight is precisely the timeless and non-dual mode of knowing. God, who knows all things by non-dual insight, knows all times—past and future—as existing in this Eternal Moment.

The confusion of time and Eternity also generates one of the most perplexing questions ever to plague man, namely, "When was the universe created?" Many modern astronomers answer something like, "There occurred x billion years ago a 'big bang' that flung matter outward into space from a very condensed pool of ionic plasma. This was the beginning of the universe." Yet ask them what happened *before* the Big Bang and you receive the Big Evasion, either "we don't know" or "let's change the subject." Nobody has yet found a beginning in time, so that now most scientists and educated laymen respond indifferently to this question by replying, "It was never created, nor will it end," without really understanding the incredible meaning of that statement— for that which has no beginning and no end in time, is and must be timeless, Eternal. That is, the universe and all things in it are being created *Now*, in what Boehme called an "everlasting beginning." Thus proclaims Eckhart:

> To talk about the world as being made by God tomorrow [or] yesterday, would be talking nonsense. God makes the world and all things in this present now.[39]

Suzuki, speaking of the Buddhist doctrine of the Void (sunyata), says:

> God is not in time mathematically enumerable. His creativity is not historical, not accidental, not at all measurable. It goes on continuously without cessation, with no beginning, with no end. It is not an event of yesterday or today or tomorrow, it comes out of timelessness, of nothingness, of Absolute Void. God's work is always done in an absolute present. . . .[40]

And Coomaraswamy explains: "In other words, God is always creating the world 'now, this instant,' and it is only to creatures of time that the creation presents itself as a series of events, or 'evolution.' "[41]

Creation is thus nowever, coming straight out of the Voidness of *this* timeless Moment—and this creation is not the creation of things, of material, or of substance, *but the creation of dualisms*. Thus is the universe created, and it is to this creation that we must soon turn.

To bring this discussion of Eternity and Infinity to a close, one major point has to be emphasized. To see the world aright, to experience Absolute Subjectivity, to know it as Infinite and Eternal, is not simply a matter of abolishing the temporal dualism of past vs. future or the spatial dualism of subject vs. object. These, like all dualisms, are not so much false as illusory, and the attempt to abolish them is not wrong but nonsensical. Time and space cannot be abolished for the sufficient reason that they do not exist!

Thus, if at this moment we carefully look so as to find even the least trace of time, we will not succeed. For, as St. Augustine said, the past is literally nothing but a memory and the future nothing but an expectation, with both memory and expectation being a *present* fact! Think of the past—that is a present act; anticipate the future—that also is a present act. Any evidence of a past exists only in the present, and any reason to believe in a future also exists only in the present. When the real past happened, it wasn't the past but the present, and when the real future arrives, it won't be the future, it will be the present. Thus, the *only* time of which we are ever aware is the *present moment*, a present which includes the past of memories and the future of expectations.

This moment, because it contains or embraces all time, is itself above time or timeless, and that is the nature of Eternity. Whether we say all time is now, or whether we say there is no time but now, it all comes to the same thing: time is a vast illusion, and *this* timeless moment is Eternity itself. Thus, Eternity is not everlasting time but the real, unfading, indestructible, and timeless Present, for, as Schroedinger said, the present is the only thing that has no end.

Similarly, the dualism of subject vs. object is as illusory as that of the past vs. the future, and its illusory nature can be as easily demonstrated. For, at this moment, can you actually find a separate self, a separate "subject" apart from its "object"? When you hear a sound, can you ever hear yourself hearing? When you taste something, can you taste the taster? Smell the smeller? Feel the feeler? When you see a tree, can you at the same time see the seer? As you are now thinking about all of this, can you simultaneously find a thinker who is thinking about it? Is all this not the clearest demonstration that there exists no separate subject apart from objects? Invariably, the sensation called "yourself in here" and the sensation called "objects out there" are one and the same sensation. As we said in connection with Yogacara, at this moment you are this page reading itself!

Now this state of ever-present non-dual awareness wherein the observer is the observed we have called Mind. It alone is always the case, for, whether we realize it or not, the subject is never actually split from the object—"The barrier does not exist," however vividly we imagine otherwise! In this chapter, we have also termed this non-dual awareness "Absolute Subjectivity." We have done so not in a descriptive fashion but in an injunctive fashion, using "Absolute Subjectivity" as a kind of signpost, as a kind of Ariadne's thread to lead us out of the maze of duality and back to Mind-only. And a useful signpost it is, as the mystics of all ages have testified, for it points to the inescapable fact that when you go "behind" the relative subject to find this Witness, this Supreme Knower, this Absolute Subjectivity, this Perceiver, *all you find are objects of perception,* which is the surest indication that the Knower is one with the universe it knows. As we have pointed out, non-dual understanding is itself Mind! And when this occurs (it is occurring *now*), then it further becomes obvious that what you thought was the split between yourself as "subject in here" and the rest of the universe as "object out there" is in fact a subtle illusion, that the universe is never really severed into a seer and a seen, but that the seer and seen are always united in the present act of seeing. Hence there is no problem in calling the real world Mind-only, or Consciousness-only, or Absolute Subjectivity, for in actuality consciousness and the universe are not separate entities. Thus, like the "Void," or the "Dharmadhatu," or "Mind-only," or "Brahman," the "Absolute Subjectivity" is just another name for the real world as *indistinct* from, and therefore true to, itself.

Because the dualisms of past vs. future and subject vs. object are not just false but illusory, it follows that we are already living in and as the real world, infinite and eternal (again, not big and everlasting, but spaceless and timeless), however much we may pretend to obscure this with symbolism. Thus all of the discussions about Mind-only, Brahman-only, the Void, the Infinite, the Eternal, Absolute Subjectivity—all of this is not an analytical prescription of the way things should be but a metaphorical description of a state of affairs that already exists. Your very state of consciousness, just as it is now, this instant, is always identical to the ultimate, for, as we have seen, in this instant you simply can't find a separate subject to be divided from reality, nor any time in which this separation could occur. Whether we realize this or not does not alter the fact of our Supreme Identity, and hence our problem is not to engineer this Reality in some future but to understand it as a present fact.

In sum, there is "within" you that which knows, the Witness, the Absolute Subjectivity, and it is none other than Mind, the Godhead itself. But this Absolute Subjectivity is not the separate subject we habitually know and feel ourselves to be, for this sense of separate subject is an illusion, demonstrated by the fact that whenever you look for this subject you find only objects of perception. Thus the real Knower is one with its universe of knowledge: everything you observe is none other than you who are observing it. When you go right down to the very base of your consciousness, you find the universe—not the false universe of objects out there, but the real universe which is no longer imagined as split into a subject vs. an object. At the very bottom of yourself you fall out of yourself into Reality. As Monoimus put it, "And if thou shouldst closely investigate all these things, thou wilt find God in Thyself, one and many; thus finding from thyself a way out of thyself."

Falling into the real world, where the observer is the observed, it becomes obvious that you and the universe are not, were not, and never will be separate entities. "Thus," to repeat the words of Schroedinger, and I assure you he means them literally, "you can throw yourself flat on the ground, stretched out upon Mother Earth, with the certain conviction that you are one with her and she with you." In other words, the *space* between you as observing subject "in here" and the observed objects "out there" is absent in Absolute Subjectivity—and that which is spaceless is Infinite. Similarly, the *time* between the past and the future simply cannot be found in Absolute Subjectivity, for there is not time but now— and that which is timeless is Eternal. In short, Absolute Subjectivity knows its universe simultaneously, not in a sequence called "time" or through a distance called "space." *And* this is a present state of affairs, whether we realize it or not. That is why the Buddhists maintain that Mind is the "Unattainable," for you cannot attain that which you already have, any more than you can go out and acquire your feet.

But most of us do not realize this. We have forgotten Mind, and forgotten we have forgotten it. Therefore, we must now take a profound journey, not backwards into time, but deeply into the present, to re-call, re-collect, re-cognize, and re-member who and what we really are. We will follow the generation of the Spectrum of Consciousness from its eternal ground in Mind-only, where we are already one with the Infinite, all the way up to the point where we actually believe ourselves to be separate and alienated egos divorced from, but trapped in, a body. We will then begin what, from our present point of view, must appear as a long and laborious descent back to Mind, healing the dualisms that obscure our Supreme Identity only to find in the end that they never existed. We will find that the journey was unnecessary, but perhaps inevitable, and so the only advice we can take with us is:

> Moment without duration, point without extension—these are the Golden Mean, and inconceivably Strait Way leading out of time into eternity, from death to immortality.[42]

REFERENCES AND NOTES

1. Nicholas Berdyaev, *Spirit and Reality* (New York: 1939), pp. 5, 53. Cf. "The sastra's purport is not to represent Brahman definitely as this or that object, its purpose is rather to show that Brahman as the eternal subject (pratyagatman, inward Self [above subject-object]) is never an object, and thereby to remove the distinction of objects known, knowers, acts of knowledge, etc., which is fictitiously created by Nescience." Shankara's commentary on the *Vedanta Sutras of Badarayana,* trans. George Thibaut.

2. Ibid., pp. 198-199.

3. Arthur Osborne, *The Collected Works of Ramana Maharshi* (London: 1959), p. 25.

4. Philip Kapleau, *The Three Pillars of Zen* (Boston: Beacon Press, 1965), p. 162.

5. After Shankara, *Crest-Jewel of Discrimination.* Prabhavananda, Swami, and Isherwood, Christopher, trans., (New York: Mentor Book, 1947), p. 52.

6. Shankara's commentary on *Kena Upanishad.* In René Guénon, *Man and His Becoming* (London: Luzac, 1945), p. 114.

7. *Lao Tze,* Chapter XIV.

8. G. S. Brown, *Laws of Form* (New York: Julian Press).

9. John Blofeld, trans., *The Zen Teaching of Huang Po* (New York: Grove Press, 1958), pp. 33, 35.

10. Y. S. Hakeda, trans., *The Awakening of Faith* (New York: Columbia University Press, 1968), pp. 50, 53.

11. *Chandogya Upanishad,* 6.8.6.

12. Ananda K. Coomaraswamy, *Time and Eternity* (Switzerland: Ascona, 1947), p. 71n.

13. For a popular account, see Alan W. Watts, *The Supreme Identity* (Vintage Books, 1972), Chap. 1.

14. Blofeld, *Zen Teaching,* p. 84.

15. T. R. V. Murti, *The Central Philosophy of Buddhism* (London: George Allen and Unwin, 1960), p. 141.

16. Thus states Coomaraswamy: "It would hardly be an exaggeration to say that a faithful account of Hinduism might well be given in the form of a categorical denial of most of the statements that have been made about it, alike by European scholars and by Indians trained in our modern sceptical and evolutionary modes of thought. One would begin, for example, by remarking that the Vedic doctrine is neither pantheistic nor polytheistic. . . ." *Hinduism and Buddhism.* p. 3. So also Suzuki: "This is to be regretted, for pantheism is something foreign to Zen. . . . Even when Zen indulges in intellection, it never subscribes to a pantheistic interpretation of the world. For one thing, there is no One in Zen. If Zen ever speaks of the One as if it recognized it, this is a kind of condescension to common parlance [to the analogical way of pointing]." *Zen and Japanese Culture.* p. 32.

17. Rollo May, *Paulus* (New York: Harper and Row), p. 87.

18. St. Dionysius, *The Divine Names,* X. 3.

19. R. B. Blakney, trans., *Meister Eckhart* (New York: Harper Torchbooks, 1941), pp. 62, 212.

20. Coomaraswamy, *Time and Eternity,* p. 112. Cf. Suzuki, "But if we do not somehow succeed in making 'was' or 'will be' turn into 'is,' we cannot have peace of mind, we cannot escape from dread. . . ." *Mysticism, Christian and Buddhist,* p. 53.

21. Nicholas de Cusa, *The Vision of God,* Chap. X.

22. Osborne, *Collected Works,* p. 73; also *The Spiritual Teaching of Ramana Maharshi* (Berkeley: Shambhala, 1972), p. 47.

23. Blofeld, *Zen Teaching,* p. 124.

24. D. T. Suzuki, *Essays in Zen Buddhism,* Third Series (London: Rider and Co., 1970).

25. Hakeda, *The Awakening of Faith,* p. 39.

26. Chang Chung-yuan, trans., *Original Teachings of Ch'an Buddhism* (New York: Pantheon, 1969), p. 100.

27. From *Sutta Nipata.*

28. Jalalu'd Rumi, *Mathnawi,* III. 1152-3, I. 132-3, and VI. 2715.

29. Erwin Schroedinger, *What is Life? and Mind and Matter* (London: Cambridge University Press, 1969), pp. 145, 165.

30. Coomaraswamy, "Physics", *Time and Eternity,* p.80.

31. Ibid., pp. 80-81.

32. Alan W. Watts, *The Wisdom of Insecurity* (New York: Vintage, 1968), p. 82.

33. Schroedinger, *What is Life?,* p. 145.

34. Bertrand Russel, *A History of Western Philosophy* (New York: Simon and Schuster, 1945).

35. René Guénon, *The Metaphysique Orientale,* pp. 17, 140.

36. A. K. Coomaraswamy, *Hinduism and Buddhism* (New York: Philosophical Library), p. 37.

37. Ludwig Wittgenstein, *Tractatus Logico-Philosophicus* (London: Routledge and Kegan Paul, 1969), p. 147.

38. Coomaraswamy, *Time and Eternity,* p.114.

39. D. T. Suzuki, *Mysticism: Christian and Buddhist* (Macmillan, 1957), p. 12.

40. Ibid., p. 13.

41. Coomaraswamy, *Time and Eternity,* p. 29n.

42. A. K. Coomaraswamy, *The Bugbear of Literacy* (London: Dobson, 1949).

V. *EVOLUTION OF THE SPECTRUM*

With this understanding, we are now in a position to describe the generation of the spectrum of consciousness "out of" the infinite and eternal Absolute Subjectivity, out of the Void Mind, out of Brahman, out of the Godhead. Throughout this volume we have been discussing, in a rather random fashion, the creation of dualistic illusions that seem to obscure Reality. What we propose to do now is to describe the generation of the major dualisms historically, step by step, *as if* this process were an evolution occurring through time, but bearing in mind always that this evolution is actually of the Moment, not of the past. In order to give this account some coherence, we have chosen a certain "marker" of dualism, namely, the level of identification. A short overview of the evolution of the Spectrum of Consciousness will clarify this concept.

In reality, there is Mind-only, "all-inclusive," non-dual, the timeless ground of all temporal phenomena, "fusion without confusion," a Reality "without duality but not without relations." At this "stage," we are identified with this All, we are one with the basic Energy of the universe. This is what we have elsewhere termed the first level of consciousness, the Level of Mind. But through the process of *maya,* of dualistic thought, we introduce illusory dualities or divisions, "creating two worlds from one." These divisions are not real, but only seeming, yet man behaves in every way *as if* they were real; and being thus duped, man clings to his first and primordial dualism, that of subject vs. object, self vs. not-self, or simply organism vs. environment. At this point, man shifts from a cosmic identity with the All to a personal identity with his organism, and we thus generate the second major level of consciousness, the Existential Level: man identified with his organism.

Like an ascending spiral, man's fragmentation through duality continues, so that most individuals don't even feel identified with all of their organism—we say not "I am a body" but rather "I *have* a body," and this "I" that "has" a body we call our self, our ego. At this point, man's identity shifts from his organism as a whole to his ego, and we have generated the third major level of consciousness, the Ego Level. Continuing this dualistic spiral, man can even attempt to disown facets of his ego that he finds undesirable, refusing to admit into his consciousness the unwanted aspects of himself. Again man's identity shifts, this time to *some* facets of his ego, generating the next level of the spectrum, a level we call the Shadow.

Here, then, we have the evolution of the spectrum of consciousness. Metaphorically, each level of the spectrum represents the seeming identification of Absolute Subjectivity with one set of objects as against all others, and *with each new level of the spectrum, this identification becomes more narrowed and exclusive.* Of course, the spectrum itself contains a vast number of bands and levels, but we have singled out a half-dozen major ones since they are easily recognizable, as will presently become evident. We must turn now to a more detailed explanation of the generation of these various levels of consciousness as well as a careful but preliminary description of each.

This will be, in other words, a study in what the Hindus and Buddhists call *maya,* a study in the distinctions "superimposed" on Reality to apparently generate phenomena. Thus it would be useful to bear in mind the general nature of *maya* itself—namely, the "magic" or "art" whereby we "create two worlds from one," a dualistic process that is very much a *creation* but an *illusory* creation, not real but "pretend", a make-believe manifestation of the Absolute *appearing* as all phenomena. *Maya* is the Godhead's creative power of emptying or reflecting itself into all things and thus *creating* all things, the power of Absolute Subjectivity to take on objective appearance. In reality the Godhead remains Void, but appears or takes form only as objects; and this power of phenomenal appearance-creation is *maya.*

In this regard, the word *maya* itself, which is usually translated as "illusion", is derived from the Sanskrit root *ma,* from which we get such English words as mother, matter, and measure, so that the "world of maya" is simply the "world of measurement"—that is, of mental and purely symbolic maps conventionally dividing and measuring the universe. By the same token, the "world of maya" is also the "world of matter," for material things, as we have seen, are nothing but a product of our mental measuring and dividing. Because all measurement is merely abstraction and, as such, an omission of part of the truth, the world of measure and matter, if mistaken for ultimate realities, is indeed a world of illusion. The point, then, is not to confuse the world as it is with the world as it is measured into space, time, objects, classes, delineations, boundaries, limits, particulars, universals, individuals, generals, or categories of any type or kind—for the simple reason that all measurement is a product of thought, not reality; just as, for example, wood is not actually composed of inches but is only conventionally and mentally measured or divided into very arbitrary units called "inches." So also, the world is not actually composed of separate things extended in space and succeeding one another in time, except as viewed through the magic illusion of *maya,* of measurement. Not to understand this trick is to condemn oneself to the perpetual frustration of trying to gather up "inches" and save them in a box.

It is in all these senses, therefore, that Coomaraswamy defines *maya* as "the maternal measure and means essential to the manifestation of a quantitative, and in this sense 'material,' world of appearances, by which we may be either enlightened or deluded according to the degree of our own maturity."[1] Thus, measure is the mother of matter—*maya:* the birth of the apparent world of separate things extended in space and time, with man "the measure of all things."

Now we cannot give a reason for the arising of *maya,* for reason itself is within *maya* and thus could not account for it. That is to say, the Godhead's "actions" are without purpose or goal, effort or volition, motive or desire, cause or effect—for all of that implies a future aim and God knows no future or past, but only an Eternal Now. All we can do is, somewhat poetically, describe the world of *maya,* so that in seeing the trick we have played on ourselves, we are free to awaken from the spell. Towards this end, we will now give a wide survey of some different accounts of the "beginning" of *maya*—not reasons for its "beginning," but descriptions of its "beginning"—which, of course, is the same as the beginning of the spectrum of consciousness. We will begin with a mathematical account and end with a psychoanalytical account, understanding, however, that we believe they are all referring to essentially the same process.

In the opening paragraph of *Laws of Form,* the brilliant mathematician G. Spencer Brown states:

> The theme of this book is that a universe *comes into being when a space is severed or taken apart.* The skin of a living organism cuts off an outside from an inside. So does the circumference of a circle in a plane. By tracing the way we represent such a severance, we can begin to reconstruct, with an accuracy and coverage that appear uncanny, the basic forms underlying linguistic, mathematical, physical, and biological science, and can begin to see how the familiar laws of our own experience follow inexorably from the *original act of severance.*[2]

It is precisely with this *original act of severance which creates the phenomenal universe* that we are now concerned: the very first movement whereby we "sever a space," create two worlds from one, and land ourselves squarely in a world of appearances. *This original act of severance we will call the Primary Dualism:* epistemo-

logically, it is the severance of the knower from the known; onto-
logically, the severance of the Infinite from the finite; theo-
logically, it is original sin; generally, we may speak of it as the
illusory split between subject and object. Of this Primary Dualism,
G. Spencer Brown states:

> The act itself is already remembered, even if unconsciously, as
> our first attempt to distinguish different things in a world
> where, in the first place, the boundaries can be drawn any-
> where we please. At this stage the universe cannot be dis-
> tinguished from how we act upon it, and the world may seem
> like shifting sand beneath our feet.[3]

This is the non-dual territory before we introduce the conventional boundaries known as maps and symbols. Most of us, however, are so lost in maps that the territory remains buried. Thus
Brown comments:

> That mathematics, in common with other art forms, can lead
> us beyond ordinary existence, and can show us something of
> the structure in which all creation hangs together, is no new
> idea. But mathematical texts generally begin the story some-
> where in the middle, leaving the reader to pick up the thread
> as best he can. Here the story is traced from the beginning.[4]

Brown then shows that the beginning of mathematics, indeed of
physics and philosophy, linguistics and biology—in fact, the universe itself—can be elegantly traced from the *original act,* which
he states as:

Let there be a distinction.

In his own words, "we have here reached a level so primitive that
active and passive, as well as a number of other more peripheral
opposites, have long since condensed together."[5] We are here at the
Level of Mind, of pure non-duality, of the coincidence of opposites,
of timeless and spaceless Reality. For no apparent reason—
because reason itself does not exist here—there occurs a
dualism—"Let there be a distinction"—and following upon this
Primary Dualism there arises, according to Brown, several "departures from the void," four of which he chooses to emphasize:
void to form, form to indication, indication to truth, and truth to
existence. Speaking of this general process, he states, "We left the
central state of the form, proceeding outwards and imagewise
towards the peripheral condition of existence. . . ."[6] Now what
Brown calls *"proceeding outwards and imagewise"* is what we have
elsewhere called *objectification through conceptualization.* Brown,
in other words, is mathematically describing the generation of the
spectrum of consciousness, and each of his "departures from the

void" may be viewed as a different band of the spectrum, starting from the level of Mind and ending at the Existential Level, the entire generation depending, of course, on the Primary Dualism. Of importance to us at this point, however, is simply the fact that the "universe comes into being when a space is severed or taken apart," and this original act of severance—"let there be a distinction"—we term the Primary Dualism.

Let us continue this survey by comparing Brown's mathematical account of the Primary Dualism with that given by Mahayana Buddhism, especially as outlined in two of the Mahayana's most profound texts, the *Lankavatara Sutra* and the *Awakening of Faith*. In a famous passage found in the *Awakening of Faith*, Asvaghosha states:

> Mind, though pure in its self nature from the very beginning, is accompanied by ignorance. Being defiled by ignorance, a defiled [state or level of] Mind comes into being. But, though defiled, the Mind itself is eternal and immutable. Only the Enlightened are able to understand this.
>
> What is called the essential nature of Mind is always beyond thoughts. It is, therefore, defined as "immutable." When the one World of Reality is yet to be realized, the Mind seems mutable and not in perfect Unity. *Suddenly, a thought arises; this is called ignorance.*[7]

Ignorance (*avidya*) in the Buddhistic and Hunduistic sense is "ignore-ance" of Reality—it has nothing to do with being literate or illiterate, intelligent or stupid. In the words of Ramana Maharshi, "Illiteracy is ignorance and education is learned ignorance. Both are ignorant of the true Aim." The "true Aim" is the non-dual mode of knowing, while being literate or illerate concerns the dualistic and symbolic mode of knowing. Ignorance, in other words, is ignorance of the non-dual and non-conceptual mode of knowing, which would instantly reveal the universe to be Mind-only. It is thus ignorance of Mind-only which literally creates the conventional and symbolic universe of separate things extended in space and succeeding one another in time; and since the major instrument of ignorance is thought, it is thought itself which is ultimately responsible for the seeming existence of the conventional universe.

The word "thought," as Asvaghosha uses it, refers not so much to the process of full-blown logical intellection that we use, for instance, in solving a math problem, but rather to the very root process whereby we create distinctions and dualisms. In this sense, the higher powers of abstract intellection follow upon this core process of creating distinctions, upon that primordial act of severance, and that core dualistic tendency is termed "thought." Thus when Asvaghosha says, "Suddenly, a thought arises," he is referring to the Primary Dualism that Brown described as "Let there be a distinction." Thought, conceptualization, ratiocination, distinctions, dualisms, measurements, symbolic-map knowledge—all are different names for that *maya* whereby we seemingly divide the One into the Many and generate the spectrum of consciousness.

Perhaps this will become clearer if we proceed to the teachings of the *Lankavatara Sutra*. Throughout this profound text passages such as the following can be found:

> It is like an image reflected in a mirror, it is seen but it is not real; the one Mind is seen as a duality by the ignorant when it is reflected in the mirror constructed by their memory. . . . The existence of the entire universe is due to memory that has been accumulated since the beginningless past but wrongly interpreted.[8]

According to the Lankavatara, the "existence of the entire universe" occurs when the one Mind is reflected upon by memory wrongly interpreted. This "reflection" creates "two worlds from one" and thus propels us into the conceptual world of space, time, and objects.

To understand this process of "reflection by memory wrongly interpreted," we need only recall that the genesis of time involves the mistaking of present memory for real knowledge of a "past." For it is only through this "memory wrongly interpreted" that we create the convincing illusion of knowing time past, and then—projecting this "knowledge" forward in expectation—we create time future, whereas all memory and expectation, and thus all time, exists nowhere but in *this* present moment.[9] In this fashion do we conjure up, out of this moment, the fantastic illusion called "time." And since "time" is just another name for space and objects (space-time-objects being a single continuum), the *Lankavatara* claims the entire universe of separate objects extended in space and succeeding one another in time is actually generated by thought-memory[10] wrongly interpreted, which "reflects" the one Mind and thus apparently "divides" that Mind, just as a mirror apparently creates two worlds from one.

In this connection, it is interesting to note that the *Lankavatara* claims that we "wrongly interpret memory" primarily because we separate the subject from the object. The psychological agent that introduces the subject vs. object dualism is called in Buddhism the *manas*, and thus it is stated:

> The function of the Manas is essentially to reflect upon [Mind] and to create and to discriminate subject and object from the pure oneness of the [Mind]. The memory accumulated in the latter is now divided into dualities of all forms and all kinds.[11]

Hence, according to the *Lankavatara,* the conventional universe of things extended in space and time ultimately results from that primordial distinction between subject and object—the dividing of the real world into one state which sees and one state which is seen.

In this respect, the Vedanta is in perfect agreement. Stated very briefly, *maya,* for the Vedanta, is "all experience that is constituted by, and follows from, the distinction between subject and object."[12] Thus the Primary Dualism for Vedanta, as well as for the Mahayana in general, is the illusory separation of subject and object.

We can continue this survey by discussing the more *mythological descriptions of the Primary Dualism,* such as those given by Hindu Autology and Christian theology. For the Hindu account, we turn again to the fabulous Ananda Coomaraswamy:

> In this eternal beginning there is only the Supreme Identity of "That One" (*tad ekam*) [i.e. Mind], without differentiation of being from non-being, light from darkness, or separation of sky from earth. The All is for the present impounded in the first principle, which may be spoken of as the Person, Progenitor, Mountain, Tree, Dragon, or endless Serpent.[13]

Then, which is now, in this eternal beginning, occurs the Passion:

> The passion is both an exhaustion and a dismemberment. The endless Serpent, who for so long as he was one Abundance remained invincible, is *disjointed* and *dismembered* as a tree is felled and cut up into logs. . . . From this Great Being, as if from a damp fire smoking, are exhaled the Scriptures, the Sacrifice, these worlds and all beings. . . . The Progenitor, whose emanated children are as it were sleeping and inanimate stones, reflects "Let me enter into them, to awaken them;" but so long as he is one, he cannot, and therefore *divides himself.* . . .[14]

Of this Passion, this Dismemberment, this Exhaustion ("to empty out"), this Dividing of Brahman, Coomaraswamy states:

> Whether we call him Person, or Sacerdotium, or Magna Mater, or by any other grammatically masculine, feminine or neuter names, "That" of which our powers are measures is a syzygy of conjoint principles, without composition or duality. These conjoint principles . . . become contraries only when we descend from the silent level of the Non-duality to speak in

terms of subject and object and to recognize the many separate
and individual existences that the All or Universe presents to
our physical organs of perception. And since this finite totality
can only be logically and not really divided from its infinite
source, "That One" can also be called an "Integral Multiplicity" and "Omniform Light."[15]

This "descent from Non-duality to ... subject and object" is
mythologically spoken of as a dismemberment, since it suggests
the figurative cutting-up or dis-membering of Brahman into the
world of opposites, and it is with this Dismemberment—which is
nothing but the Hindu's description of the Primary Dualism—that
a universe of "separate things" comes into temporal and spatial
existence.

> There is thus an incessant multiplication of the inexhaustible
> One and unification of the indefinitely Many. Such are the
> beginnings and endings of worlds and of individual beings:
> *expanded from a point without position or dimensions and a*
> *now without date or duration.*[16]

Moving to Christian theology, one finds an equally elaborate
system of mythopoetic imagery designed to present to our finite
intellect some hint of the ineffable infinite. Many Christians become noticeably uncomfortable when such events as the Virgin-
birth, the Resurrection, and the Fall are spoken of as mythology.
But this is an unnecessary concern, because mythology does not
mean a system of fairy tales completely divorced from reality—it is
rather, as we have pointed out, one of the three ways of verbally
speaking *about* that reality of which in actuality nothing can be
said. Myth is one form of the analogical approach to the absolute,
and represents a clothing of the Infinite in positive, metaphorical,
and finite terms. Since of Reality nothing can be predicated,
mythology is a potent analogy, so potent, in fact, that a famous
philosopher has remarked that "Myth embodies the nearest approach to absolute truth that can be stated in words."[17] To the
extent that we form any positive mental conception of God, *that*
conception must be a myth, for as St. Augustine himself noted: "If
any one in seeing God conceives something in his mind, *this is not*
God, but one of God's effects." You cannot think about God because
he is doing the thinking, and if you try, you will see only concepts
and objects, never God Himself. But to the extent we insist on
trying to form images about the Imageless, myth becomes an
important tool, provided that we do not confuse the myth with the
actuality. Thus we can examine Christian mythology in an attempt to divine what the mythopoetic symbols *mean,* and forget for
the time being whether or not these mythic events actually oc-

curred as a matter of historic fact. This is the approach taken by
the most illustrious Church Fathers, from St. Clement to St. Augustine to St. Thomas, and it is the approach we shall follow here.

> In the beginning God created the heaven and the earth. And
> the earth was without form, and void; and darkness was upon
> the face of the deep. And the Spirit of God moved upon the face
> of the waters (Genesis 1:1-2)

Now this is not the description of a historical fact, for "In the
beginning" means eternal and *beyond* time, not an event *in* time.
Thus we shall have to look a little deeper for its meaning, and to do
so, we need only call upon the universal language of mythology.
Recall, from Hindu mythology, that "before" the Dismemberment,
God is a "syzygy of conjoint principles." Let us now continue the
story from there:

> The conjoint principles; for example, Heaven and Earth, or
> Sun and Moon, man and woman, were originally one. Onto-
> logically, the conjugation is a vital operation, productive of a
> third in the image of the first and nature of the second.[18]

This is equally true in Christian mythology, for in theological
accounts, all creation is from the conjugation of the masculine
Spirit and the feminine water,[19] as in the following:

> In the beginning the Spirit conceived, the waters gave birth,
> and the world which was born from their conjugation was the
> first material image of the Word, of God the Son, the Logos
> who was the ideal pattern after which the creation was
> molded.[20]

Now Logos is simply word-and-thought,[21] that primordial power
of dualism, the Supreme Divider, and so did Logos "divide the light
from the darkness" (Genesis 1:4) and "divide the waters from the
waters" (Genesis 1:6) and "divide the day from the night" (Genesis
1:14); so also in Proverbs (8:27) do we find that "when he prepared
the heavens, I was there; when he set a compass upon the face of
the deep." The compass points out the measuring and dividing, the
dis-membering, whereby the Godhead "indivisibly divides" himself into all creation. And this measurement is precisely *maya,*
which, being etymologically similar to the words measure, meter,
matrix, matter, and mother, explains the creation of the world out
of Prima Materia and Virgin Matter as well as the Christ-birth
from the Virgin Mother: matter, mother, maya—the creation by
measurement and distinctions performed by Logos the Supreme
Divider.

In the microcosm of the first Adam, the story is repeated, for
when Adam is set to sleep, he becomes divided into male and

female, where previously he was hermaphroditic. The meaning is strictly mythological:

> In mythology male and female ... signify duality rather than sexuality, and the Fall is the subordination of the human mind to the dualistic predicament in thinking and feeling—to the insoluble conflict between good and evil, pleasure and pain, life and death.[22]

The division of Adam into male and female made possible the Fall, which specifically occurred when Humanity, compounded in the first couple, ate from the tree of knowledge, a knowledge that was of good and evil: and there is no mistaking *that* knowledge—it is dualistic. Man's Fall is into dualism, and thus "Suddenly a thought arises; this is called ignorance;" is here seen as "Suddenly dualistic knowledge arises; this is called the Fall."

The modern day students of man's Fall are, by and large, the psychologists and psychiatrists, and although the language they utilize is much more sophisticated, the story they tell is in all essential respects another variation of the generation of dualisms:

> At the mother's breast, in Freudian language, the child experiences that primal condition, forever after idealized, "in which object-libido and ego-libido cannot be distinguished;" in philosophic language, the subject-object dualism does not corrupt the blissful experience of the child at the mother's breast. . . . The primal childhood experience, according to Freud, is idealized because it is free from all dualisms. . . . Psychoanalysis suggests the eschatological proposition that mankind will not put aside its sickness and its discontent until it is able to abolish every dualism.[23]

We will draw heavily upon psychoanalytical insights when we discuss the dualisms arising *within* the self (subject) *after* it has been severed from the other (object), so for the moment we need only note that for psychoanalysis the Primary Dualism arises when the distinction of self vs. other is drawn, so that, in the words of Freud, "the ego-feeling we are aware of now is thus only a shrunken vestige of a far more extensive feeling—a feeling which embraced the universe and expressed an inseparable connection of the ego with the external world."

Now throughout this survey we have been concerned with the "initial" movement of Mind into a world of phenomena, and since we have discussed this *maya* from a variety of angles, it might prove helpful to summarize the essentials of this process. *A universe of temporal-spatial particulars is created with the original act of severance,* which we have called the Primary Dualism. This severance is not, however, a historical event; *there is no First*

Cause here, but rather an "everlasting beginning," an event occurring now-ever, without cause, motivation, or purpose (Asvaghosha's "suddenly" means "spontaneously"[24]); a severance which creates time and space and is itself therefore above time and space. This severance is variously spoken of as a self-reflection, a dismemberment, creation by the word-and-thought of Logos, manifestation, projection, reflection of Mind by memory wrongly inter-preted, art, play, magic, illusion—to name a few. All of these refer to the creative but illusory process whereby we measure "two worlds from one" and render Reality apparently "distinct from, and therefore false to, itself." And this process of dismemberment is intimately connected with our symbolic and dualistic form of knowing, so that the Primal Act, the Original Severance, the Primary Dualism is being repeated at this moment by our very use of this form of dualistic knowledge—"and this is the original sin of the Gods, in which all men participate by the very fact of their separate existence and their manner of knowing in terms of subject and object, good and evil, because of which the Outer Man is excluded from a direct participation in 'what the Brahmans understand by Soma.' The form of our 'knowledge,' or rather 'ignorance,' dismembers him daily. . . ."[25]

The "two halves" of this Primary Dualism may be called by many names: subject and object, male and female, inside and outside, Heaven and Earth, something and nothing, Sun and Moon, Ying and Yang, fire and water, self and other, ego-libido and object-libido, organism and environment. The most useful terms, from the point of view of identify, are subject and object, self and other, or simply organism and environment, for with the Primary Dualism man now finds himself identified exclusively with his organism as against his environment, forgetting altogether that he himself has imposed this illusory limitation, and so it is from this limitation, as we will see, that man seeks liberation:

> Truly there is no cause for you to be miserable and unhappy. You yourself impose limitations on your true nature of infinite Being, and then weep that you are a finite creature. Hence I say know that you are really the infinite, pure Being, the Self absolute. You are always that Self and nothing but that Self. Therefore, you can never really be ignorant of the Self; your ignorance in merely a formal ignorance.[26]

Nevertheless, we imagine the Primary Dualism to be real, and the generation of the spectrum of consciousness begins.

To better understand this Primary Dualism and its creative

power of *maya,* a simple illustration might help. Let the blank space below represent Mind or the non-dual Void:

This blank space does not mean that Mind is a featureless nothingness—it is only a representation of the fact that Reality is non-conceptual, non-dual, non-objective, etc. Now let us super-impose conceptualization upon this Void by placing a grid "over" it, as follows:

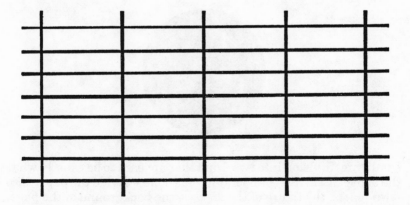

Upon the "blankness" of the Void we have traced several *distinctions* represented by the crossed lines of the grid. Thus this grid itself represents Logos, word-and-thought, symbolic elaboration, superimposition, dismemberment, *maya,* dualism, measurement, conceptualization, maps—everything implied in the word "thought", since it is by thought, the dualistic mode of knowing, that we fabricate these distinctions and "dismember him daily."

But notice what has happened. The "unity" (strictly, the "non-duality") that underlies the grid is no longer directly visible; it has become obscured—the distinctions of the grid have "split" the underlying unity, and this unity then becomes unnoticed, implicit, unexpressed, and thus *repressed*. This underlying unity now *appears* or *manifests itself* or *projects itself* as a world of "separate" objects extended in space and time. In the figure, these "objects" are represented by the squares of the grid, each of which has boundaries or distinctions that set it apart from the other "square-things." The underlying unity, in other words, is now *projected* as a multiplicity of separate "things." Thus dualism, to the extent that we forget its "underlying ground" of non-duality, *represses* that non-duality and then *projects* it as multiplicity. Dualism-Repression-Projection: this is the threefold process of *maya*. And *this* is the process which will concern us.

Now the grid we have drawn represents *several* distinctions; and so, to clarify this subtle process of Dualism-Repression-Projection (maya), as well as to emphasize its importance, we will single out *one* distinction and demonstrate in detail how this process operates. To begin with, let us draw one "thing," a "disk," marked-off from the page itself by *one* distinction, namely, the disk's boundary. Thus:

Duality is "division into two," and that appears to be exactly what the above distinction or boundary has done—divide the paper into "two" parts: the figure of the disk vs. the background of the page. Thus, I most probably imagine that I can see very clearly the "thing" which is called a "disk." This, however, is pure illusion, a mental sleight-of-hand, for never at any time am I actually aware of a separate "disk-thing"—what I see in fact, in concrete fact, is the entire visual field or gestalt of figure-plus-background, disk-plus-page (and indeed, some surrounding area!) My eye doesn't see a "disk," it sees a disk-page!

In other words, the two "things," the disk and the page, are not so separate after all. They are "different," but *not* separate. They are, that is, mutually correlative and interdependent—they are not two, non-dual. The boundary of the disk is certainly there, but it does not actually divide the disk from the page. To borrow a phrase from G. S. Brown, the two are really united by virtue of their common boundary. Inescapably, the perception of the "separate disk" is not an act of discovery, but an act of creation. To repeat the words of William James, "out of what is in itself an undistinguishable, swarming continuum, devoid of distinction or emphasis, our senses make for us, by *attending* to this motion and *ignoring* that, a world full of contrasts, or sharp accents, of abrupt changes, of picturesque light and shade."

Thus, through the power of narrowed and selective attention, which is nothing other than the thought process—the first mode of knowing—we focus and seize upon the "disk," mentally separate it from its background, completely ignore the unity of the gestalt, and then imagine that this state of affairs existed all along! In so doing, we have introduced a dualism which *represses* the non-duality of the field or gestalt and *projects* it as the disk vs. the page. Yet this vision of separateness, of duality, is a pure illusion, for just try to imagine seeing the disk by itself, without any sort of background at all! Conversely, try to imagine a background without any figure with which to contrast it! Inescapably, the one cannot exist without the other—they are united in nature, and separated in thought only.

Thus each dualism is accompanied by a *repression* and a *projection*: a dualism "severs" a process, *represses* its non-dual or "unitary" character, and *projects* that process as two apparently antagonistic opposites, such as the figure of the disk vs. the background of the page. The Primary Dualism, therefore, is actually the Primary Dualism-Repression-Projection. "Let there be a distinction," and the non-dual awareness (Absolute Subjectivity) is repressed, thereupon projecting itself as the opposites subject vs. object or organism vs. environment. This general process of dualism-repression-projection is an important one, for it repeats itself numerous times throughout all subsequent levels of consciousness, each time generating a new band of the spectrum and increasing man's ignorance of his Supreme Identity.

With the Primary Dualism-Repression-Projection we move "upward" as it were from the Level of Mind to the Existential Level, wherein the organism is clearly believed and actually felt to be distinctly separate from the environment. We might pause here to mention that the bands between the Level of Mind and the Existential Level we call the Transpersonal Bands. Here are found Jung's collective unconscious, extrasensory perception, the transpersonal witness, astral projection, out-of-the-body experiences, plateau experiences, clairaudience, and other such occurrences. That is, they occur in the bands of the spectrum where the boundary between self and other has not been completely crystallized. Whether or not all of these phenomena actually exist is of no pressing concern to us—but if they do, they occur on these Transpersonal Bands. Eventually we will have more to say about these bands and about the real difficulties involved in exploring them, but at this point we must pick up the story at the Existential Level, for it is the first level that we can recognize without difficulty.

The Existential Level is generated with the Primary Dualism-Repression–Projection: Mind is severed, its non-duality is repressed, and it is then projected as organism vs. environment, with man centering his identity in his organism as existing in space and time. See Fig. 1. Man's identity shifts from the All to his organism. Man's illusory Fall thus comprises a seeming descent not only from non-duality into duality, but also from Eternity into time, from Infinity into space, from Absolute Subjectivity into a world of subjects and objects, and from a cosmic identity to a personal one. The actor, the Sole Actor, common *in* and *to* us all, Blake's eternal Man, becomes so absorbed in his role, in his Psychodrama, that He pretendingly renders unremembered the counsel of Philosophia, "You have forgotten who you are." And thus, in truly heroic fashion, Man's drama is played out on the raging stage of *space* and of *time.*

For notice immediately that this separation of subject from object *marks the creation of space: the Primary Dualism itself creates space.* The Absolute Subjectivity is sizeless or spaceless, and therefore infinite; but with the rise of the Primary Dualism, the subject is illusorily separated from the object, and that separation, that "gap" between seer and seen, is nothing other than space itself. Man, in identifying exclusively with his organism as separated from his environment, necessarily creates the vast and grand illusion of space, the gap between man and his world.

And further—necessarily connected with the creation of space is, of course, the creation of *time,* since space and time form an inter-related continuum. Now we have already examined the *how* of time's genesis—we saw it was created as a by-product of man's linear, serial, memory mode of viewing the world. So let us turn now to the *why* of time's genesis—and we will see that it is nothing other than man's *avoidance of death.*

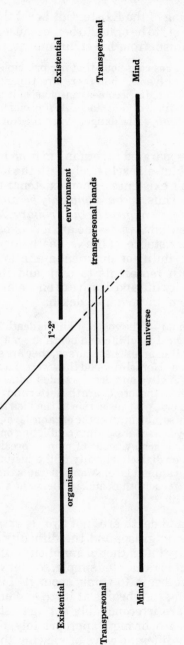

Figure 1

It is with the arising of the Existential Level that there occurs the infamous debate of "to be or not to be;" because, at the moment man severs his organism from his environment, then

> Suddenly he becomes conscious that *his* principle is not the principle of the universe, that there are things that exist independently of him, he becomes conscious of it in suffering from contact with the world-obstacle. *At this moment appears conscious fear of death,* of the danger which the Not-Self represents for the Self.[27]

Because man has separated his organism from his environment and then identified himself exclusively with the former, the problem of the organism's existence or non-existence now becomes of paramount concern. Thus, *because and only because the organism is separated from the environment by the Primary Dualism,* there is generated the existential *angst*—the anxiety of being vs. nullity, of existence vs. non-existence, of life vs. death. Man cannot accept nor even face the possibility of imminent annihilation, of the total extinction that death represents to him; and thus, not understanding that in reality life and death are one, man severs them in his frantic flight from an imagined death:

> Freud's own formula—"The goal of all life is death"—suggests that at the biological level life and death are not in conflict, but are somehow the same. That is to say, they are some sort of dialectical unity, as Heraclitus said they were: "It is the same thing in us that is alive and dead, awake and asleep, young and old: by a reversal the former are the latter and the latter in turn are the former." We thus arrive at the idea that life and death are in some sort of unity at the organic level, that at the human level they are separated into conflicting opposites. . . . It is the distinctive achievement of man to break apart the undifferentiated or dialectical unity of the instincts [of Life and Death] at the animal level. Man separates the opposites, turns them against each other, and, in Nietzsche's phrase, sets life cutting into life.[28]

The fact that life and death are "not two" is extremely difficult for most individuals to grasp, and the difficulty lies not in the direction of complexity but rather of simplicity—it is not too complex to understand, it is rather too simple, so that we miss it at the very point where we begin to think about it. Life is ordinarily taken to be something that begins at birth and ends at death, so that life and birth are irreconcilably set against death. But in actuality, life and death, or more appropriately, birth and death, are nothing but two different ways of viewing the reality of the present Moment. As we have seen, in the absolute Present there is no past, and that which has no past is something which is just born. *Birth is the condition of having no past.* Further, in the absolute Present there is no future either, and that which has no future is something which has just died. *Death is the condition of having no future.* Thus the present Moment, because it has no past, is newly born; and, because it has no future, it is simultaneously dead. Birth and death, therefore, are simply two ways of talking about the same timeless Moment, and they are illusorily separated only by those "who cannot escape from the standpoint of temporal succession so as to see all things in their simultaneity." In short, birth and death are one in *this* timeless Moment.

But man, in identifying solely with his organism and thus initiating the illusory debate of being vs. nullity (for this debate is impossible when the organism is one with the environment), man cannot bear the possibility that the outcome might be annihilation—he cannot accept what appears to him as death. Thus, following upon the Primary Dualism, there arises the Second major Dualism-Repression-Projection: *man severs the unity of life-and-death, represses that unity, and projects it as the war of life against death.*

Yet in severing and denying the unity of life-and-death, man simultaneously severs and denies the unity of the present Moment, for life, death, and the Now—moment are all one. Thus is *time* created, *for in refusing death man refuses to have no future and therefore refuses the reality of the future-less Moment, the timeless Moment*—he can no longer exist Now, he must exist in time; he no longer is joyous over living today, for he must also live tomorrow. In the words of Emerson (from "Self-reliance"):

> These roses under my window make no reference to former roses or to better ones; they are for what they are; they exist with God today. There is no time for them. There is simply the rose; it is perfect in every moment of its existence. . . . But man postpones or remembers; he does not live in the present, but with reverted eye laments the past, or, heedless of the riches that surround him, stands on tiptoe to forsee the future. He cannot be happy and strong until he too lives with nature in the present, above time.

But this is just the problem, for to live in the Present above time is to have no future, and to have no future is to accept death—yet this man cannot do. He cannot accept death and therefore neither can he live in the Now; and not living Now, he lives not at all.

> This incapacity to die, ironically but inevitably, throws mankind out of the actuality of living, which for all normal animals is at the same time dying; the result is the denial of life

(repression). The incapacity to accept death turns the death instinct into its distinctively human and distinctively morbid form. The distraction of human life to the war against death, by the same inevitable irony, results in death's dominion over life. The war against death takes the form of a preoccupation with the past and the future, and the present tense, the tense of life is lost—the present which Whitehead says "holds within itself the complete sum of existence, backwards and forwards, that whole amplitude of time, which is eternity."[29]

Thus, in fleeing death, man is thrown out of the Now and into time, into a race for the future in an attempt to escape the death of the timeless Moment. The Secondary Dualism-Repression-Projection, because it severs the unity of life-and-death, simultaneously severs the unity of the Eternal Moment; for life, death, and eternity are one in this timeless Now. In other words, the separation of life and death is ultimately and intimately the same as the separation of past and future, and *that* is time! *Hence is the Secondary Dualism the progenitor of time.* And this means that the life in time is the life in repression, specifically, the Secondary Repression. In the words of Brown:

> The consequence of the disruption of the unity of Life and Death in man is to make man the historical animal. . . . Man, the discontented animal, unconsciously seeking the life proper to his species, is man in history: repression and the repetition-compulsion generate historical time. Repression [the secondary repression] transforms the timeless instinctual compulsion to repeat into the forward-moving *recherche du temps perdu.* . . . And conversely, life not repressed . . . is not in historical time . . . only repressed life is in time, and *unrepressed life would be timeless or in eternity.*[30]

Here on the Existential Level, man's flight from death also generates the blind Will to Life, which is actually the blind panic of not having.a future, the panic that is death. But man's flight from death has numerous other consequences, for it is destined to color every subsequent action that man will make—foremost among which is the creation of an idealized image called the "ego." For the anxiety generated by this flight from death—"anxiety is the ego's incapacity to accept death"—this anxiety is the cause of yet another dualism-repression-projection. Under the anxiety of fleeing death, *the life of the organism itself is severed, its unity repressed and then projected as a psyche vs. a soma,* as a soul vs. a body, as an ego vs. the flesh.

> The truth of the matter, according to Freud's later theory, is that the peculiar structure of human ego results from its

incapacity to accept reality, specifically the supreme reality of death. . . .[31]

The theory is complex, but the point can be put simply: in the debate of being vs. nullity, of existence vs. non-existence, of life vs. death—that is, the Secondary Dualism—man, not accepting death, abandons his mortal organism and escapes into something much more "solid" and impervious than "mere" flesh—namely, ideas. *Man, in fleeing death, flees his mutable body and identifies with the seemingly undying idea of himself.* Corrupt but flattering, this idea he calls his "ego," his "self." In the words of Hubert Benoit:

> The two parts of man [psyche and soma] being unable to reunite naturally . . . he sets himself to adore an image that has no reality, the Ego. In default of a proper love of his abstract part for his animal part man has only an ersatz, self-respect, love of his abstract part for an ideal image of himself.[32]

This "ideal image of himself," this "ego," seems to promise man something that his mutable flesh will not: immortality, the crystal everlastingness of innumerable tomorrows embodied in pure ideas, ideas that will not die, nor ever be susceptible to corrosion and decay. Man's flight from death is a flight from his body, and thus is created the third (or "tertiary") major Dualism-Repression-Projection: *the organism is severed, its unity repressed and then projected as a psyche vs. a soma.* See Fig. 2.

Thus, on the Ego Level, man imagines he *has* a body, that he *possesses* it much as he would a car or a house. In fact, he applies property rights to aspects of his organism, thereby diminishing his intrinsic worth in his own eyes. Here, on the Ego Level, man is only vaguely conscious of what he now calls "body awareness," and this impoverished body awareness is all that remains of the Existential Level, which in turn is all that remains of Mind.

Now, in ways I will try to explain, the *exclusive* identification with the ego and the simultaneous alienation of the body literally forces man into the exclusive use of the first mode of knowing, the totally dualistic, symbolic, linear, and temporal mode of knowing. There are, of course, numerous other consequences of this tertiary dualism—all equally significant—but since we have spoken so often of this first mode of knowing, we must at least examine its maturation in the context of the Spectrum of Consciousness. For the first mode of knowing is really nothing other than a *negation* of much broader and more inclusive modes of awareness.

We may follow this entire process if we can only understand what I would like to call *organismic awareness*. Organismic

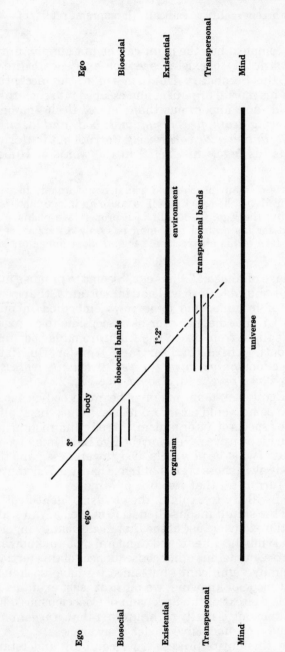

Figure 2

awareness is what we—on the Ego Level—ordinarily, but clumsily, refer to as seeing, touching, tasting, smelling, and hearing. But in its very purest form, this "sensual awareness" is non-symbolic, non-conceptual, momentary consciousness. Organismic awareness is awareness of the Present only—you can't taste the past, smell the past, see the past, touch the past, or hear the past. Neither can you taste, smell, see, touch, or hear the future. In other words, organismic consciousness is properly *timeless,* and being timeless, it is necessarily spaceless. Just as organismic awareness knows no past or future, it knows no inside or outside, no self or other. *Thus pure organismic consciousness participates fully in the non-dual awareness called Absolute Subjectivity.*[33]

Organismic consciousness and cosmic consciousness are thus one and the same. Hence we need not erroneously assume that organismic consciousness is confined *within* or encapsulated *by* the skin-boundary of the organism. On the contrary, there is nothing, absolutely nothing, given to you in your direct experience that indicates any boundary to your awareness. Your actual field of awareness, of organismic consciousness, has no boundary for the simple reason that, for you, there is nothing *outside* your awareness—and thus, strange as it first sounds, nothing *inside* your awareness. There is just awareness, with no inside nor outside—no boundary at all!

As an almost silly, nevertheless revealing, example, can you actually *smell* the supposed difference between inside and outside? Is that difference really given in your awareness? Can you *taste* the boundary between self and other? Or is there just a process of tasting, with no inside and outside to it? If you relax, close your eyes, and listen carefully to the sounds "around" you, can you actually hear the difference between inside and outside—or do the sounds seem to come just as much from "inside" your head as from "outside"? And if there does seem to be a real difference between "inside" and "outside", can you actually *hear* it? Not at all! Rather, this primary dualism of inside vs. outside is merely an idea you have been taught—an idea you use to interpret and thus distort your basic awareness. The supposed split or boundary isn't really there! As Schroedinger remarked, "The world is given to me only once, not one existing and one perceived. Nothing is reflected. The original and the mirror-image are identical." The point is that organismic awareness is non-dual awareness. It is Mind itself.

The repression of organismic awareness begins immediately with the primary and secondary dualisms, for with the illusory separation of inside from outside and of past from future, man's Supreme Identity apparently becomes *bounded* and *limited:* it shifts from a non-dual universal one to a personal one enclosed "in here." That is to say, man's identity shifts to *within* the conventional boundaries of his organism as against all else, *even though this identity is nowhere given in his real organismic awareness*.

So although we say that on the Existential Level man is identified with his total organism as against his environment, this most definitely does not mean that he is in direct touch with what we are calling "organismic awareness." For real organismic consciousness, as we have just seen, is spaceless and timeless, it is the same as the Level of Mind, and it is not in any way confined within the skin-boundary of the organism. It is only with the rise of the primary and secondary dualisms that man *imagines* his awareness to be so confined and skin-encapsulated, and consequently his identity also collapses onto his own organism as against what is equally his own environment. And *that* is the state of awareness we are calling the "Existential Level"—man identified solely with his organism as existing in space (primary dualism) and time (secondary dualism).

Appropriately enough, we may call the awareness at this stage "existential awareness," an awareness that seems to be bounded by the skin of the total organism, an awareness centered on man's separate existence in space and time. Thus, in an unfortunately technical language, one might say that the primary and secondary dualisms transform unbounded organismic awareness (Absolute Subjectivity) into existential awareness. In short, they transform cosmic consciousness into rudimentary individual consciousness.

Now on the Existential Level man is, as we have seen, in flight from death. That is, he refuses to live without a future in the timeless Now—he wants a *future moment* as a promise that death won't touch him now. He doesn't want *this* timeless present alone, he wants the promise of yet *another* present *ahead* of him. Thus he arranges for *this* present to *pass* on to yet *another* present, and he harbors the secret wish that all his moments will flee into future moments forever. For precisely this reason, none of his present moments seem timeless, eternal, and complete in themselves. Rather, they seem to *pass on,* they seem to *flee into, other* moments. The eternal moment, which *is* always, *therefore appears as a series of fleeing moments,* a series of durations lasting a mere 2-3 seconds. Thus, with the rise of the secondary dualism, the *nunc stans* or eternal Present appears as the *nunc fluens* or passing present. In flight from death we demand a future, and thus our moments pass.

Thus existential awareness is indeed an awareness which involves time and space, but only in the most vividly concrete sense. It involves the *passing present* and is not, therefore, easily lost in ruminations over yesterday and tomorrow. Hence, on this level, a person grasps, in the passing present, his naked existence, shorn of all but the most subtle and deep-rooted symbolic maps. The mode of knowing on the Existential Level is thus *primarily* a type of *global prehension,* or series of direct grasps of a person's own separate existence in space and time. He prehends *his* being (Primary dualism), and *his* immediate *duration* (secondary dualism), without any extra overlay of abstractions or symbolic interpretations. These prehensions are three-dimensional grasps of the passing present in all its possibilities. Only the most basic dualisms corrupt these prehensions, and thus we say that the Existential Level is but a step, albeit often a giant step, away from Mind and the timelessness of organismic awareness.

Further, at this Existential Level, the generation of time, mostly in the form of the passing present, is intimately connected with the generation of the Will. For we have seen that here man *wills* to have a future as a promise that death won't touch him. He *wills* to move globally into an immediate future. He *wills* to avoid eternity. And this Will is the prototype of all subsequent tendencies, all wishes, all inclinations, all intentions, all desires, inasmuch as they all involve a time component, which is why we say that the Existential Level is also the home of man's Will, specifically his Will to life against death. But this Will is not to be confused with will-power, which blossoms on the Ego Level. Will-power is a linear, concerted effort on the part of the Ego or Persona to subdue aspects of the organism or environment while in pursuit of others. But the Will is much more basic and fundamental—it is a three-dimensional act of the total organism to globally move in time towards some future end. Will-power is merely what remains of the Will once the tertiary dualism occurs, while the Will itself is an act of the person's total being. The Will is a *moving* prehension. It is an intentionality, as demonstrated by Rollo May in *Love and Will.*

But all this theoretical paraphernalia aside, the only point I wish to emphasize now is that all these aspects of the Existential Level are what Mind looks like after the Primary and Secondary Dualisms have occurred. Karuna is apparently transformed into trishna, the *nunc stans* into the *nunc fluens,* non-dual awareness into prehension, spontaneous *lila* into the Will and intentionality. And with the rise of the Ego Level, each of these will in turn be transformed into different consciousness dimensions.

All we need remember at this point is that existential awareness is organismic awareness contaminated with the basic splits of inside vs. outside and past vs. future (primary and secondary dualisms). The very saving grace of this Existential Level, however, is that man is still at least in touch with his total organism, with his psychosomatic unity, even if he erroneously assumes it to be separate from the environment. Hence, at this stage, at this Existential Level, man does not yet feel himself to be an intelligent soul separated from his stupid animal body, as if he were merely a chauffeur stuck in a corruptible chassis or a horseman separated from his unruly horse. Rather, he directly feels himself to be a mind-body unity, a truly undivided psycho-somatic being. To help remind us of this fact, we will also be calling existential awareness by the name "centaur awareness": the awareness not of a horseman ruling over his horse, but rather of a centaur, a total, self-governing organism. As such, man on the Existential Level is still one with his senses and his body, even if he misunderstands them by way of the primary and secondary dualisms. Existential or centaur awareness is, so to speak, only a step away from cosmic consciousness, from organismic awareness, from Mind itself—even though, for some, this single step appears a giant leap across an unfathomable abyss.

But with the generation of the Tertiary Dualism, the centaur itself is literally broken: the mind is split from the body, and the body hastily is abandoned. Man, in flight from death, surrenders his mortal flesh and flees in fear into a world of static symbols. Instead of existing as his total psychosomatic organism, man substitutes, and identifies with, *a purely mental or psychic representation of his total psychosomatic being*. He identifies, in short, with his ego.[34] A wedge is driven deep into the centaur, and man emerges as the rider and controller divorced from his horse-body, a flesh-less and therefore life-less psyche precariously perched atop what now seems an unruly and passion-riddled soma. And that wedge, that split between the psyche and the soma, is precisely the tertiary dualism—and with its generation, man finds himself squarely on the Ego Level.

Centaur awareness is, as we have said, but a step away from Mind, from non-dual organismic consciousness. So as man severs and represses the Centaur, he severs all remaining links with organismic consciousness, and any possibility of non-dual awareness. In breaking apart his Centaur and abandoning his body, he suffocates even the chance for non-dual awareness. Speaking rather freely, we may say that on the Existential Level, man is still in touch with organismic awareness, although he misunderstands it, while on the Ego Level he is not even in touch with it. Rather, he is now completely out of any contact with the timelessness of organismic awareness. Indeed, he is even out of touch with the passing present—more than ever, he is living solely in time, and thus retreats enthusiastically to the temporal, linear, instrumental, and purely dualistic mode of knowing, accomplished by drawing from his memory concepts and symbols which he now inserts between himself and Reality. Instead of non-dual organismic consciousness, instead even of prehensions, man is forced to a pale substitute: intellection, fantasy, imagination, symbolic-map knowledge—and thus the first mode of knowing is finally and fully crystallized.

> The more specific and concrete mechanism whereby the body-ego becomes a soul is fantasy. . . . Fantasy, as a hallucination of what is not there dialectically negating what is there, confers on reality a hidden level of meaning, and lends a symbolical quality to all experience. The *animal symbolicum* (Cassirer's definition of man) is *animal sublimans,* committed to substitute symbolical gratification of instincts for real gratification. . . . By the same token the *animal symbolicum* is the animal which has lost its world and life, and which preserves in its symbol system a map of the lost reality. . . .[35]

Hubert Benoit further explains:

> One sees clearly the double role played by the imagination. . . . It plays the role of protector towards the egotistical and revendicative illusions of the abstract portion [the ego], and the role of destroyer towards the animal machine [organismic awareness] by abandoning it to the fear of death. It protects the Ego, which is illusory, and crushes the machine, which is real.[36]

With this "crushing of the machine, which is real," man's non-dual awareness, his second mode of knowing, is also finally crushed, since, as we have just been saying, organismic consciousness and the non-dual mode of knowing are one and the same. On the Ego Level, all that is left of organismic awareness shows up as a greatly impoverished body awareness. On this level, man does not know, cannot know, that this body awareness is but the ragged tip of a submerged but priceless jewel of daybreak knowledge. Man's flight from death and his body is hence a flight from the only mode of knowing capable of revealing reality. Man's first mode of knowing—symbolic—which was latent in the primary dualism as "thought" (in Asvaghosha's sense), *now matures and is fully functioning.* Thus is completed the equipment for the ego's life-long project—avoiding the Now-moment by symbolically mapping the past onto the present. Man's identity shifts from his total psychosomatic organism to his mental picture of himself, his ego, which—ironically enough—is thoroughly based on the past and therefore thoroughly dead. And so it comes to pass that man kills himself by degrees in order to avoid an illusory death.

The completion of the Tertiary Dualism-Repression-Projection of the psyche vs. the soma marks the generation of the Ego Level.

We will temporarily leave the story of the evolution of the spectrum here, to return to it, and the Ego Level, later. Our concern now is with the Existential Level—here man is more or less still in touch with his total organism, his psycho-somatic unity, the centaur itself. He is not, to repeat, fully in touch with pure organismic consciousness, for this consciousness has been contaminated with the rudimentary ratiocinations of the primary and secondary dualisms. Thus self vs. other (organism vs. environment) and life vs. death are the major dualisms present on this Level.

You can "locate" the Existential Level for yourself by retiring to a quiet place, free from external distractions, and chasing away all ideas and concepts that you have formed about yourself. Forget for the moment whether you are male or female, intelligent or dumb, happy or distressed, and then notice the feeling—not so much the thought, but the "feeling"—that persists "under" or "behind" these ideas, namely that core feeling that you somehow are existing and are alive at this moment. That is the Existential Level, and that simple feeling of existence is neither mental nor physical, for the tertiary dualism of psyche vs. soma is not active at this level—that feeling is simple, clean, neutral existence.

Nevertheless, if while resting on this Existential Level you gently look about for dualisms, the one you will most prominently notice is that of self vs. other. That is, your root feeling of identity and existence (your "self") seems to be separate from the universe around you (the "other"). This is the primary dualism of organism vs. environment, and it is, of course, characteristic of the Existential Level.[37] Were it to suddenly dawn on you that your existence is actually identical to that of the universe, then the dualism of self vs. other would have vanished and you would have temporarily shifted "down" to the Level of Mind. But the fact that you feel your existence to be fundamentally separate from the rest of existence indicates with certainty that the Primary Dualism has occurred and that you therefore are on the Existential Level.

This dualism of self vs. other is most interesting, because numerous factors—some biological, most sociological—act to shape it, color it, mold it, fashion it. It is here, on what might be called the "upper limits" of the Existential Level, that the cultural premises of an organism are absorbed, and these premises color all subsequent transactions between the organism and the environment. This "pool" of sociological factors, of cultural ideologies, this social gloss, as Talcott Parson calls it, determines to a large extent not only how the organism perceives the environment but also how it acts towards the environment—in short, it dictates broad guidelines for an organism's overall behavior.

Each individual, on this level, carries with him a vast network of relations that represents society "internalized." It is of an extra-ordinary complex nature, little understood, comprising a matrix of language and syntax, the introjected structure of the individual's family, cultural beliefs and myths, rules and metarules. In a very general manner, it can be viewed as the sum total of all the basic sociological information that the organism has accumulated. In the words of R. D. Laing:

> One's body is of unique significance because it is *the* range for "introjective" mappings from all domains: and these intro-jective sets provide a "pool" for projections in turn *to* any domain. . . .[38]

This "pool of introjective sets," this "internalized society," be-cause it is mapped or transferred from society onto the biological organism, we will call the Biosocial Band. It represents the upper limits of the Existential Level, as man begins to move upwards and away from his centaur awareness by operating upon it so as to translate it into socially meaningful and acceptable terms.

Most of the Biosocial Band is, in one sense or another, un-conscious. It is rather too close for us to see clearly, so it is only as we begin to study other cultures that we realize that what we unconsciously took for reality is actually nothing more than a social convention, or, in Castenada's phrase, reality is an agree-ment. This can most easily be seen in the phenomenon of language, which is perhaps the most basic of the various sets of relations constituting the Biosocial Band. In this regard, no one was as keenly aware of the ways in which language and grammar *uncon-sciously* mold our experience as was Benjamin Lee Whorf. In his words:

> We all hold an illusion about talking, an illusion that talking is quite untrammeled and spontaneous and merely "expresses" whatever we wish to have it express. This illusory appearance results from the fact that the obligatory phenomena within the apparently free flow of talk are so completely autocratic that speaker and listener are bound unconsciously as though in the grip of a law of nature. The phenomena of language are background phenomena, of which the talkers are unaware or, at the most, very dimly aware. . . . The forms of a person's thoughts are controlled by inexorable laws of pattern of which he is unconscious. These patterns are the unperceived in-tricate systematizations of his own language.[39]

Language is to us as water is to a fish—a background phenom-enon so constant in our experience that we are unaware of it. It is true that we are usually aware of some of the functions of language—we can be conscious, for instance, of manipulating and choosing symbols to convey meaning to others, and most of us are at least vaguely aware of the grammatical rules by which we formulate our sentences. But language performs one all-pervading. function of which we are almost totally unaware: it creates distinctions. That is, language—and its offspring, abstract intellection—are the major source of man's dualisms. Again, in the words of Whorf:

> *Segmentation of nature is an aspect of grammar.* . . . We cut up and organize the spread and flow of events as we do, largely because, through our mother tongue, we are parties to an agreement to do so, not because nature itself is segmented in exactly that way for all to see. . . . *We dissect nature along lines laid down by our native languages.* The categories and types that we isolate from the world of phenomena we do not find there because they stare every observer in the face; on the contrary, the world is presented in a kaleidoscopic flux of impressions which has to be organized by our minds—and this means largely by the linguistic systems in our minds. We cut nature up, organize it into concepts, and ascribe significances as we do, largely because we are parties to an agreement to organize it in this way—an agreement that holds throughout our speech community and is codified in the patterns of our language.[40]

Thus, with our linguistic processes we slice up reality, unconsciously introducing dualisms that we then naively imagine have existed all along.

> In English we divide most of our words into two classes. . . . Class 1 we call nouns, e.g. "house, man;" Class 2, verbs, e.g. "hit, run." Many words of one class can act secondarily as of the other class, e.g., "a hit, a run," or "to man (the boat)," but, on the primary level, the division between the classes is absolute. Our language thus gives us a bipolar [dualistic] division of nature. *But nature herself is not thus polarized.*[41]

Because the very tool we use to represent nature is itself dualistic, we soon come to believe that nature herself is so constructed. But then, if the only tool one has is a hammer, one tends to see everything as a nail. The very real problem with this is that the form of the universe is not necessarily that of our language and logic, and as we force the former to conform with the latter, a subtle but pernicious violence is unconsciously perpetrated upon nature. As one example:

> We are constantly reading into nature fictional acting entities, simply because our verbs must have substantives in front of them. We have to say "It flashed" or "A light flashed,"

setting up an actor, "it" or "light," to perform what we call an action, "to flash." Yet the flashing and the light are one and the same! . . . By these more or less distinct terms we ascribe a semifictitious isolation to parts of experience. English terms, like "sky, hill, swamp," persuade us to regard some elusive aspect of nature's endless variety as a distinct THING. . . . Thus English and similar tongues lead us to think of the universe as a collection of rather distinct objects and events corresponding to words.[42]

This incredible fact lead L. L. Whyte to comment that "this procedure is so paradoxical that only long acquaintance with it conceals its absurdity." But we have elsewhere explained how language-and-thought populates the world with fictitious entities, things, and objects, and we needn't dwell on it here. The point is that the Biosocial Band, as the repository of sociological institutions such as language and logic, is basically, fundamentally, and above all else a *matrix of distinctions,* of forms and patterns conventionally delineating, dissecting, and dividing the "seamless coat of the universe."

Thus the Biosocial Band, if it isn't directly responsible for all dualisms, nevertheless definitely reinforces all dualisms, and so perpetuates illusions that we would ordinarily see through. The primary example of this is that the subject/verb cleavage in our language reinforces the Primary Dualism of organism vs. environment, for there is no acceptable way to describe a unitary transaction of the organism-environment field without ascribing the action to either the organism or the environment, thus presenting the convincing illusion that the two are actually separate. Language—the most basic constituent of the Biosocial Band—is the prototypical reinforcer of dualisms, for it operates by dividing and classifying the "kaleidoscopic flux" of nature, repressing its non-dual or seamless nature, and projecting it as apparently discrete and separate objects. The Biosocial Band, as a matrix of distinctions, is thus like a vast screen that we throw over reality. Its usefulness, of course, is not contended, but if we confuse this screen for reality itself, that screen becomes a blind, and we are lost in the darkness of our own shadows.

In passing, we will briefly mention three other functions of the Biosocial Band. First, it forms part of that core feeling of being a separate and distinct being, since it confers on the organism a basic yet unconscious orientation towards the environment, and subsequently molds and hardens the dualism of self vs. other. Second, it acts as a reservoir for abstract intellection, furnishing the symbols, syntax, and logic for higher thought. It is by reflecting upon this matrix of distinctions that we obtain "distinctions on distinctions," that is, ideas. Gregory Bateson, in fact, has defined an idea as "a difference that makes a difference." Third, just as the Biosocial Band offers "food for thought," it likewise offers "food for the ego." That is to say, it acts as a reservoir from which many of the characteristics of the ego are fashioned. As George Herbert Mead has demonstrated, man's self-consciousness is gained only as he becomes a sociological object to himself by viewing himself through the attitudes of others (the so-called "generalized other"). The Biosocial Band, as society internalized, acts as the reservoir for the formation of the ego, its roles, values, status, contents, and so on.

We are now in a position to pick up the story of the generation of the spectrum of consciousness at the Ego Level. The Primary Dualism has occurred, repressing Mind and projecting it as the organism vs. the environment, generating the Existential Level as Man identifies with his organism as against the environment. This triggers the Secondary Dualism of life against death, which in turn generates the Tertiary Dualism of psyche vs. soma, which marks the emergence of the Ego Level. (Fig. 2)

Thus—and we will be amplifying this in much greater detail in subsequent chapters—we have defined the Existential Level as a more-or-less total, felt identity with the entire psychosomatic organism as it exists in time and space. We define the ego as a more-or-less accurate mental and symbolic *representation* of the total (but *biosocialized*) psychosomatic organism. We might say, in a loose fashion, that the ego is what "remains" of the centaur when it is biosocialized and the Tertiary Dualism placed upon it. In short, the ego is a fairly accurate (according to *convention*), fairly acceptable, and therefore fairly "healthy" self-image.

One of the most significant features of the ego, of the self at this level, is that more than any other level it is, in essence, nothing but a bag of edited memories. Thus:

> The conventional "self" or "person" is composed mainly of a history consisting of selected memories, and beginning from the moment of parturition. According to convention, I am not simply what I am doing now. I am also what I have done, and my conventionally edited version of my past is made to seem almost the more real "me" than what I am at this moment. For what I *am* seems so fleeting and intangible, but what I *was* is fixed and final. It is the firm basis for predictions of what I will be in the future, and so it comes about that I am more closely identified with what no longer exists than with what actually is![43]

That this is so can be easily verified: just ask yourself, "Who am I?" and notice that your answer will consist predominantly of things you have done in the past. Only occasionally will someone answer, "What I am now is a process of reading this sentence." It is one thing to remember the past, but quite another to actually *identify* with it! It is as if a bird in flight, tracing an imaginary path through the sky, were to be so confused that it identified with its path. No bird is that dumb. In this regard, the following Zen story, told by an American psychotherapist, is revealing:

> I rose and walked about, rotating my feet to move my aching ankles. Relieved, I returned to my sitting position.
> The *Roshi* [master] looked at the place where I had walked.
> "Are you able to see the footsteps?" the *Roshi* asked.
> "No."
> He nodded his head. "They were not there before and are not there now. There was nothing in your life before and nothing in the future, only"—and he burst forth again with "ah!"

We, however, have identified with our tracks, our path, our illusory past. The attempt to live this way, always glancing furtively over our shoulder to the mirage of yesterday, is—in Marshal McCluhan's phrase—like driving a car using only the rear view mirror. The terrifying anxiety so produced can lead us to exclaim with Stephen (in James Joyce's *Ulysses*) that "History is a nightmare from which I am trying to awake."

Illusions, such as of the past, offer no satisfaction and in an attempt to alleviate the frustration, the ego looks to the future where it imagines that some ultimate happiness awaits it, that there lies ahead a great goodie at the end of the rainbow of time. The solution, however, is spurious, for what happens is that all happiness comes to be based solely on the future. That is, the ego is happy today only if promised a happy tomorrow, and the best news for the ego is that it has a "bright future," not that it has a bright present. Thus the ego can endure incredible misery in the present if it believes that there lies ahead a joyful future—but *that* future will never be enjoyed, for it doesn't exist now, and when it does arrive, by definition the ego will then be content only if promised yet another happy future! It is very much the proverbial case of dangling a carrot on a stick in front of a donkey, so that the poor beast will always run forward but never be rewarded.

Furthermore, I—as ego—spend so much time running forward to future happiness that very soon I come to identify happiness with the very process of running forward. I confuse happiness with the pursuit of happiness. Then all I am capable of doing is just pursuing and running, so much so that I cannot *stop* running, and hence, should that future goodie actually show up, I cannot stop myself from running right past it. I am never completely living in the present, and so I can never completely enjoy myself. And if I can't enjoy the present, I won't enjoy the future when it becomes present. I am forever frustrated, and my only apparent alternative is to run faster, so that I am thrown into a vicious circle of working for my chronic frustration. But then, you can't stop progress—only one begins to wonder if progress is not rather more a cancer. Chides John Maynard Keynes:

> Purposiveness means that we are more concerned with the remote future results of our actions than with their own quality or their immediate effects on our own environment. The "purposive" man is always trying to secure a spurious and delusive immortality for his acts by pushing his interest in them forward into time. He does not love his cat, but his cat's kittens; nor, in truth, the kittens, but only the kittens' kittens, and so on forward for ever to the end of cat-dom. For him jam is not jam unless it is a case of jam to-morrow and never jam to-day. Thus by pushing his jam always forward into the future, he strives to secure for his act of boiling it an immortality.[45]

The crux of all of this is that joy, which is only of the present Moment, the ego can never taste to the full, for joy of the present Moment knows no future, and that which knows no future is death. In this sense, joy is Blakes's "Eternal delight," timeless delight, delight that knows no future, and thus delight that must entail the acceptance of death. The ego, however, cannot accept death, and so it cannot find happiness. In the words of Goethe:

> As long as you do not know
> How to die and come to life again,
> You are but a sorry traveler
> On this dark earth.

Thus man, at the Ego Level, attempts to avoid the death of the timeless Moment by living in a past that doesn't exist and seeking a future that will never arrive. The primary tool for this attempt is, of course, man's symbolic-map knowledge. We need hardly mention again that this mode of knowing is "negative" and "illusory" *only* if we confuse its reports with the territory itself. It is perfectly legitimate and positively helpful to use a road-map if I am traveling cross-country, as long as I realize what I am doing. Trouble is, most of us have long since run off the road and into the ditch, but we haven't yet looked up from our road-maps long enough to notice. Likewise, most of us are in the same ditch with symbolic-map knowledge—we have looked towards ideas about reality so persistently that we no longer have the slightest direct knowledge of reality itself. Nevertheless, we have made great strides in representational thought, especially as evidenced in science and medicine, even if we no longer know the reality so represented. Symbolic-map knowledge has, with a few glaring exceptions, made beneficial contributions to agriculture, pharmacology, medicine, and pure sciences. The glaring exceptions, such as the ecological crisis, mostly came about because we could not see the actual territory very clearly, and so we nearly destroyed it before we realized what we were doing. At any rate, the point is that it is here on the Ego Level that the symbolic, linear, dualistic, objective, and conceptual mode of knowing dominates; whether it is used correctly or not is another matter.

Symbolic-map knowledge is also a major ingredient in the process of information transfer that we generally know as "communication," and it is to this process that we now must turn in explanation of the genesis of the final major dualism, as well as the final major level of the spectrum of consciousness. Now communication can be a very complex phenomenon, especially as set forth in information theory, cybernetics, and the like, but we needn't pursue these subtleties. We should, however, point out an important but usually overlooked fact: *communication can operate on several different planes.* For instance, John says to Mary, "You're a creep," and then he adds, "Ah, I'm really kidding." John has sent two messages to Mary, and these messages are on different planes because *the second message is about the first message;* the second message tells Mary that the first message was not meant seriously. Messages, such as this second one, which are about other messages are called "meta-messages"—they operate on a different plane, a "meta-plane." Most of us are very familiar with this phenomenon, even if we have never thought of it in such terms. Body-language, for instance, is now a commonly discussed topic, and much of body-language really acts as "body metalanguage," that is, it acts as a message about our verbal messages. Thus, to return to the example, if John says to Mary, "You're a creep," but he is relaxed and smiling, then his tone of voice and his bodily gestures will serve as a meta-message telling Mary that he is kidding her. On the other hand, if he is tense and flushed and screams out "You're a creep!" then it will be quite obvious to Mary that she is in trouble. In both cases the verbal message was the same (i.e., "You're a creep"), but the meta-message changed its meaning drastically. This suggests that, in many cases, *for us to understand any message we must accurately identify its context by assigning an appropriate meta-message to it.*

Usually an individual can do this with very little trouble, unconsciously, spontaneously, effortlessly, accurately. Occasionally, however, an individual will develop certain "tangles" in his meta-communicative processes—he will have difficulty handling those meta-messages that would ordinarily help him understand other messages. He therefore may not be able to figure out if the world is for or against him; he may not be able to assign labels (or meta-messages) to his *own* messages about what he is really feeling; or, similarly, he might not be able to assign the correct contexts to others' actions towards him. He may even have trouble *identifying the source of some messages*—do they originate within him or in the external world? In other words, he is having trouble with his meta-communicative habits, and we start to see here the genesis of the Fourth or Quaternary Dualism-Repression-Projection.

These tangles in communication usually develop in situations technically known as "double-binds."[46] We have seen that to correctly perceive a situation we need messages and meta-messages; in a double-bind situation, however, *the messages and the meta-messages contradict each other*. Further, if the individual does not realize what is happening, then he will have to distort and invalidate either the message or the meta-message, and occasionally both. His communication processes thus become hopelessly tangled. Let us clarify this with an example.

A young child has just performed some horrid act, such as pouring honey all over the living room rug. Mother is understandably furious, and she grabs the child and proceeds to thrash the little rascal. But as she is doing this, she tells the child something like, "Now dear, I love you very much. I'm doing this for your own good, and I want you to know that even now I love you." That is her verbal message to the child, and it is one of supposedly pure love. But her voice is shaking, her face is red with rage, and on top of all that she is hitting the child. These, of course, act as a meta-message, but this meta-message is definitely and unmistakably one of anger and temporary hatred. Thus mother has given the child messages on two different planes: one is verbal in character and expresses overt loving affection, and the other is a non-verbal meta-message of rage—and this meta-message denies and contradicts the first message!

Now what is the child to do? If he correctly discerns that at this moment mother actually hates him, and he tells her so, she would mobilize the force of her authority and "sincerity" to convince the child that he is wrong, that at this moment mother really does love him, that mothers always love their children. The child is persuaded to believe that his accurate appraisal of the situation is actually incorrect. Thus, if he correctly discriminates her message, he is shown to be wrong. But what if he now acts on this, if he believes mother loves him at this moment and he responds accordingly by trying to befriend her? Well, at this moment, mother is *not* in an affectionate mood, and she would put him off, either with "Go to your room," or "Be quiet," or just plain "Leave me alone." Obviously, mother is not very affectionate, and so even if he incorrectly discriminates her message of "anger" by calling it "love," he is still shown to be wrong. He is damned-if-he-does and damned-if-he-doesn't. He is in a bind, and he simply "can't win." His one way out of this tangle would be to comment on it, to say, "Something is really fowled-up here," but to mother this is "backtalk!" The child has no way out (short of running away)—and he is thus in a double-bind.

Now there are two possible consequences of being repeatedly placed in double-bind situations such as this. One, the individual will learn to mis-label messages, both his and others, as when mother teaches the child to see anger as "love." In this case, *the individual's meta-communicative processes become tangled,* and so he can no longer accurately determine the meaning of certain messages. Two, in really severe and oft-repeated double-binds, the individual may totally surrender all attempts at meta-communications; since he "can't win" whether he does it correctly or not, why should he even try? This is relatively rare, but it usually results, according to Bateson *et al*,[47] in what is called "schizophrenia."

We will, for the time being, confine our attention to the first consequence, that is, to tangled and distorted meta-communicative processes, because these are instrumental in creating the quaternary dualism. For many meta-messages concerning information about the ego are in effect messages that punctuate the ego's stream of experience—it is not enough to know that anger is present (message), one must also know to whom the anger belongs (meta-message). It is not enough that the stream of experience reports an emotion (message), the stream must also be accurately punctuated (meta-message) so as to place that emotion within the ego boundary. For example, many people experience negative emotions such as "evilness" (message), but because of a meta-communicative tangle, they do not see this emotion as belonging to themselves—they correctly perceive the emotion (message), but they punctuate (meta-message) the stream so as to see the emotion as residing not in the ego but in others. Other people now start to look "evil," and we have the basis of the well-known witch-hunts. As another example, a child sits down to dinner with his parents—his stream of experience contains the message "desire to eat." But if the parents start in with, "You'd better eat because *we* say you *must*," then the child might start perceiving the message "desire to eat" as originating *outside* himself—he believes that only his parents want him to eat. His meta-communicative process is fowled, so that he punctuates (meta-message) the stream of experience so that the "desire to eat" (message) lies outside the ego. Understandably, he will not eat a thing. He has correctly perceived the impulse, but incorrectly located its source, due to a meta-communicative tangle, a tangle in the messages that would ordinarily locate the source of other messages.

Now I don't want to give the impression that communication and meta-communication are confined solely to the Ego Level, for of course they are not. It's only that they predominate the Ego Level. Neither are double-binds or impasses confined solely to the Ego Level. As we shall see, any dualism presents consciousness with a double-bind or impasse situation, so that every level of the Spectrum (except Mind) has its own peculiar double-binds, since each level has its own dualisms.

At any rate, we need now only note that meta-communicative processes are instrumental in defining a working ego boundary by punctuating the stream of experience correctly. In being repeatedly placed in binds, double-binds (which in Gestalt therapy are known as "impasses"), or similar situations, an individual can develop tangles in his meta-communicative processes. The stream of experience is punctuated so that certain aspects of the ego appear to exist in the environment. In effect, the individual splits off facets of his own psyche, facets which he now perceives as existing external to him, usually in other people. The individual correctly perceives these facets, ideas, emotions, drives, qualities and other messages, *but his meta-communicative processes incorrectly identify the source of the messages,* so that the individual disowns or alienates aspects of himself and then projects or appears to perceive them in the environment.

But, and this is crucial, these types of tangles and misappraisals leave the individual with a *distorted* self-image, an impoverished self-image that does not accurately represent the total psychophysical organism, a fraudulent self-image composed of only fragments of the true ego. In an attempt to make his self-image acceptable, the person renders it inaccurate. Now this inaccurate and impoverished self-image we will be calling the *Persona;* and the disowned, alienated, and projected facets of the ego which now appear to be external, we will call the *Shadow.*

Thus, in the ultimate act of severance and fragmentation, man imposes a *dualism* or split upon his own ego, *represses* the underlying unity of all his egoic tendencies, and *projects* them as the persona vs. the shadow. Such then is the generation of the Quaternary Dualism-Repression-Projection. (See Fig. 3)

It is the nature of every dualism-repression-projection that it presents an apparent or illusory reality, that it reveals things as

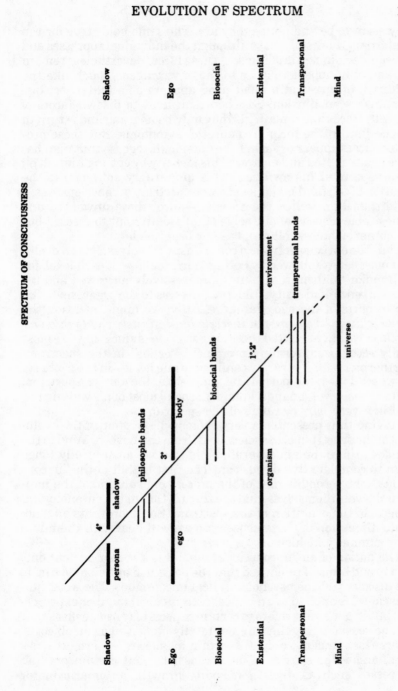

SPECTRUM OF CONSCIOUSNESS

Figure 3

they seem to be and not as they are. The same holds true for the quaternary dualism, and so although the individual represses and projects certain facets of himself, those facets nevertheless remain his and only appear to exist in the environment, much like the reflection of a tree in a quiet pond appears as a real object but remains as an illusion. So when man tries to disown facets of himself, since they remain his they only boomerang and return to plague him in the form of "neurotic" symptoms. But these projected facets appear or seem to be outside the ego, so that man has once again shifted and narrowed his identity by cutting himself off from aspects of his own self. This quaternary split marks the creation of the final major level of the spectrum of consciousness, a level that Jung called the *Shadow*—all of those unwanted and undesirable aspects of our selves that we attempt to discard but which nevertheless follow us as our own Shadow.

Thus the entire spectrum of consciousness evolves. It is an evolution most easily followed by noting Man's *identity* at each level, for each major dualism results in a progressively narrowed and restricted sense of identity, from the universe to the organism to the ego to parts of the ego. Parenthetically, we might mention the obvious: *these levels are not discrete but infinitely shade into one another;* we have selected these six basic levels since they are most easily recognized, forming prominent "nodes" in the spectrum. Furthermore, Man is rarely confined to one level—in the course of a twenty-four-hour period, he may span the entire spectrum. Usually, however, an individual will spend most of his waking life within a very narrow range of the spectrum.

Having thus presented a very sketchy description of the evolution of the spectrum of consciousness, from the Level of Mind to the Shadow, there remain several points that we must briefly touch upon to complete this discussion. The first is that of the "unconscious," the second is that of the process of evolution of the individual levels themselves, and the third is that of the chronological aspects of the evolution of the spectrum. Space prevents an elaborate discussion of these aspects, so we will deal with them in a very summary fashion.

The notion of an "unconscious" in man is a rather ancient one, and Freud himself remarked that the poets had anticipated him in the discovery of the psychoanalytical unconscious. The word "unconscious" is applied to an almost astronomical number of processes, but in general it refers to certain aspects of consciousness that for one reason or another are not totally perceived as an object of awareness. Thus not only are certain memories, experiences, desires, and ideas spoken of as unconscious, but certain organic processes such as digestion, bodily growth, automatic motor skills—these also are unconscious, in the sense that we do not normally control them in a conscious fashion. Psychoanalytically, the unconscious contains wishes (and ideas if they are linked with a wish) that are banished from consciousness by the mechanism of repression, so that wherever there occurs a type of repression, there necessarily occurs a type of unconscious. But our analysis of the spectrum of consciousness suggests that the psychoanalytical repression is but one of several types of repression that operate throughout the spectrum, so that wherever we encounter another type of repression we can expect to find another type of unconscious. Each level of the spectrum, since it is generated by a particular dualism-repression-projection, is always accompanied by particular and specific unconscious aspects. In other words, each level has its own unconscious, generated by the superimposition of one of the four major dualism-repression-projections. As we have seen, each major dualism-repression-projection operates by imposing a severance upon an underlying non-duality or "unity," repressing this unity, and then projecting or manifesting it as dual opposites. *This repressed non-duality or "unity" therefore becomes unconscious.* Or, to say the same thing from a slightly different angle, each particular unconscious represents some aspect of the universe with which we have dis-identified ourselves.

All of this, and all of what we are about to say now, can really be summed up very simply: psychologically, *dualism means unconsciousness.* "Light is always light in darkness; that is what the unconscious is all about."[48] That, indeed, is the whole point. All opposites are mutually interdependent and inseparable, non-dual, *coincidentia oppositorum,* and he who imagines otherwise does so at the price of sending reality underground.

In most instances—as in the example of the disk-figure and the page-background at the beginning of this chapter—we usually imagine that we can perceive the figure all by itself, and this notion leads us to the conclusion that separate figures, separate things, must exist by themselves, since that is apparently the way we perceive them. But as we know, that is an illusion: we actually perceive the entire visual field of figure-plus-background in all its infinite richness and interwoven detail. The figure and background are separated only in symbolic fantasy, never in reality. Yet in a very similar fashion, we imagine that the figure of good can be fundamentally separated from its background of evil, that right is irreconcilably set apart from wrong, that truth will out over falsity. We are perhaps willing to see the inseparability of the disk-figure and the page-background, for that seems a relatively inconsequential insight, but how we recoil at the thought of the hidden conjunction, the *coniunctio oppositorum,* between God and

Satan, life and death, pain and pleasure, will and won't, vice and virtue! Yet we must realize, and in our deepest hearts we already know, that the perception of one without the other is not just meaningless but impossible—physically, logically, sensually. One might as well speak of boxes with insides but no outsides. In imagining that the figure has really won over the background, all we have actually succeeded in doing is slicing-out and repressing certain aspects of the non-dual field of awareness, delivering it up, mutilated, on a dualistic platter. And thus, inevitably, the reality of the non-dual field remains unconscious!

It seems, then, that between what our organisms see and what our dualistic, symbolic processes think we see, there is a vast gulf: and that gulf is the base metal of which the unconscious is fashioned. In short, we pay for duality with the sleep of unconsciousness, as our fathers and their fathers before them did: "when Adam fell, he fell asleep".

For the sake of elaboration, let us now briefly run up the spectrum of consciousness and outline the major unconscious processes associated with the four major dualisms. In so doing, we will also have occasion to comment on some of the more important unconscious processes *derivative* of these major dualisms, such as the "philosophic unconscious" and the "biosocial unconscious." We will, of course, be dealing with these topics in more detail at the appropriate place, and so what follows may serve as a type of summary introduction.

Beginning with the primary dualism-repression-projection, which generates the Existential Level, recall that it severs the "unity" of subject and object, of self and other, of organism and environment, so that this unity—that is, Mind itself—is rendered underlying, implicit, unnoticed, unconscious. In other words, most of us are simply unaware that what we are is Mind. The experience of Mind-only is nevertheless always present—in fact, it is the *only* experience ever-present—but, due to the primary dualism, we repress it, ignore it, forget it and then forget we forgot it. In short, we render Mind unconscious.

Yet it should be emphasized that in saying that Mind is the fundamental unconscious, we do not mean that final enlightenment, the ultimate undoing of all repression, consists in dredging up Mind from the depths and taking a good hard realistic and objective look at it. That, indeed, is unnecessary and even impossible. The undoing of the primary repression requires not that we objectively look at Mind, which in any event is not possible, but that we consciously live as Mind, which in a certain sense we are already doing anyway. Because Mind can never become an object of consciousness, it is frequently referred to as "the Unconscious," but this carries a slightly different connotation than that of the statement that we are presently "unconscious" of Mind. The latter, as we have just explained, means that we are presently unaware of and ignore-ant of the fact that we are always living as Mind, and this is a state of affairs which is "reversed" with the lifting of the primary repression. In the former case, in which Mind is the Unconscious, it is a state of affairs which cannot and need not be reversed. Mind is the Unconscious (*wu hsin, wu nien*) because, as Absolute Subjectivity, as non-dual awareness, as the Supreme Knower, it cannot be known *as an object of consciousness*. Nevertheless, it is highly conscious—as a matter of fact, it is pure consciousness—it is just never conscious of itself, as an eye does not see itself. In the words of Wei Wu Wei:

> What, then, could be inconceivable, what in fact is and must be inconceivable? Only that which is conceiving is itself inconceivable, for only what is conceiving cannot, when conceiving, conceive itself.[49]

In our terminology, the Level of Mind, being pure consciousness, is never conscious of itself, and so is Unconscious. The conceiver is inconceivable; the thinker is unthinkable; consciousness is Unconscious. Thus the Level of Mind is "Unconscious" in two similar yet slightly different senses: unconscious because we are ignorant of its "existence," and unconscious because we cannot know it dualistically—we know Mind by *being* it, and in no other way.

In short, the primary dualism renders the Unconscious unconscious. And that implies—and we mean it to!—*that the very root "layer" of the unconscious is the universe itself.* The sun, moon, and stars, the mountains, clouds, and waters, even the cars, planes, and trains: these truly are some of the "contents" of our base unconscious.

At this point it should be at least noted that this base unconscious is a "product" of not only the primary dualism but also the secondary dualism. For, as we will eventually discover, the secondary dualism is actually the flip-side of the primary dualism—the former dualism constituting time and the latter constituting space, so that the distance between subject and object, which obscures infinity, is the same as the distance between past and future, which obscures eternity. For the moment, however, we need only recall that the secondary dualism, which occurs on the Existential Level, severs the unity of life and death, past and future, being and nullity, and hence propels man into a life of time, thereby obscuring and rendering unconscious the *nunc stans,* the Eternity of the present moment, the vast and magical world of the non-historical. And with this, the now-consciousness that Goethe described suddenly escapes us:

> At each moment (Nature) starts upon a long, long journey and at each moment reaches her end. . . . All is eternally present in her, for she knows neither past nor future. For her the present is eternity.
>
> (*Fragments on Nature*)

Thus the fundamental unconscious is the infinite and eternal universe, which is rendered unconscious by the primary and secondary dualisms. The base unconscious: all the worlds—past, present, future—lying in the unfelt Heart of man. "The unconscious is rather that immortal sea which brought us hither; intimations of which are given in moments of 'oceanic feeling'; one sea of energy or instinct; embracing all mankind, without distinction of race, language, or culture; and embracing all the generations of Adam, past, present, and future, in one . . . mystical . . . body." For "the unconscious is the true psychic reality; and the unconscious is the Holy Spirit."[50]

Now to say that the primary and secondary dualisms render Mind unconscious is only another way of saying that these two dualisms mark the repression of organismic consciousness, for, as we have already indicated, organismic consciousness participates fully in Absolute Subjectivity by virtue of the fact that its operations are spaceless and timeless. Remember, there is nothing in your pure sensory awareness that even vaguely corresponds to space or time. You cannot, for example, hear the past or future, nor smell the difference between inside and outside. Silly as that sounds, it happens to be true! At any rate, the primary and secondary dualisms repress and obscure this pure organismic consciousness—Mind itself—by convincing you that the boundaries between inside and outside and between past and future are very real, whereas, like all boundaries, they are merely symbolic conventions.

Thus organismic awareness is *transformed* into centaur awareness. But for the average person, even this centaur awareness, this total prehension of existence in the passing present, will succumb to repression with the rise of the tertiary dualism, which shatters the coherency of the centaur itself. But, as we have seen, it is not just the tertiary dualism which obscures centaur awareness, for between the Existential Level and the Ego Level there lies a vast matrix of introjected social distinctions which greatly contribute to the obscuration of centaur consciousness. We are speaking, of course, of the Biosocial Bands.

The Biosocial Band is certainly derivative of the primary and secondary dualisms, in the sense that culture molds and is molded by the tenor of self vs. other (the primary dualism), and in the sense that culture is what man does with death (the secondary dualism).

But fundamentally, this Band of the Spectrum is a complex matrix of distinctions, a vast field of dualities, and since in all cases dualism means unconsciousness, the Biosocial Band inexorably contributes to the repression of existential awareness—which means nothing more than that the Biosocial Band acts as a major filter of reality. Those aspects of experience which cannot penetrate this social filter (of language, law, ethics, taboos, logic, rules and meta-rules, etc.) simply remain unconscious. Thus, as we start to move towards the upper limits of the Existential Level by operating on centaur consciousness so as to translate it into socially meaningful terms, a vast expanse of reality is laid waste, rendered unconscious, by this very socialization of existential awareness. And, we might add, the major ingredient of this wasteland, this "biosocial unconscious," is a reservoir containing much of our centaur awareness and the patterned reality it would otherwise reveal. In the words of Erich Fromm:

> But the effect of society is not only to funnel fictions into our consciousness, also to prevent the awareness of reality. . . . Every society, by its own practice of living and by the mode of relatedness, of feeling, and perceiving, develops a system of categories which determines the forms of awareness. This system works, as it were, like a *socially conditioned filter;* experience cannot enter awareness unless it can penetrate this filter. . . . *I am aware* of all my feelings and thoughts which are permitted to penetrate the threefold filter of (socially conditioned) language, logic, and taboos (social character). Experiences which can not be filtered through remain outside of awareness; that is, they remain unconscious.[51]

What remnants of centaur consciousness there are that survive the filtering of the Biosocial Band are finally and almost completely rendered unconscious with the generation of the Ego Level. For even on the Biosocial Band, where existential awareness is greatly obscured, man still acts as, and fundamentally feels himself to be, a centaur, a mind-body: his ego is more-or-less a body-ego and his thinking is more-or-less body-thinking. But with the appearance of the tertiary dualism, man surrenders the body and forfeits all conscious contact with centaur consciousness. The tertiary dualism severs and represses the centaur, projecting it as the psyche vs. the soma, so that man is no longer aware of himself as a unified centaur but as a horseman divided from his horse, beating or praising it in order to extort the desired actions from this, his "animal" body, his poor brother ass. The centaur is not killed, however. It is just buried alive.

Such, then, is the emergence of the ego, which, it must be emphasized, is simply the fruition of the separate-self sense born with the primary dualism. Now we might also mention that closely connected with the ego is what could be called the individual's "philosophic unconscious," which consists of all of one's unexamined metaphysical assumptions, one's personal but unexposed philosophical paradigms, one's intellectual root premises and maps so taken for granted that they are no longer ordinarily up for critical scrutiny. This band of the Ego Level forms, as it were, a type of personal analogue to the social filter of the Biosocial Band. This is what Fromm has in mind when he states that "in addition to the social taboos there are individual elaborations of these taboos which differ from family to family; a child, afraid of being 'abandoned' by his parents because he is aware of experiences which to them individually are taboo, will, in addition to the socially normal repression [of the Biosocial Band], also repress those feelings which are prevented from coming to awareness by the individual aspect of the filter."[52]

In their broadest sense, the philosophic bands are simply a *personal matrix of distinctions,* over and above the social matrix of distinctions constituting the Biosocial Band. Obviously, in many cases the philosophic bands are instrumental in the generation of the quaternary dualism-repression-projection, and in all cases they are instrumental in its maintenance. For, generally speaking, the philosphic bands act as a personal filter which screens out those experiences which are inconsistent with its mesh. Should the experience thus screened-out be of an "external event," then conventional egoic perception of that event is distorted; but should the experience screened-out be of a personal origin, then straightaway material for the Shadow results. And it matters not whether this personal filter contains philosophical structures judged true or false by conventional standards, for in all cases "there are more things in heaven and earth than are dreamt of in your philosophy," and if any of these "more things" are of personal origin, they end up in the Shadow. Thus the quaternary dualism is born.

Hence, on the Ego Level, the quaternary dualism-repression-projection severs the psyche, represses its essential unity, and thus creates the unconscious Shadow—all of the repressed traits and wishes that the ego has attempted to vanquish by pushing them out of consciousness. Specifically, it is the unity or harmony (*concordia discors*) of psychic tendencies that is now rendered unconscious, while the banished aspects of the psyche are generally, but somewhat unsatisfactorily, spoken of as the "contents" of this unconscious. Of course, we are in some sense aware of this Shadow, but only in an indirect and hence distorted fashion, for we project it onto people or objects "out there" and so fancy ourselves innocent of it.

Thus we see that for each level of the Spectrum there is a corresponding unconscious—or rather, some corresponding unconscious aspects or processes. *Each level of the Spectrum has intrinsically different characteristics*—different needs, different symbols, different modes of awareness, different motivations, different compensations, and so on. *When a particular level is rendered unconscious, so are the major features of the characteristics of that level.* Thus, *the unconscious is stratified,* and for the very same reasons that the Spectrum itself is stratified.

But fundamentally, upon whatever level of the Spectrum we exist, the "total" unconscious consists of the sum of all those characteristics and aspects of the universe with which—at that level—we are no longer identified, as well as the dualistic maps which are so instrumental in screening our identity with those aspects. Furthermore, under the general conditions of repression—at whatever level—those aspects with which we are no longer identified can enter the field of awareness only in an indirect and distorted fashion, appearing as alien and potentially threatening objects "out there." At the Shadow Level, for example, we have already lost direct contact with the environment, with the body, and even with parts of the ego—and hence we are aware of all of these now "unconscious" aspects only in an illusory fashion: they appear as objects out there, external, alien, potentially threatening; they are hazy reflections of paradise lost and union forgotten. As Philosophia said to Boethius in his distress, "You have forgotten who you are."

Now we hasten to add that, distinct as these levels of the unconscious may be, they *all* ultimately stem from the primary dualism. Once the seer is severed from the seen, that seer becomes a blind-spot of the universe, for the simple reason that the seer cannot see itself seeing. No observing system can observe all of itself, and so under these circumstances something always gets left out (which we earlier saw as Incompleteness and Uncertainty Principles, and which we see now operating psychologically). The universe takes a turn on itself and gets lost. For in turning back on itself, it appears to generate the "other" and thus to be alien to itself. It is exactly this primordial blind-spot which acts, so to speak, as a type of seed-crystal around which grows, with each successive level of the spectrum, a new layer of "something-left-out-ness," of unconsciousness, with each layer being nothing more than an "enlargement," through a new dualistic twist, of the original blind-spot. That, in short, is the evolution of the spectrum of consciousness.

The second point which we must mention is that of the evolution of the individual levels themselves, for it should be obvious that not only does the spectrum evolve "upwards and outwards" in a type of vertical movement away and out of the Level of Mind, but also do the individual levels themselves evolve and "expand" in a type of horizontal movement. The ways in which our intellects, our language processes, our self-images, our bodily awareness, and other phenomena pertaining to individual levels—the ways in which these processes are growing and evolving, in individuals as well as in the species as a whole, are being intensely investigated by scientists and educators, anthropologists and sociologists. Further, the ways in which these changes affect our "breakthroughs to cosmic consciousness" have been elaborated by such renowned explorers as Teilhard de Chardin, Bucke, Sri Aurobindo, Jean Gebser, William I. Thompson, Rozak, von Weizacher, and others. The point is that although the Level of Mind does not itself actually evolve—being timeless and spaceless—nevertheless the ways in which it seems to manifest the other levels of the spectrum do indeed appear to be evolving.

The third point concerns the chronological aspects of the evolution of the spectrum, a point which is difficult to comprehend because of what Schroedinger called the "peculiar time-table of Mind," namely, it knows no past or future, no before or after.[53] Therefore, as we have tried to point out, the evolution of the spectrum is not a real evolution of Mind through space and time, but a pretend evolution of Mind into space and time, a pretend evolution of Mind manifesting itself as space and time. Thus the description of the evolution of the seven bands of the spectrum and of the four major dualisms, as if they occurred in time is nothing but a concession to our rutted patterns of thought and language that necessarily translate the simultaneity of events occurring in the timeless Moment into the terms of linear and temporal representation. The temporal evolution of the spectrum of consciousness is nothing but a description, a setting-forth-in-linear-terms, of the Eternal Simultaneity. To the student of the Hindu science of Self (*adhyatmavidya*), this idea will present no difficulty, for it is very much analogous to the *Adhyatmavidya* doctrine of the involution (*Nivritti Marga*) and the evolution (*Pravritti Marga*) of the Self, the Atman-Brahman.

> The life or lives of man may be regarded as constituting a curve—an arc of time-experience subtended by the duration of the individual Will to Life. The outward movement of this curve—Evolution, the Path of Pursuit—the *Pravritti Marga*—is characterized by self-assertion. The inward movement—Involution, the Path of Return—the *Nivritti Marga*—is characterized by increasing Self-realization. The

religion of men on the outward path is the Religion of Time; the religion of those who return is the Religion of Eternity.[54]

The process of the Self's involution and evolution is viewed as a universal drama of the eternal play (*lila, krida, dolce gioco*)[55] of hide-and-seek, of creation and redemption, of manifestation and dissolution, of anabolism and catabolism, but the sole actor in this drama is the one and only Self, playing an infinite number of roles (such as you and me) without ceasing in the least to completely remain itself, spaceless and timeless, whole and undivided. In our limited and temporal state, we divide this drama into two stages—that of involution and that of evolution—while in reality both phases are one aspect. In highest truth, there is no involution and evolution through time, for whether we realize it or not, the Self remains always above time in the Eternal Moment. The same holds true for the apparent evolution of the spectrum of consciousness, for we have actually done nothing more than explain the *pravritti marga* in more modern terms. For this reason, we have studiously avoided assigning actual chronologies to the four major dualisms. From the standpoint of time, we have only suggested that the four major dualisms do occur in the order that we have outlined, beginning with the primary and ending with the quaternary dualism. This is not to say, however, that these dualisms, as they appear to evolve in history, do not constitute a legitimate field of study. On the contrary, the field is a most important one. The primary dualism, for example, has been approached anthropologically by investigators concerned with that period in man's evolution when he learned to separate himself from his environment. It has also been followed in the individual development of the infant, as the child learns to separate himself from his immediate surroundings. The work of such scholars as Freud, Piaget, Werner, Cassirer, Arieti, and others in this area represents a most valuable contribution.

We are not primarily interested in these temporal aspects, however, for *man re-enacts his major dualisms in this very moment*, and it is only as he views them through the squinting eye of time that he is persuaded to establish a time-table for what actually remains timeless. How, in this very moment, we illusorily separate ourselves from our universe, our bodies, and even our thoughts—that is our primary concern. This separation, this Fall, is part and parcel of our implicit faith that the universe proceeds in a line, in a one-dimensional sequence that we call "time", and so our redemption is ultimately a release from the illusion of history, of the tunnel-vision that presents Eternity as strung out in a sequence called the past-present-future. And here, no amount of history will deliver us from history, from that nightmare from which Stephen and all sensitive beings must eventually awake.

REFERENCES AND NOTES

1. A. K. Coomaraswamy, *Hinduism and Buddhism* (New York: Philosophical Library).

2. G. S. Brown, *Laws of Form* (New York: Julian Press), p. v.

3. Ibid., p. v.

4. Ibid., p. v.

5. Ibid., p. 84.

6. Ibid., p. 104.

7. Y. S. Hakeda, trans., *The Awakening of Faith* (New York: Columbia University Press, 1967), p. 50.

8. D. T. Suzuki, *Studies in the Lankavatara Sutra* (London: Routledge and Kegan Paul, 1968), p. 133.

9. What has been called "the one defect in the mystic tradition" is supposedly "its tendency to flee the responsibilities of history and engage in premature adventures into eternity." This is most incorrect, for the true mystic does not flee history, he just refuses to be bound by it. The difference between the two is vast, and it is also the difference between pseudo and pure mysticism. Actually, we could argue that the mystic *alone* is the one who does not flee the reality of the Present, and thus he alone is capable of seeing history in its true context. Besides, all of this overlooks the fact that "eternity is in love with the productions of time."

10. Vasana is also similar to "bija", so-called "memory seeds", different in degree, not kind, from "everyday" memory-thought.

11. Suzuki, *Studies in the Lankavatara Sutra,* p. 190.

12. E. Deutsch *Advaita Vedanta, A Philosophical Reconstruction* (Honolulu: East-West Center Press, 1969), p. 28.

13. Coomaraswamy, *Hinduism and Buddhism,* p. 6.

14. Ibid., p. 7.

15. Ibid., p. 11.

16. Ibid., p. 9.

17. Ibid., p.33.

18. Ibid., p. 12.

19. E.g.: In the "next major creation," the Spirit again conceives, and the waters (as Virgin Mother Mary, Star of the Sea) again give birth to the Word (Logos) made flesh, the Christ. Thus also "Except a man be born of water and the Spirit, he cannot enter into the kingdon of God." (John 3:5) Thus is a man reborn, re-created, which is the "third major creation."

20. Alan Watts, *Myth and Ritual in Christianity* (Boston: Beacon Press, 1970), p. 47. Cf: from the *Pancavimsa Brahmana,* VII, 8, 1—
    "The Waters [Prima Materia, virgin matter] being ripe unto conception, Vayu [i.e., the Wind, Masculine Spirit, who conceives by spiration] moved over their surface [cf. Thomas Aquinas, *Summ. Theol.,* I. 74, "the Spirit of the Lord signifies the Holy Ghost, Who is said to move over the water—that is to say, over what Augustine holds to mean formless matter" (i.e., Prima Materia. . . .] wherefore came into being a lovely thing [Logos, world image-matrix], there in the Waters Mitra-Varuna beheld themselves reflected." Quoted in *Transformation of Nature in Art,* p. 210. Note also the connection between maya and narcissism, genesis by God's self-reflection, as in Boehme's *Selbstabbildung*—all division (and hence creation) being in effect a Self-reflection, "motivated" by loving exuberance (karuna), "For God so loved the world" which was nevertheless His Image. Such Divine Narcissism is a creative illusion, a playful dividing of the Integral Multiplicity of That One into the duality of the original and the mirror image (Primary Dualism), a play in which, according to our degree of maturity, we are invited to participate. Hence, Buddhist discipline is designed to transmute trishna, or egoic narcissism, into Karuna, Divine Narcissism; that is, to transmute self-love, which excludes love of others, into Self-love, which *is* love of others.

21. Thus does Lao Tzu proclaim that "Naming (word and thought) is the Mother of 10,000 things (the world)."

22. Watts, *Myth and Ritual in Christianity,* p. 52.

23. Norman O. Brown, *Life Against Death, the Psychoanalytical Meaning of History* (Middletown: Wesleyan University Press, 1959), p. 52.

24. The nowever creation is totally without cause, volition, movement, work, or effort. It is spontaneous, without reference to past or future, *sahaja, tzu jan.* Thus "The Tao's principle is spontaneity." (Lao Tze, XXV.) Effort or work implies resistance, and there is nothing outside of Godhead to offer resistance, hence his activity is "motion without locomotion," the unmoved mover, dynamic immobility: Cf., Eckhart, "When God created the heavens, the earth, and creatures, he did no work; he had nothing to do; he made no effort." Thus Eckhart describes God's activity as play, and "This play was played eternally before all creatures." Yet "play and audience are the same." Similarly Brahman's activity is "lila", play, a spontaneous game—cf. Coomaraswamy, "All this implies that what we call the world-process and a

creation is nothing but a game that the Spirit plays with itself, and as sunlight 'plays' upon whatever it illuminates and quickens, although unaffected by its apparent contacts." *Hinduism and Buddhism*, p. 14. The Creation is Psychodrama.

Inexorably, then, if man's Fall is into work and effort ("Adam fell when this play became serious business."), it is finally from work and effort that he will be delivered—delivered not from activity but from volitional activity. Hence the Bodhisattva's life is "anabhogacarya," one of purposeless, effortless deeds—motivated not by laziness but by Karuna, universal compassion: volition, purpose has meaning only in time. So also is prajna effortless, being dimensionless knowledge, as the Bodhisattva "enters in one Moment and with effortless knowledge into the realm of [Reality] gained by the omniscient." *Dasabhumika Sutra*.

25. Coomaraswamy, *Hinduism and Buddhism*, p. 9.

26. *The Spiritual Teaching of Ramana Maharshi* (Berkeley: Shambhala, 1972), p. 92.

27. Hubert Benoit, *The Supreme Doctrine* (New York: Viking Press, 1955), pp. 33-4. (My italics.)

28. Brown, *Life against Death*, pp. 84, 100.

29. Ibid., p. 284.

30. Ibid., p. 91, 93.

31. Ibid., p. 159.

32. Benoit, *Supreme Doctrine*, p. 35.

33. Thus, Eastern traditions do not shun sensual knowledge, but rather sensual knowledge contaminated by conceptualization. Thus Sengtsan, in the *Hsin hsin Ming*, maintains that "When you are not antagonistic to the senses, it turns out to be the same as complete enlightenment." Hence, Suzuki: *"Because of conceptualization,* our sense-experiences inform us with an incorrect picture of the world." *Zen and Japanese Culture*, p. 175. And elsewhere: "I have come to think that 'feeling' is a better term than 'intuition' for the experience Zen claims to have—'feeling,' psychologists generally distinguish from other activities of the mind." Ibid., p. 219. This "pure feeling" not contaminated with conceptualization is what we are calling "organismic consciousness."

34. Psychoanalytically, this repression of bodily awareness results in its concentration in the genital area. Cf., N. O. Brown: "If normal adult sexuality is a pattern which has grown out of the infantile delight in the pleasurable activity of all parts of the human body, then what was originally a much wider capacity for pleasure in the body has been narrowed in range, concentrated on one particular (the genital) organ. . . . Then the pattern of normal adult sexuality (in Freud's ter-

minology, genital organization) is a tyranny.... Children are poly-
morphously perverse [i.e., they take blissfull delight in the entire life
of the organism, while] adult sexuality is an unnatural restriction of
the erotic potentialities of the human body." Psychoanalytically, to
live on the Ego Level is to possess genital organization, and thus the
classic (if incredible) psychoanalytical formula: soul = phallus. If this
seems somewhat fantastic, many sages, such as Krishnamurti, claim
to possess polymorphous perversity.

35. Brown, *Life against Death,* p. 167.

36. Benoit, *Supreme Doctrine,* p. 42.

37. We should note here that the Existential Level, as the embodiment of
the Primary and Secondary Dualisms, is very much a cramp or perturbation, *the* cramp or perturbation, lying at the root of man's "self"-
identity. Further, it is this cramp, which Benoit calls a spasm and
Franklin Jones calls a contraction, that is the fundamental motor of
all man's activities. And the fuel for this motor is of one type only: the
desire to return to the Garden, to reunite with God, which is, of course,
God's desire to find himself. With the rise of the Primary and Secondary Dualisms, man is thrown out of the Garden (i.e., God goes out
of himself, "kenosis"), and hence God becomes unconscious (i.e., the
Primary Unconscious which is Mind, corresponding with the Primary
Dualism. "But the unconscious is the true psychic reality; and the
unconscious is the Holy Spirit." Brown, *Love's Body,* p. 195). Man, the
mask of God, then seeks reunion, but this is now impossible, for the
movement of seeking implies the real duality of the seeker vs. the
sought, and God lies where this primary duality is not. Thus man is
driven to "substitute-gratifications," basically symbolic, in which he
seeks to recapture the non-dual Garden. Man, however, does not
know that what he seeks is the Garden. His desire is "unconscious."
He thinks he wants success, prestige, money, etc. Further, since he
can never find Mind through this dualistic search, he is never completely at home with himself; hence, the basic spasm, the primordial
cramp that is the Existential Level; man, the discontented animal,
seeking reunion in a way that prevents it.
    There is a psychoanalytical correspondence. The infant is poly-
morphously perverse, under sway of the pleasure principle, erotic and
playful reality, in touch with pure organismic consciousness, which in
Sanskrit is called "prana," Greek "pneuma," Arabic "ruh," Chinese
"chi." Under repression prana goes underground and man is driven to
"substitute gratificaiton," but he "remains unconvinced because in
infancy he tasted the fruit of the tree of life, and knows that it is good,
and never forgets." Freud never fully understood that this "prana"
can be awakened in a mature form, that man needn't regress to return
to the Garden. The correspondence is that "prana" is an exact equivalent of the Holy Spirit.

38. R. D. Laing, *The Politics of the Family* (New York: Pantheon, 1971), p.
117.

39. B. L. Whorf, *Language, Thought, and Reality* (Cambridge: M.I.T. Press, 1956), pp. 221, 252.

40. Ibid., pp. 240, 213.

41. Ibid., p. 215.

42. Ibid., pp. 243, 240.

43. Alan Watts, *The Way of Zen* (New York: Vintage, 1957), p. 6.

44. Gardner Murphy, and Lois B. Murphy, (ed.), *Asian Psychology* (New York: Basic Books, 1968), p. 213.

45. John Maynard Keynes, *Essays in Persuasion.* Quoted in note 23, p. 107-8. Cf., Chung Tzu put it, "you see your egg and expect it to crow."

46. G. Bateson, *Steps to an Ecology of Mind* (New York: Ballantine, 1972), p. 201.

47. Ibid.

48. T. Rozak, ed., *Sources* (New York: Harper and Row, 1972), Chap. V.

49. Wei Wu Wei, *Posthumous Pieces* (Hong Kong: Hong Kong University Press, 1968), p. 5.

50. Norman O. Brown, *Love's Body* (New York: Vintage, 1966).

51. E. Fromm, D. T. Suzuki, and R. DeMartino, *Zen Buddhism and Psychoanalysis* (New York; Harper and Row, 1970).

52. Ibid. The "philosophic bands" are similar, but by no means identical to, the Freudian super-ego. Our interpretation of the psycho-analytical theory of the generation of the super-ego (following Norman O. Brown) is as follows: the infant, after constructing the primary dualism, is faced with the immanent possibility of death, and thus in fantasy seeks to avoid death, repress it, escape it. This construction of the secondary dualism of life vs. death blossoms into the Oedipal project, which is the infant's attempt *to avoid death by becoming,* in fantasy, *the father of himself.* The libido is concentrated in the genital region for just this purpose. That project, however, is brought to a swift end with the castration complex, which halts forever the infantile *bodily* solution to the Oedipal complex. But the attempt continues in *fantasy* solutions. For, with the castration complex, the infant internalizes the parents as the super-ego and thus succeeds, in fantasy fashion, in becoming father in himself. In a sense, he becomes his own Parent, but at the cost of remaining his own Child. And, as mentioned, the castration complex also results in the severing of the ego from the body, since the *bodily* solution to the Oedipal gives way to purely *mental* solutions. This is, of course, the tertiary dualism. Thus, on the Ego Level, we find a tripartite ego divorced from the body: the super-ego, the adult ego, and the infantile ego, *all* supported by the flight from death (secondary dualism). This tripartite ego structure has been noted by many researchers. Transactional

Analysis refers to them as the ego states of Parent, Adult, and Child; while Perls called them the Topdog, centered self, and Underdog. We agree with this basic tripartite structure of the Ego Level.

Now, on the Ego Level, it is not so much the existence of the Parent-Adult-Child that is problematic, for *all* people possess them as an inevitability of bio-civilization. It is rather whether or not we understand them, are aware of them, and are consciously utilizing them, as opposed to being their unwitting instruments. For the moment they are "unconscious", they become Shadow (quaternary dualism), and just *that* is the problem. Since I have dealt with all this in great detail in a paper presently being prepared for publication ("A Working Synthesis of Transactional Analysis and Gestalt Therapy," *Psychotherapy: Theory, Research, and Practice)* I have omitted extended discussion of it here. Let me only add that the philosophic bands contain the premises and paradigms added throughout life, and not just those of the Parent-Child added in the first five years of life, important as those may be. The philosophic bands are the home of personal premises (including those of the Parent and Child) and as a premise is a *meta-message,* its relation to the Shadow is obvious.

53. Need we mention that this completely undercuts the notion of causality? If there is no before or after, there is no cause or effect.

54. Ananda K. Coomaraswamy, *The Dance of Shiva* (New York: Noonday Press, 1957), p. 10.

55. Again, "play" because Godhead's activity is spontaneous, without reference to time, unmoved, unmotivated, effortless. We might also mention that because Mind's activity is purposeless, effortless, and timeless, this precludes any doctrine of emanation, which holds the manifestation is necessary. Even "manifestation" as we are using this word is liable to be misunderstood, for it erroneously suggests that phenomena "come out" of Mind, while there is actually nothing outside Mind. Emanation, which is after all a form of pantheism (*see* note IV. 16), is untenable, inasmuch as it is dualistic (the many emanate from the One, as if the two were separate), and hence imposes spatial-temporal limitations on Mind. Phenomena do not emanate from Mind—each phenomenon *is* Mind, a fact obscured by our dualistic mode of knowing.

VI. *SURVEYING THE TRADITIONS*

America's master psychologist and greatest philosopher, William James, has stated our basic (metaphorical) contention very precisely:

> Let us take outer perception, the direct sensation which, for example, the walls of these rooms give us. Can we say that the psychical and the physical are absolutely heterogenous? On the contrary, they are so little heterogenous that if we adopt the common-sense point of view, if we disregard all explanatory inventions—molecules and ether waves, for example, which at bottom are metaphysical entities—if, in short, we take reality naively, as it is given, an immediate; then this sensible reality on which our vital interests rest and from which all our actions proceed, *this sensible reality and the sensation which we have of it are absolutely identical one with the other at the time the sensation occurs. Reality is apperception itself.* . . . In this instance, the content of the physical is none other than the psychical. Subject and object confuse, as it were.[1]

That Reality is this pure non-dual awareness (apperception, as James calls it) is simple enough, but it certainly remains difficult to fully comprehend, for it implies that with the rise of the primary dualism (and the consequent dualisms) our perception of the world as well as ourselves is rendered, in some sense, illusory. As Brown pointed out, the "world undoubtedly is itself (i.e., is indistinct from itself)," but as soon as the primary dualism arises, the world has acted "so as to make itself distinct from, and therefore false to, itself." But this "falseness" cannot be real, since the world nevertheless, always, and actually remains indistinct from itself, and so the distinction must be illusory—that is the sense in which we use this word.

On the face of it, this hardly seems good news, and it so vitiates common sense that most of us recoil in shock. Add to this the fact that this non-dual awareness is not at all an idea, but much closer to what we mean by "pure experience,"[2] so that strictly speaking we cannot fully characterize it in words (since words themselves are *part* of experience), and the average soul beats a hasty retreat into any number of comfortable ideologies. To compound the apparent difficulty, any time a writer, from Schroedinger to Ramana Maharshi—in an attempt to awaken us from this dream—tries to describe non-dual awareness, knowing full well that it is a necessary but ultimately futile gesture, then the paradoxes and logical contradictions that necessarily result inevitably make him prey to any member of the Wise Guy School of philosophy that wants to take a shot at him. The following anecdote told of Shankara, the renowned Indian sage and author of the Vedanta, will illustrate.

> A certain king in India, who was of a very realistic and logical mind, went to Shankara to receive instructions as to the nature of the Absolute. When Shankara taught him to regard all of his kingly wealth and power as no more than mere phenomenal illusions arising out of the absolute Self which is the ground of all things, the king was incredulous. And when he was told that the one and only Self appeared multiple only because of the dualisms of his ignorance, the king straightaway decided to put Shankara to a test and determine if the sage really felt this existence was no different from a dream.
>
> The following day, as Shankara was approaching the palace to deliver his next lecture to the king, a huge and heat-maddened elephant was deliberately turned loose and aimed in Shankara's direction. As soon as the sage saw the elephant charging, he turned and fled in an apparently very cowardly fashion, and as the animal nearly reached him, he disappeared from sight. When the king found him, he was perched at the top of a lofty palm tree, which he had ascended with remarkable dexterity. The elephant was caught and caged, and the famous Shankara, perspiration pouring off him, came before his student.
>
> The king naturally apologized for such an unfortunate and nearly fatal accident. Then, with a smile breaking across his face, but pretending great seriousness, he asked why the venerable sage had resorted to physical flight, since surely he was aware that the elephant was of a purely illusory character.
>
> Shankara replied, "Indeed, in highest truth, the elephant is non-real and illusory. Nevertheless, you and I are as non-real as that elephant. Only your ignorance, clouding the truth with this spectacle of non-real phenomenality, made your Highness see illusory me go up a non-real tree.[3]

The point is that the non-dual awareness of Self is not a luminous mush of undifferentiated jelly, so that the universe melts down into one huge monistic lump of clay. Indeed, the universe exists exactly as we perceive it (where sense and sensibility are still non-dual), but not necessarily as we name and divide it into separate things extended in space and time. "Seeing! Seeing! Seeing!" as Rumi declared. And it is this "Seeing"—before we divide it into seer and seen—this non-dual "apperception" that James declares is reality itself—it is THIS that we are to discover.

To help orient us to this discovery, we will now devote ourselves to briefly elaborating in a diagrammatical fashion what we have heretofore explained in a more logical and linear fashion. We will utilize images, diagrams, and schematics—that is, the imaginative type of symbolic elaboration used in the analogical way—to supplement the somewhat formal descriptions that were previously presented. Then, with the aid of these diagrammatic representations, we will compare the spectrum of consciousness with the psychologies of the great metaphysical traditions.

The simplest diagram representing the spectrum of consciousness is that given in Fig. 3 of the last chapter. In this schematic the four major dualisms as well as six of the bands of the spectrum are traced out, so that they can be easily compared with linear descriptions given earlier. It must be emphasized that the major drawback in this and every diagram is that the Level of Mind is made to look as if it were simply another level of the spectrum, which in this sense it is not. Perhaps it would be better to let the paper itself represent Mind, and then draw the levels as superimposed upon the paper. (This, as we shall see, is exactly what the late Zen Master Harada used to do.) But if one simply remembers that the Level of Mind is not a particular level among other levels, but is rather that "no-level" which is the "ground" of all levels, then Fig. 3 may prove useful.

The three-dimensional diagram shown in Fig. 5 is an attempt to represent the same spectrum from a slightly different angle, and is roughly based upon the classic metaphor of Plato's Cave. Plato maintained that man, in his natural state (*avidya*), is as if situated in a cave with his back facing the opening of the cave. Outside this opening itself lies the Light of Eternal Reality, but man—because his back is to this light—sees only the shadows of reality that dance across the back of the cave, and with his attention thus occupied, he sees only dreams and reflections, never reality itself. So fascinated is man with these shadows, that he builds great systems of "science" and philosophy around these illusory phantoms. Then one day, somebody escapes from the cave, sees Reality, returns and says, "Guys, you're not going to believe this, but. . . ." As we have presented it, the shadows represent the symbolic-map knowledge, the pictures we form of reality, the dualistic mode of knowing; while the Light represents non-dual awareness, Absolute Subjectivity, I-I, Brahman. These are labeled in Fig. 4.

Now we have extended Plato slightly by suggesting — throughout this volume—that there are *levels* of shadows, represented by the various bands of the spectrum of consciousness. These bands are therefore superimposed upon Fig. 4 and the resultant schematic is given in Fig. 5, which is simply a combination of Figs. 3 and 4.

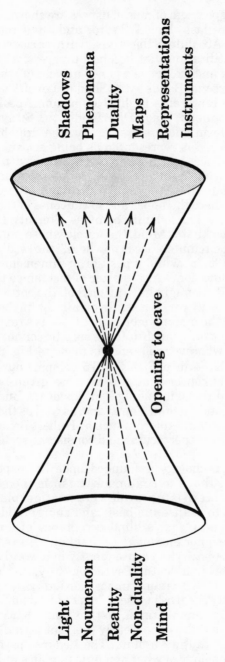

Shadows
Phenomena
Duality
Maps
Representations
Instruments

Opening to cave

Figure 4

Light
Noumenon
Reality
Non-duality
Mind

The bands of the spectrum of consciousness are shown in the upper half of the hour-glass-shaped figure, and they represent the identification of Absolute Subjectivity with various objects and subjects, an identification that becomes progressively more narrowed, restricted, and exclusive as one "moves up" the spectrum from the Transpersonal Bands to the Shadow Level. The lower half of the hour-glass represents Light, Noumenon, Absolute Subjectivity, Mind, Godhead, Tao, Dharmadhatu, Sunyata, Brahman—whatever term one prefers. Again, the drawback in this diagram is that Mind is represented as being set apart from the other levels by space; and further, it is drawn with the spatial dimensions of a cone—both of these representations are misleading. To alleviate these very real difficulties, we have labeled the single point where the upper and lower cones of the hour glass intersect—we have labeled this point as Eternity-Infinity, the absolute Here-Now that is Mind, the "circle whose center is everywhere and whose circumference is nowhere," the "still point of the turning world," a "point without position or dimensions and a now without date or duration." As a matter of fact, since this point of Here-Now *is* Mind, we might have just left off the bottom half of the hour glass—this, however, is a strain on almost anybody's imagination, and since the metaphor of Plato's Cave is so expressive, we have left in the bottom cone. But these specific connotations must be born in mind wherever reference is made to Fig. 5.

Let us now, with the aid of Figs. 3 and 5, compare our description of the spectrum of consciousness with those given by the great metaphysical traditions, including Zen, Yogacara Buddhism, Vedanta Hinduism, and Tibetan Vajrayana, as well as those set forth by renowned individual explorers such as Hubert Benoit. [4] We will begin with that most spectacular and consistent system, the Advaita Vedanta.

The Vedanta psychology is founded upon the experimentally verifiable insight that the Brahman-Atman is the sole Reality, and its primary concern is to provide a pragmatic explanation as to "why" man fails to realize his basic and supreme identity with Brahman. In general, man's blind acceptance of dualisms and distinctions is the ignorance (*avidya*) that lands him squarely in a world of illusions (*maya*) and consequently in a world of suffering (*samsara*, round of birth-death). Psychologically, this ignorance of Brahman is marked by the superimposition (*adhyasa*) of what are technically called "sheaths" (*kosas*) "over" or "upon" the underlying reality of Brahman-Atman, so that man identifies himself with these *kosas* and thus apparently (i.e., not actually) obscures his real identity with the Absolute. The Vedanta psychology is a detailed phenomenology of what amounts to man's universal case

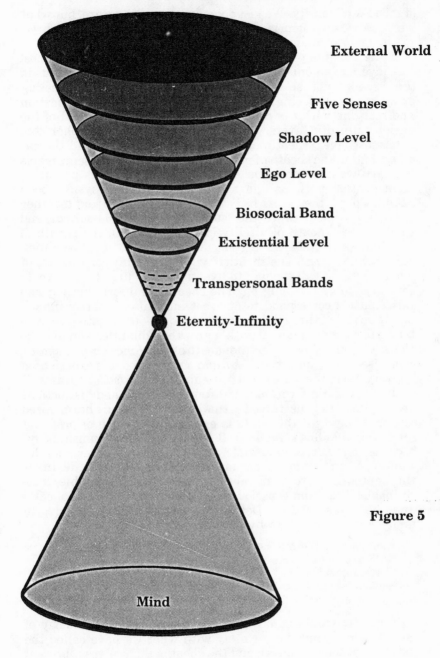

External World

Five Senses

Shadow Level

Ego Level

Biosocial Band

Existential Level

Transpersonal Bands

Eternity-Infinity

Mind

Figure 5

of mistaken identity. We just do not realize who we are, but what we *think* we are comprises several sheaths (*kosas*) with which we, in our ignorance, inadvertently identify.

In the Vedanta psychology, the sheaths are looked upon almost like layers of an onion, with the reality of the Atman "buried" in the very center of the onion, so that liberation results from peeling away (or simply seeing through) these levels of mis-identification and merging with the center which is the actual ground of the various illusory layers.[5] Continuing with this metaphor, the outermost layer, sheath, or "skin" of the onion is called the *annamayakosa*, the sheath of material existence. It represents man's ordinary waking consciousness (*jagarita-sthana*), his primitive identification with an ego encapsulated in his physical body (*sthula-sarira*, the "gross body"). The next three layers together constitute what is called the "subtle body" (*suksma-sarira*), and they are the sheath of vitality (*pranamayakosa*), the sheath of discrimination (*manomayakosa*), and the sheath of ratiocination (*vijnanamayakosa*). The sheath of vitality roughly corresponds to what we might call the will to live, that blind urge to survive, to continue, to go on going on. The sheaths of discrimination and ratiocination correspond to our root inclination—partly innate, partly acquired through language and logic—to dichotomize existence, to overlay the Real with a growth of dualities and distinctions. The innermost layer, the sheath of bliss (*ananda-mayakosa*), comprises the "causal body" (*karana-sarira*), and it is experienced by everyone in the state of deep, dreamless sleep (*susupti*), as well as during certain forms of meditation. Dualities and distinctions are not completely destroyed at this level, but they are harmonized so completely that this state is experienced as one of profound relaxation and bliss (*ananda*). It is also called the "causal body" because it is the ground and "cause" of all the other sheaths. Finally, when this last sheath is peeled away, the pure Reality of the Center alone remains, absolute non-duality, ineffable, indescribable, Brahman-consciousness, underlying the five sheaths and the three bodies.[6] Deutsch points out that the Advaitic analysis of the Self into five sheaths

> shows that there is no discontinuity of consciousness, that there is but one consciousness, namely, that associated with Atman, which appears in different states because of various upadhis or mis-identifications of self with one or more aspects of phenomenal selfhood.[7]

By now it should be obvious that the Vedanta psychology of sheaths corresponds very closely with what we have called the spectrum of consciousness, and the sheaths themselves represent different levels of the spectrum. Thus the outer sheath of the "gross body" corresponds to the Ego Level, to the self, divided from and therefore a slave to, the physical or gross body. The three middle sheaths of the will and the ratiocinative processes (the "subtle body") correspond to the Existential Level, where the repression of death produces the blind will to live ("vitality sheath") and where the root discriminative processes (the sheaths of discrimination and ratiocination) initiate the hardening of dualisms. The inner sheath of bliss (the "causal body"), wherein man transcends his ego and his physical body, corresponds to the Transpersonal Bands, and finally the very Center, the absolute Brahman-Atman, corresponds to our "no-level" of Mind.

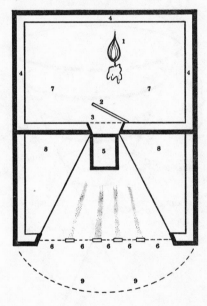

Ramana's Explanation		(Spectrum of Consciousness)
1. Flame	Self	Level of Mind
2. Door	Sleep	Susupti-Transpersonal Bands
3. Doorway	Intellectual principle	Root discrimination (Existential level)
4. Inner Wall	Ignorance	Primary Dualism
5. Mirror	Ego	Ego Level
6. Windows	Five Senses	Five Senses
7. Inner Chamber	Causal Body	Transpersonal Bands
8. Middle Chamber	Subtle Body	Existential Level
9. Courtyard	Gross Body	Ego Level

Figure 6

Figs. 6 and 7 show the close similarity between the Vedanta psychology of sheaths and the spectrum of consciousness. Fig. 6 is a sketch of Vedanta psychology made by the illustrious Sri Ramana Maharshi.[3] The legend contains Ramana's explanation, and the correspondence with the spectrum of consciousness is enclosed in the parentheses following his explanatory notes. Thus the Light corresponds with the Level of Mind, the doorway corresponds with the Existential Level, the mirror with the Ego Level, and so on, as indicated in the figure. Fig. 7 shows the same correspondence, but here the diagram of the spectrum of consciousness is presented with the parallel sheaths of the Vedanta psychology labeled.

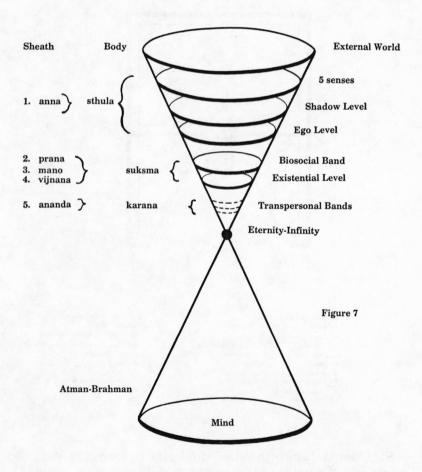

Sheath   Body   External World

                                                      5 senses

1. anna } sthula {   Shadow Level

                                                      Ego Level

2. prana }   Biosocial Band
3. mano   } suksma {
4. vijnana }   Existential Level

5. ananda } karana {   Transpersonal Bands

                                                      Eternity-Infinity

                                                      Figure 7

Atman-Brahman

                        Mind

There are, as one would naturally expect, some differences between the Vedanta psychology of sheaths and our description of the spectrum of consciousness, but in essentials the two are in perfect agreement, reflecting the universal nature of the *philosophia perennis*, of that "philosophical consensus of universal extent." Moving from the psychology of Vedanta Hinduism to that of Mahayana Buddhism, it is therefore no surprise to discover that the spectrum of consciousness is in broad agreement with the psychology of the Mahayana, especially as set forth by Asanga and Vasubandhu, and elaborated upon in such texts as the *Lankavatara Sutra*, the *Awakening of Faith*, and the *Platform Sutra*. D. T. Suzuki summarizes the essential drift of Mahayana psychology:

> The mind, inclusive of Citta, Manas, and the other six Vijnanas [these are all levels of the spectrum of consciousness, as we will explain], is in its original nature (*svabhava*) quiet, pure, and above the dualism of subject and object. But here appears the principle of particularization known as "Vishaya," which comes from the root *vish* meaning "to act," "to work;" and with the rise of this wind of action, the waves are agitated over the tranquil surface of the mind. It is now differentiated or evolves (*vritti*) into eight vijnanas [or levels]: Alaya, Manas, Manovijnana, and the five senses; and simultaneously with this evolution the whole universe comes into existence with its multitudinous forms and with its endless entanglements.[9]

In essential aspects, this is very similar to our description of the evolution of the spectrum of consciousness, and so as we now describe the eight *vijnanas* of Mahayana psychology, we will simultaneously point out the corresponding levels of the spectrum of consciousness. Thus the *Citta* or Mind corresponds with the Level of Mind, the absolute and non-dual consciousness. With the rise of the Primary Dualism, the eight *vijnanas* evolve, the first of which is the *alaya-vijnana*, the "storehouse consciousness," so named because it is here that the phenomenal "seeds" (*vasanas* or *bija*) or archetypes of all of man's actions (*karma*) are collected and stored, eventually to influence all future deeds. Thus the *alaya* is similar to the causal body of Vedanta, and many investigators feel that it is roughly equivalent of Jung's collective unconscious. In any case, being supra-individual, it corresponds with the Transpersonal Bands.

The next *vijnana* or level, moving "upwards and outwards" from the pure Citta, is called the *manas*, from the root *man* meaning "to think" and "to intend." According to the Mahayana psychology, the *manas* performs three interrelated functions. First, it is the seat of man's core dualistic tendencies. Thus:

The function of Manas is essentially to reflect upon the [Mind] and to create and to discriminate subject and object from the pure oneness of the [Mind]. The memory accumulated (*ciyate*) in the latter is now divided (*viciyate*) into dualities of all forms and all kinds.[10]

The second function of the *manas* stems from the first; that is, the *manas* itself "grows to be the source of great calamity when it creates desires based upon its wrong judgements [i.e., dualism], such as when it believes in the reality of an ego-substance and becomes attached to it as the ultimate truth. For Manas is not only a discriminating intelligence, but a willing agency, and consequently an actor."[11] *Manas* is thus the general source of will, and specifically the source of the will to live. In other words, this corresponds with the second major dualism, wherein man severs life-and-death and is hurled into the blind compulsion to survive. These two functions, of root discrimination and willing, give rise to the third function of *manas*—in Kapleau's words, it serves as the persistent source of I-awareness, the pernicious feeling that "I" exist as the isolated subject of all my experiences. Thus the *manas* is easily recognized as the Existential Level.

The evolution of the *vijnanas* continues: "As soon as Manas evolves the dualism of subject and object out of the absolute unity [then] Mano-vijnana and indeed all the other Vijnanas begin to operate."[12] Now the next level, the *manovijnana*, is generally translated as "intellect," as the sum total of our symbolic and abstractional powers. The *manovijnana* is said to reflect on the core dualisms of the *manas*, and from this process issue all of our more abstract and rarefied conceptualizations. In other words, intellection, which is latent in *manas*, blooms full in the *manovijnana*. Hence, with the *manovijnana*, man is identified with his intellect and consequently with his intellectual appraisal of himself, that is, with his ego. Thus does the *manovijnana* correspond with the Ego level. Finally, the remaining five *vijnanas*, simply enough, correspond to the five senses. Suzuki admirably sums up the Mahayana psychology of the eight *vijnanas*:

In the beginning [i.e., the "everlasting beginning" of the eternal moment] there was the memory amassed in the Alaya [the so-called "seeds"] since the beginningless past as a latent cause, in which the whole universe of individual objects lies with its eyes closed; here enters Manas with its discriminating intelligence, and subject is distinguished from object [Primary Dualism]; Manovijnana reflects on the duality, and from it issues a whole train of judgements with their consequent prejudices and attachments, while the five other vijnanas force them to become more and more complicated not only intellectually but affectively and conatively. All the results of these activities in turn perfume the Alaya [i.e., "reseed" it], stimulating the old memory to wake while the new one finds its affinities among the old. In the meantime, however, the Alaya itself remains unmoved retaining its identity.[13]

As always, the *Alaya*—which in the above passage is used as synonymous with *Citta*, absolute Noumenon— the *Alaya*, like Atman and the Level of Mind, actually retains its identity but apparently evolves into numerous levels, much like a candle set in a hall of mirrors will appear to reflect and evolve into numerous candles while all the time retaining its identity.

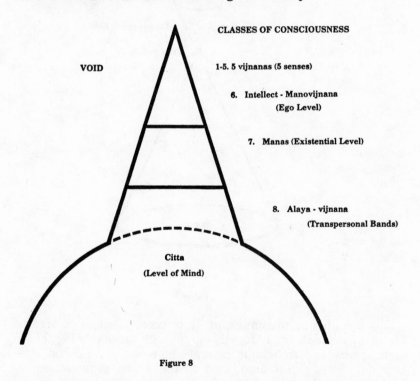

CLASSES OF CONSCIOUSNESS

VOID

1-5. 5 vijnanas (5 senses)

6. Intellect - Manovijnana
    (Ego Level)

7. Manas (Existential Level)

8. Alaya - vijnana
    (Transpersonal Bands)

Citta
(Level of Mind)

Figure 8

Fig. 8 is adapted from a sketch by the Zen Master Harada, showing the relation of the eight *vijnanas*. The correspondence between the *vijnanas* and the levels of the spectrum are again shown in parentheses. To make the correspondence clearer, Fig. 9 is included—it is the diagram of the spectrum of consciousness with the corresponding *vijnanas* labeled along-side the various levels.

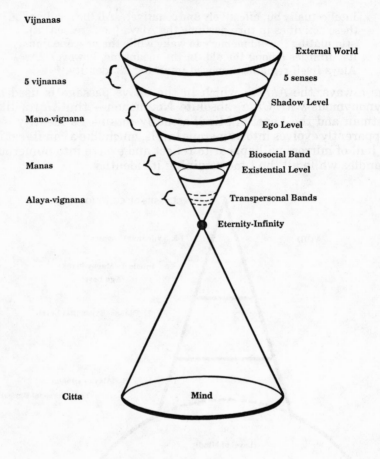

Figure 9

Zen Buddhism, inasmuch as it is recognized as a sect of Mahayana Buddhism, naturally agrees with the psychology of the eight *vijnanas*. Throughout the ages, however, several Zen Masters developed what amounted to their own personal interpretations of the psychology of eight *vijnanas*, elaborating and adapting it to better suit their own particular style of teaching. Foremost among these masters was Hui-neng, the sixth patriarch of Ch'an, whose profound psychological insights are set forth in the *Platform Sutra*. Hui-neng's psychology is summarized in Fig. 10, which is a schematic made by Dr. Suzuki to explain the essentials of Hui-neng's doctrine. The diagram contains five levels, which we have labeled "A" through "E" for convenient reference.

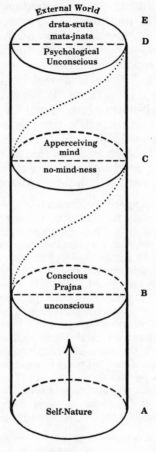

Figure 10

Now how do these levels correspond to those of the spectrum of consciousness? Let us begin with level "A," which is labeled "Self-nature." "Seeing into one's Self-nature" was the hallmark of Hui-neng's teachings, and it has remained to this day the fundamental issue of Zen. "Self-nature" is synonymous with "Buddha-nature," which the *Nirvana Sutra* declares is inherent in all beings, and thus "seeing into one's Self-nature" is nothing less than the attainment of Buddhahood. As we might expect, this seeing is accomplished by *prajna,* the non-dual mode of knowing, and thus Self-nature and *prajna* are very important terms in Hui-neng's thought. Ultimately, of course, Self-nature and *prajna* are identical, since in the infinity and eternity of Buddhahood, *knowing* and *being* coalesce, but they are *conventionally* spoken of sepa-rately. Thus level "A" and level "B," respectively labeled "Self-nature" and "*prajna*," are actually one and the same ("Self-nature is *prajna*"),[14] and they correspond with the Level of Mind.

The conventional separation of Self-nature and *prajna* into two levels (levels "A" and "B") is, however, highly significant, espe-cially since the *prajna* level (level "B") is cut in half by a dashed line, whereas the Self-nature level (level "A") is not. The dashed line of level "B" represents the first severance, the primary dualism, whereby the void and non-dual Self-nature is *seemingly* split into subject and object. Because this dualism is seeming and illusory, the Self-nature level contains no dashed line. Suzuki, commenting on Hui-neng's thought, explains it thus:

> When we have an experience, for example, of seeing a tree, all that takes place at the time is the perceiving of something. We do not know whether this perception belongs to us, nor do we recognize the object which is perceived to be outside ourselves. The cognition of an external object already presupposes the distinction of outside and inside, subject and object, the per-ceiving and the perceived. When this separation takes place . . . the primary nature of the experience is forgotten . . . [This primary nature or self-nature] refers to the time prior to the separation of mind and world, when there is yet no mind standing against an external world and receiving its im-pressions through the various sense channels. Not only a mind, but a world, has not yet come into existence. This we can say is a state of perfect emptiness . . . [Then] there rises a thought in the midst of Emptiness; this is . . . the separation of unconsciousness and consciousness, or, logically stated, the rise of the fundamental dialectical antithesis.[15]

The statement "there rises a thought" is exactly Asvaghosha's "Suddenly a thought arises" and G. S. Brown's "let there be a distinction;" and as we explained earlier, it refers not so much to full-blown intellection as to the root tendency to dichotomize which results in the Primary Dualism, which Suzuki explains as the separation of the inside and the outside, the subject and object, the perceiver and the perceived, the conscious and the uncon-scious. With this separation, man is now set apart from the world and thus finds himself on level "C," the "apperceiving mind," which is explained as follows:

> Prajna, the conscious, develops into the apperceiving mind where Self-nature comes in communication with the external world which acts upon the psychological mind, and is in turn acted upon by the latter. The apperceiving mind is where we form the notion of selfhood. . . . [16]

Thus the "apperceiving mind" is not exactly a "mind" in the sense of being the seat of lofty intellection and abstraction, but is rather the core dualistic tendency now operating on the personal level so that it forms our persistent and irreducible feeling of existing as an isolated self. It is thus very similar to the *manas* and the "subtle body," and corresponds to the Existential Level.

Level "D" is what we generally would label mind or intellect, and Suzuki calls it the plane of sense (*drista-sruta*) and thought (*matajnata*). It is here that we form our intellectual abstractions about life and reality, and so it is here that we form our intellectual picture of ourselves. Level "D," in other words, corresponds to the Ego Level. Further:

> The unconscious mind has its pathological states on the plane of sense (*drista-sruta*) and thought (*mata-jnata*), corresponding to the "Unconscious" of Analytical Psychology or Psychoanalysis ... The psycho-analytical Unconscious cannot go deep enough to include the question of no-mind-ness [Self-nature, Mind].[17]

These "pathological states" will be recognized as the Shadow Level. (As a concluding summary, the formal correspondence between Hui-neng's thought and the spectrum of consciousness is shown in Fig. 11).

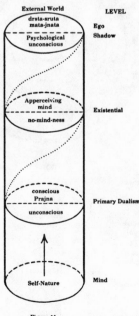

Figure 11

Moving to the psychology of Tibetan Buddhism, we again find strict similarities with the spectrum of consciousness. In fact, the psychology of Tibetan Buddhism is almost identical to that of Vedanta Hinduism, for both psychologies are built around the doctrine of the five sheaths. Thus we needn't go into the details of the Tibetan Buddhistic psychology, for we would only be repeating the commentary of the Vedanta psychology. Suffice it to say that for centuries the greatest sages of Tibet have found this psychological system to well represent the facts of consciousness, and we believe that in all essentials it perfectly agrees with the spectrum of consciousness. Fig. 12 is a diagram by the fabulous Lama Govinda illustrating the psychology of the five sheaths from the Tibetan view. [18] The sheaths themselves are the same as those of the Vedanta; nevertheless we have included the diagram itself because it so clearly shows the "onion-like" nature of the five sheaths.

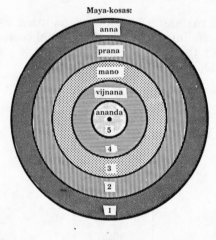

SHEATH	BODY	LEVEL (corresponding)
1. anna-maya-kosa (material)	sthula-sarira (gross)	Ego
2. prana-maya-kosa (vitality)		
3. mano-maya-kosa (discrimination)	suksma-sarira (subtle)	Existential
4. vijnana-maya-kosa (ratiocination)		
5. ananda-maya-kosa (bliss)	karana-sarira (causal)	Transpersonal
Brahman-Atman		Mind

Figure 12

Overall, then, we conclude that the psychological systems of the great metaphysical traditions—from Vedanta to Zen—are in essential, formal agreement with the spectrum of consciousness as we have described it. This fact has recently led me to suggest that there exists a *psychologia perennis*,[19] a "perennial psychology", which, it appears, God has nowhere and nowhen left without a witness. The Spectrum of Consciousness, in fact, is a modern presentation of this perennial psychology, but drawing equally upon Western as well as Eastern insights. For if our presentation of the spectrum of consciousness agrees in essentials with these Eastern psychologies, it nevertheless differs in emphasis. From the view of these Eastern approaches, all of the levels of the spectrum (except the "no-level of Mind") do exist, but only in an illusory fashion, just as the images seen on a television screen are unreal as actual events but exist as mere pictures. Their overriding concern has always been with the Level of Mind, and thus they never systematically investigated the pathologies that could occur on any individual level. On the other hand, the Western world—especially since the 17th century—has almost completely ignored the Level of Mind, and consequently Western psychology has concentrated exclusively on the distress-causing abnormalities that can occur on particular levels, and especially on that of the Ego Level. Further, investigators in the West have recently been increasingly interested in pathologies occurring on the Existential and Biosocial Levels, as evidenced in the growth of such disciplines as existential psychology, family therapy, and communications psychiatry. Taken together, then, these Eastern and Western approaches form an uncanny complementarity, for—generally speaking—the levels that the West has heretofore ignored have been thoroughly investigated by the East, and vice versa. Thus the East has extensively explored those paths leading to Absolute Noumenon, while the West has restricted itself to scientific investigations of phenomenal psychology. Man, as Absolute Subjectivity, is the Godhead—this is the concern of the East; man, as an object of knowledge, is the phenomenal ego—this is the concern of the West. Taken together they span the entire spectrum of consciousness. If Western investigators, confirmed as they are to the Existential, Ego, and Shadow Levels, feel that they shall have the last word in consciousness, then so much the worse for them and their delusions of adequacy. On the other hand, the Eastern investigators—who do have the final say on consciousness—nevertheless sorely neglect the levels of the spectrum on which most of us are destined to remain. So while we completely agree with the pronouncements of the Eastern sages, we have slightly shifted emphasis by supplementing their psychologies with the findings of Western scientists. The weary chemist, the frantic businessman, the depressed housewife—they neither understand enlightenment nor seek it. If they do, so much the better; if not, shouldn't we address ourselves to the levels on which they now exist?

Now this complementarity can also be approached epistemologically. We have already seen that man has two major forms of knowing, one being symbolic-map knowledge and the other being non-dual awareness. The Madhyamika calls the former *samvritti*, which is responsible for the relative truths of science and philosophy, while the latter is referred to as *paramartha,* which results in the knowledge of Absolute Truth. Later systems, such as the Yogacara and Vedanta, elaborated upon this essential two-fold doctrine and restated it in the form of a *three-fold* division of knowledge. In this system, the first or symbolic-map mode of knowing is subdivided into two classes: one class, called *parikalpita* by the Yogacara, results in pure imaginary knowledge, such as viewing a rope and thinking that it is a snake; the second class, called *paratantra,* is responsible for what we would call objective truth, such as seeing a rope and correctly calling it a rope. Finally, the last of the Yogacara's three forms of knowledge is the same as the Madhyamika's *paramartha*: it is what we are calling non-dual awareness "of" absolute truth. The Yogacara simply re-names it as *parinishpanna,* and, as we just said, it corresponds with the second mode of knowing and is thus responsible for absolute truth, for seeing the rope and knowing that one is seeing one's own True Self, Mind-only.

The only difference, then, between the two-fold and three-fold divisions of truth is that the latter expands upon the former by separating symbolic-map knowledge (*samvritti*) into a relatively false (*parikalpita*) and a relatively true (*paratantra*) conventional knowledge. In this sense, the scientist is working with the relatively true instrumental form of knowledge (*paratantra*), with finding adequate and useful symbolic and objective representations of reality. But although scientific knowledge is relatively true, it is still a form of dualistic knowledge, of *samvritti*, and from the absolute point of view it is as illusory as any other form of dualistic knowledge.

Western intellectual pursuits such as science and philosophy have wandered in the land of *samvritti,* of symbolic-map knowledge, and their primary aim has been to separate the relatively false knowledge of *parikalpita* (snake) from the relatively true knowledge of *paratantra* (rope). Reality for the West has been *paratantra,* a matter of finding objective "truth." The Eastern approaches of Vedanta and Mahayana Buddhism, however, realizing *paratantra* to be relatively true but absolutely unreal, have instead pursued the path of *paramartha,* of Absolute Truth. Now the point is: *what happens when these epistemological considerations are transposed into the realm of psychopathology?*

Psychopathology has always been considered—in one sense or another—as resulting from a distorted view of reality. *But what one considers to be psychopathology therefore must depend upon what one considers to be reality!* Hence East and West, with different notions of reality, developed different notions of psychopathology. Thus, for Western psychology, psychopathology has always been connected with *parikalpita* (snake), with viewing reality in a way that is considered to be false by those who subscribe to the *paratantra* (rope) point of view. A person is indeed "sick" if he looks at a rope and always sees a snake, if he experiences hate and calls it love, represses sex and calls it hunger. The "cure," on the other hand, is supposed to result when the individual shifts from the *parikalpita* (snake) view to the *paratantra* (rope) view, when he sees ropes as ropes, hate as hate, and sex as sex. In other words, the epistemological division between the relatively "true" knowledge of *paratantra* and the relatively "false" knowledge of *parikalpita* also became the dividing line between sanity and insanity.

For these Eastern approaches, however, reality was not a matter of distinguishing between *parikalpita* (snake) and *paratantra* (rope), for these both belong to the realm of *samvritti,* of relative (and illusory) symbolic-map knowledge, so that ultimately to shift from *parikalpita* (snake) to *paratantra* (rope) is simply to shift from wearing iron chains to wearing gold chains. Their concern was instead to shift completely from *samvritti* to *paramartha* (or *parinishpanna*), from relative knowledge—true or false—to absolute knowledge, which recognizes no such distinctions. Their "psychopathology" was thus connected not with *parikalpita* (snake) but with *samvritti* (snake and rope): the person who sees a rope as a snake as well as the person who sees the rope as a rope are equally "deluded" and "asleep," and the "cure" results when both see the rope for what it is—a manifestation of Brahman, an objectification of Mind, so that both the snake and the rope are ultimately illusions. "By and by comes the Great Awakening," says Chuang Tzu, "and then we shall find out that life itself is a great dream. All the while fools think that they are awake, busily and brightly assuming that they understand things. Making nice discriminations, they differentiate between princes and grooms [opposites in general]. How stupid! Words like this will be labeled the Supreme Swindle."[20]

By most Western investigators, this Great Awakening was usu-

ally viewed, psychologically at least, as a Great Nervous Breakdown, for they officially recognized only the *parikalpita* (snake)
and *paratantra* (rope) forms of knowledge, and therefore an individual had to subscribe to either one or the other. Thus when
anyone happened upon the *paramartha* (absolute) form of knowledge, he had to be viewed as going crazy. In the words of R. D. Laing:

> Attempts to wake before our time are often punished, espe-
> cially by those who love us most. Because they, bless them, are
> asleep. They think anyone who wakes up, or who, still asleep,
> realizes that what is taken to be real is a 'dream' is going
> crazy.[21]

But surely we can now recognize the existence of all three forms
of knowledge, and hence realize that differentiating between
parikalpita (snake) and *paratantra* (rope) is a matter of conventional and relative "sanity", while differentiating between *samvritti* (relative) and *paramartha* (absolute) is a matter of Enlightenment. Again we see the complementarity of approaches—in Fig.
13—for Western psychologists will enable us to see a rope where
formerly we saw a snake, while Eastern sages will show us Brahman where formerly we saw only a rope.

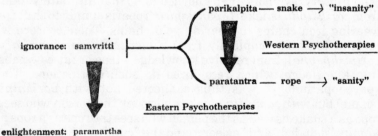

EPISTEMOLOGY AND PSYCHOPATHOLOGY

Figure 13

Now to conclude this overview of the spectrum of consciousness, let us briefly touch upon the works of some of the more "Western" explorers of consciousness, such as Gurdjieff, Fischer, and Benoit. To begin with Gurdjieff, we note that his psychological system— which was apparently based on Sufi teachings—has had its greatest proponent in Ouspensky, and more recently has been adopted by such gifted researchers as Oscar Ichazo and John Lilly.[22] Gurdjieff maintained—rightly, we believe—that consciousness can best be viewed as a multi-leveled continuum of different vibratory bands or states. For ease of identification, each level is assigned a "vibratory number", either 3, 6, 12, 24, 48, or 96. Thus, as Dr. Lilly describes it, level 3 is "fusion with universal mind, union with God," and this we instantly recognize as the Level of Mind. The next level in Gurdjieff's continuum, called vibratory state 6, is "point of consciousness, astral travel, traveling clairaudience, traveling clairvoyance, fusion with other entities in time," which clearly corresponds with the Transpersonal Bands. Vibration state 12 represents the lower limits of the Existential Level, for it is "heightened bodily awareness, highest function of bodily and planetside consciousness, being in love;" while vibration state 24 represents the upper limits of the Existential Level, that is, the Biosocial Band, for here "all the needed programs are in the unconscious of the biocomputer, operating smoothly, the self is lost in pleasurable activities that one knows best and likes to do." The next level, vibration state 48, is simply the Ego Level, or "the neutral biocomputer state, the state for the absorption and the transmission of new ideas; for the reception and transmission of new data and new programs." Finally, vibration state 96, which is a "negative state; pain, guilt, fear, doing what one has to but in a state of pain, guilt, fear," we recognize as the lower limits of the Shadow Level.

We should mention at this point that one can get, as it were, very "far out" on the spectrum of consciousness, into the very upper reaches and furthest limits of the Shadow Level. This can occur under conditions of extreme pain, hyperphrenia, schizoid states, certain drug experiences, and so on. In the Gurdjieff system, these upper vibratory levels are numbered 192, 384, and 768. Now in these upper limits of the Shadow Level, a most peculiar phenomenon can occur: almost instantly one can "rebound" or "slingshot", so to speak, from one of these bands to a corresponding *lower* level of the spectrum to consciousness. As one example, consider the following story told by C. G. Jung:

> A woman patient, whose reliability and truthfulness I have no
> reason to doubt, told me that her first birth was very difficult.

After thirty hours of fruitless labor the doctor considered that a forceps delivery was indicated. This was carried out under light narcosis. She was badly torn and suffered great loss of blood. When the doctor, her mother, and her husband had gone, and everything was cleared up, the nurse wanted to eat, and the patient saw her turn round at the door and ask, "Do you want anything before I go to supper?" She tried to answer, but couldn't. She had the feeling that she was sinking through the bed into a bottomless void ... The next thing she was aware of was that, without feeling her body and its position, she was *looking down* from a point in the ceiling and could see everything going on in the room below her: she saw herself lying in the bed, deadly pale, with closed eyes. Beside her stood the nurse. The doctor paced up and down the room excitedly, and it seemed to her that he had lost his head and didn't know what to do ...

The next thing that happened was that she awoke from her coma and saw the nurse bending over her in bed. She was told that she had been unconscious for about half an hour. The next day, some fifteen hours later, when she felt a little stronger, she made a remark to the nurse about the incompetent and "hysterical" behavior of the doctor during the coma. The nurse energetically denied this criticism in the belief that the patient had been completely unconscious at the time and could therefore have known nothing of the scene. Only when she described in full detail what had happened during the coma was the nurse obliged to admit that the patient had perceived the events exactly as they happened in reality.[23]

In other words, from the Shadow Level of considerable pain and fear, the woman had "rebounded" into what was clearly one of the Transpersonal Bands. This rebounding can, and frequently does, occur from the upper bands of the Shadow Level to a corresponding lower level of the spectrum. John Lilly is well aware of this Shadow Level "slingshot effect", for he takes the Gurdjieff vibration levels 96, 192, 384, and 768 (that is, all of the bands of the Shadow Level) and re-numbers them respectively as -24, -12, -6, -3, to emphasize the *potential correspondence of these negative Shadow states with their counterparts at the opposite end of the spectrum.* This potential correspondence can be so intimate that , in some cases, certain of the upper bands of the Shadow Level actually take on the characteristics of their rebound levels lower on the spectrum, with the exception, of course, that these Shadow bands are extremely negative and painful, forming, as it were, malevolent caricatures of their counterpart levels. It is with this in mind, then, that Lilly defines each of the Shadow bands, such as -6, as "similar to +6 except that it is extremely negative."

In this connection, let it be noted that Roland Fischer's experimental research at the Maryland Psychiatric Institute[24] offers what amounts to a physiological correlate not only of this rebound effect but also of the spectrum-like nature of consciousness. Fischer has found that, as an almost "instinctual defense mechanism", an individual's central nervous system, when stimulated (naturally or artificially) to states of hyper-arousal, can automatically rebound to a corresponding state of hypo-arousal. As for consciousness itself, Dr. Fischer has abundant experimental evidence that it exists as a type of *continuum* or spectrum, with the Absolute Self metaphorically "located" at one end of the continuum (Mind) and the normal ego awareness at the other (Ego). Further, "each consecutive layer of self-awareness with diminishing objectivity 'out there' is accompanied by an increase in subjective 'Self'-awareness . . . ", so that there exists "many layers of self-awareness, each with its characteristic 'Self'-to-'I' ratio", which we have expressed as "levels of identity". This also implies, as we have suggested, that there are numerous levels of unconscious processes; and, in fact, Fischer's data lead him to the conclusion that, "instead of postulating *one* subconscious, I recognize as many layers of self-awareness as there are levels of arousal and corresponding symbolic interpretations in the individual's interpretive repertoire."

Finally, let us turn now to that most penetrating psychoanalyst and interpreter of Eastern philosophy, Hubert Benoit. Dr. Benoit's thought is so very judicious and subtly profound that we would not do him justice by simply summarizing his views. Rather, we must let him speak for himself, and intersperse our comments among his quotations. We will not dwell upon Benoit's levels of consciousness, for they are essentially identical to those of the spectrum, and anything we might say would be repetitious. We will only mention here that the Level of Mind, the Existential Level, the Ego Level, and the Shadow Level are all recognized by Benoit, and he terms them, respectivity, Absolute Principle, subjectal-emotive consciousness, objectal consciousness, and the Devil. Rather, we must extensively elaborate upon Benoit's use of "Energy" as a metaphor of the Absolute, for it is the most direct way to get a "feel" for the operation of the spectrum of consciousness in our everyday lives.

In the following, Hubert Benoit is outlining his psychology, which he begins with a common example:

> To that end let us start with a concrete observation. A man annoys me; I become angry and I want to hit my adversary. Let us analyse what takes place in me in the course of this scene. We will see that my inner phenomena are divided into two different reactions that we will call primary reaction and secondary reaction.[25]

We will eventually see that these two different reactions correspond to the two basic forms of knowing: the primary reaction
refers to the non-dual mode, while the secondary reaction refers to
the symbolic mode. Benoit continues with the analysis of the
mobilization of anger:

> The primary reaction consists in the awakening, in me, of a
> certain amount of vital energy; this energy was lying, latent,
> in my central source of energy until it was awakened by my
> perception of an energy manifested in the Not-Self against
> Self [Primary Dualism]. The foreign aggressive energy stirs
> up in me the manifestation of a reactive force which balances
> the force of the Not-Self. This reactive force is not yet a move-
> ment of anger, it has not yet a precise form; it is compatable
> with the substance which is going to be poured into a mould
> but which has not yet been released. During an instant, with-
> out duration, this budding force, mobilised at my source, is not
> yet a force of anger; it is an informal force, a pure vital force.[26]

Now this primary reaction, this pure, informal (i.e., "without
form"), vital force represents the non-dual mode of knowing, and of
course its associated non-dual consciousness, as Benoit explains:

> This [primary] reaction corresponds to a certain perception of
> the outer world, to a certain knowledge. It corresponds there-
> fore to a certain consciousness, but quite different from what is
> habitually so called. It is not the mental consciousness, intel-
> lectual, clear, evident [of the Ego Level]. It is an obscure
> consciousness, profound, reflex, organic . . . [an] organic con-
> sciousness which "knows" the outside world in a non-
> intellectual manner. Besides, this is corroborated by an in-
> ward observation: I feel anger *going to my head* where it will
> proceed to build up a thousand images; I feel it rising from
> below, from my organic existence. This primary reaction is
> extremely rapid and it escapes my observation if I am not very
> attentive, but if, after my anger, I examine in detail what has
> happened in me, I realize that, *during a short moment, a pure
> anonymous organic force, coming from an organic conscious-
> ness, has preceded the play of my intellectual consciousness,
> formulator of images of anger.*[27]

This organic or primary consciousness we have elsewhere called
organismic consciousness, and insofar as it is "anonymous",
"pure", "without form"—that is, uncontaminated by conceptualization—it participates fully in cosmic consciousness or the Level of
Mind, for it operates, as Benoit points out, in "an instant without
duration." This vital Energy is therefore of the timeless Moment,
of Eternity, and thus of Brahman, Mind, Tao. It is Reality itself.
   Initially it might seem odd to describe the Godhead as Energy,

but on reflection, the word "energy" is no less accurate than any number of other descriptive words, all of which are doomed by their finiteness and duality to fail in grasping the infinite and non-dual, for even the word "non-duality" is dualistic because it excludes "duality." We are using "non-duality" in its "absolute" sense of "not two, not one," as being synonymous with *sunyata*, void, and in this sense "energy" will do just as well. As Coomaraswamy noted:

> This is the predicament of the positivist or "nothing-morist," that in acknowledging the reality only of that which can be grasped, he is attributing "reality" to things that cannot be grasped because they never stop to be, and is driven, in spite of himself, to postulate the reality of some such abstract entity as "Energy"—a word that is nothing but one of the names of God.[28]

One would hardly imagine that in picking up a college physics textbook, one is actually handling a "religious" document that has carefully been scrubbed clean of all dirty words such as intuition, eternity, and Godhead. But the central concern of physical science revolves around the concept of energy and its transformations, whether these transformations occur in molecules, biological systems, or computers. And how is this Energy described? It can neither be created nor destroyed, put together nor taken apart, and on the whole it is neither increasing nor decreasing, remaining always constant. This, in fact, is the First Law of Thermodynamics. Further, the Energy of the universe, which remains forever constant, nevertheless undergoes "transformations" or "manifestations," for all types of energy and matter, whether kinetic, thermal, or molecular, are spoken of as "Forms of Energy." As a matter of fact, all phenomena in the universe are ultimately nothing but forms of Energy, so that this Energy more or less "underlies" all material things. This is pure physics, but it sounds strangely familiar, and one begins to wonder whether we are discussing physics or Hinduism. Ultimately, it matters not one whit whether we say that all things are forms of Energy or forms of Brahman.

Now Benoit, in using "Energy," makes it much easier for us to orient ourselves towards this reality, for we all have, however dimly, an inward feeling of this mobilization of energy, as in the example of anger. Proceeding with this example, Benoit states:

> The dynamic modification of my being constituted by the primary reaction, this mobilization of my energy in response to the energy of the outside word [in this case, the man annoying me], will release a secondary reaction [which is] the reactive play of my intellectual consciousness; and this secondary

reaction will tend to re-establish in me the original immobility by disintegrating the mobilized energy.[29]

This secondary reaction corresponds to our symbolic mode of
knowing, to the process whereby we translate our pure organismic
consciousness into the dualistic terms of thought and language.
Now Benoit's formulation of these two modes of knowing is ingenious, for it allows us to understand how, in *this* moment, our
organismic and non-dual mode of knowing disintegrates into the
symbolic mode, thereby obscuring our Supreme Identity which
this pure organismic consciousness would otherwise reveal. We
will return to this point at the appropriate time, but let us now
revert to Benoit's explanation of the two modes of knowing:

> Let us recall what we have called our primordial demand, or
> claim to be-absolutely-as-a-distinct-being, to exist-absolutely.
> At the bottom of our intellectual understanding of the Uni-
> verse, there is the irreducible discrimination between Self and
> Not-Self [that is, the Primary Dualism]. It is this discrimina-
> tion that one evokes when one speaks . . . of identification
> with our psyco-somatic organism [Existential Level]. In so far
> as I am an organic consciousness I do not discriminate [non-
> duality], but, in so far as I am an intellectual consciousness, I
> discriminate.[30]

Benoit then elaborates on these two modes of knowing, and then
brings forth a most important conclusion:

> *In my organic consciousness I am as much identified with the
> Not-Self as with the Self* [this is the Level of Mind]; in my
> intellectual consciousness I am identified with the self [Ego
> Level], I affirm that only the self exists. My intellectual con-
> sciousness only knows self. When I think that I have an intel-
> lectual knowledge of the outside world, I only have knowledge
> in reality of the modifications of my self in contact with the
> outside world. Philosophers call that "the prison of my subjec-
> tivity," disregarding *my organic consciousness which does not
> discriminate between subject and object and thanks to which I
> am already virtually free.*[31]

"I am already virtually free" because my pure organismic consciousness, this vital Energy that wells up within me, which does
not recognize the Primary Dualism, which is intemporal and
therefore infinite, necessarily participates fully in cosmic consciousness or Mind, the realization of which constitutes liberation
(*moksha*). But his organismic consciousness cannot be located
within the body, for this is most dualistic; and, as Schroedinger
himself pointed out, "we do not usually realize this fact, because we
have entirely taken to thinking of the personality of a human

being ... as located in the interior of its body. To learn that it cannot really be found there is so amazing that it meets with doubt and hesitation, we are very loath to admit it. We have got used to localizing the conscious personality inside a person's head—I should say an inch or two behind the midpoint of the eyes .... It is very difficult for us to take stock of the fact that *the localization of the personality, of the conscious mind, inside the body is only symbolic,* just an aid for practical use."[32]

This, however, in no way implies that consciousness lies *outside* the body, a misguided belief very popular with exponents of astral projection, out-of-the-body experiences, and similar phenomena (which *can* occur on the Transpersonal Bands but are *not* to be confused with Mind). The belief that consciousness exists outside the body is just the mirror-image of the dualism inside-outside, the flipside of a worthless coin. When Ramana Maharshi was told by a student that he occasionally had flashes of consciousness whose center seemed outside the normal self and body, the Maharshi guffawed—

> Outside! For whom is the inside or outside? These can exist only so long as there are the subject and object. ... On investigation you will find that they resolve into the subject only. See who is the subject; and this enquiry leads you to pure Consciousness beyond the subject.[33]

So when Benoit speaks of this Consciousness as Energy arising within the organism, it is nothing but a concession to popular parlance. In that "instance without duration" when pure, informal, anonymous, and non-dual force arises, it knows neither inside nor outside and is thus incapable of being localized. But when this energy disintegrates into images, that is to say, when we intellectually reflect upon this élan vital, the primary dualism has already occurred, and thus it certainly *appears* to us that this energy has its Source within our body. But Suzuki cautions us that "this conception of Great Source as existing separately somewhere is the fundamental mistake we all make in our attempt intellectually to interpret our experience."[34] We should therefore bear this in mind whenever reference is made to the mobilization or organismic energy.

Let us now continue with Benoit's description of how this mobilized Energy, this organismic consciousness, this non-dual awareness disintegrates into images, into concepts, into the symbolic mode of knowing; and then we will return to the organismic consciousness, this vital Energy "thanks to which I am already virtually free." Thus:

> In the course of the secondary reaction, my intellectual need to

"be" [i.e., the idea of my ego being strong, immovable, permanent, stable, etc.]is thwarted by this mobilisation of energy in
me, for this mobilisation implies the acceptance of the outside
world [rendered impossible by the primary dualism] .... My
secondary reaction to the mobilisation of my energy can only
be, therefore, a refusal opposed to this mobilisation. But this
opposition to the cosmic order could not succeed; the force
which is mobilised in me could not return to non-manifesta-
tion. My refusal of the mobilised energy cannot result, therefore, in anything but *the destruction of this energy by its
disintegration.*[35]

Further, Benoit adds that this *"disintegration of the energy
mobilised is realized by the imaginative-emotive processes."*[36] That
is, this Energy disintegrates into mental images and their corresponding bodily emotions, a process that is roughly equivalent to
sublimation, for, as Norman O. Brown stated, the *animal symbolic*
is the *animal sublimans*. Now this process, whereby our Energy,
our non-dual mode knowing, our organismic consciousness disintegrates and dissipates into the symbolic mode of knowing, into
concepts, into images, into thoughts and distinctions—*this process
is exactly that by which we "dismember Brahman daily."* We will,
at the appropriate time, return to this point and carefully elaborate it, but now we must return to the Level of Mind, to organismic
consciousness, about which Benoit states:

To the two reactions correspond, as we have said, two different
consciousnesses, to the primary reaction my organic consciousness [Level of Mind], to the secondary my mental, or
intellectual, or imaginative consciousness [Ego Level] ... My
imaginative consciousness is dualistic, the imaginative-
emotive processes which take place therein being affirming or
denying, pleasant or unpleasant [front or back]. My organic
consciousness, on the contrary, is not dualistic since the vital
force which wells up in it is informal [i.e., without form],
anonymous, always the same, *independent of the dualistic
forms which it will animate thereafter.* ... We have seen that
the organic consciousness does not discriminate between the
self and not-self, that its play implies an essential identity
between these two poles and in consequence a ... *knowledge
of the Universe in general, in its unity.* ... In short, my organic
consciousness alone knows the Universe.[37]

The organismic consciousness, as Benoit states, knows the universe in its unity, but only because its operation is space-less and
time-less and therefore infinite and eternal, and because *all* of
infinity-eternity is simultaneously present at *every* point of space
and time, then "knowing THIS you know all." Knowing the absolute Now you know all time; knowing the absolute Here you know

all space—and knowing them both (for they really aren't separate) then you know the universe in its unity. This certainly doesn't mean that you will know all the *facts* that can be gained by symbolic-map knowledge, that you will know exactly all of the information contained in all of the books ever written—far from it! Rather, you will *know* and *be* the *reality* of individual facts, the reality of which abstract "facts" are mere reflections. You will never know all of these facts, these reflections—but you will vividly know the sole reality which is reflected.[38] The *Chandogya Upanishad* (6.1.4-5) poetically states it thus:

> Just as by one piece of clay everything of clay may be known—the differences being merely verbal distinctions, names; the reality is just "clay"—just as by one piece of copper everything made of copper may be known—the differences being merely verbal distinctions, names; the reality is just "copper"—so, my friend, is this teaching.

And thus does Lao Tzu (chapter 47) proclaim:

> Without going outside, you may know the whole world
> Without looking through the window, you may
>   see the ways of heaven.
> The farther you go, the less you know.
> Thus the sage knows without traveling . . . .

In a similar vein, Bernard Lonergan, in his monumental study on insight and understanding, stressed one major point:

> Thoroughly understand what it is to understand, and not only will you understand the broad lines of all there is to be understood but also you will possess a fixed base, an invariant pattern, opening upon all further developments of understanding.[39]

Understand this and you understand all—stand under this and you stand under all.

Towards this end, Benoit's concept of Energy and organic consciousness is most useful, for it is precisely this informal Energy that "stands under" all of our mental and bodily phenomena. It is useful because it points to that "in" us which lies beneath and animates all of the passing forms of our conscious attention; just as in Benoit's example of anger, the mobilized Energy, as it first begins to well-up, is without form, pure, homogenous, and only after a few seconds does it disintegrate into images and forms, only after a few seconds do you feel "anger." As such, "Energy" is a metaphor closely resembling that of "Absolute Subjectivity," of Mind, for "Energy is a word that is nothing but one of the names of God." Energy lies "within," completely upstream of all conceptual elaboration which it will later animate; it is without form, nebulous, unknown as an object or concept, but nevertheless something that we can know directly, non-dualistically, immediately, non-conceptually: "thanks to which I am already virtually free."

We have seen that the spectrum of consciousness represents identifications of the Absolute Knower with certain known objects, in Patanjali's words, "Ignorance is the identification of the Seer with the instruments of seeing." An original identification with the All becomes progressively narrowed and restricted, with each restriction generating a new level of the spectrum. Our "aim" is thus to cease identifying exclusively with particular complexes of objects so that we may discover our supreme identity with *all* phenomenal manifestation. (Fig. 3 represents those objects with which we have identified, an identity that becomes progressively more exclusive towards the top of the diagram). In Benoit's words, "this identification is not mistaken, but is merely incomplete in that it excludes my equal identification with the rest of the Universe. The egotistical illusion does not consist in my identification with my organism but in the exclusive manner in which this identification is realized."[40]

Let us now follow the evolution of the spectrum of consciousness using the metaphor of *Energy and its disintegration instead of Absolute Subjectivity and its objectifications*. In a simplistic fashion, we can envision this as follows: Energy mobilized at the Level of Mind is pure, without form (i.e., void), intemporal, infinite, but as it "rises up" through the levels of the spectrum, it begins to disintegrate by taking on dualistic images and forms. Each level is therefore characterized by the nature of dualistic disintegration that occurs there. Thus at the Existential Level, the Energy has disintegrated and fragmented into "self" energy vs. environmental energy; at the Biosocial Band, this self energy starts to take form, picking up the trappings and colorings of that Level; while at the Ego Level it has further disintegrated into bodily energy vs. psychic energy. The Shadow Level simply represents a continuance of this disintegration, where psychic energy itself becomes split and fragmented.

As an example of this entire movement, let us again use the mobilization of anger, as when a person strikes me. The actual strike itself, in its simplest form, is just a movement of the universe, but as the primary dualism starts to occur, I sense a mobilization of energy arising *within* me. At this stage—before the primary dualism hardens— this energy is still pure, informal, intemporal—it operates in an "instant without duration" and it comprises that still moment before I name what is happening. But this intemporal mobilization starts to take on duration as it "passes" the Biosocial Band, for it is here that this energy takes the *form* of anger and therefore *endures* in time. This *form* is molded by the internalized relations of the family and society that exist here on the Biosocial Band. This energy, now in the form of anger, "rises to my head," where I *verbalize* it as "anger" (Ego Level). If the quaternary dualism occurs at this point, I will then project this anger and aggression and hence feel fear (Shadow Level). At any rate, by these or other mechanisms (denial, displacement, retroflection, splitting, replacement, regression, scotomatization, rationalization, etc.) my Energy is finally dismembered, dispersed, and disintegrated.

Such then is the mobilization and disintegration of my Energy, the evolution and involution of Brahman, a "play played eternally before all ,creatures," coming straight out of voidness and fading back into' voidness, leaving no real tracks, no traces, a path-less play that comprises the creation-dissolution of the universe now-ever, a creation-dissolution not of matter but of dualisms, the eternal rise-fall of the Spectrum of Consciousness, the simultaneous spontaneity of moment to moment that nevertheless remains always already *this* moment—for there is none other.

> The world as unity of opposites,
> From the formed towards the forming,
> Is essentially a world
> From present to present.
> The moment of the eternal present
> Which is the unity of opposites.... [41]

Viewed temporally and psychologically, this creation is mirrored exactly in the mobilization of Energy—the non-dual mode of knowing—and its disintegration into forms, objects, concepts—the symbolic mode of knowing. Thus is the *objective* universe created now by the form of my dualistic knowledge, for "the form of our knowledge dismembers him daily." To return to Benoit's example of anger and restate this again in skeletal fashion: a man annoys or even strikes me, but I do not instantly feel anger—I feel instead a stillness, a clear awareness, a pellucid alertness, and only after this, perhaps a few seconds later, do I feel a rush of emotions and thoughts that I collectively term "anger," for then my Energy has disintegrated into and animated images. During those few seconds of silent awareness, I am directly in touch with Reality—there is no screen of thought, no painted veil, no conceptual "outflows" (*asrava*); it is pure non-dual awareness, timeless organismic Energy, the "wisdom of non-outflowings" (*jnanam-anasravam*), "originally pure" (*prakriti-prabhasavaram*); it is Ch'an's "initial consciousness" (*yeh-shih*), which operates without reference to space or time, dimensions or extensions, thanks to which I am already virtually free. It is Mind itself, the non-dual mode of knowing. But—for reasons we will soon investigate—it disintegrates, dissipates, manifests, and projects into mental objects-concepts, animating dualisms and creating the world of patterned phenomena. This is the birth of worlds, the birth of the symbolic universe, the birth of dualistic and inferential knowledge, the birth of the spectrum of consciousness, a process which in our meager example we drastically narrowed down to the simple birth of "anger," but which actually occurs in all manifested dimensions—now, this moment, every moment. "Such are the beginnings and endings of worlds and of individual beings: expanded from a point without position or dimensions and now without date or duration."

Parenthetically, it should be obvious that whenever we speak of "contacting" this in-formal Energy (or organismic consciousness) before it disintegrates into dualistic forms, this is simply another way of referring to that energy, awareness, or level of consciousness wherein the universe has not yet disintegrated into observer vs. observed. It comes to the same thing to speak of Absolute Subjectivity or Mind, for this is nothing but the same energy or awareness before it is imagined as split into subject vs. object. So it matters not whether we speak of Energy and its disintegrations or Absolute Subjectivity and its objectifications—both are simpy two ways of pointing to Mind, to that everpresent level of consciousness wherein the universe has not yet become distinct from, nor false to, itself.

We will return to this presently, but it should be obvious that to see clearly what is happening, to understand fully how my levels or sheaths or layers are re-animated and re-generated at every moment of my life, to know that Reality lies upstream of all conceptualization at the very Source of my Energy, at Absolute Subjectivity itself—surely this points out the door, the opening in the cave of shadows, through which we all must pass if we are to catch a glimpse of the Light of the Universe, of that within which is beyond.

REFERENCES AND NOTES

1. John J. McDermott, *The Writings of William James* (New York: Modern Library, 1968), p. 186. We would amend his last statement to conform to that of Eckhart: subject and object fuse but are not confused.

2. Cf. Suzuki, "It starts from the absolute present which is pure experience, an experience in which there is yet no differentiation of subject and object." Pure experience does not imply, however, a naive realism, a view that reality is nothing but the simple objects of our senses—for the view that our senses perceive "objects" is already an idea screening the Real. Thus, "in point of fact, to say 'pure experience' is to commit oneself to something already posited somewhere, and thus it ceases to be pure."

3. Henrich Zimmer, *Philosophies of India* (London: Routledge and Kegan Paul, 1951), p. 20.

4. Due to space, I have eliminated comparisons with Roberto Assagioli's Psychosynthesis and Stanislov Grof's work. These "pluridimensional" approaches have much to recommend them, and I feel that in essentials they are most compatible with the spectrum of consciousness. *See* Assagioli, R., *Psychosynthesis,* and—for Grof's brilliant experimental work into the realms of the Transpersonal Bands, *see* *The Journal of Transpersonal Psychology.*

5. Actually there is no merging with the Center. We are always merged with the Center. It is rather an understanding of this eternal union now, and not a manufacture of it tomorrow.

6. Again, the idea of the Atman "underlying" the sheaths is pure metaphor. The Atman underlies or overlies nothing. It *is* the sheaths—it is the real nature of every sheath. The metaphor is courtesy, not reality.

7. E. Deutsch, *Advaita Vedanta, A Philosophical Reconstruction* (Honolulu: East-West Center Press, 1969), p. 63.

8. A. Osborne, ed., *The Collected Works of Ramana Maharshi* (London: Rider, 1959), pp. 22-24.

9. D. T. Suzuki, *Studies in the Lankavatara Sutra* (London: Routledge and Kegan Paul, 1968), p. 175.

10. Ibid., p. 190. Manas acts, in other words, to reflect and thus objectify Mind.

11. Ibid., p. 190.

12. Ibid., p. 191.

13. Ibid., pp. 191-192.

14. D. T. Suzuki, *The Zen Doctrine of No Mind* (London: Rider, 1970), p. 46.

15. Ibid., p. 133.

16. Ibid., pp. 143-144.

17. Ibid., p. 144.

18. Lama Govinda, *Foundations of Tibetan Mysticism* (New York: Samuel Weiser, 1973), pp. 148-149.

19. Ken Wilber, "Psychologia Perennis: The Spectrum of Consciousness," *Journal of Transpersonal Psychology,* vol. 7, no. 2, (1975).

20. *Chuang Tzu,* Chap. 2.

21. R. D. Laing, *The Politics of the Family* (New York: Pantheon, 1971), p. 82.

22. John Lilly, *The Center of the Cyclone* (New York: Julian Press, 1972).

23. C. G. Jung, *Psyche and Symbol* (New York: 1958).

24. These quotes are taken at random from the illuminating papers of Roland Fischer, Maryland Psychiatric Research Center.

25. H. Benoit, *The Supreme Doctrine* (New York: Viking Press, 1955), p. 179.

26. Ibid., p. 179.

27. Ibid., p. 179. (My italics.)

28. A. K. Coomaraswamy, *Time and Eternity* (Switzerland: Ascona, 1947), p. 68n.

29. Benoit, *Supreme Doctrine,* p. 180.

30. Ibid., p. 180.

31. Ibid., p. 180. (My italics).

32. Erwin Schroedinger, *What is Life? and Mind and Matter* (London: Cambridge University Press, 1969), p. 133. (My italics.)

33. *The Spiritual Teachings of Ramana Maharshi* (Berkeley: Shambhala, 1972).

34. Suzuki, *Zen Doctrine of No Mind,* p. 134.

35. Benoit, *Supreme Doctrine,* pp. 180-1. (My italics.)

36. Ibid., pp. 180-1. (My italics.)

37. Ibid., pp. 184-5. (My italics.)

38. Thus in the *Prajnaparamita* literature, prajna is *sarvajnana,* "all-knowledge."

39. Bernard J. F. Lonergan, *Insight, A Study of Human Understanding* (New York: Philosophical Library, 1970), p. xxviii.

40. Benoit, *Supreme Doctrine,* p. 175.

41. Kitaro Nishida, *Intelligibility and the Philosophy of Nothingness* (Honolulu: East-West Press, 1958), pp. 165-7. I have put this into verse form.

PART TWO INVOLUTION

Thou shalt know God without image, without semblance, and without means. So long as this he and this I, to wit, God and the soul, are not one single here, one single now, the I cannot work with nor be one with that he.

Meister Eckhart

There is neither creation nor destruction, neither destiny nor free-will; Neither path nor achievement; this is the final truth.

Sri Ramana Maharshi

Some have declared that it lies within our choice to gaze continually upon a world of equal or even greater wonder and beauty. It is said by these that the experiments of the alchemists in the Dark Ages are, in fact, related not to the transmutation of metals, but to the transmutation of the entire Universe. This method, or art, or science, or whatever we choose to call it (supposing it to exist, or to have existed), is simply concerned to restore the delights of the primal Paradise; to enable men, if they will, to inhabit a world of joy and splendour. It is perhaps possible that there is such an experiment, and that there are some who have made it.

Hampole

VII. *INTEGRATING THE SHADOW*

At the beginning of his career as a "nerve doctor," Sigmund Freud traveled to Nancy in eastern France in order to witness the celebrated works of the hypnotist Dr. Bernheim. What Freud saw there was eventually to mold the main currents of all Western psychotherapy, from Alder to Jung to Gestalt to Maslow. In a typical experiment performed by Bernheim, the patient was placed in a deep hypnotic trance and then told that, upon a certain signal, he will pick up an umbrella from beside the door, open it, and place it over his head. When the signal was given, the patient did indeed pick up and open the umbrella. When the doctor asked him why he opened the umbrella indoors, the patient would reply with a good reason, such as, "I wanted to see to whom it belonged," or "I just wanted to make sure it was working correctly," or "I was interested in the brand name" or some such. Now these were all good reasons, but they obviously weren't the correct reason. The patient was performing an act, but he had absolutely no idea why he was really doing it! In other words, the patient most definitely had a reason for opening the umbrella but he was unaware of it—his real reason was unconscious, and he was being moved by forces which apparently were not in his conscious mind.

Freud built his entire psychoanalytic system around this basic insight, the insight that man has needs or motivations of which he is unconscious. Now because these needs or instincts are unconscious, the person is not fully aware of them, and thus he can never act upon them to gain satisfaction. In short, *man doesn't know what he wants*; his real desires are unconscious and therefore never adequately satisfied. Neuroses and "mental illness" result, just as if you were completely unconscious of your desire to eat, you would never know you were hungry, and consequently you would never eat, which would indeed make you quite ill. Now this is a superlative idea, the essence of which has been confirmed again and again in clinical observations. The problem, however, is that although everybody agrees that man has unconscious needs, nobody agrees as to what these needs are.

The confusion began with Freud himself, who three times changed his mind as to the nature of man's desires or instincts. Initially he felt they were sex and survival; then he thought they were love and aggression; finally, he stated they were Life and Death. Ever since, psychotherapists have been trying to figure out what man's "real" needs are. Whether they call them needs, instincts, wishes, drives, motivations, desires or whatever, the story is the same. Thus Rank felt it is the need for a strong and constructive will; Adler, the search for power; Ferenczi, the need for love and acceptance; Horney, the need for security; H. S. Sullivan, biological satisfactions and security; Fromm, the need for meaning; Perls, the need to grow and mature; Rogers, self-preservation and enhancement; Glasser, the need for love and self-worth; and so *ad infinitum*.

We have no intention of adding to this confusion by describing what we feel are man's "real needs," for although the different schools of psychiatry and psychotherapy postulate essentially different human needs, they all subscribe to the same basic premise, namely, that man is unaware of, or alienated from, or unconscious of, or tangling communication with some aspects of his "self." These alienated aspects of man's self we have called the Shadow, and we propose here to explore some of the more viable methods whereby man can re-contact and eventually re-own his alienated Shadow. This involves, in other words, an attempt to re-unite the persona, or inaccurate self-image, with the shadow, or alienated facets of self, so as to evolve an accurate and acceptable self-image, the Ego.

We will not, however, stop with these Ego Level therapies, for there exists today a veritable zoo of psychotherapeutic techniques, systems, methods, schools, and disciplines, which in itself is not necessarily a regretable state of affairs, for, as will soon become obvious, there is good reason for the existence of so many different schools. But the problem—and it is a pressing one, for professional and layman alike—is to discern a semblance of order and a synthesizing structure for this vast complexity of different and frequently contradictory psychological systems. Now we believe that, using the spectrum of consciousness as a model, this hidden semblance of order can in fact be demonstrated.

One of our major contentions is that consciousness, the non-dual universe, can appear to function in several different but continuous modalities, states, or levels. Using this model, we maintain that it becomes possible to integrate, in a fairly complete and comprehensive fashion, not only most of the major schools of Western psychology-therapy, but also what are generally called "Eastern" and "Western" approaches to consciousness. For, if there be any truth at all to the Spectrum of Consciousness and to the great metaphysical traditions that unanimously subscribe to its basic theme, then it immediately becomes obvious that *each of the major but differing schools of "psychotherapy" is simply addressing a different level of the Spectrum*.

Thus, a primary reason so many different, and yet seemingly

valid, schools of psychology exist is not, as is generally assumed, that they are all viewing the same level of consciousness and arriving at contradictory conclusions, but that they are each approaching a *different* level of consciousness and thus arriving at *complementary* conclusions. We thus start to discern some method in this madness of innumerable and apparently contradictory psychological systems. For if we agree with the great metaphysical traditions that consciousness is pluri-dimensional (i.e., apparently composed of numerous levels), and if we then *add* the insight that pathology can and does occur on any of these levels (except, of course, the Level of Mind), we will thereupon discover that the *various schools of psychotherapy, East and West, fall naturally into an order that spans the entire Spectrum of Consciousness*.

Thus we are provided with a truly encompassing and integrative guide to the vast number of psychotherapies available today. Now to help us implement this guide, we will, over the next several chapters be devoting ourselves to a study of the pathologies, or more correctly, the dys-eases, that commonly occur on the major levels of consciousness, as well as the therapies that have evolved to deal with these dys-eases. This study is not meant to be either exhaustive nor finally authoritative, for new psychological insights into the various levels are turning up daily. Rather, this study offers only a basic skeleton, an invariant pattern, upon which we may add new flesh as our knowledge grows.

Recall that each level of the spectrum of consciousness is generated by a particular dualism-repression-projection, which results (among other things) in a progressive narrowing of identity from the universe (Mind) to the organism (Existential) to the psyche (Ego) to parts of the psyche (Persona). Thus each level of the spectrum is potentially productive of a certain class of dys-eases, for each level represents a particular type of alienation of the universe from itself. Speaking very generally, the nature of these dys-eases gets progressively "worse" as one ascends the spectrum, because with each new level there appears more aspects of the universe with which the individual no longer identifies and which therefore seem alien and potentially threatening to him. For example, at the Existential Level, man imagines himself separated from and therefore potentially threatened by his own environment. At the Ego Level, man fancies that he is also alienated from his own body, and thus the environment as well as his own body seem possible threats to his existence. At the Shadow Level, man even appears divorced from parts of his own psyche—thus his environment, his body, and even his own mind can appear foreign and threatening. Each of these alienations, created by a particular dualism-repression-projection, is thus potentially productive of a specific class of dys-eases. Or, if you prefer, a specific class of repressions, or projections, or unconscious processes, or dualisms, or fragmentations—from the point of view of the spectrum of consciousness, these terms all refer to the same basic process of creating-two-worlds-from-one which repeats itself, with a new twist, on each and every level of the spectrum.

Thus, to say that each level is created by a particular dualism-repression-projection, or to say that each level is marked by a narrowing of identity, or to say that each level has particular unconscious processes, is only to say that each level has a characteristic set of potential dys-eases. Our task, as was just noted, will be to point out these major sets of dys-eases peculiar to each level, as well as the therapies that have adapted themselves to that level. In so doing, we will also have occasion to comment on the various "needs" and "drives" of each level, on the potential for growth on each level, on the "positive virtues" of each level, on the unconscious processes of each level, and so on. As for the therapies themselves, we will discover in the end that since each level of the spectrum is generated by a particular dualism-repression-projection, the therapies of each and every level share the common goal of healing and whole-ing that level's major dualism. We will return to this at the appropriate place.

One last point. We will start with the Shadow Level and conclude with the Level of Mind, following precisely the reverse order in which the levels evolved. As we will eventually discover, there is good reason for this procedure. Right now, we need only recognize that we are beginning the psychological path of involution, of return to the source, of remembrance of Mind: the descent of the Spectrum of Consciousness. Thus we will start with the therapies aimed at moving from the Shadow to the Ego Level, then descend the spectrum to examine those therapies concerned with the Biosocial Band, then move to those working on the Existential Level, then descend once more to those aimed at the Transpersonal Bands, and conclude with those working at the Level of Mind. One may therefore descend the spectrum as little or as much as one wishes.

To make full use of the methods for integrating the Shadow Level, it would be best to recall how it is generated. With the quaternary dualism-repression-projection, the Ego is severed, its unity repressed, and the shadow—which originally was an integral facet of the Ego—is now projected as foreign, alien, disowned. Generally, we can think of the Shadow as all of our ego-potentials with which we have lost contact, that we have forgotten, that we have disowned. Thus the Shadow *can* contain not only our "bad," aggressive, perverse, wicked, "evil," and demonic aspects that we have tried to disown, but also some "good," energetic, god-like, angelic, and noble aspects that we have forgotten belong to us. Although we attempt to disown and alienate these aspects, they nevertheless remain our own, and the gesture is ultimately as futile as trying to deny our elbows. And just because these facets do remain our own, they continue to operate, and we therefore continue to perceive them, but since we *believe* that they are not ours, we see them as belonging to other people. We have therefore read our own qualities into other people to such an extent that we have lost track of them in ourselves.

On the Ego Level, this alienating of certain aspects of our self has two basic consequences. One, we no longer feel these aspects are ours, and so we can never use them, act upon them, satisfy them: our base of action is thus drastically narrowed, reduced, and frustrated. Two, these facets now *appear* to exist in the environment—we have given our energy to others, and so that energy now seems to turn on us, to boomerang. We loose it in ourselves and "see it" in the environment where it threatens our being. In the words of psychiatrist G. A. Young, "In this process the individual will make himself less than he is and the environment more than it is."[1] We end up clobbering ourselves with our own energy. As Fritz Perls, founder of Gestalt Therapy, puts it, "Once a projection has occurred, or once we have projected some potential, then this potential turns against us."[2]

How our projected energy or potential turns against us can be easily seen—suppose, for example, that an impulse or push-to-action arises within the self, such as the impulse to work, eat, study, play. Now what would this impulse or drive-to-action feel like if, due to the quaternary dualism, we projected this push or drive? The drive would still arise, but we would no longer feel that it belonged to us—the drive would now appear to arise externally to us, in the environment, and we would therefore no longer feel a drive towards the environment but the environment driving us! Instead of pushing to action we would feel pushed into action; instead of having drive we would feel driven; instead of interest, we would experience pressure; in place of desire, obligation. Our energy remains ours, but because of the quaternary dualism, its *source* appears external to us, and so instead of possessing this energy we feel hammered by it, buffeted and slammed around by what now appears to be "external" forces, so that we are driven mercilessly like a helpless puppet, with the environment *apparently* pulling the strings.

Moreover, we can project not only our *positive* emotions of interest, drive, and desire, but also our *negative* feelings of anger, resentment, hatred, rejection, etc. The same thing results, however: instead of being angry at someone, we will feel the world is angry at us; instead of temporarily hating a person, we will sense that the person hates us; instead of rejecting a situation, we will feel rejected. Becoming unaware of our little bit of negative tendencies, we project them onto the environment and thus populate our world with imaginary but quite frightening boogey men, devils, ghosts: we are frightened by our own shadows.

Now besides projecting positive and negative *emotions*, we can also project positive and negative *ideas* or qualities or traits. When a person projects his positive qualities of value and self-worth onto another person, he has surrendered some of his own "goodies" and sees them residing in the other individual. This person therefore feels that he is worthless compared to this other individual, who now appears as a superman, possessing not only his own goodies but also those projected onto him. This projection of positive tendencies and ideas happens frequently in romatic love—be it heterosexual or homosexual—so that the person in love gives all his potentials to his beloved and then is overwhelmed by the supposed goodness, wisdom, beauty, etc. of the beloved. Nevertheless, "Beauty is in the eye of the beholder," and the person who is romantically in love is really in love with the projected aspects of his own self, and he believes that the only way he can re-own these projected goodies is to own and possess his beloved. The same mechanism is operating in cases of wild admiration and envy, for again we have given our potentials away, consequently feeling that we ourselves lack them, and seeing them instead as belonging to others. We become "worthless," and the world appears to be populated with people who are capable, important, awesome in our eyes.

Similarly, we can project negative qualities , consequently feel ourselves to lack them, and instead see them as belonging to others. This is a most common occurrence, because our natural tendency when faced with an undesirable aspect of ourselves is simply to deny it and push it out of consciousness. This, of course, is a futile gesture, for these negative ideas nevertheless remain our own, and we can only pretend to get rid of them by seeing them in other people. The witch-hunt is on. Communists under every bed; the Devil waiting at every corner; Us, the Good Guys, versus Them, the Bad Guys. Our impassioned fight with the devils of this world is nothing but elaborate shadow-boxing.

To those unfamiliar with projection on the Ego Level, this mechanism initially seems most perplexing and occasionally ridiculous, for it implies that those things which most disturb us in other people are really unrecognized aspects of ourselves. This idea is usually met with resentful, bitter opposition. Yet, as Freud pointed out, violent denial is the very mark of projection; that is, if we didn't deny it, we wouldn't be projecting! The fact remains, however, that "it takes one to know one," and our carping criticisms of other people are really nothing but unrecognized bits of autobiography. If you want to know what a person is really like, listen to what he says about other people.

All of this really stems from Freud's original insight that all emotions are intra-psychic and intra-personal, not inter-psychic and inter-personal—that is to say, emotions are experienced (*on the Ego Level* at least) not between me and thee but between me and me.

The so-called neuroses thus result with the arising of the quaternary dualism, where the integrity of the Ego Level is severed, its unity repressed, and then certain facets projected onto the environment. With this quaternary projection, we disown and alienate some of our own tendencies—we forget them, and then forget that we have forgotten them. Therapy on the Ego Level therefore entails a re-membering and re-owning of our forgotten tendencies, a re-identifying with our projected facets, a re-uniting with our shadows. In the words of Dr. Perls:

> Much material that is our own, that is part of ourselves, has been dissociated, alienated, disowned, thrown out. The rest of potential is not available to us. But I believe most of it *is* available, but as projections. I suggest we start with the impossible assumption that whatever we believe we see in another person or in the world is nothing but a projection. . . . We can reassimilate, we can take back our projections, by projecting ourselves completely into that other thing or person. . . . We have to do the opposite of alienation—identification.[3]

Let us give several examples to fully clarify these points. We will present the examples in four groups, representing the four major classes of projection: positive emotions, negative emotions, positive qualities, and negative qualities. We will deal with them in that order.

(1) *Projection of positive emotions* — such as interest, desire, drive, motivation, eagerness, excitement, etc. John has a date with Mary. He is terribly excited about it, and eagerly looks forward to picking her up at her house. As he rings the doorbell he is trembling slightly with excitement, but when her father opens the door, John gets panicky and very "nervous." He forgets his original excitement about meeting with Mary, and consequently instead of being interested in the environment, he feels that the environment—especially Mary's father—is inter-

ested in him. Instead of *looking* he feels *looked at*, and it seems that the situation is very much zeroed in on him. John is clobbering himself with his own energy (although he will probably blame it on the environment, in this case, the "evil eye" stare of Mary's father. Nevertheless, there is nothing in the situation *per se* that "causes nervousness," for many men positively love meeting parents and trying to get to know them—the tangle lies not in this situation but in John himself).

Besides clobbering himself with his own energy, John will end up in a vicious circle, for, as in all projections on the Ego Level, the more he projects, the more he will tend to project: the more he forgets his excitement, the more he projects it, and thus the more the environment seems zeroed in on him. This increases his excitement, which he again projects, making the environment seem even more zeroed in on him, causing him yet more excitement. . . . The only way out of this uncomfortable situation is for John to regain his interest, to re-identify with his excitement and thus *act upon it instead of being acted upon by it*. Usually this will occur as soon as Mary walks into the room—John instantly regains his interest and acts upon it by rushing over to greet her, thereby integrating his alienated interest, for he is now looking at the environment instead of being looked at by it.

The moment John began to feel panic and anxiety, he was losing touch with his basic biological excitement (not sexual excitement, but simply excitement in general)—he blocked it, disowned it, projected it. Under these conditions, excitement is experienced as anxiety, and conversely, whenever we feel anxiety we are simply refusing to let ourselves be excited, vibrant, alive. The only way out of this type of situation is to get back in touch with our interest and excitement—to let our body get excited, to breathe and even gasp deeply, instead of tightening our chest and restricting our breathing; to shake and vibrate with energy, instead of "playing cool" and trying to hold back our excitement by stiffening and becoming "uptight;" to let our Energy mobilize and flow instead of damning it up. Whenever we feel anxiety, we need only ask ourselves "What am I excited about?" or "How am I preventing myself from being naturally excited?" A child simply feels joyously excited, but an adult feels uncomfortably anxious, only because as the Energy wells up, adults shut it off and project it, while children let it flow. "Energy is eternal delight," and children are eternally delightful, at least until they are taught the quaternary dualism, after which children as well as adults alienate their natural excitement. Energy continues to mobilize and well up, but—thanks to the quaternary dualism—it appears to arise *externally* to us, where it takes on a threatening nature. Anxiety, then, is nothing but blocked and projected excitement and interest.

This can most easily be experimented with when one is alone, for one can "let go" without fear of condescending comments from stuffy onlookers. If a feeling of anxiety is present, don't try to get rid of it (i.e., alienate it even more), but instead get into it fully—shake, tremble, gasp for air, follow your bodily action. Get in touch with this anxiety by letting it explode into excitement. Find that Energy that wants to be born, and feel it out completely, for anxiety is birth denied to excitement. Give that Energy birth, re-own it, let it flow, and anxiety will yield to vibrant excitement, to energy freely mobilizing and directed outward, instead of blocked and projected, boomeranging back on us as anxiety.

Another example of the consequences of projecting a positive emotion, let us take the alienation of desire. Jack wants very much to clean out the garage—it's a mess and he has been thinking about cleaning it for quite some time. Finally he decides he'll do it this coming Sunday. At this point Jack is very much in touch with his desire, he wants to get the job done; but when Sunday arrives, Jack starts to have second thoughts about the matter. He putters around for several hours, day dreams, fidgets about—he is starting to lose touch with his desire. Now that desire is still present, because if it weren't, Jack would simply leave the job and do something else. He still wants to do it, but he is beginning to alienate and project that desire, and all he needs to really finish the projection is any available person onto which he can "hang" the projected desire. So when his wife pokes her head in and casually asks how the job is going, Jack snaps back that she should "get off his back!" He now feels that not *he*, but his wife who wants him to clean the garage! The projection is completed. Jack starts to feel that she is pressuring him, but what he is actually experiencing is his own projected desire, for all "pressure" is nothing but displaced eagerness.

At this point, most of us object that we are in situations that really do impose a tremendous pressure upon us, that pressure is due not to our projecting desire but to the very nature of the situation itself (such as an office job, the "obligations" of a family, etc.), and consequently we find little desire for our work. But that is precisely the point—the very fact that we are unaware of our desire leads to our feelings of pressure! We usually reply to this that we would certainly like to find ourselves really desiring to work, cook, do laundry, or whatever, but that the desire is just not present. The fact of the matter, however, is that *desire is present, but we are feeling it as external desire or pressure*. That pressure is our own disguised desire, and *if we didn't have that desire, we simply wouldn't feel pressured*. If desire weren't present, we would feel bored, lackadaisical, or perhaps apathetic, but never pressured. Similarly, in our previous example, if John really had no interest in dating Mary, then when he picked her up he would never feel anxiety—he just wouldn't care, he would feel neutral or maybe slightly annoyed, but never anxious. John's anxiety was possible only because he really was interested in Mary but projected that interest, and likewise pressure is experienced *only* where there is a projected desire.

Hence Jack will continue to feel pressured and nagged by his wife until it dawns on him that the only person who is pressuring him to clean the garage is Jack himself, that the battle is between Jack and Jack and not between Jack and his wife. If he realizes this, he will act on his desire instead of fighting it, and end up cleaning the garage—which is what he wanted in the first place. The Putneys admirably summarize it thus:

> The autonomous alternative is to move beyond pressure by recognizing that any sense of insistent pressure is one's own projected drive. The man who recognizes that what he feels is his own drive will neither resent nor resist the pressure; he will act.[4]

Thus, if we are feeling pressured, we needn't try to invent or create desire so as to escape pressure—we are already experiencing the needed desire, only we have mis-labeled it "pressure."

(2) *Projection of negative emotions*— such as aggression, anger, hatred, rejection, resentment, etc. The projection of negative emotions is an unbelievably common occurrence, especially in the West, where the prevailing moral atmosphere of popular Christianity demands that we try to fight all "evil" and negative tendencies in ourselves and others; and even though Christ counseled us to "resist not evil," to love it and befriend it, since "I am the Lord, and there is none else. I form the light, and create darkness; I make peace, and create evil; I the Lord do all these things;" nevertheless, very few of us love our "evil" tendencies. On the contrary, we despise and loathe them, they shame and embarass us, and we consequently seek not to integrate them but to alienate them. With the arising of the quaternary dualism, this alienation becomes possible; rather, it seems to become possible, for although we deny these tendencies consciousness, they remain ours nevertheless. We push them from consciousness so that they *appear* in the environment—it then seems that *we* lack them but the environment is swarming with them. Actually, when we survey other people and are horrified by all the

evils we "see" in them, we are but gazing unerringly into the mirror of our own souls.

Egoic "health and sanity" thus demands that we re-own and re-integrate these "evil" and negative tendencies. Once we have done so, a most startling thing happens: we discover that these negative tendencies we were so loathe to admit in ourselves, once they are re-integrated become harmoniously balanced with our positive tendencies and therefore loose their supposed evil coloring. In fact, these negative tendencies of hatred and aggression assume a really violent and evil nature only when we alienate them, only when we separate them from their counterbalancing positive tendencies of love and acceptance and then fling them into the environment where, isolated from their balancing context, they can indeed appear most vicious and destructive. When we incorrectly imagine these demonic aspects to actually exist in the environment—instead of realizing that they exist in us as the necessary counter-balance of our constructive positive tendencies—when we do imagine they exist in the environment, then we react most violently and viciously to this illusory threat, then we are driven into frenzies of frequently brutal crusading, then do we kill "witches" for their own good, start wars to "maintain peace," establish inquisitions to "save souls." In short, an alienated and projected negative tendency, because it is severed from its balancing context and given a life of its own, can take on a very demonic nature and result in truly destructive actions, while that same tendency, reintegrated in us and placed along side its balancing positive tendency, takes on a mellow and cooperative nature. In this sense, it is a moral imperative that to be Christ-like one must befriend the Devil.

Further, we rarely realize that not only do good and evil tendencies balance one another when they are integrated, but also that—like all opposites—they are necessary for one another, that not only does evil harmonize with good but that *evil itself is necessary for the very existence of the good*. As Rilke put it, "If my devils are to leave me, I am afraid my angels will take flight as well." Says Lao Tzu:

> Is there a difference between yes and no?
> Is there a difference between good and evil?
> Must I fear what others fear? What nonsense!
> Having and not having arise together
> Difficult and easy complement each other
> Long and short contrast each other
> High and low rest upon each other
> Front and back follow one another.[5]

And Chung-tzu draws the conclusion:

> Thus, those who say that they would have right without its
> correlate, wrong; or good government without its correlate,
> misrule, do not apprehend the great principles of the universe,
> nor the nature of all creation. One might as well talk of the
> existence of Heaven without that of Earth, or of the negative
> principle without the positive, which is clearly impossible. Yet
> people keep on discussing it without stop; such people must be
> either fools or knaves.[6]

People hate the darkness of their negative tendencies just as
children hate the darkness of the night, but just as if there were no
dark of night we would never recognize the light of day, so also if
we possessed no negative aspects we would never recognize our
positive ones. Our negative and positive tendencies are thus like
the valleys and the mountains of a beautiful landscape—there can
be no mountains without valleys, and vice versa, so that those who
would misguidedly seek to annihilate the valleys must in the same
stroke level the mountains.

Trying to rid ourselves of negative tendencies, trying to destroy
them and eliminate them, would be a fine idea—if it were possible.
The problem is, that it is not, that the negative tendencies in
ourselves to which we try to shut our eyes nevertheless remain
firmly ours and return to plague us as neurotic symptoms of fear,
depression, and anxiety. Cut off from consciousness, they assume
menacing aspects all out of proportion to their actual nature. We
can tame evil only by befriending it, and we simply inflame it by
alienating it. Integrated, evil becomes mellow; projected, it becomes quite vicious, and thus those who would seek to eliminate
evil have added substantially to its victory. In the words of Ronald
Fraser:

> Let me ask you to remember some day that I have told you that
> the hatred of evil strengthens evil, and opposition reinforces
> what is opposed. This is a law of an exactitude equal with the
> laws of mathematics.[7]

Or from theologian Nicholas Berdyaev:

> Satan rejoices when he succeeds in inspiring us with dia-
> bolical feelings to himself. It is he who wins when his own
> methods are turned against himself. . . . A continual de-
> nunciation of evil and its agents merely encourages its growth
> in the world—a truth sufficiently revealed in the Gospels, but
> to which we remain persistently blind.[8]

As an example of the projection of negative emotions, let us
begin with that of hatred. Martha is leaving home to attend a

"sophisticated" girl's college in the East. While she was in high school she was very much in touch with her negative emotions of hatred, so that this hatred was not at all of the violent or vicious type, but was rather mellow and easy-going, which we could call rascality, orneriness, whimsy, or gentle cynicism:

> This attitude of gentle cynicism has always been characteristic of highly cultured and humane people, and in the fellowship of those who can "let their hair down" with each other and express the warmest friendship in such terms as, "Well, you old rascal!" The whole possibility of loving affection between human beings depends upon the recognition and acceptance of an element of irreducible rascality in oneself and others. . . . The power of fanaticism, "effective" as it may be, is always bought at the price of unconsciousness, and whether its cause be good or evil it is invariably destructive because it works against life: it denies the ambivalence of the natural world.[9]

The point, again, is that when we are conscious of our little bit of hatred, it really isn't hatred as such, for it is blended and harmonized with our positive emotions of love and kindness, so that integrated hatred takes on very gentle and frequently humorous overtones. Bob Young, a psychiatrist, greets his intimate friends with "Hi, you ole bastard!" and has even formed a club named YRENRO DRATSAB, which is "ornery bastard" spelled backwards, whose sole aim is to "promote the gentle art of *brotherly unlove*."

Now Martha was in touch with her whimsical and devilish side, her integrated hatred, and so it formed a very constructive part of her character. But as she arrives at college, she is thrown in with an overly zealous "prim and proper" group of friends where any expressions of whimsical rascality are looked upon with disdain. In a very short time, Martha starts to loose touch with her hatred and therefore she begins to project it. Hence, instead of whimsically and gently hating the world, she feels the world is hating her. She predictably looses her sense of humor and has disquieting feelings that absolutely nobody likes her—"I hate the world" has become "the world hates me," but where the former makes for a world of whim, the latter makes for a world of grim.

Many of us go through life (or at least high school) feeling that "nobody likes us," and we think this is terribly unfair because we, of course, dislike nobody. But these are precisely the two distinguishing marks of projection on the Ego Level: we see it in everybody else but imagine ourselves to lack it. We feel the world hates us *only because* we are unaware of the small part of ourselves that gently hates the world.

The same general phenomenon occurs when we project such negative emotions as aggression, anger, and rejection. Instead of gently and humorously attacking the environment, we turn these emotions back on ourselves and then feel that the environment is maliciously attacking us. Aggression, for example, is a most useful personality trait when we are fully conscious of it, for it allows us to meet the environment and grapple with it effectively. If we are not just to "swallow" everything we are told, or all experiences that come to us, we must actively attack them, tear into them, thoroughly "chew" them—not maliciously, but with drive and interest.

> If you can realize the necessity for an aggressive, destructive, and reconstructive attitude toward any experience that you are really to make your own, you can then appreciate the need . . . to evaluate aggressions highly and not to dub them glibly "anti-social."[10]

As a matter of fact, violent anti-social aggressive acts are a result not of integrated aggression but of suppressed and alienated aggression, for by "holding it in" the force of aggression greatly increases, just as the tighter you clamp on the lid of a pressure cooker the greater the force of steam becomes, until it finally results in violent explosion. Again, it appears a moral imperative to integrate and make conscious our aggressive tendencies. Yet most of us do just the opposite—we seek to deny our aggressive tendencies and push them out of consciousness. It should be obvious by now, however, that these tendencies nevertheless remain our own, and nevertheless continue to operate in us, but we now experience them as if they originated outside of us in the environment, and consequently it appears that the world is attacking us. In short, we experience fear. "The projector is connected . . . with his projected aggression by fear." As projected excitement is felt as anxiety, as projected desire is felt as pressure, projected aggression is felt as fear.

"Well," some of us might reply, "I certainly feel afraid at times, but my problem is just that I'm not the aggressive type—I often feel fear, but I just never feel aggression." Precisely! We don't feel aggression because we have projected it and are consequently feeling it as fear! The very experience of fear is nothing but our masked feeling of aggression which we have turned back on ourselves. We don't have to invent aggression—*it is already there as fear*, and so all we have to do is call fear by its correct name: *aggression*. Thus the statement, "the world is emotionally attacking me," is much more accurate if read backwards.

If projected aggression is felt as fear, then projected anger is felt as depression. Angry rejection of the world—which we all experience at moments—is useful in spurring us into constructive action, but if it is alienated and projected, we begin to feel that the world angrily rejects us. Under these circumstances, the world looks very dark and understandably we become very depressed. Outrage becomes inrage as we turn anger back on ourselves and then suffer terribly under its lash. M-A-D has become S-A-D, and we become the depressed victims of our own anger. The person who is depressed need only ask himself, "What am I so mad at?" and then learn to spell "sad" correctly: M-A-D.

(3) *Projection of positive qualities* — such as kindness, strength, wisdom, beauty, etc. Besides projectng emotions we can also project personal traits, qualities, and characteristics, so that we then feel ourselves totally lacking in these characteristics while everybody seems to have an over-abundance of them. When these characteristics happen to be positive and good, such as beauty or wisdom, we feel ourselves awed by the number of supermen who seem to surround us, for we have given them all of our goodies. This is the basis of romantic love, but it also occurs frequently in marriages and friendships, between doctor and patient, between professor and student. There is a story of a woman undergoing psychotherapy who had projected all of her goodies onto her therapist and so consequently felt complete and utter adoration and admiration for him. As a token of her thanks, she decided to buy him a gorgeous sky blue tie because, in her words, "it matches your beautiful blue eyes that are so full of wisdom." Now it so happened that the therapist had *brown* eyes, and so when she presented him the tie that matched his supposedly blue eyes of such wisdom, the therapist grabbed a mirror and held it to her face. "Now," he demanded, "Just who has the beautiful blue wisdom eyes?" The woman's eyes, of course, were beautifully deep blue. As always, beauty, as well as wisdom, is in the eyes of the beholder, and whenever we feel an over-blown awe for someone, we have built them a pedestal out of our own potential.

(4) *Projection of negative qualities* — such as prejudices, snobbishness, devilishness, prudishness, meanness, etc. Like the projection of negative emotions, the projection of negative qualities is very common in our society, for we have been duped into equating "negative" with "undesirable." Thus instead of befriending and integrating our negative traits, we alienate and project them, seeing them in everybody else but ourselves. As always however, they nevertheless remain ours, so that

The accusations which A hurls at B are embarrassing bits of

A's autobiography. The insights which A has into B's sick motivations reveal the motives of A, for one person can have insight into another only by analogy to his own experience. Whether or not the projections fit, the accusations and the insights are best applied where they originate—within the self.[11]

As an example, nine out of a particular group of ten girls love Jill, but the tenth girl, Betty, can't stand her because, as Betty explains it, Jill is a prude. And Betty hates prudes. So she will go to lengths to try to convince her other friends of Jill's supposed prudishness, but nobody seems to agree with her, which further infuriates Betty. It is perhaps obvious that Betty hates Jill only because Betty is unconscious of her own prudish tendencies; and projecting them onto Jill, a conflict between Betty and Betty becomes a conflict between Betty and Jill. Jill, of course, has nothing to do with this argument—she simply acts as an unwanted mirror of Betty's own self-hatred.

All of us have blind spots—tendencies and traits that we simply refuse to admit are ours, that we refuse to accept and therefore fling into the environment where we muster all of our righteous fury and indignation to do battle with them, blinded by our own idealism to the fact that the battle is within and the enemy is much nearer home. And all it takes to integrate these facets is that we treat ourselves with the same kindness and understanding that we afford to our friends. As Jung most eloquently states:

> The acceptance of oneself is the essence of the moral problem and the epitome of a whole outlook upon life. That I feed the hungry, that I forgive an insult, that I love my enemy in the name of Christ—all these are undoubtedly great virtues. What I do unto the least of my brethren, that I do unto Christ. But what if I should discover that the least among them all, the poorest of all the beggars, the most impudent of all offenders, the very enemy himself—that these are within me, and that I myself stand in the need of the alms of my own kindness—that I myself am the enemy who must be loved—what then?[12]

To summarize this discussion and place it in its context of the spectrum of conscious: Our Energy (*Brahman*, Level of Mind) mobilizes and wells up, passing the Transpersonal Bands and eventually reaching and passing through the Existential Level and then the Biosocial Band, where it takes on *form as idea and direction as emotion*. Our Energy, now clothed in ideas and emotions, reaches the Ego Level, where, if the quaternary dualism-repression-projection has occurred, these ideas, qualities, and emotions, both positive and negative, will be alienated and projected, so that they will now appear to have their origin not in the self but in the environment. This final major dualism, which creates the Shadow Level, has been the subject of our concern, and it is succinctly described by Perls, Hefferline, and Goodman:

> A projection is a trait, attitude, feeling, or bit of behavior which actually belongs to your own personality but is not experienced as such; instead, it is attributed to objects or persons in the environment and then experienced as directed *toward* you by them instead of the other way around. The projector, unaware, for instance, that he is rejecting others, believes that they are rejecting him; or, unaware of his tendencies to approach others sexually, feels that they make sexual approaches to him.[13]

The consequences of this quaternary dualism are always two-fold: one, we come to believe that we totally lack the quality which we are projecting, and thus it is unavailable to us—we do not act upon it, utilize it, or in any way satisfy it, which causes a chronic frustration and tension. Two, we see these qualities as existing in the environment, where they assume awesome or terrifying proportions, so that we end up clobbering ourselves with our own energy.

Projection on the Ego Level is very easily identified: if a person or thing in the environment *informs* us, we probably aren't projecting; on the other hand, if it *affects* us, chances are that we are a victim of our own projections. For instance, Jill might very well have been a prude, but was that any reason for Betty to hate her? Certainly not; Betty was not just *informed* that Jill was a prude, she was violently *affected* by Jill's prudishness, which is a sure sign that Betty's hatred of Jill was only projected or extroverted self-contempt. Similarly, when Jack was debating whether or not to clean the garage, and his wife inquired how he was doing, Jack over-reacted. Had he really not desired to clean the garage, had he really been innocent of that drive, he would have simply answered that he had changed his mind. But he did not—instead he snapped back at her—"imagine, *she* wants him to clean the garage!" Jack projected his own desire and then experienced it as pressure, so that his wife's innocent inquiry did not just *inform* Jack, it strongly *affected* Jack: he felt unduly pressured. And *that* is the crucial difference—what I see in other people is more-or-less correct if it only *informs* me, but it is definitely a projection if it strongly *affects* me emotionally. Thus if we are overly attached to somebody (or something) on the one hand, or if we emotionally avoid or hate someone on the other, then we are respectively either shadow-hugging or shadow-boxing, and the quaternary dualism-re-pression-projection has most definitely occurred.

The undoing of a projection represents a move or a shift "down" the spectrum of consciousness (from the Shadow to the Ego Level), for we are enlarging our area of identification by re-owning aspects of ourselves that we had previously alienated. And the first step, the primary step, is always to realize that what we thought the environment was mechanically doing to us is really *something we are doing to ourselves—we are responsible*. In the words of Laing:

> There is thus some phenomenological validity referring to such "defenses" [such as projection] by the term "mechanism." But we must not stop there. They have this mechanical quality because the person as he experiences himself is dissociated from them. He appears to himself and to others to suffer from them [as if they were "external" to him]. . . .
>
> But this is so only from the perspective of his own alienated experience. As he becomes de-alienated [integrating his projections] he is able first of all to become aware of them, if he has not already done so, and then to take the second, even more crucial, step of progressively *realizing that these are things he does or has done to himself.*[14]

Thus, if I am feeling anxiety, I would usually claim that I am a helpless victim of this tension, that people or situations in the environment are *causing* me to become anxious. The first step is to become fully aware of anxiety, to get in touch with it, to shake and jitter and gasp for air—to *really feel it*, invite it in, express it— and thus realize that I am responsible, that I am tensing, that I am blocking my excitement and therefore experiencing anxiety. I am doing this to myself, so that anxiety is an affair between me and me and not me and the environment. But this shift in attitude means that where formerly I alienated my excitement, split myself from it and then claimed to be a *victim* of it, I now am *taking responsibility for what I am doing to myself*. This can be clearly seen in the following dialogue between Gestalt therapist Fritz Perls (F) and his "patient" Max (M), where Max begins by disclaiming any responsibility for his "symptoms":

> M: I am tense. My hands are tense.
>
> F: Your hands are tense. They have nothing to do with you.
>
> M: *I* am tense.
>
> F: You are tense. How are you tense? What are you doing? You see the consistent tendency towards [alienating aspects of ourselves by] reification—always trying to make a thing out of a process. . . .
>
> M: I am tensing myself.
>
> F: That's it. Look at the difference between the words "I am

tensing myself" and "There's a tenseness here." When you say "I feel tenseness," you're irresponsible, you are not responsible for this, you are impotent and you can't do anything about it. The world should do something—give you aspirin or whatever it is. But when you say "I am tensing" you take responsibility, and we can see the first bit of excitement of life coming out.[15]

Max's tenseness and anxiety quickly change into excitement, and Perls comments on this:

Of course, taking responsibility for your life and being rich in experience and ability [are] identical. And this is what I hope to do here in this short seminar—to make you understand how much you gain by taking responsibility for every emotion, every movement you make, every thought you have—and shed responsibility for *anybody* else. The world is not here for your expectation, nor do you have to live for the expectation of the world. We touch each other by being honestly what we are, not by intentionally *making* contact.[16]

Dr. Perls then summarizes the whole drift of this discussion most clearly:

As long as you fight a symptom, it will become worse. If you take responsibility for what you are doing to yourself, how you produce your symptoms, how you produce your illness, how you produce your existence —the very moment you get in touch with yourself— growth begins, integration begins.[17]

If the first step in the "cure" of shadow projections is to take responsibility for the projections, then the second step is simply to *reverse* the direction of the projection itself and gently do unto others what we have heretofore been unmercifully doing unto ourselves. Thus, "The world rejects me" freely translates into "I reject, at least at this moment, the whole damn world!" "My parents want me to study" translates into "I want to study." "My poor mother needs me" becomes "I need to be close to her." "I'm afraid of being left alone" translates into "Damned if I'll give anybody the time of day!" "Everybody's always looking at me critically" becomes "I'm an interested critic of people."

We will return to these two basic steps of responsibility and reversal in just a moment, but at this point let us note that in all these cases of shadow projection we have "neurotically" tried to render our self-image acceptable by making it inaccurate. All of those facets of our self-image, our ego, which are incompatible with what we superficially believe to be our best interests, or all those aspects which do not mesh with the philosophic bands, or all those facets which are alienated in times of stress, impasse, or double-bind—all of that self-potential is abandoned. As a result we narrow our identity to only a fraction of our ego, namely, to the distorted and impoverished *persona*. And so by the same stroke are we doomed to be haunted forever by our own Shadow, which we now refuse to give even the briefest conscious hearing. But the Shadow always has its say, for it forces entry into consciousness an anxiety, guilt, fear, and depression. The Shadow becomes symptom, and fastens itself to us as a vampire battens on its prey.

To speak somewhat figuratively, it may be said that we have split the *concordia discors* of the psyche into numerous polarities and contraries and opposites, all of which for convenience sake we have been referring to collectively as the quaternary dualism, that is, the split between the persona and the Shadow. In each of these cases, we associate ourselves with only "one-half" of the duality while casting the banished and usually despised opposite to the twilight world of the Shadow. The Shadow, therefore, exists precisely as the *opposite* of whatever we, as persona, consciously and deliberately believe to be the case.

Thus it stands to good reason that if you would like to know just how your Shadow views the world, then—as a type of personal experiment—simply *assume exactly the opposite of whatever you consciously desire, like, feel, want, intend, or believe*. In this way you may consciously contact, express, play, and ultimately re-own your opposites. After all, you will own them, or they will own you—the Shadow always has its say. This, if anything, is what we have learned from every example in this chapter: we may wisely *be aware* of our opposites, or we will be forced to *beware* of them.

Now to play the opposites, to be aware of and eventually re-own our Shadows, is not necessarily to *act* on them! It seems that nearly every person is most reluctant to confront his opposites for fear they might overpower him. And yet it's rather just the other way round: we end up, totally against our will, following the dictates of the Shadow only when it's unconscious.

As a very skeletal example, let us imagine that Ann is convinced that the one thing she wants out of life is to become a lawyer. So convinced is she that Ann won't even let the least doubts about the matter cross her mind. Now the thought of this prospective career is very pleasing to Ann, and by all accounts she should be rather happy with her situation. And yet she is miserable because, as Ann explains it, she knows her husband won't approve. Of course, it's really none of his business, and Ann knows he wouldn't actually try to prevent her from pursuing law. Yet she just knows he would disapprove, and that disapproval—for various reasons—would simply be crushing for her, turning a difficult profession into an impossible one.

Now as it turns out, Ann hasn't exactly asked her husband what he does think about her becoming a lawyer, because, says she, it's unnecessary—he would flatly oppose it. And thus for some time—and its not at all uncommon for situations like this to drag on for years—Ann lives in semi-agony, secretly resenting her husband on the one hand, and openly playing the martyr on the other, all to the immense confusion and frustration of hubby. Finally and inevitably the conflict breaks open, and Ann angrily confronts her husband with his supposed rejection of her desired career, only to find, to Ann's complete befuddlement, that he is honestly not at all opposed to her wishes! Superficial as this example is, it nevertheless represents a very basic drama something similar in which each of us has participated at one time or another.

Then what, we may ask, was really behind this tragedy? Ann's conscious orientation was one of supposedly pure desire to become a lawyer. Yet Ann could not have known she liked law unless a small part of her also disliked it! An image does not stand out in consciousness unless there exists a contrasting ground against which to realize it. But to Ann, an awareness of her own little bit of "to hell with it" seemed tantamount to acting exclusively on it! Thus, she attempted to deny her minor but absolutely necessary dislike of law, but only succeeded—as is always the case with projections—in denying *ownership* of it. It nevertheless remained hers, and hence this banished opposite continued to clamor for her attention. Thus she knew that *somebody* was increasingly trying to voice a rejection of her proposed career in law, but since it obviously wasn't her, she had only to pick a candidate. And anybody would do—but she needed at least one! Thus, to her greater but miserable glory, in walked hubby, and there, out in the environment, in the person of her spouse, blown up and perceived as if through a psychic magnifying glass, she beheld nothing other than the face of her own Shadow, her alienated opposite. "The *nerve* of that bastard, not wanting *me* to attend law school!"

Because Ann would not confront her opposite, but instead projected it, the opposite actually had the final say: for God knows how long, Ann, in behavior at least, rejected law and failed to pursue that career. When it finally came to light that hubby actually thought law a superb idea, Ann was left with her projection dangling. If, at this point, she has the good sense to finally confront her opposite, she will, for the first time, be in a position to realistically and consciously weigh her own likes and dislikes and thus make a sound decision. Whatever her decison, she will now be free to make it, not forced to.

The point is that to make any valid decision or choice we must be fully aware of both sides, of both opposites, and if one of the alternatives is unconscious, our decision will probably be a less

than wise one. In all areas of psychic life, as this and every example
in this chapter has shown, we must confront our opposites and
re-own them—and that doesn't necessarily mean to *act* on them,
just to be *aware* of them.

By progressively confronting one's opposites, it becomes more
and more obvious—and this point can hardly be repeated too
often—that since the Shadow is a real and integral facet of the ego,
all of the "symptoms" and discomforts that the Shadow seems to be
inflicting on us are really symptoms and discomforts which we are
inflicting on ourselves, however much we may consciously protest
to the contrary. *It is very, very much as if I, for instance, were
deliberately and painfully pinching myself but pretending not to*!
Whatever my symptoms on this level may be—guilt, fear, anxiety,
depression—all are strictly the result of my "mentally" pinching
myself in one fashion or another. And this directly implies, incredible as it may seem, that *I want this painful symptom, whatever its
nature, to be here just as much as I want it to depart*!

Thus, the first opposite you might try confronting is your secret
and shadowed desire to keep and maintain your symptoms, your
unawares desire to pinch yourself. And may we be impudent
enough to suggest that the more ridiculous this sounds to you, the
more out of touch you might be with your Shadow, with that side of
you that *is* doing the pinching?

Hence, to ask, "How can I get rid of this symptom?" is to goof
immediately, for that implies that it is not *you* who are producing
it! It is tantamount to asking, "How can I stop pinching myself?" As
long as you are asking how to stop pinching yourself, or as long as
you are *trying* to stop pinching yourself, then you quite obviously
have not seen that it is *you* who are doing the pinching! And so the
pain remains or even increases. For if you clearly see that you are
pinching yourself, you don't ask how to stop—you just stop, instantly! To put it bluntly, the reason the symptom doesn't depart is
that you are trying to make it depart. This is why Perls stated that
as long as you fight a symptom, it will get worse. Deliberate change
never works, for it excludes the Shadow.

Thus, the problem is *not* to get rid of any symptom, but rather to
deliberately and consciously try to increase that symptom, to deliberately and consciously experience it fully! If you are depressed,
try to be more depressed. If you are tense, make yourself even
tenser. If you feel guilty, increase your feelings of guilt—and we
mean that literally! For by so doing you are, for the very first time,
acknowledging and even aligning yourself with your Shadow, and
hence are doing consciously what you have heretofore been doing
unconsciously. When you, as a personal experiment, consciously
throw every bit of yourself into actively and deliberately trying to

produce your present symptoms, you have in effect *thrown your persona and Shadow together*. You have consciously contacted and aligned yourself with your opposites, and, in short, re-discovered your Shadow.

So, deliberately and consciously increase any present symptom to the point where you consciously see that *you* are and always have been doing it, whereupon, for the first time, you are spontaneously free to cease. Just as when Max clearly saw he was tensing himself, then—and only then—was he free to *stop* tensing himself. If you can make yourself *more* guilty, it dawns on you that you can make yourself *less* guilty, but in a remarkably spontaneous way. If you are free to depress yourself, you are free not to. My father used to cure hiccups instantly by producing a twenty-dollar bill on the spot and demanding in return that the victim immediately hiccup just one more time. So also, allowed anxiety is no longer anxiety, and the easiest way to "un-tense" a person is to challenge him to be as tense as he possibly can. In all cases, conscious adherence to a symptom delivers you from the symptom.

But you mustn't worry about whether the symptom disappears or not—it will, but don't worry about it. To play your opposites for the sole reason of trying to erase a symptom is to fail miserably at playing your opposites. In other words, don't play the opposites half-heartedly and then anxiously check to see whether or not the symptom has vanished. If you hear yourself saying, "Well, I tried to make the symptom worse, but it still didn't go away and I wish like hell it would!" then you have not contacted the Shadow at all, but merely rifled off some quick-fire lip service to placate the gods and demons. You must become those demons, until with the entire force of your conscious attention you are deliberately and purposefully producing and holding on to your symptoms.

So—in the beginning at least—every time you find yourself slipping back into deliberately trying to silence a symptom, or eradicate it, or ignore it—play your opposite: hold on to the symptom, increase it, express it, play it up! It's very much as if you were starting to fall on a bicycle, and against all your better judgements you turn right into the direction of the fall, and miraculously the bike rights itself. We fall over our "symptoms" all the time simply because we turn in the wrong direction.

Thus, if the first goof is trying to get rid of a symptom, the second goof is trying not to get rid of the symptom in order to get rid of the symptom. So, to repeat, we needn't worry or even hope that the symptom will go away. That, as we have seen, is a half-truth anyway. Rather, we need only concern ourselves with fully and completely experiencing and playing up the symptom, contacting the Shadow, confronting our opposites, and then the symptom

will—without any coaxing from us and in its own sweet time—
spontaneously depart. And this for the simple reason that the
psyche is a spontaneously self-organizing system which, finally
given the correct information that it is pinching itself, will automatically stop it!

That, in essence, is the *first step*—the playing of your opposites,
the assuming responsibility for your Shadow, your symptoms. And
as your opposites become more and more conscious—your loves
and hates, likes and dislikes, good qualities and bad qualities,
positive emotions and negative emotions—and as your symptoms
become more and more experienced—your moods and fears, your
twitches and shakes, your depressions and anxieties—then you
will be able to proceed, where necessary, to the *second step* and
reverse the direction of the projections, using the broad guidelines
set forth in this chapter as to whether your projections are of
positive or negative qualities, or positive or negative emotions.

Now as a general rule it is only with the projected emotions and
not the projected qualities that this second step is needed, i.e., that
the *direction* of the projection has to be reversed. The reason is
that, freely speaking, emotions are not only qualities, but *qualities
with a direction*. So when we project a particular emotion, not only
do we flip the *quality* of that emotion outside ourselves, we also flip
the *direction* of that emotion. For instance, if I project a positive
emotion, such as interest, not only do I project the quality of
interest itself (and so fancy myself innocent of that quality), I also
project or flip the direction of that interest: instead of my looking at
others, I feel others looking at me! Or if I project my sexual desire
for someone, both the quality and the direction flip: I'm not sexu-
ally aroused but that person's out to rape me! Or I project my drive:
I have no drive but everybody is driving and pressuring me! Similarly with negative emotions: "I reject others" flips to "Others
reject me." "I hate the world" flips to "The world hates me." "I'm
fighting mad" flips to "People are out to crucify me!" We project the
quality of the emotion and so feel ourselves to lack it ("Why, I have
no hatred at all"), and we project the direction of the emotion ("But
he viciously hates *me*!"). To put it all simply, when we project an
emotion we also flip its direction.

So in contacting my symptoms and deliberately trying to identify with them, I will want to keep in mind that any particular
symptom—if it has an emotional nucleus—is the visible form of a
Shadow which contains not only the opposite quality but also the
opposite direction. Thus, if I feel terribly hurt and mortally
wounded "because of" something Mr. X said to me, and I consequently am in agony—although I consciously harbor nothing
but goodwill toward X—the first step is to realize that I am doing

this to myself, that literally I am hurting myself. Taking responsibility for my own emotions, I am now in a position to reverse the direction of the projection and to see that my feelings of being hurt are precisely my own desire to hurt X. "I feel hurt by X" finally translates correctly into "I want to hurt X." Now this doesn't mean that I go out and thrash X to a pulp—the awareness of my anger is sufficient to integrate it (although I might like to brutalize a pillow instead). The point is that my symptom of agony reflects not only the opposite quality, but also the opposite direction. Hence, I will have to assume responsibility both for the anger (which is the opposite quality of my conscious goodwill toward X) *and* for the fact that the anger itself is *from* me *towards* X (which is the opposite of my conscious direction).

In a sense, then, we have *first*—in the case of projected emotions—to see that what we thought the environment was doing to us is really something we are doing to ourselves, that we are literally pinching ourselves; and then, as it were, to see that this is actually *our own disguised desire to pinch others!* And for the "desire to pinch others", substitute—according to your own projections—the desire to love others, hate others, touch others, tense others, possess others, look at others, murder others, contact others, squeeze others, capture others, reject others, give to others, take from others, play with others, dominate others, deceive others, elevate others. You fill in the blank, or rather, let your Shadow fill it.

Now this *second* step of reversal is absolutely essential. If the emotion is not fully discharged in the correct direction, you will very quickly slip back into the habit of turning that emotion back on yourself. So as you contact an emotion, such as hatred, every time you start to turn the hatred back on yourself, then play the opposite direction! Turn it out! That is now your choice: to pinch or to be pinched, to look or to be looked at, to reject or to be rejected.

Taking back our projections is somewhat simpler—but not necessarily easier—when it comes to projected qualities, traits, or ideas, because they do not themselves involve a direction, at least not one as pronounced and as moving as that of the emotions. Rather, positive or negative traits, such as wisdom, courage, bitchiness, wickedness, stinginess, and so on, seem to be relatively much more static. Thus we have only to worry about the quality itself, and not so much about any direction of the quality. Of course, once these qualities are projected, we may react to them in a violently emotional manner—and then we may even project these reactive emotions, and then react to them, and so on in a dizzying whirl of shadow boxing. And it may well be that no qualities or ideas are projected unless emotionally charged. Be all that as it may, considerable re-integration can nevertheless be accomplished if we simply consider the projected qualities by themselves.

As always, the projected traits—just like the projected emotions—will be all those items we "see" in others that don't merely inform us but strongly affect us. Usually these will be the qualities which we imagine another to possess and which we utterly loathe, qualities we are always itching to point out and violently condemn. Never mind that we are but flinging our condemnations at our own little black heart, hoping thereby to exorcise it. Occasionally the projected qualities will be some of our own virtues, so that we cling to those onto whom we hang our goodies, frequently attempting to feverishly guard and monopolize the chosen person. The fever comes, of course, from the powerful desire to hold onto aspects of our own selves.

In the last analysis, projections come in all flavors. In any case, these projected qualities—just like the projected emotions—will always be the opposite of those we consciously fancy ourselves to possess. But unlike the emotions, these traits themselves do not have a direction, and thus their integration is straight-forward. In the very first step of playing your opposites, you will come to see that what you love or despise in others are only the qualities of your own Shadow. It is not an affair between you and others but between you and you. Playing your opposites you touch the Shadow, and in so understanding that you are pinching yourself, you stop. There is no direction to the projected traits themselves, and so their integration does not demand the second step of reversal.

And so it is that through playing our opposites, through giving the Shadow equal time, that we eventually extend our identity, and thus our responsibility, to all aspects of the psyche, and not just to the impoverished persona. In this fashion, the split between the persona and Shadow is "wholed and healed," and in this fashion I spontaneously evolve an accurate and therefore acceptable unitary self-image, that is to say, an accurate mental representation of my entire psychosomatic organism. Thus is my psyche integrated; thus do I descend from the Level of Shadow to that of Ego.[18]

Now most "psychotherapies" that have developed in the West are primarily aimed at descending to and working with the Ego Level—in one way or another, they are dealing with the quaternary dualism-repression-projection, with so-called intra-psychic conflict: integrating the Shadow, however the Shadow may be conceived. We suggest, in our simplistic fashion, that despite their many real differences in form, style, and content, and despite their various differences in apparent effectiveness, they are all essentially dealing with this fourth major dualism in an attempt to "make conscious the unconscious," "to strengthen the ego," to develop an accurate self-image, and so on. Certain aspects of Gestalt therapy, psychoanalytic ego psychology, reality therapy, rational therapy, transactional analysis, psychodrama, the plethora of ego psychologies—to name a few—would all have us confront the Shadow, eventually re-own it, and thus see what we would not see before: in the old enemy, a friend.

REFERENCES AND NOTES

1. Personal Communication.

2. Frederick S. Perls, *Gestalt Therapy Verbatim* (Lafayette: Real People Press, 1969), p. 99.

3. Ibid., pp. 67, 100.

4. Snell Putney, and Gail J. Putney, *The Adjusted American: Normal Neuroses in the Individual and Society* (New York: Harper Colophon, 1966), p. 163.

5. *Tao Te Ching*, Chapter 2.

6. Lin Yutang, ed., *The Wisdom of China and India* (New York: Modern Library), p. 686.

7. From *Bird Under Glass*.

8. Nicholas Berdyaev, *Freedom and the Spirit* (London), p. 182.

9. Alan W. Watts, *The Two Hands of God* (Collier Books, 1969), p. 17.

10. Frederick Perls, Ralph F. Hefferline, and Paul Goodman, *Gestalt Therapy* (New York: Dell, 1951), p. 190.

11. Putney and Putney, *Adjusted American*, p. 50.

12. Carl Jung, *Modern Man in Search of a Soul* (London), pp. 271-272.

13. Perls, Hefferline and Goodman, *Gestalt Therapy*, p. 211.

14. R. D. Laing, *The Politics of Experience* (New York: Ballantine Books, 1967), p. 35.

15. Perls, *Gestalt Therapy Verbatim*, p. 107.

16. Ibid., p. 65.

17. Ibid., p. 178.

18. In this chapter I have not distinguished between retroflection and projection, nor have I included a discussion of the tripartite structure of the Ego Level and its relation to the Shadow Level. I have dealt with these topics in detail elsewhere. *See* "A Working Synthesis of Transactional Analysis and Gestalt Therapy," *Psychotherapy: Theory, Research, and Practice* (In press). *See* also note V. 52.

VIII. *THE GREAT FILTER*

Almost as soon as Freud began to establish a circle of followers and fellow researchers around him, he began to run into doctrinal difficulties with them, so much so that these difficulties ultimately led to many of his disciplines simply leaving the Master, starting with Adler and ending with Jung. The reasons for these mutinies were numerous, but an outstanding concern—one that is very much alive today—revolved around the emphasis that should be placed upon social conditioning in the forming of an individual's personality, as opposed to Freud's purely biological forces. Starting with Alfred Adler and Otto Rank, and continuing with H. S. Sullivan, Karen Horney, and Eric Fromm, therapists increasingly began to give more and more attention to the sociological factors that seemed to be present in the molding of the human personality. Adler, for instance, felt that an individual could best be understood in terms of his life goals in society rather then his (Freudian) infantile past, while Rank emphasized social relationships in the etiology of emotional distress. Sullivan went even further with his "interpersonal therapy," claiming that the process of becoming human is the process of becoming socialized, and Fromm has detailed the vast interrelationships between psychic make-up and social structure. Furthermore, there has been a recent expansion of interest in the fields of social phenomenology, family therapy, interpersonal and transactional analysis, and other related areas, all of which invariably point to an increasing concern with what we have called the Biosocial Band of the spectrum of consciousness.

We propose now to briefly explore some of the insights reported by these researchers on this Band of the spectrum. Since we are at this point concerned with "therapies," we will dwell on "what can go wrong" on the Biosocial Band, but this should in no way be misinterpreted as a Rousseauistic indictment of this Band—the existence of virtually every civilization, culture, society, and individual depends intimately and directly upon it, a fact that needs no further comment. It is not the existence of the Biosocial Band that we must explore, but rather its misuse.

Now the Biosocial Band lies, so to speak, right above the Existential Level, or we might say that it represents the upper limits of the Existential Level. As such, the dualisms most prominent on this Band are those of life vs. death (or past vs. future) and self vs.

225

other (or organism vs. environment). Man thus feels himself to be a fundamentally separate organism existing in space and enduring in time. Investigators of the Biosocial Band are therefore concerned with those factors, some biological, most sociological, that mold this basic existential awareness, as well as those factors that influence the interaction or transaction between self and other, between two or more people, between a person and his environment. On the Ego Level we are concerned with "I"; on the Biosocial Band we are concerned with "I and you."

This is obviously an area we can ill-afford to overlook, for the way in which an individual experiences reality and subsequently *himself* is profoundly influenced by sociological factors—by language structure, by social value systems, by the implicit and unconscious rules of communication, to name but a few—influenced, in short, by the *maps* that he is given by society to translate and transform reality. Now what an individual personally does with these maps is a phenomenon of the Ego Level, but the general matter of the maps themselves is clearly a phenomenon of the Biosocial Band.

There are a rather immense number of these symbolic maps constituting the Biosocial Band, for it is the home of such all-pervading social conventions as a culture's peculiar language structure and syntax, its logic, its laws, and its popular ethics; its basic religious outlook, its family structure, and its powerful taboos; its goals, rules of communication, game plans, and common sense assumptions about reality; its ideas of meaning, value, self-worth, and prestige—in short, all of those symbolic relationships that distinguish a particular society, and all of which any individual more-or-less internalizes by virtue of his membership in that society. Thus does the Biosocial Band mark the first really massive accumulation of symbols in man's awareness.

Different as they may be, all of these deeply-rooted symbolic maps basically serve the same purpose, namely, to mold an individual's prior awareness into conventional forms acceptable and meaningful to his society. In ways we are just starting to realize, these conceptions mold his perceptions! He learns, in effect, to edit and translate reality into the social terms held in common with others. Obviously an individual must learn to transform his experience into socially meaningful units if he is to at all communicate with those around him. This, in fact, is the meaning of "membership" in a society (or culture, or sub-culture, or group, or family), for a person becomes a member of his society when he has successfully internalized the maps, or the sets of symbolic relations, constituting that society. To put it simply, a person is in society when society is "in" him.

At this band of the spectrum, then, we are primarily concerned with what could be called the socialization of existential or centaur awareness—that is to say, the operating on experience and reality via symbolic maps so as to transform them into socially recognized forms. In a word, this means learning to see and respond to the world as we believe others believe we should!

This conventionalization of reality seems to entail, among numerous other things, learning to make a socially verifiable one-to-one correspondence between the symbol and what is symbolized, between the world and our description of it. On the simplest level, for example, we must learn to associate particular "objects" with the correct conventional words that society uses to represent those objects. Thus, for instance, when I ask for "a glass of water," you understand that I am requesting a vessel full of that clear, tasteless, odorless liquid we have all implicitly agreed to represent with the vocal sound "wôt ´-er." Through this and other similar language games we eventually learn an astoundingly immense number of associations which allow us to perceive and act on the world in a common and mutually understood fashion. After all, you and I are just not going to get along very well if I ask for a glass of water and you bring me a pound of sugar.

Now through this process of association we learn to take a basically *meaningless* vibration or set of vibrations, such as the vocal vibration "wôt ´-er," and socially *give it a meaning*. For the sound "wôt ´-er" itself carries no real meaning—it points to nothing beyond itself, and inherently it signifies nothing in particular. Plainly, it is just a noise, a sound vibration which, taken by itself, is as meaningless as "thorgle," "whiplittle," or "hinderthrumptie." If you are not totally clear about this, then repeat the word "water" quickly for thirty seconds, whereupon you will strip it of all associations and hence reduce it to its inherently meaningless vibrations. Yet we *give* this neutral vibration "wôt ´-er" a "meaning" by *agreeing* to have it represent the "real" water.

But notice also that, as far as we are concerned, the "real" water itself is likewise just another type of meaningless vibration or group of vibrations. These vibrations we variously call "wet," or "clear," or "cool," or some such, but *in themselves* these vibrations are meaningless—they point to nothing, signify nothing, mean nothing, save perhaps themselves. And so it turns out that the "real" water itself is just as meaningless as the sound "wôt ´-er". Thus, in assigning meaning to the sound "wôt ´-er", we are in effect implicitly agreeing to have one meaningless vibration point to another meaningless vibration! At this simple level, then, the very act of *pointing* establishes meaning. In other words, we transform a meaningless vibration into a meaningful sign by making a so-

cially verifiable one-to-one correspondence between one experienced vibration and another. Or, if we may state it in yet
another way, one vibration gains meaning when we conventionally agree to have it *point beyond itself* to another vibration.

Now the vibration which *points* is generally called a *symbol*, and
the vibration which is pointed to, its *meaning*. Thus, if I ask you
what the meaning of the symbol "tree" is, you will run me outdoors
and simply point to one, explaining that there is the object we have
all agreed to call a "tree". And so it is through this type of association process, carried out to infinitely complex and deviously intri-
cate levels, that our experience and our reality eventually become
socialized and symbolized.

Now notice more carefully just what this process of symbolization entails. As we have just seen, one experienced vibration, such
as the sound "wôt ´-er", takes on meaning *only* as we agree to have it
point beyond itself to another experienced vibration—namely, the
"real thing", such as the water itself. Yet, as far as we are aware,
both of these vibrations are *equally complete experiences,* so that
what is actually happening in the establishment of meaning is
that the coherence of experience is being broken down into two
fragments, one of which points to the other! In this fashion, the
wholeness of experience is necessarily split, severed, and disjointed. After all, if something is to take on meaning or significance, that is, if it is to *point beyond itself,* then the universe has
necessarily to be split into at least two fragments: one which
points, and one which is pointed to—the pointer vs. the pointee!
And is not this just another example of the way in which the
universe seems to become distinct from, and therefore false to,
itself? To wánt my life to have meaning is to want my experience
and my reality to be profoundly fragmented.

Surely we can now see that the real world has no meaning, it
points to nothing because there is nothing outside of it to which it
can point! The real world is point-less. As Wittgenstein said, "In
the world everything is as it is and happens as it does happen. *In* it
there is no value—and if there were, it would be of no value."
Naturally, this at first sounds rather shocking, for we are used to
associating meaninglessness with unreality or morbidity or absurdity or what not—but this reflects only the temporary panic of
no longer interpreting and evaluating experience in the ways we
were told to. To say the real world is meaning-less, point-less, or
value-less, is not, however, to say that it is moronic, chaotic,
absurd, etc., for these are just more values, more meanings, only
negative in tone. Rather, it is to say that the real world points to
nothing nor can be pointed to, and thus is profoundly beyond

meaning and evaluation, whether positive or negative.

The real world, then, is point-less, value-less. It is an end in itself without purpose or goal, future or result, meaning or value—a dance with no destination other than the present. This is precisely the insight the Buddhists express with the term *tathata,* the world as it is in its "suchness" or "thusness", which Eckhart called "isness," the Taoists called *"tzu jan,"* the Hindu *sahaja,* and Korzybski, more to the point, called the "unspeakable." For the real world, the world of the Tao, because it is Void of concepts, symbols, and maps, is necessarily Void of meaning, value, and significance. For this reason, *tathata* is actually just another name for the Absolute, Sunyata, Mind. But we must remember that in saying Reality is void of concepts, we do not mean that in reality all concepts simply disappear, but only that our concepts and ideas do not mirror reality as we so naively suppose, and hence they do not carry the meaning we imagine them to. We may somewhat clumsily say that the real world is pure, non-dual territory, wherein all events, being mutually interdependent and inseparable, cannot point to anything and hence carry no meaning—or, looking at it from another angle, they point to everything and hence carry no meaning. They exist just as they are in their suchness, their "self-so-ness". They make no reference. Thus we say that the meaning of the word "tree" is the real tree itself, but what in turn is the "meaning" of that real tree? To what does it point? Asked to summarize the entire essence of Buddhism, a Zen Master said nothing but "Ah, This!"

At the same time, our ideas and concepts are equally aspects of this non-dual territory, for in their suchness they likewise inherently signify nothing. They happen in the mind just as clouds happen in the sky. And so isn't it odd that we force some aspects of nature, those which we call "ideas", to represent other aspects, such as "things and events"? This is actually very much like having the flower represent the mountain, or saying the meaning of the fish is the rabbit. As a matter of fact, an excellent, if not conclusive, argument can be made to the effect that this manufacturing of meaning and value is the sole source of all fundamental problems, logical as well as psychological. As Shakespeare put it, nothing is good or bad, but thinking makes it so. In the words of Seng-tsan, "The concern between right and wrong is the sickness of the mind." There is no Problem of Life because there is fundamentally nothing *wrong*.

At any rate, we can establish meaning in the pure suchness of the territory only by fragmenting it, for to have meaning is to point, and to point is to split, to dichotomize—and that is precisely what symbolization does! A map, plainly enough, is constructed by drawing a boundary.

Now that is the essential nature and function of all of these social maps—to establish meaning, pointers, and values by dichotomizing existence. A map, after all, is something which *points* to something else, and which has meaning only by virtue of that power to indicate and to point. Realize at once, however, that this dichotomization is not only between signifier and signified, but also between agent and action, cause and effect, before and after, good and evil, true and false, inside and outside, opposites and contraries and contrasts in general—and these in turn are inseparably bound up with our language, logic, taboos, and other social maps.

This implies, then, that meaning, symbols, and maps in general are all of a piece with the illusion that the world is broken. And so, through the internalization of these various social maps, we are eventually persuaded that the real world actually exists as a collection of disjointed fragments, some of which have meaning because they point to others! But the world seems to be this fractured affair only because those are now the terms in which we perceive it. We approach it by slicing it to bits and then hastily conclude that this is the way it has existed all along. In a very real sense, our social conceptions have become individual perceptions.

At this stage of the social game we have thoroughly overstepped the usefulness of the map by almost totally confusing it with the actual territory. Our maps are fictions, possessing as much or as little, reality as the dividing of the earth into lines of latitude and longitude or the splitting of the day into units of hours and minutes. Yet social fictions die hard. Useful as they are, untold confusion results when they are mistaken for facts. In 1752 the British government rearranged the standard calendar by changing September 2 to September 14, with the result that Westminster was stormed by people who were absolutely horrified that eleven days had just been taken off their lives! So also, every year in America, when certain localities go off daylight savings time, an unbelievable number of "little ole' ladies" rush City Hall, outraged in their belief that their begonias have actually lost an hour of sunlight.

These fictions are perhaps easy enough to see through, but many others, such as the separation of life and death and the existence of an objective world "out there", are much more difficult to penetrate. The reason is that we have been thoroughly brainwashed, by well-intentioned but equally brainwashed parents and peers, into mistaking a description of the world for the world as it is in its suchness, its voidness. Is this not the entire essence of the teachings of the sorcerer Don Juan? As Castenada tells it,

For a sorcerer, reality, or the world we all know, is only a description.

For the sake of validating this premise don Juan concentrated the best of his efforts into leading me to a genuine conviction that what I held in mind as the world at hand was merely a description of the world; a description that had been pounded into me from the moment I was born.

He pointed out that everyone who comes into contact with a child is a teacher who incessantly describes the world to him, until the moment when the child is capable of perceiving the world as it is described. According to don Juan, we have no memory of that portentous moment, simply because none of us could possibly have had any point of reference to compare it to anything else. . . .

For don Juan, then, the reality of our day-to-day life consists of an endless flow of perceptual interpretations which we, the individuals who share a specific *membership,* have learned to make in common.[1]

Once we have accepted the social description of the world as reality itself, it is only with the very greatest of difficulty that we can perceive any other aspects of reality. Our eyes become glued to our maps without us realizing what in fact has happened. Thus, as we have already indicated, all of these social maps basically serve to mold an individual's awareness into conventional units meaningful to that society, and, disastrously enough, all of those aspects of experience and reality which do not conform to this pervasive social mold are simply screened out of consciousness. That is to say, they are repressed—they are rendered unconscious—and this occurs not to such and such an individual but to *all* members of a particular society by virtue of their common subscription to that society's pictures of the world—its language, logic, ethics, and law.

And so it comes about that, despite its numerous other functions, the Biosocial Band acts, in Fromm's words, as a major *filter* of reality, a prime repressor of existential or centaur awareness. As anthropologist Edward Hall explains it, "Selective screening of sensory data admits some things while filtering others, so that experience as it is perceived through one set of culturally patterned sensory screens is quite different from the experience perceived through another."[2] Even more revealing, however, is psychoanalyst Laing's comment that "If our wishes, feelings, desires, hopes, fears, perception, imagination, memory, dreams . . . do not correspond to the law, they are outlawed, and excommunicated."[3]

However outlawed and excommunicated, these experiences do not simply disappear. Rather, they go underground, where they form, so to speak, the contents of this, the biosocial unconscious. It is not surprising, then, that Lévi-Strauss has defined "the" unconscious as the locus of the symbolic function, and Jacques Lacan maintains that it is "structured like a language." Consider, among other things, that only in language can one say "no", and "no", as Freud saw, is a form of repression. At any rate, our social maps, words, and symbols are almost universally dualistic, and—as in all cases—dualism means unconsciousness.

In a most general fashion we can therefore say that the biosocial unconscious represents that vast gap between the territory of existential awareness and the abstract maps-and-meanings that we so innocently believe to "report" it. Listen to Fromm on the "contents" of the unconscious, but bear in mind that what he says here we must emphatically take as representative of *only* the Biosocial Band—for, as we have seen, there are levels of the unconscious:

> The individual cannot permit himself to be aware of thoughts or feelings which are incompatible with the patterns of his culture, and hence is forced to repress them. *Formally* speaking, then, what is unconscious and what is conscious depends (aside from the individual, family-conditioned elements and the influence of humanistic conscience) on the structure of society and on the patterns of feeling and thoughts it produces. As to the *contents of the* [biosocial] *unconscious,* no generalization is possible. But one statement can be made: it always represents the whole man, with all his potentialities for darkness and light; it always contains the basis for the different answers which man is capable of giving to the question which existence poses. . . . The [biosocial] unconscious is the whole man—minus that part of man which corresponds to his society.[4]

Remember that with the rise of the Existential Level, that is, with the appearance of the Primary and Secondary Dualisms, man's fundamental identity shifts from the cosmos to his organism, so that man basically feels himself to be a separate self extended in space and enduring in time. He is still, however, more or less in touch with the whole organism, the centaur, even if he suffers the illusion that the centaur is divorced from its environment. With the rise of the Biosocial Band, however, the centaur is slowly buried under the weight of a host of social fictions.

Consider, as only one example, the seminal insight of Jacques Lacan that the infant's learning of language condemns him to the perpetual inability to express, and in most cases satisfy, the "biological needs" of his total organism. In the words of Lacan's most distinguished American interpreter, Anthony Wilden:

> Demand *re*-presents needs that are originally biological but

that the child cannot satisfy alone. Because the child must respond to the desire of the Other that he learn to speak . . . these needs eventually will be translated into words. Words transform a biological relationship into a human one—but the inadequacy of language either to represent the I who speaks or to define relationships leads to the paradox of an unconscious desire that is known (analogically), but that cannot be expressed (in digital forms).

The child's first appeal to the Other is by crying. A particular Other will satisfy a need, such as hunger, but cannot satisfy the demand. For what is the message that crying translates? Even though we all know what it is, *it is impossible to say*. But it is always possible to say something—this something is a metaphor for the inexpressible desire created by the inability of language to express all that has to be said. . . . Speech or discourse thus flows in chain upon metonymic chain of connected words in an impossible attempt to fill up the hole in being created by language itself.[5]

Furthermore, we must recognize at once that this socialization of awareness outlaws not only much of the centaur but also many of those aspects of reality that have thus far managed, as it were, to survive the Primary and Secondary Dualisms. Language, for example, filters the "external world" as much as it does the centaur. Thus an obvious result of this filtering is a tremendous reinforcement of the Primary and Secondary Dualisms. After the rise of these two major dualisms, the world seems "external", or "out there"—the organism appears fundamentally alone in time and space. Technically, we say that non-dual organismic awareness, which recognizes neither space nor time, is transformed by the Primary and Secondary Dualisms into existential awareness, into centaur awareness, which has been classically defined by Tillich as man's awareness of his "predicament in space and time". The important point, however, is that under the filter of the Biosocial Band, even this existential awareness, this centaur awareness, is slowly suffocated. Now that means nothing more than that social factors profoundly mold an individual's sense of basic existence. And as existential awareness becomes socialized and symbolized, this necessarily reinforces the Primary and Secondary Dualisms—for all social maps basically subscribe to the primary dualism of inside vs. outside and the secondary dualism of before vs. after. In short, the Primary and Secondary Dualisms are sealed as the centaur is buried under social shams. Finally—under the burden of these social fictions and still in flight from death—the centaur surrenders the ghost, called "ego", and man kisses his poor brother ass good-bye. For at this momentous point, the centaur is no longer simply obscured, it is totally entombed; and man, of course, imagines the angel-beast to be split: the tertiary dualism establishes a seemingly unbridgeable hiatus between the soul and the soma.

The import of what has been said thus far is that out of suchness or voidness we manufacture meanings and engineer complex games by agreeing to divy up nature's chips and set a price on them, and then we collectively confuse this social contract with the real world itself. Those experiences that do not play the game nor follow the law are now simply outlawed. This measuring out of nature and this choosing of sides both begin, of course, on the Existential Level with the Primary and Secondary Dualisms, but this whole process is sealed, vastly extended, and even compounded to result in this, the biosocial unconscious.

Now it is quite beyond the scope of this chapter to detail all the intricacies of the biosocial unconscious. For one thing, they are simply too numerous and too complex. Rather, we have approached this phenomenon from a very basic angle: the Biosocial Band, as a matrix of social distinctions or social maps, necessarily screens and filters certain aspects of awareness, for the obvious reason that the whole organism is much richer in experience than any social abstraction or definition of it, and those aspects of awareness not embraced in the social maps form the "contents" of the biosocial unconscious. In other words, it is not this map or that map which causes the problem, but the very nature of social maps themselves. Maps mean dualism, and dualism means unconsciousness.

Yet notice immediately another consequence of the inherently dualistic nature of our social maps. These maps, just because they are dualistic, always mold awareness, but frequently do so in *contradictory* directions, so that pressed into action they necessarily have contradictory results. To put it crudely, in manufacturing dualistic meaning out of non-dual suchness, something has to back-fire. A dualistic map of a non-dual territory just has to be booby-trapped. The implication of this, which we must now briefly explore, is that dualism means not only unconsciousness, but also double-binding. As a result, we end up saddled with paradoxical or self-contradictory social maps and meanings, ones that *implicitly* point in *two* contrary directions. The effect is, to say the least, dramatic. It is a funny situation, but unfortunately the joke is on us all.

To follow this effect, let us begin by repeating that the Biosocial Band is fundamentally a vast network or matrix of conventional distinctions; that our symbols, our maps, our root ideas and our social meanings all share a common feature: *they govern the manner in which we divide and delineate reality*. Now the relation between this matrix of distinctions and a person's behavior can be easily seen, *for a division or distinction in action is a rule,*[6] and a rule in turn governs subsequent action. For example, if we imagine the "mind" to be separate or completely distinct from the "body", then this distinction will lead to the rule that we can ignore the body when studying the mind, and our subsequent action guided by this rule will be to study only the mind. Thus the distinction (mind vs. body), when acted upon, leads to a rule (ignore the body) which itself leads to further action (study only the mind). Stated simply, a distinction in action is a rule which governs subsequent action. Thus the Biosocial Band is the most basic, profound, and pervasive mold of not only man's awareness but also his behavior, because *as a person divides Reality, so he acts.*

In this fashion, the Biosocial Band determines how we operate on our experience in order to socialize it, conventionalize it, clothe it in units of meaning, symbolize it, evaluate it, screen it, delineate it, divide it, punctuate it—and further, through the rules implicit in those distinctions, it governs the direction of our subsequent action. In short, the Biosocial Band is a matrix of distinctions embodying rules which in turn govern behavior.

Let us now take this one step further. Activity governed by a specific set of rules is a *game.* This is not to imply that all of our activities are just trivial and frivolous; rather, the word is used with its widest possible connotation: our social activities are games in the sense that they depend upon rules which in turn always rest upon certain distinctions. Draw a distinction between the all-saving God and the all-sinful man, and this will lead to a rule that man can be saved only by getting in touch with God—this is the Religion Game. Draw a distinction between valuable success and humiliating failure, and this will lead to a rule that to be valuable one must avoid failure—this is the Competition Game. In a word, *distinctions lead to rules which in turn form games.*

The point of all this will be glaringly obvious if we now ask a simple question: what happens if we draw inappropriate distinctions? Straightforwardly, an inappropriate distinction can lead to contradictory or paradoxical rules which in turn can lead to self-defeating and self-frustrating games. And a society built on such self-defeating games is an ideal breeding ground for neuroses and psychoses. That is, the distinctions, rules, and games of a society can themselves be concealed contradictions and paradoxes, so that trying to act upon them places the double-bind on us all, for this type of game has rules that insure that we will never win the game! As a few examples:

> Society, as we now have it, pulls this trick on every child from earliest infancy. In the first place, the child is taught that

he . . . is a free agent, an independent origin of thoughts and actions—a sort of miniature First Cause. He accepts this make-believe for the very reason that it is not true. He can't help accepting membership in the community where he was born. He has no way of resisting this kind of social indoctrination. It is constantly reinforced with rewards and punishments. It is built into the basic structure of the language he is learning. It is rubbed in repeatedly with such remarks as, "It isn't like you to do a thing like that." Or, "Don't be a copy-cat; be yourself!" Or, when one child imitates the mannerisms of another child whom he admires, "Johnny, that's not you. That's Peter!" The innocent victim of this indoctrination cannot understand the paradox. He is being told that he *must* be free. An irresistable pressure is being put on him to make him believe that no such pressure exists. The community of which he is necessarily a dependent member defines him as an independent member.

In the second place, he is thereupon commanded, as a free agent, to do things which will be acceptable only if done voluntarily! "You really *ought* to love us," say parents, aunts, uncles, brothers, sisters. "All nice children love their families, and do things for them without having to be asked." In other words, "We demand that you love us because you want to, and not because we say you ought to." . . . Society as we know it is therefore playing a game with self-contradictory rules . . . with the result that children raised in such an environment are almost permanently confused.[7]

A "game with self-contradictory rules" is another name for the double-bind, and as we have seen, the double-bind is the prototypical situation for generating mental confusion. But the double-binds with which we are now concerned are not so much those imposed on one person by another, but those built into the very foundations of some of our social institutions and therefore imposed on us all! If this be true, the dismal conclusion is that, in this sense at least, society as we know it is mad. "Thus," states Watts, "it is hard to avoid the conclusion that we are accepting a definition of sanity which is insane."[8] Neitzsche put it simply: "Insanity in individuals is something rare—but in groups, parties, nations, and epochs, it is the rule."[9] Even H. S. Sullivan used to tell his psychiatric students, "I want you to remember that in the present state of our society, the patient is right and you are wrong."[10] And it has been stated most violently, yet eloquently, by the psychoanalyst Laing:

Long before a thermonuclear war can come about, we have had to lay waste our own sanity. We begin with the children. It is imperative to catch them in time. Without the most

thorough and rapid brainwashing their dirty minds would see
through our dirty tricks. Children are not yet fools, but we
shall turn them into imbeciles like ourselves, with high I.Q.'s
if possible.

From the moment of birth, when the Stone Age baby confronts the twentieth century mother, the baby is subjected to
these forces of violence, called love, as its mother and father,
and their parents and their parents before them, have been.
These forces are mainly concerned with destroying most of its
potentialities, and on the whole this enterprise is successful.
By the time the new human being is fifteen or so, we are left
with a being like ourselves, a half-crazed creature more or less
adjusted to a mad world. This is normality in our present
age. . . .

The condition of alienation, of being asleep, of being unconscious, of being out of one's mind, is the condition of the
normal man.

Society highly values its normal man. It educates children
to lose themselves and to become absurd, and thus to be normal.

Normal men have killed perhaps 100,000,000 of their fellow
normal men in the last fifty years.[11]

Normal men, of course, have good reasons for their behavior—
normal men always have good reasons for their behavior. We are
taking the only *realistic* approach possible, or so we huddle together to reassure ourselves. Perhaps the only answer possible to
this is in the words of Schroedinger: "Reality? A strange reality.
Something seems to be missing."

The point, however, is not that there exist certain "insane"
individuals parading as normal persons. On the contrary, the
problem on this level, this Biosocial Band, concerns not individual
egos but the very social institutions that underlie all egos. As the
Putney's expressed it in the preface to their work on this subject:
"This is not a book about *them* (whose foibles we can view with
detachment or even a certain relish); it is a book about *us*—the
normal, the adjusted of our society. Its basic concern is with certain neuroses which are normal. . . ."[12] In short, the bricks in the
walls of our egos are cemented together with the mortar of madness, and it is this universal mortar, not the particular walls, that
we must examine.

As an example of a socially universal game with self-contradictory rules, take the following: if we make a hard and fast
distinction between the organism and the environment—which
our society most unmistakably does—this will lead to a rule that
one may ignore the environment in search of personal success.
This is the basis of the Top-Dog Game, the unending attempt to be

King of the Mountain, to be one-up on all other organisms, and it is a game inculcated in children from a very early age. Jules Henry, anthropologist and sociologist, clearly describes the numerous self-contradictions of this cultural game, beginning with a case in point, an example taken from elementary education:

> Boris had trouble reducing $^{12}/_{16}$ to the lowest terms, and could only get as far as $^6/_8$. The teacher asked him quietly if that was as far as he could reduce it. She suggested he "think." Much heaving up and down and waving of hands by the other children, all frantic to correct him. Boris pretty unhappy, probably mentally paralyzed. The teacher quiet, patient, ignores the others and concentrates with look and voice on Boris. After a minute or two she turns to the class and says, "Well, who can tell Boris what the number is?" A forest of hands appears, and the teacher calls Peggy. Peggy says that four may be divided into the numerator and denominator.[13]

Henry comments on this in brutally honest terms:

> Boris's failure made it possible for Peggy to succeed; his misery is the occasion for her rejoicing. This is a standard condition of the contemporary American elementary school. To a Zuni, Hopi, or Dakota Indian, Peggy's performance would seem cruel beyond belief, for competition, the wringing of success from somebody's failure, is a form of torture foreign to those noncompetitive cultures.[14]

Some of the self-contradictions of this game now become obvious:

> Looked at from Boris's point of view, the nightmare at the blackboard was, perhaps, a lesson in controlling himself so that he would not fly shrieking from the room under enormous public pressure. Such experiences force every man reared in our culture, over and over again, night in, night out, even at the pinnacle of success, to dream not of success, but of failure. In school the external nightmare is internalized for life. Boris was not learning arithmetic only; he was learning the essential nightmare also. *To be successful in our culture one must learn to dream of failure. . . .*
>
>   In a society where competition for the basic cultural goods is a pivot of action, people cannot be taught to love one another. It thus becomes necessary for the school to teach children how to hate, *and without appearing to do so,* for our culture cannot tolerate the idea that babes should hate each other. How does the school accomplish this ambiguity?[15]

Ambiguity is right! It is a whopping self-contradiction, for, as someone once remarked, nothing fails like success. To try to get one-up on the environment is ultimately to try to get one-up on one's own self as well, since self and environment are actually one process. And *that* is as impossible as trying to lift oneself off the ground by pulling up on one's ankles. We are duped into playing this game without being told that we can never win it—so if we play the game, we lose, and if we stop playing, we lose. Damned-if-we-do and damned-if-we-don't, and that is the double-bind, the game with self-contradictory rules.

Placed in such a situation we naturally are bamboozled, because we assume that the fault must lay in our own inept actions. We go over and over and over the problem with no apparent success, but not because we are too dumb to arrive at the answer, but because there is no answer. The problem, as Wittgenstein would say, is nonsensical, and we drive ourselves to the depths of neuroses and occasionally psychoses in search of the non-existent answer.

Not realizing the problem is nonsensical, however, we are in the position of the poor drunk, who, leaving his favorite bar and heading towards home, collides head-on with a lamp post. Staggering back several paces, he looks around, tries to re-adjust his course, and proceeds to smack into the lamp post once more, this time with such force that it knocks him flat. Resolutely, he picks himself up and charges forward again, only to repeat the collision. Defeated, he cries out, "Oh, it's no use. I'm fenced in." There is no physical barrier, no actual basis to our problem—the difficulty lies in the tangle of our thoughts, not in reality.

But instead of making these rules open and explicit, parents and grandparents, siblings and cousins, aunts and uncles keep them concealed, implicit, unconscious, because they in turn have also been so duped. Consequently, the "internalized society" of the Biosocial Band contains many concealed rules, messages, and meta-messages that are paradoxical and self-contradictory, aside from those that are useful or unuseful. That is, there are numerous double-binds built into the very fabric of the Biosocial Band, and these can—and almost universally do—result in varying degrees of mental confusion, neuroses, and psychoses.

It is important to remember that these double-binds are placed on us all by simple virtue of our membership in society. They are intimately derivative of the very morphology and syntax of our language, law, logic, and ethics: the grammatical convention that separates nature into nouns vs. verbs and subjects vs. objects; the commonsense logic that refuses to relinquish the Law of the Excluded Middle and therefore refuses to see the *coincidentia oppositorum;* the popular ethic to "do good always and avoid evil," which amounts to driving through a city trying to "turn left always and avoid right." They are built into our roles, our status, our value systems, our popular philosophical paradigms: living for a future that does not exist, so that in living for tomorrow we will never be able to enjoy it; identifying with a purely abstract and superficial role, so that the more "identity" we have the more we shall actually feel lost; seeking success by fearing failure, so that the more success we gain the more we fear failure—in short, all the games that fail if they work and which we lose if we win.

The point is that not only can social communications between individuals on the Ego Level contain double-binds, but also the very rules of communication in general can themselves be contradictory, paradoxical, and hence generative of double-binds. Thus we might say that the particular double-binds that generate intense problems and projections on the Ego Level are just nodes in the disturbed Biosocial Band where the self-contradictions are most intense, or that acute emotional disturbances result in places where the double-binds imposed by society in general are greatly compounded or intensified by particular double-binds imposed in certain family or educational situations. At any rate, the Biosocial Band is itself the source of numerous emotional-intellectual difficulties, of our "normal neuroses," of our collective insanity, and it is to this level that communications psychiatrists, family therapists, social phenomenologists, and others of their genre are addressing themselves.

The difficulty, although it certainly involves games with self-contradictory rules, actually goes somewhat deeper than the games and rules themselves, for as we have suggested, a self-contradictory rule in turn rests on the drawing of inappropriate distinctions. Our conventional distinctions and divisions of Reality, carried out by language, logic, and symbolic maps, do not report Reality, *they edit it,* and here is the crux of the problem.[16]

For example, since our action *is* an action of the universe, it is meaningless to try to act *on* the universe—we just aren't in a position outside of it to be able to do this. But when we edit reality by severing our action from the environment's action, we get the convenient illusion that we can act apart from our surroundings. This inappropriate distinction leads to the self-contradictory rules of the Top-Dog Game and its various derivatives.

We fall for this nonsense only because we are hypnotized by our symbolic knowledge. We say a meteor crashes into the moon, but it is equally true that the moon crashes into the meteor; or we say a train moves across the ground, but it is equally true that the ground moves under the train. There is but one action here, yet if we try to make a single statement about it, the statement might seem self-contradictory because we are trying to incorporate two opposite viewpoints at once, and this is something our language and logic are just not prepared to do.

Yet just because Reality is non-dual, the coincidence of opposites, then the inappropriate distinctions and dualisms that we make invariably lead to rules that generate actions with contradictory results, for the banished opposite must paradoxically return. For instance, we sever life from death, an inappropriate distinction that leads to the self-contradictory rule that we *must* go on living, that we must fight tooth and nail to eradicate death. But since life and death are actually one, to win this game is to lose our life, so if we succeed we fail. It's very much like one doorway: it can simultaneously serve as both an entrance and an exit, so that if we block the exit we also block the entrance. In escaping death it kills us.

Thus it is these types of inappropriate distinctions which underlie the self-contradictory rules and self-defeating games of many of our social institutions, and these in turn are the fuel for the fires of our collective insanity. We have, throughout this text, pointed out four major inappropriate distinctions, and numerous corollary ones, but again it must be emphasized that an inappropriate distinction is *any* distinction we take to be ultimately real. It is fine to make distinctions, dualities, and divisions, provided we know and feel the reality that we are dividing. Problem is, we do not—and consequently our distinctions become inappropriate, leading ultimately to double-binds and all that they entail: *maya* becomes madness.

Hopefully it will be obvious that we are all the more prone to take our distinctions to be ultimately real if we don't realize that it is *we* who make them, that—in the words of Sullivan, referring to the inappropriate distinction of space vs. time—"Nature, it appears, knows nothing of the distinction we make between space and time. The distinction we make is, ultimately, a psychological peculiarity of ours." We would only add that nature knows nothing of *any* distinction that we make, and consequently our distinctions screen and obscure it in ways of which we are only vaguely aware. That is, these distinctions, these primordial maps, are usually implicit, unnoticed, concealed, and unconscious, which is only to say that many of our maps are not realized as maps, and so we erroneously assume that we are dealing with the territory itself. Because these primitive maps, these distinctions, are unconscious, we almost invariably commit the Fallacy of Misplaced Concreteness without realizing it. In short, we are unconscious of Reality because we are unconscious of the ways in which we obscure Reality. We divide reality, forget we have divided it, and then forget that we have forgotten it.

In sum, our social maps, in establishing meaning, dichotomize existence and hence screen or filter awareness, a process which results, at this level, in the biosocial unconscious. Further, because the territory these dualistic maps represent is actually non-dual, in many cases their so-called "meanings" are really meaningless or self-contradictory or paradoxical, and trying to act under their influence is double-binding. Note also that in most instances these maps themselves are also unconscious, because if we knew that these maps were in fact nothing but maps, we would automatically start looking for the territory itself. But this is precisely what is outlawed! Thus, there are even maps which deny the existence of other maps! Or, taboos against knowing about certain taboos, or laws against knowing about other laws, or, in the words of Laing, rules against seeing the rules—and even rules against the rules against seeing the rules, for "to admit the rules would be to admit what the rules and operations are attempting to render non-existent." And that would be horrible—after all, we might wake up.

Family therapy, communication psychiatry, semantic therapy, some forms of very fundamental inter-personal therapies, social phenomenology, and the like, all in their own ways are striving to make these unconscious maps conscious, so that even if they continue to obscure reality, we at least realize that reality *is* being obscured—and here is the beginning of insight. As Chung Tzu put it, "He who knows he is a great fool, is not such a great fool." In seeing our maps as maps, we are finally in a position to go beyond them to the territory itself, to relinquish the hold these social dreams exercise over us, to see through "the texture of the fabric of these socially shared hallucinations that we call reality."[17] If we do not succeed, then these social fictions will be taken for real, so that "around us are pseudo-events, to which we adjust with a false consciousness adapted to see these events as true and real, and even as beautiful."[18] The result is what one analyst called "an institutionalized nightmare that everyone is having at once," but only because "everyone believes everyone else believes them."

It is therefore to the Biosocial Band that most of these therapies are directed. Although it is not the sole creator of distinctions and dualisms, it is certainly the most pervasive, especially since it is the home of our dualistic language and logic. It is this vast matrix of distinctions which, if taken for real, not only screens awareness, but also leads to self-contradictory rules, self-defeating games, and hence neuroses and psychoses. Thus its importance in behavior cannot be overlooked.

For as a person divides Reality, he so acts.

REFERENCES AND NOTES

1. C. Castaneda, *Journey to Ixtlan* (New York: Simon and Schuster, 1972).

2. Quoted in John White, ed., *The Highest State of Consciousness* (New York: Anchor, 1972).

3. R. D. Laing, *The Politics of the Family* (New York: Pantheon, 1971), p. 74.

4. E. Fromm, D. T. Suzuki, and R. DeMartino, *Zen Buddhism and Psychoanalysis* (New York: Harper and Row, 1970).

5. A. Wilden, *Psychology Today*, vol. 5, no. 2, (May 1972).

6. Cf. Laing, *Politics of the Family*, p. 91, "Rules are themselves distinctions in action."

7. A. W. Watts, *The Book: On the Taboo Against Knowing Who You Are* (New York: Collier, 1970), pp. 65-66.

8. A. Watts, *Psychotherapy East and West* (New York: Ballantine, 1969), p. 53.

9. Quoted in Putney and Putney, *Adjusted American*, p. xi.

10. Cf. Brown, *Love's Body*, p. 159: "It is not schizophrenia but normality that is split-minded; in schizophrenia the false boundaries are disintegrating . . . schizophrenics are suffering from the truth."

11. R. D. Laing, *The Politics of Experience* (New York: Ballantine, 1967), pp. 58, 28.

12. Putney and Putney, *Adjusted American*, 9, p. ix.

13. Jules Henry, *Culture Against Man* (New York: Random House, 1963), p. 27.

14. Ibid., pp. 295-296.

15. Ibid., pp. 293, 296.

16. Thus Bateson came to identify double-binds with contextual breeches.

17. Laing, *Politics of Experience*, p. 73.

18. Ibid., p. 1.

IX. *MAN AS CENTAUR*

Before exploring the Existential Level, let us get our bearings: at the upper limits of this Level is the Biosocial Band, and "above" that lies the levels of the Ego and Shadow; while directly "beneath" the Existential Level are the Transpersonal Bands and the Level of Mind. We must remember that the Primary Dualism of organism vs. environment or self vs. other, and the Secondary Dualism of life vs. death or being vs. non-being—these are the two major dualisms marking this Level, so that here our identity is with our total organism as it exists in space and time. Also, it is significant that the Tertiary Dualism of psyche vs. soma or mind vs. body is not present—at least not prominently—and hence this Level represents our total existential prehension of existence as opposed to our fragmentary ideas-about-existence which compose the Ego Level.

Since, in fact, it is the Tertiary Dualism of mind vs. body that propels us away from the Existential Level towards the Ego Level, it is precisely by healing this split, this tertiary dualism, that we center ourselves in the total organism of mind-body called the Existential Level, just as by healing or whole-ing the quaternary dualism between persona and shadow we descend to the Ego from the Shadow Level. As we have previously explained, this shift to the Existential Level can temporarily be effected by simply resting in a quiet place, chasing away all mental concepts about oneself, and plainly sensing one's basic existence. But to establish one's identity on this Level on a more or less permanent basis *usually* requires some form of existential "therapy," such as hatha yoga, bioenergetic analysis, structural integration, existential psychology, polarity therapy, humanistic psychology, logotherapy, massage therapy—to name a prominent few. Despite their wide divergence of external forms, all of these therapies aim essentially at getting us in touch with the "authentic being" of our total organism by *integrating the tertiary dualism.*

Now because our approach *towards* the Existential Level is usually *from* the Ego Level *through* the tertiary dualism of mind vs. body, these "therapies" generally fall into two broad classes, reflecting the dualism itself: those that proceed primarily through the "mind," such as existential analysis, humanistic therapies, logotherapy, etc.; and those that proceed basically through the "body," such as structural integration, hatha yoga, polarity therapy, and so on. Some approaches, of course, work "from both ends" at once, mind and body, such as bioenergetic analysis and Orgone therapy. But whether proceeding through the mind or the body or both, all alike share a common goal: the integrated organism, the Existential Level, man as Centaur.

Both major approaches—through the mind or through the body—have their special merits, their peculiar advantages and disadvantages. But both alike are based on a principle that is becoming more and more obvious to researchers on this level, a principle that can loosely be stated as follows: *for every mental "problem" or "knot," there is a corresponding bodily "knot," and vice versa*, since, in fact, body and mind are not two.

As an example of a bodily knot and its corresponding mental knot, we may take the following story about John Lilly. As a youth, Lilly had accidentally sunk a chopping ax deep into his foot, a trauma so severe that he had "repressed" the pain of the ax cut—he saw the ax bury into his foot, but felt no pain. His "mind," of course, recorded this incident and its concomitant pain, but it repressed this trauma from his consciousness. Years later, Lilly was undergoing structural integration under Peter Melchior, who instantly noticed the brutal scar on his foot. As he started working toward this scar, deeply massaging and pounding the tissue to loosen the bodily kinks, Lilly began to get visibly anxious and tense. When he finally attacked the scar itself, the whole painful occurrence of the accident flashed into Lilly's mind, and for the first time he actually felt the pain of the original ax cut, a pain that had been buried in his "unconscious" all those years.

> Suddenly I realized that I had blocked the pain in the original experience. This scar had held the potential of that pain ever since. It also had a basic traumatic memory, a tape loop [mental "hang-up"] attached to it. I had favored that foot, favored that region of the foot, and had not completed the hole that was left in my body image here. The Rolfing [structural integration] allowed this hole to fill in. . . . [1]

The point is that *through an attack on the body, a mental knot was loosened*.

As an example of the reverse—of mental knots producing corresponding bodily knots—we need only mention the work of Wilhelm Reich on the character armor and Fritz Perls on retroflection. Essentially, both of these researchers maintained that a person suffering from a neurosis, such as the quaternary dualism, will manipulate, squeeze, and tighten his own bodily musculature as a substitute for what he would really like to do to others. Reich especially felt that neurotics choke off their "nasty" sexual impulses by squeezing and compacting the muscles of the pelvic region, so that after a while true sexual release is next to impossible; while Perls emphasized that alienated aggression is turned onto the body by a general locking of the muscles involved, so that a person who wants to choke someone might retroflect the aggression and stammer instead, or a person who wants to "squeeze the daylights" out of others might instead stiffen and tighten his entire body. Thus, "in the mind", aggression is alienated by repressing and projecting it, but "in the body", aggression is repressed only by *locking all of the muscles opposed to those which would normally discharge that emotion.* The result is stalemate, spasm, blockage—large amounts of energies pulling in equal but opposite directions, with a net movement of zip.

So it slowly becomes obvious that what *in the mind is a war of attitudes, in the body is a war of muscles!* Thus, a person who represses his interest and excitement must, at the same time, repress his bodily breathing: he must lock his chest, stiffen his diaphragm and stomach, and clamp his jaws. Someone who represses his anger must lock all the muscles opposed to those which would strike out at the world: contract and pull in his shoulders, clench his chest, and lock the musculature of his arm. One who wishes to repress crying or screaming must violently tense his eye, neck and throat muscles, as well as restrict breathing and block off all sensations of the gut. In order to repress all sexual impulses, one has to tighten the muscles of the pelvis, lock the lower back muscles, and studiously avoid any awareness of the entire mid-section of the body. In all of these cases, a mental knot has produced a bodily knot, which an attack on the mind can loosen. (Actually, to ask whether mental knots produce bodily knots or whether bodily knots produce mental knots is probably a wrong question—the most we should say is that they arise together, and can be cured by an "attack" through either "end," since mind and body are not two).

Dr. Lilly, who has had extensive experience on the Existential Level, clearly recognizes these two major approaches—through the mind or through the body—for he states:

> Thus I realized that the human biocomputer includes the muscle systems and the way these are held by central nervous system patterns of activity is a function of fixation in childhood. Trauma causes hiding of the causes of the trauma, thus setting up a tape loop in the central nervous system, which goes on perpetually activated until broken into either at the brain end or at the muscle end.[2]

Now to simplify this discussion, any of those approaches, such as hatha yoga, polarity therapy, and structural integration, that aim at healing the tertiary split between mind and body by working primarily through the "body", through the "muscle end", we will call a *somatic-existentialism;* while any of those approaches proceeding basically through the "mind", through the "brain end", such as existential analysis and logotherapy, we will term a *noetic-existentialism*. Theoretically at least, one approach, either somatic or noetic, if carried out completely and conclusively, can result in thorough contact with the Existential Level. Ideally, however, a combination of the two is highly desirable and most efficacious, a point to which we will presently return.

As an example of a typical somatic-existential approach, let us take structural integration or "Rolfing" as it is called after its founder, Dr. Ida Rolf. She writes:

> In any attempt to create an integrated individual, an obvious starting place is his physical body, if for no other reason than to examine the old premise that a man can project only that which is within. To the medical specialist, this body, and this alone, *is* the man. To the psychiatrist, this body is less than the man; it is merely the externalized expression of personality. Neither of these specialists has accepted as real a third possibility; namely, that in some way, as yet poorly defined, *the physical body is actually the personality,* rather than its expression, is the energy unit we call man. . . . [3]

That is to say, the aim of "Rolfing" is to experience the integrated organism wherein the mind *is* the body and the body *is* the mind, which unmistakably refers to the healing of the tertiary dualism. Now many of us will find this somewhat difficult to understand, especially since we are so used to placing our "mind," and consequently our identity, *in our head,* and we feel that our body just sort of dangles along after us. Yet any student of Rolfing, hatha yoga, or massage therapy very soon starts to experience his identity as not being *in* his body but *as* his body, *with* his body, and he has consequently started to dissipate the tertiary dualism and hence to establish himself on the Existential Level. Even Albert Einstein, in all seriousness, claimed that he thought with his muscles!

Rolfing itself is a series of exercises and deep massages designed to reawaken our usually benumbed body so that we can begin to reintegrate it, re-own it, and hence take delight in it, as once we had done as children—before we were taught the tertiary dualism, before we were taught that the body housed animal and disgusting passions, that it should be hidden from our sight by binding and suffocating clothing, that while the "mind" produced noble ideas, the body produced nothing but "brute" force or "foul" excretions, that bodily disease was evil and something to feel ashamed of, and that sooner or later our body would just rot out from under us, eaten up by such unspeakable horrors as cancer. The whole weight of our social indoctrination is aimed at placing as much distance between our "minds" and our "bodies" as possible. But this maneuver inevitably backfires, for as Freud, Blake, and others have so clearly explained, all joy is of the body, of the senses, so that in exiling our bodies we simultaneously exile all possibility of real joy and happiness. To recover this possibility, we must descend from the Ego to the Existential Level, there to awaken the life and energy of the body, for "Energy is eternal delight . . . and is from the Body."

In this respect, what was said of Rolfing is essentially applicable to the other somatic-existential approaches, although naturally the techniques, the outer forms, and the "philosophy" of each varies considerably. Hatha yoga, for instance, has always had as its basic aim the awakening of the body and its uniting with the psyche (which is not to be confused with the "higher" yogas such as *raja* yoga that aim at the Level of Mind). Hatha yoga selects the breath for special attention, since it is most clearly the function where mind and body unite, where conscious mental control and unconscious bodily processes unite—as such, the breath is the royal road to mind-body union. The word "yoga" itself means "union," and hatha yoga is designed specifically to unite mind and body into an integrated psychophysical organism. Hatha yoga is thus the epitome of somatic-existentialism, but at heart it differs not at all from the other therapies aimed at contacting the Existential Level by healing the tertiary split.

With this understanding, let us turn now to some of the aspects of noetic-existential psychology. Notice that, in the first place, noetic-existentialism in general is working with the same level that somatic-existentialism is, but its techniques and philosophy are decidedly different, although—we must emphasize—clearly complementary. Now the number of different noetic-existential approaches is formidable, but they all aim, in their own fashions, to actualize the "authentic being" of the *total organism*, to undercut the tertiary dualism and face one's stark existence, shorn of all egoic ideas, objects of cognition, and intellectual crutches. Jean-Paul Sartre, for instance, who is a brilliant but fanatical noetic-existentialist, persuasively argues that the isolated ego, the solitary "I," is a deceptive fiction we conjure up in order to hide ourselves from the constant flux of our real existence. The Ego Level is therefore viewed, rightly we believe, as an existential hemorrhage, as a major source of "bad faith" obscuring our existence. Further, Sartre has always inveighed against the "type and degree of abstraction and reification employed in various theories, wit-

tingly or unwittingly," because of "the violence done perceptually
and conceptually to the human reality in its concrete fullness."[4]

It is this "concrete full being" not cut asunder and fragmented
into a psyche and a soma that the noetic-existentialists are seeking
to authenticate. The whole approach of conventional psychotherapy, where the human personality is viewed as an isolated
"ego" or even a multiple complex of "egos" must be superceded by a
more encompassing approach if we are to reach, or "descend to,"
the fullness of the Existential Level. In the words of that most
compassionate existential psychologist, Rollo May:

> The concept of the ego, with its capacity for being broken up
> into many discrete egos is tempting for experimental psychol-
> ogy, for it invites the "divide and conquer" method of study
> that we have inherited in our traditional dichotomized scien-
> tific method. . . .
> If it is countered that this picture of the multitude of egos
> reflects the fragmentation of contemporary man, I would re-
> join that any concept of fragmentation presupposes some
> unity *of which* it is a fragmentation. . . . For neither the ego,
> nor the unconscious, nor the body can be autonomous. Au-
> tonomy by its very nature can be located only in the *centered
> self*. . . . Logically as well as psychologically we must go be-
> hind the ego-id-superego system and endeavor to understand
> the "being" of whom these are expressions.[5]

Dr. May maintains that the separate ego and alienated body, as
well as other fragmentations, are—as he puts it— "expressions" of
the total being, or, as we have explained it, *projections* of the total
organism made possible by the tertiary dualism-repression-
projection. And behind these projections, these expressions, these
manifestations, behind this, the Ego Level, lies the Existential
Level, our "centered self," our "total being," the "unity of which"
the psyche and soma represent a fragmentation. Again, it is precisely this "total being" that the noetic-existentialists seek to
actualize. We must leave the Ego Level, tuck away all of our
cherished ideas about existence, come back to our bodies, and *live*.
In the explosive words of the "existentialist" author Fyodor Dostoyevsky:

> But listen to me for a moment. I'm not trying to justify myself
> by saying *all of us*. As for me, all I did was carry to the limit
> what you haven't dared to push even halfway—taking your
> cowardice for reasonableness, thus making yourselves feel
> better. So I may still turn out to be more *alive* than you in the
> end. Come on, have another look at it! Why, today we don't
> even know where real life is, what it is, or what it's called! Left
> alone without literature, we immediately become entangled

and lost—we don't know what to join, what to keep up with; what to love, what to hate; what to respect, what to despise! We even find it painful to be men—real men of flesh and blood, and *our own private bodies;* we're ashamed of it, and we long to turn ourselves into something hypothetical called the average man. We're stillborn, and for a long time we've been brought into the world by parents who are dead themselves: and we like it better and better. We're developing a taste for it, so to speak. Soon we'll invent a way to be begotten by ideas altogether.[6]

And *that* requires no comment.

We are starting to understand that the descent to the Existential Level involves an expansion of identity from the Ego to the Centaur, the total organism. Of course, to those who live their waking lives on the Ego Level, this project seems most enigmatic. For on the Ego Level, one naturally has the tendency either to claim that one is already in complete identity with the body, and so dismiss the entire humanistic movement as much ado about nix, or to claim that such a feat is theoretically sweetness and light, but otherwise a sheer impossibility, since man is mind and that is that. Those who claim the former will frequently retort that they give an immense amount of attention to their bodies (especially when it comes to sex), which only goes to prove they are *not* identified with their bodies but obsessed *by* them. On the other hand, those who claim the later—that man is mind—usually maintain that there's absolutely nothing of interest going on in their bodies, so that centering awareness there is a dull adventure indeed—which shows precisely how much they have totally numbed their sense of existence.

These prejudices are buried so deeply in the philosophic and biosocial unconscious that they tend to incite, even in scholars, nothing but panicked emotions. Worse still, the tertiary dualism is firmly rooted throughout the fields of medicine, education, athletics, and sadly enough, orthodox psychology. Education exercises one's "mind", while athletics exercises one's "body"; psychology heals one's "mind", while medicine heals one's "body". Thus, the antagonism between education and athletics on the one hand, and psychology and medicine on the other hand, is a startling reflection of the divorce between mind and body. This is particularly apalling in the area of psychology and medicine—Freud, after all, was never truly accepted by orthodox medicine, nor is he today, as evidenced in the most disgracefully superficial lip service given to psychosomatic medicine.

And so it is that those sciences, such as biofeedback, somatology, and humanistic psychology that are today trying to pull the two ends of man back together are looked upon by both sides as being probably well-intentioned but basically incompetent. The ingratiating fact is that the repression of the centaur has been, and still is, both thorough and pandemic.

But we are today seeing the outlines of a science of the Existential Level slowly starting to emerge. As Thomas Hanna explains it, "Fundamental to this movement is an understanding that human self-awareness [is] not a vacuous and disembodied 'epiphenomenon,' but [is] a holistic awareness of the self which [is] embodied and always aware of the state of its embodiment. From this viewpoint, self-awareness . . . is the function of experiencing the whole state of one's organic structure. As that organic structure changes, so does our basic self-awareness—and vice versa." Thus, on the Existential Level, man's awareness, his centaur awareness, "is a living, integral part of a somatic, organic whole. . . ; a self-aware, self-controlling organism, an organic unity of many functions which have traditionally been thought of separately as 'bodily' and 'mental'."[7]

In view of all this, let us now return to the descent from the Ego Level to the Existential Level. Recall that in discussing the descent to the Ego Level from the Shadow Level, we saw that this process entailed a progressive expansion of identity that eventually resulted in an accurate self-image, one that included all of the facets of the psyche once thought alien, threatening, and completely beyond control. Now the very same process occurs in the descent to the Existential Level—we again expand our boundaries of identification to include all of the aspects of our total organism that once seemed foreign, threatening, or at least beyond control. We are taking back our bodies, and thus reviving the Centaur.

That, in short, is precisely the aim of noetic-existentialism. As Perls, Hefferline, and Goodman clearly state, "The aim is to extend the boundary of what you accept as yourself to include *all organic activities.*"[8] It is fine to have and live as an accurate mental representation of one's entire psychosomatic organism—but it is much better to actually *be* that total organism. Dr. Perls was therefore even more forceful in stating the aims of existential therapy: "Loose your mind and come to your senses!" That is, come to the centaur. As Dr. Lowen expresses it, "As long as the body remains as object to the ego, it may fulfill the ego's pride, but it will never provide the joy and satisfaction that the 'alive' body offers." And as for the purely ego-oriented approach to "therapy", Lowen states:

> It is hoped [in ego therapies] that if a person can consciously accept the irrational in his personality, he will be free to

respond naturally and spontaneously to life situations. The weakness in this concept is that the conscious acceptance of a feeling does not lead, necessarily, to the ability to express this feeling. It is one thing to recognize that one is sad, it is another to be able to cry. To know that one is angry is not the same as to feel angry. To know that one was incestuously involved with a parent does little to release the repressed sexual feeling locked in the body. . . .

On some level [people] are aware that the body is a repository of their repressed feelings, and while they would very much like to know about these repressed feelings, they are loathe to encounter them in the flesh.[9]

In other words, a major difference (there are many) between ego and existential approaches is between *accurately representing* the total organism and *actually being* the total organism, and although to the Ego it might sound trivial, that difference is vast indeed.

Yet this is not at all to say that the Existential Level therapies shun the work to be done on the upper levels of the Spectrum. Quite the contrary, they employ a wide variety of techniques to heal the quaternary dualism, to integrate the Shadow, but, wherever possible, this is always done with an eye to continuing the integrative process so as to reach a *felt identity* with the entire organism.

This can be clearly seen in the work of Dr. Perls, who rather effectively used the Shadow level techniques not as an end in themselves but in order to steer the "patient" into an explosion from the Existential Level, wherein ego and body, psyche and soma, unite in the awareness of the total self. So whereas on the Ego Level one may receive an undoubtedly beneficial insight *about* one's repressed anger, on the Existential Level one *becomes* the anger, one disappears into anger, in the flesh, as body and soul fuse into the now released spontaneity of the centaur.

These releases can be dramatic. Perls felt that these explosions—which actually reflect the release of Energy trapped in the tertiary dualism—were the embodiment of the total organism, the centered self, and hence were neither of the mind nor of the body, but of the entire organism. (They are, in short, glimpses of the awakening centaur). Perls felt these explosions were basically of four types: anger, joy, orgasm, and grief. We may take these as four of the characteristic potentials of existential awareness, from an explorer who knew this territory well. To these we may add, as facts warrant, such characteristics as spontaneity, organic faith, existential meaning, prehension, intentionality, and so forth, as elaborated by other researchers of this level, such as Rogers and Maslow.

Now we should at least mention that a true existential therapy must take into account the screening power of the Biosocial Band. The Biosocial Band is, after all, the major fllter of existential awareness. This battle to undercut the Biosocial Band can again be seen in the work of Perls, who fought constantly against the bewitchment of the centaur by the powers of language and logic. "It language" must be turned into "I language"; "thing language" into "process language"; either/or logic into experiential directness; questions into demands; dream interpretation into dream identification; gossip into confrontation. All were direct attempts to lift the screen of the Biosocial Band and plunge into the immediateness of existential awareness. Of course, once the screen is lifted, one is still free to use it—one is no longer, however, forced to use it.

To return to our main point: the progressive dissolution of the tertiary dualism, of the split between ego and body, is a progressive expansion of identity, and therefore responsibility, to one's entire organism, to *"all organic activities."* Now this does not mean that I will therefore exercise absolute volitional control over all my organic activities, so that I can, for example, make my blood flow backwards or my bones grow faster. It means I recognize and accept *all organic* activities as *mine*, so that they no longer stand outside of me.

The first step to or against me taking back the body and eventually reviving the centaur is simply to contact the body itself, to give it some awareness, to explore its feelings, urges, tinglings, responses, and vibrations. Confront, and then contact, your body.

> A body is forsaken when it becomes a source of pain and humiliation instead of pleasure and pride. Under these conditions the person refuses to accept or identify with his body. He turns against it. . . .
> I have repeatedly stressed how afraid people are to feel their bodies. On some level they are aware that the body is a repository of their repressed feelings, and while they would very much like to know about these repressed feelings, they are loathe to encounter them in the flesh. Yet, in their desparate search for an identity, they must eventually confront the state of their bodies.[10]

Although the confronting of the body is initially an Ego Level exercise—because you as ego seem to be different from the body you are confronting—this is nevertheless the first step to re-owning the body and descending to the Existential Level. So you might begin to confront the state of your body. Simply lie down, close your eyes, and explore. Explore the body's feelings, its impulses, its energies, its muscle tones, and especially its breathing. Stay alert for ways the ego will avoid this simple experiment in bodily awareness: getting drowsy or even falling asleep; becoming bored, restless, or distracted; trying the experiment for about two minutes, proclaiming "All's well", then quitting.

Sooner or later you will more than likely stumble upon an unexpected and disheartening fact: in many areas of your body you will have little or no feeling whatsoever. There will exist only a numbness, a blankness, a hole in your body awareness—these are the sites of bodily projections (somatic counterparts of "mental " shadow projections). Thus, some people have no eyes, others no genitals, or no heart, or no guts, no ears, no spine, no breasts, no legs, no head, no hands, no mouth. Finding these gaps, one need do no more than concentrate awareness on them. The point is not to alter the situation, just to directly feel the situation, whereupon—if needed—it will correct itself. Spending an hour or more a day on body awareness is not at all a waste of time. Very few people loose their minds, but most have already lost their bodies.

In other areas of the body you will discover bands of tightness and strong tensions, muscles locked against each other in a stalemated combat—these are the sites of bodily retroflections (the motor anchors of many shadow projections). Upon discovering them, one's natural inclination is simply to relax them, which works fine—for about one minute. Rather, the *impulses locked in these muscles must be thoroughly felt out, mobilized, exaggerated if necessary, and then discharged in the appropriate activity,* which is whatever the body actually feels like doing: crying, laughing, screaming, hitting, trembling, jumping for joy, making love. To try to simply relax these tensions—to "make them go away"—implies that *you* are not responsible for, nor identified with, them. And that is always the great mistake. So we again must understand that we are pinching ourselves—this time *physically* and not just mentally—and in so understanding, we *spontaneously* cease. The goal, remember, is to extend identity and responsibility to all organic activities.

As a useful guide to what you may discover in the blocked body, as well as in the free-flowing body, I have included two schematic charts adapted from Alexander Lowen's *Depression and the Body.* We may take them as maps of the Existential Level drawn up by a gifted explorer. Fig. 14 shows "the kinds of feelings one has in the different segments of one's body when the flow of excitation . . . is full and free." Fig. 15 represents "feelings which develop when the flow is blocked by chronic muscular tension. Not only is the flow interrupted, but within each segment there is a stagnation of the excitation which produces bad feelings. . . ."

All in all, then, this descent to the Existential Level entails accepting as yourself not only what you do deliberately and on purpose (Ego), but also everything "your" organism is doing spontaneously, beyond "your" control. You will come to feel, for instance, not "I have a headache" but "I am hurting myself in the head". Not "My heart is pumping blood" but "I am pumping blood with 'my' heart". You will come to feel, in short, that you don't exist *in* your body, but *as* your body. This is again a *confronting and playing of one's opposites*, but on a level continuous with and yet also so much deeper than that of the purely mental persona.

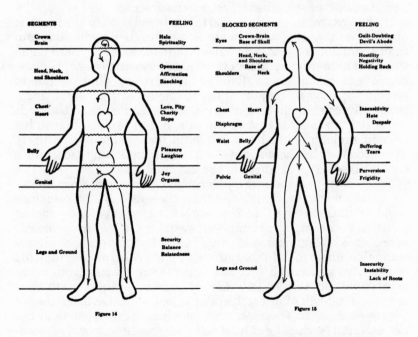

UNINTERRUPTED FLOW OF EXISTENTIAL FEELING

DISRUPTION OF FEELING BY CHROMIC MUSCULAR TENSIONS

Figure 14

Figure 15

(Illustration adapted from Dr.. Alexander Lowen, *Depression and The Body,* Coward, McCann & Geoghegan, Inc. 1972, N.Y.)

(Adapted from and illustration in *Depression and The Body,* Dr. Alexander Lowen; Coward, McCann & Geoghegan, Inc. 1972)

It should be obvious by now that noetic-existentialism and somatic-existentialism can (and, we might add, should) be used in a complementary fashion, since both seek to authenticate the centaur, the total psychophysical organism, and to extend responsibility "to *all organic activities.*" In practice, however, this has been a relatively rare occurrence. Many noetic-existentialists, for all their good intentions and their otherwise direct approach to the total human being, nevertheless tend to continue in the merely talk-shop line of psychotherapy, and thus subscribe to the popular suspicion that "mere bodily exercise" or awareness is relatively useless. They tend to be unaware of the extraordinary power of yoga, Rolfing, or sensory awareness to center a person in his organism. Furthermore, some "mental problems" are so deeply and chronically anchored in the musculature of the body that they simply must be approached through bodily techniques—otherwise, a patient can lie on the couch and talk for fifteen years with no noticeable improvement. Some somatic-existentialists, on the other hand, commit the reverse error and tend to dismiss all noetic approaches as a lot of very hot air, and hence they easily slide into that plague of true-somatic existentialism, namely, mere calisthenics. For mere calisthenics is not a true somatic-existentialism, because it seeks not to dissolve the tertiary dualism but to strengthen it by perpetuating the illusion that the "mind" independently commands and controls and exercises the "body." It seeks not to reveal man as a centaur, but to confirm him in his ancient prejudice that he is instead a horse-man (ego) entirely divorced from his horse (body), an angel grafted by God into a corruptible body, the ghost in the machine.

True noetic and somatic existentialists, however, even if they personally do not practice both approaches, will at least recognize their complementarity. In this regard, there exist encouraging signs that the mild contempt between the noetic and somatic approaches is starting to dissolve. This contempt is perhaps understandable, given the ill-fated adventures of Wilhelm Reich and his orgone therapy, which was the first dramatic attempt to unite psychoanalytic "talk" with bodily maneuvers. At this time there is actually a rebirth of interest in Reich, not, we believe, because of his psychoanalytic theories, some of which were peculiar in the extreme, but because he at least saw the complementarity of somatic and noetic approaches.

Some existential analysts are picking up where Reich left off, and we see in them the emergence of a true *amphi-existentialism,* that is, a true union of noetic and somatic approaches to the Existential Level. The existentialists are in a perfect theoretical position to do this, for one of the core concepts of noetic-existentialism is that of the three dimensions of personal reality, namely, the *Umwelt* or biological world, including one's body, the *Mitwelt* or social world, and the *Eigenwelt* or world of the psychic and egoic processes. A truly encompassing existentialism will thus embrace not only the individual's social world and the world of his egoic processes—the two worlds most noetic-existentialists stress—but also the *Umwelt*, his own body. In this sense the Bioenergetic Analysis of Alexander Lowen is a perfect example of amphi-existentialism, utilizing the noetic approach to deal with the *Mitwelt* and the *Eigenwelt,* and combining that with a powerful set of exercise and analyses aimed at exploring the *Umwelt*—thus approaching the Existential Level from "both ends."

Turning now to the more purely philosophical aspects of noetic-existentialism—to what is actually called "existential philosophy"—we find a rather bewildering conglomeration of technical vocabulary, definitions, and ideas. Existentialism stresses the individual, especially his "subjective" experience of existential truth, and maintains that any objective statement or generalization is erroneous. Thus each existentialist has his own terminology, his own methodology, and his own conclusions, none of which match very well with those of any other existentialists. And although the existentialists on the whole usually maintain that they all agree with one another, nodody else is ever quite sure just what it is that they all agree on. Nevertheless certian recurrent themes continue to surface in existentialism, and their discussion becomes greatly simplified if we recall that this movement is grounded on the Existential Level, a level that is marked by two major dualisms: that of self vs. other and that of being vs. nullity. Noetic existentialism is thus *an attitude of squarely facing and dealing with these two major dualisms*. It does not completely undercut these dualisms, but—once they have occurred—it deals with them in the soundest possible fashion.

That existentialism—at least as it is reflected in existential psychology—is based on the primary and secondary dualisms is clearly reflected in its two major concerns, namely, those of being-in-the-world and being vs. nothingness. Being-in-the-world refers to an authentic encounter between man's total being and his environment, that is to say, *an encounter between the two sides of the primary dualism,* the organism and its environment. Similarly, being vs. nothingness refers to the encounter of the two sides of the secondary dualism, and specifically to the possibility that in this encounter one's existence, one's being, may be overwhelmed by the negative side of this dualism, by feelings of emptiness, nullity, and "sickness unto death." The problem with taking existentialism as absolutely true, however, is that neither of these opposites *encounter* one another, they *are* one another.

To be sure, many people believe that they experience the clash of these opposites, the "dialectic of crisis," but that in no way justifies mistaking them as a basic fact of reality. They are instead a phenomenon of the Existential Level—and they must be dealt with in this context. The existentialists crashed down on this level of the spectrum, and they have perceived very clearly the nature of the two basic dualisms constituting this level—the "clash" between self and other ("Hell is others") and between being and nullity ("Sickness unto death"), as well as the "fear and trembling" that this clash, this debate, seems to entail. But this debate is a source of *angst* only to the extent man believes it actually to exist. Thus the existentialists clearly perceived the debate, but they missed its illusory character.[11]

Nevertheless, the existentialists have gone a long way towards "reuniting" these apparently estranged opposites. If the existentialists do not see that my being *is* the world, they do see that my being is always being-in-the-world. If they do not see the complete non-duality of life and death, they have at least stressed that death completes and makes authentic my being.

At the same time, however, one might say that existentialism's shortcomings are, from another angle, its strengths, that contemporary existential psychology, especially as evidenced in Rollo May, the earlier Maslow (before he switched his attention to the Transpersonal Bands), Rogers, Lowen, Perls, Boss, Binswanger and the like, is the only sound approach to living on the Existential Level. On this level, the primary and secondary dualisms seems to rend and violate the very fabric of reality, and we appear in danger of being overwhelmed by the dark side of living, by the threatening otherness of the world and the suffocating blackness of our possible annihilation. And it is precisely here that the counsels of the existentialists are of such value, for they point out that on *this level* at least, I can find meaning in my life only by facing these two major dualisms through an act of *will* (which is not surprising, since the will is generated on this level). This entails the realization that *if I cannot choose my fate, I can nevertheless choose my attitude towards it,* and herein lies my existential freedom. In effect, I choose to be what I am—"we are our choices." This does not necessarily "change the fate, but it greatly changes the person."[12] And there is no asking how this is to be accomplished—one simply does it, for that is our freedom: "My first act of free will is to believe in free will."

Thus existentialism handles these two major dualisms by coming to grips with them, by courageously encountering them through an act of will, through choosing my attitude in the face of fate; and exactly here, as we have suggested, is its value and its message for man. For in the context of the spectrum of consciousness, existentialism is an attempt, by facing and accepting the primary and secondary dualisms, *to forestall further fragmentation upwards towards the levels of the Ego and the Shadow*—a fragmentation caused, as we have seen, precisely by refusing to face these dualisms! In more decidedly analytical terms, psychological repression (the tertiary and quaternary repressions) results from the complex debate between life and death, between being and non-being. In the words of Rollo May:

> On this level, we shall find that the simple mechanism of repression, which we blithely started with, is infinitely less simple than it looks; that it involves a complex struggle . . . of the individual's *being* against the possibility of *non-being*. . . .[13]

By accepting and dealing with the anxiety necessarily generated by this secondary dualism of being vs. non-being, this anxiety is not pushed into the tertiary and quaternary dualisms. Existentialism deals with *angst* immediately as it arises, and thus man remains whole, finding here the "courage to be." For example, if I accept the inevitability of my annihilation, I will not be persuaded to escape into the spurious immortality of ideas, to "invent a way to be begotten by ideas altogether." In short, I will have descended from the Ego Level to the Existential Level.

Having said this much, we are immediately faced with another major movement that has had as its ground the Existential Level—namely, that of exoteric religion. For both religion and existentialism alike spring directly from man's reaction to the primary and secondary dualisms. Perhaps this is why so many existentialists—Tillich, Jaspers, Marcel—are *theistic* existentialists. At any rate, where existentialism handles the primary dualism of self vs. other by *participating* with the other, exoteric religion handles it by *appeasing* the other, in this case, the Great Other (God). And where existentialism handles the secondary dualism of life vs. death by *facing* death, religion handles it by *denying* death. Despite what one may think of the relative merits of either approach, it is obvious that they are both direct attempts to answer these two major dualisms.

Hence the Existential Level is also the level of exoteric religion, of man's attempts to establish a relationship "across" the primary dualism with an all-powerful, all-knowing, all-present Great Other (which is usually the way Mind presents itself after the primary dualism has occurred). Now the actual phenomenon of religion, as is well known, is quite complex, but if we adopt the thesis proposed by Schuon, Guénon, and Coomaraswamy—namely the "transcendent unity of religions"—and then translate this thesis into the terms of the spectrum of consciousness, we can introduce a considerable parsimony to an otherwise bewilderingly complex filed. Let us begin with the core concept of the transcendent unity of religions with the following from Huston Smith, who is discussing the works of Schuon,

> It is *a priori* evident that everything both resembles and differs from everything else: resembles it at least in existing; differs, or there would be no multiplicity to compare. *Pari passu* with religions: Had they nothing in common we would not refer to them by a common noun; were they undifferentiated we would not speak of them in the plural. Everything turns on how this empty truth is filled with content. Where is the line between unity and plurality to be drawn, and how are the two domains to be related?
>
> Schuon draws the line between the esoteric and the exoteric [see Fig. 16]. The fundamental distinction does not lie between religions; it is not, so to speak, a line which, reappearing, divides religion's great historical manifestations vertically—Hindus from Buddhists from Christians from Muslims, etc. The dividing line is horizontal and occurs but once, cutting across the historical religions. Below the line lies esotericism, above it exotericism.[14]

Now in the terms of the spectrum of consciousness, *this dividing line between esotericism and exotericism is the primary dualism*. "Above" the primary dualism lies the Existential-Biosocial Level while "below" it lies the Level of Mind. Any individual who experiences the Level of Mind and then ascends to the Existential-Biosocial Level to talk about it, will have to clothe that "religious" experience in the only symbols available to him, namely those supplied by his Biosocial Band. The diversity of exoteric religions thus reflects the diversity of cultural ideologies, idiosyncrasies, and paradigms—in short, the diversity of Biosocial Bands. Thus Schroendinger, Christ, and Shankara—who all experienced Mind—would speak of it in different terms, reflecting not a difference in Mind but a difference in symbolic elaborations of Mind. Schroedinger used the terms of physical theory; Christ, those of Hebrew theology; and Shankara, those of Hindu Autology—yet this Reality remains one and the same. Hence the Existential Level is the level of the various exoteric religions, while the Level of Mind is the level of the "transcendent unity" of esoteric religion. Religions diverge at the Existential Level and converge at the Level of Mind.

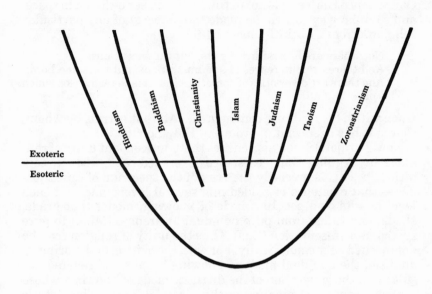

Figure 16

Many fundamentalist Christians gag in horror when any mention is made of the fact that all religions are identical in esoteric essence, for it implies that Christianity is not THE ONLY WAY, and hence the fuel for their "proselytizing fury" evaporates, leaving them, so to speak, holding the bag. The greatest stumbling block for fundamentalists is the belief in the historicity of Christ, that Jesus was an event in history that somehow confers salvation upon all who would embrace his historical reality. But to place Christ in history is to place him in the *past,* and the past is thoroughly dead. Under these circumstances, the Holy Spirit becomes the Holy Ghost, and in the eyes of many, the Holy Spook. Christ never was, nor will he be; he will never come again because he never was— rather, he always *is,* above history, above time, Eternal, for "before Abraham *was,* I *am.*"

And God said unto Moses, I AM THAT I AM: and he said, thus
shalt thou say unto the children of Israel, I AM hath sent me
unto you. (Exodus 3:14)

Christ, since His being is not in time, can neither be found in space,
and so in no way can He be made the property of any particular
religion. From I Corinthians (12:4-6):

Now there are diversities of gifts, but the same Spirit.
And there are differences of administrations, but the same Lord.
And there are diversities of operations, but it is the same God which
worketh in all.

Upon which St. Ambrose commented, "All that is true, by whom-
soever it has been said, is from the Holy Spirit."

Now Frithjof Schuon approaches this transcendent unity of religions by arguing that "existence is graded, and with it, cognition."[15] This is precisely the crux of the spectrum of consciousness—that existence is graded into several levels, and that each
level has its own peculiar mode of knowing, modes that grade,
shade, and range from pure non-dual awareness (Mind) to pure
symbolic representation (Ego). Thus the unity of religions can be
approached epistemologically. For with the arising of the primary
dualism, the non-dual mode of knowing is split and severed, resulting in the generation of the dualistic mode of knowing, whose
symbolic content is supplied by the Biosocial Bands. The esoteric
non-dual mode of knowing is superceded by the exoteric symbolic
mode. Thus when Huston Smith comments on Schuon's work by
stating that "the issue of unity and diversity in religions is converted into a question of psychological types: the esoteric and
exoteric,"[16] we would simply translate that as follows: the issue of
unity and diversity in religions is converted into a question of the
mode of knowing: the non-dual and the symbolic-map. (This is
shown in Fig. 17.)

Hence the Existential Level is the exoteric level—the level of
many different selves symbolically knowing many different Gods,
with the contents of that knowledge supplied by many different
Biosocial Bands; while the Level of Mind is the esoteric level, the
level of the Universal Godhead, the non-dual awareness wherein
many selves and many Gods unite in the timeless omniscience of
Reality. And the single dividing line is the Primary Dualism.

Thus far, in our "descent" of the spectrum of consciousness, we
have seen that those therapies addressing the Ego Level have as
their common aim the healing of the quaternary split between the
persona and the shadow to give the whole psyche (the Ego Level).
Going deeper, we have just seen that the various existentialisms
aim at healing the tertiary split between the whole psyche and the

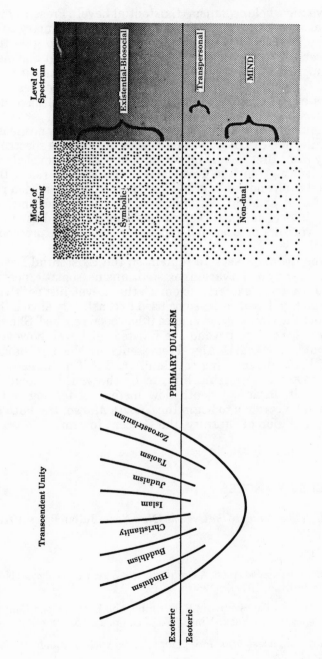

Figure 17

body, to give the whole organism (Existential Level). Presently we will see that mysticism goes still deeper to heal the primary split between the whole organism and the environment to give the entire universe (Level of Mind). Again, the point is that one may use these approaches singly or in combination, and thus one may descend the spectrum as much or as little as one's desires and capabilities allow, drawing on techniques such as we have described to *reach and then enrich* the desired level.[17]

We might mention, in passing, that as a general but by no means iron-clad rule, one can descend to a deeper level of the spectrum more easily if one first "heals" or "straightens-out" the level above it, so that healing the Ego Level makes it easier to reach the Existential Level, and healing that level in turn makes it easier to reach the Level of Mind. Put somewhat crudely, "healing" or "whole-ing" a level makes it easier to leave or transcend, for then our energies are not preoccupied and bound up with the problems of that level.

Should the *jivatman* seek to remain on the Existential Level, then he can use any of the various existentialisms (somatic, noetic, or amphi) or theisms (exoteric) to enrich that Level, just as "therapies" for the Ego Level can also be used to constantly enrich the potentials of that vibratory level once it has been reached. Should the *jivatman* seek to go beyond the Existential Level, however, then he should know that this level represents the "deepest" he can descend without surrendering the familiar. But if he is ready to know God instead of worship him, to be the world instead of encountering it, to accept death now instead of fearing it tomorrow, then he is ready to begin the *Nivritti Marga,* the Path of Return, the Religion of Eternity, the Descent to Mind.

REFERENCES AND NOTES

1. John Lilly, *The Center of the Cyclone* (New York: Julian Press, 1972), p. 102.

2. Ibid., p. 100.

3. Quoted in Severin Peterson, *A Catalog of the Ways People Grow* (New York: Ballantine, 1971), p. 250.

4. Cooper's appraisal of Sartre, in R. D. Laing, and D. G. Cooper, *Reason and Violence.* (New York: Vintage, 1971), pp. 14-15.

5. Rollo May, ed., *Existential Psychology* (New York: Random House, 1969), pp. 33-35.

6. Fyodor Dostoyevsky, *Notes From the Underground* (New York: New American Library, Signet, 1961), p. 203.

7. T. Hanna, *Main Currents,* vol. 31, no. 3, 1974.

8. F. Perls, R. Hefferline, and P. Goodman, *Gestalt Therapy* (New York: Dell), p. 84.

9. A. Lowen, *The Betrayal of the Body* (New York: Macmillan, 1967).

10. Ibid.

11. Cf. Brown, *Love's Body,* p. 143: "The boundary line between self and the external world bears no relation to reality . . . The net effect of the establishment of the boundary between self and external world is inside-out and outside-in; confusion. The erection of the boundary does not alter the fact that there is, in reality, no boundary. The net-effect is illusion, self-deception; the big lie. Or alienation."

12. May, *Existential Psychology,* p. 42.

13. Ibid., p. 19.

14. Huston Smith, "The Relation Between Religions," *Main Currents,* vol. 30, no. 2, p. 52. I have inverted his diagram and hence switched the words "above" and "below" in the quote.

15. Ibid., words of Smith.

16. Ibid., p. 53.

17. That "therapy" can be used for enriching a level as well as "curing" a level is a positive achievement of Humanistic Psychology. Thus, on each level, but in ways still poorly defined, "satisfying deficiencies avoid illness; growth satisfactions produce positive health." A. H. Maslow, *Toward a Psychology of Being,* p. 32. There is abundant room for psychogogic (Schwarz) work on each level.

X. *A NO-MAN'S LAND*

Between the Existential Level and the Level of Mind lies the most mysterious, unexplored, misunderstood, fear-inducing, and generally puzzling portion of the spectrum—the Transpersonal Bands. They can be experienced as the "dark night of the soul" or the boundless light of Amitabha; here one can meet visions of bodhisattvas and angels, or be accosted by the legions of Mara, the archetypal Evil One; one can discover here the Inner Guides, or fall into the hands of the terrible Dweller on the Threshold. One's identity can shift to out of the body or one can be whisked away to astral travel. It is here that paranormal occurrences of ESP, clairvoyance, and clairaudience are found (if, indeed, they exist), that one can relive "past lives" or project oneself into future occurrences. If ever existed a no-man's land, the Transpersonal Bands are it.

These Bands historically have not been as widely studied as the others, for several reasons: (1) They scare the daylights out of most people; (2) Orthodox psychiatry considers them as signs of a very disturbed psyche; and (3) Enlightened Masters consider them *makyo*—illusions of the most deceptive nature. In general, we agree with the Masters. This is not to say that the Transpersonal Bands are totally worthless as a subject of investigation, only that—for those pursuing the Level of Mind—they are pernicious distractions, something that must be quickly passed through. Nevertheless, we will briefly comment on them, especially since interest in these bands is rapidly growing.

An essential point to remember about these bands is that when an individual breaks the Primary Dualism *incompletely* and hence enters the Transpersonal Bands, he usually "carries" with him the maps he has received on the Biosocial and Ego Levels, and these maps will, to a large extent, determine how he views this territory. Most importantly, many people have maps that tell them that these bands either do not exist or are at least pathological, so that if they occasionally break into these bands they instantly fear for their sanity, an over-reactive attitude that could actually act to "stick" them on one of these bands for a prolonged time, an experience that is rarely harmful but always terrifying. We believe that these bands do indeed exist (although not necessarily all the phenomena that supposedly occur here) and that, in themselves, these bands are not pathological—although many people

266

who are diagnosed "mentally ill" may be lost in these bands for want of an adequate guide, and thus react as any normal English-speaking person might react if dumped into Germany without a translator. To be sure, these bands do not represent Absolute Reality, but then neither do any of the other levels above it. Orthodox psychiatrists do not discover madness on these levels, they invent it on these levles by so defining it, reflecting the incredible fact that the level of consciousness rendered accepta-ble by social conventions is very much a political affair—the politics of consciousness.

Yet to see the beneficial side of the Transpersonal Bands, we have only to look to the purer forms of Tibetan Mysticism or, for those more at home with Western traditions, to Jung's Analytical Psychology. Both of these subjects would require several volumes in themselves, and consequently our comments can only be most disgracefully superficial. On the other hand, at the Transpersonal Bands, we are all somewhat beyond our depth, but we will nevertheless hazard a few hypotheses based upon the work of Jung and certain Eastern mystical traditions, particularly the Tantra.

Jung's idea of the "collective unconscious," if somewhat in-credible, is nevertheless simple enough. Just as a man's body universally contains ten fingers, one spleen, two kidneys, and so on, Jung believed that man's "mind" might contain universal symbols or "archetypes" that, because they were biologically given to the whole species, could not be merely personal or individual and hence were transpersonal or "collective." Jung states:

> The other part of the unconscious [besides personal] is what I call the impersonnal or collective unconscious. As the name indicates, its contents are not personal but collective; that is, they do not belong to one individual alone but to a whole group of individuals, and generally to a whole nation, or even to the whole of mankind. These contents are not acquired during the individual's lifetime but are products of innate forms and instincts. Although the child possesses no inborn ideas, it nevertheless has a highly developed brain which functions in a quite definite way. This brain is inherited from its ancestors; it is a deposit of the psychic functioning of the whole human race. The child therefore brings with it an organ ready to function in the same way that it has functioned throughout human history. In the brain the instincts are pre-formed, and so are the primordial images which have always been the basis of man's thinking. . . .[1]

Of these primordial images, these archetypes, Jung states:

> There are as many archetypes as there are typical situations in life. Endless repetition has engraved these experiences into our psychic constitution, not in the form of images filled with content, but at first only as *forms without content*, representing merely the possibility of a certain type of perception and action. When a situation occurs which corresponds to a given archetype, that archetype becomes activated. . . .[2]

Jung believed that the activation of an archetype produced pathological results only if the individual refused to cooperate with its elaboration or amplification, that is, refused to establish a conscious relation with the images and myths that it animates, seeking their meaning for the individual. If, on the other hand, he did cooperate with the archetype's elaboration, it could provide a powerful, beneficial, and meaningful guide to life. Thus Jung looked upon the archetypes as something like a primitive "mental instinct," so that—like all other "instincts" or needs—if they are heeded they result in fulfillment, while if shunned, neurosis.

We have already noted the similarity of the archetypes of the collective unconscious with the *vasanas* or *bija* or seed-forms of the *alaya-vijnana*. It is not surprising, then, that just as Jung's psychology seeks to handle the archetypes not by intellectually or logically analyzing them away but by amplifying them through dream and mythological imagery, so also certain forms of Eastern mysticism seek to utilize these primordial forms for spiritual growth by amplifying them through imagery and religious mythology. The spiritual growth that results, the contact with the Level of Mind, "cannot be achieved," states Lama Govinda,

> through building up convictions, ideals, and aims based on reasoning, but only through conscious penetration of those layers of our mind which cannot be reached or influenced by logical arguments and discursive thought.
> Such penetration and transformation is only possible through the compelling power of inner vision, whose primordial images or "archetypes" are the formative principles of our mind. Like seeds they sink into the fertile soil of our subconscious in order to germinate, to grow and to unfold their potentialities.[3]

Both Jungian analysis and Tibetan visualization techniques utilize these primordial forms for beneficial growth by seeking to elaborate and not shun them. In Jung's system, this is accomplished through the use of key dreams or images that reflect universal mythological motifs, so that one can establish a conscious relationship with the archetypes molding all human action instead of being their unwitting instrument. Similarly, Tibetan Buddhism uses key images, such as the *Dhyani* or Visualization Buddhas, to become

> conscious of the world and of those forces which create it, [so that] we become their master. As long as these forces remain dormant and unperceived within us, we have no access to them. For this reason it is necessary to project them into the realm of the visible in the form of images. The symbols which serve this purpose act like a chemical catalyst, through which a liquid is suddenly converted into solid crystals, thus revealing its true nature and structure.[4]

Anyone who has seriously practiced these or other similar "archetype-elaboration" exercises will testify that they apparently tap a source of vast energy and strength which profoundly influences one's basic feeling of existence. As P. W. Martin states, in narrating Jung's "discovery" of this process:

> In short, [Jung found that] the unconscious was producing today, in the psychologist's consulting room, symbols which, far away and long ago, had brought new energy and new insights; and the modern Europeans and Americans through whom this activity was operating were likewise experiencing a *dynamic renewal of life.*[5]

These exercises, despite considerable differences in content, nevertheless share several formal characteristics, for they all seek to help elaborate and amplify these primitive "seeds" and then to consciously integrate them. Thus the Tibetan visualization techniques, for example, consist of two major phases: The first is that of elaboration or creation of the mythological image (*sristi-krama*); the second is that of dissolving or integrating (*laya-krama*) these images "into the normal stream of life and consciousness."[6] *This twofold process of conscious contact and then re-integration reflects the very same principle used "therapeutically" on every other level we have examined,* from contacting and integrating the shadow to contacting and integrating the body. Thus these exercises on the Transpersonal Bands result in a "dynamic renewal of life" just as similar exercises based on the same principle produced an analogous "dynamic renewal of life" on the Ego and Existential Levels.

But what more can we say about this "dynamic renewal of life" surging up from the Transpersonal Bands themselves? To begin with, listen once again to Jung on the archetypes:

> Do we ever understand what we think? We understand only such thinking as is a mere equation and from which

nothing comes out but what we have put in. That is the manner of the intellect. But beyond that there is a thinking in primordial images—in symbols that are older than historical man; which have been ingrained in him from earliest times, and, eternally living, outlasting all generations, still make up the groundwork of the human psyche. It is possible to live the fullest life only when we are in harmony with these symbols; wisdom is a return to them. It is a question neither of belief nor knowledge, but of the agreement of our thinking with the primordial images of the unconscious.[7]

And so, Jung would ask, by what myth do you live? For mythological imagery springs from the collective unconscious, the transconscious, and, among other things, it is therefore not contaminated nor perverted by merely social conventions, language, logic, or the illusions of any particular cult or individual. Furthermore, the language of mythology is associative and integrative, and not like ordinary thought dissociative and analytical, and hence it more clearly and truly reflects the actual physical reality of the seamless coat of the universe, of the mutual interdependence and interpenetration of all things and events. Myth, remember, embodies the nearest approach to absolute truth that can be stated in words. For these reasons, it confers upon the individual an intimation of his universality, a direct pointer to his fundamentally joyous unity with all of creation, a wholeness that whisks him far beyond the dismally petty affairs of day-to-day routine and plunges him into the vast and magical world of the transpersonal.

Myth, short —which Jung felt to be the direct embodiment of archetypes—is integrative and patterned, holistic and encompassing, a truer representation of Reality than we will find in any other symbolic system. Although it does not itself *abolish* all dualisms, it does *suspend* them, and herein lies the incredibly life-renewing power and eternal fascination of true mythology. Remember that the Hindu calls these Transpersonal Bands the "ananda-maya-kosa", the level of pure bliss, blissful precisely because the war of opposites is temporarily suspended.

Now these mythological archetypes, or bijas, or vasanas exert a profound effect upon every level of the Spectrum existing "above" the Transpersonal Bands. This is, of course, a general phenomenon seen throughout the spectrum: the vicissitudes of *any* level dramatically affect all of the levels above it. But we wish to emphasize again that the Transpersonal Bands can themselves be *directly* experienced. This holds not only for the more obvious cases of out-of-the-body experiences, astral travel, traveling clairaudience, and so on, but also for the archetypes themselves, which are one aspect of the Transpersonal Bands. Carl Jung himself realized this, for he stated that "Mystics are people who have a particularly vivid experience of the processes of the collective unconsious. Mystical experience is *experience of archetypes*."[8]

Parenthetically, we must amend Jung's statement by saying that certain "lesser" mystical states are the direct experience of the archetypes. "True" mysticism is beyond even the archetypes, the vasanas; it is of the Level of Mind, wherein all vasanas are "destroyed." Correspondingly, the Hindu differentiates between savikalpa samadhi and nirvikalpa samadhi. Savikalpa samadhi is the generally blissful experience of the ananda-maya-kosa, the collective unconscious. It is from this level that one gains an understanding of saguna Brahman, which is nothing other than the archetypal or mythological image of nirguna Brahman, the Godhead itself. It is usually ecstatic because all dualisms (except the primary dualism) are suspended as the self contemplates reality. But nirvikalpa samadhi is beyond even that: it is a direct experience "of" the Level of Mind, nirguna Brahman itself. One no longer contemplates reality, one becomes reality! All dualities and images are totally and cleanly removed. So the one state is the truest image of reality, while the other is reality itself. That, in essence, is the major distinction between the "lesser" mystical states characteristic of the Transpersonal Bands, and the "true" mystical state which is Mind. But our main point is that the archetypes themselves can, in certain cases, be directly experienced.

In the context of the spectrum of consciousness, how are we to view the bijas or vasanas or archetypes themselves? Let us begin with the following statement of Jung:

> Again and again I encounter the mistaken notion that an archetype is determined in regard to its content, in other words that it is a kind of unconscious idea (if such an expression is admissible). It is necessary to point out once more that archetypes are not determined as regards their content, but only as regards their form and then only to a very limited degree. A primordial image is determined as to its content only when it has become conscious and is therefore filled out with the material of conscious attention.[9]

In the spectrum of consciousness, then, the archetypes, as the primordial forms devoid of content, *represent the first point where—during its mobilization or "welling-up"—our pure, formless Engergy starts to take on and animate form.* This form will later solidify and pick up *content* on the Existential-Biosocial Level as images, ideas, and maps in general. They are thus the primordial but potential source of dualism that we re-activate and crystallize every moment of our lives, especially as the primary dualism. Thus in Buddhist psychology, these archetypes represent the seed-potentialities that manifest the phenomenal universe by *objectifying* Mind.

In sum, the archetypes or bijas or vasanas are the first point where our formless or seamless organismic consciousness starts to take on and animate form. As such, dualisms are present—especially some form of the primary dualism—but are more-or-less suspended or harmonized: they are present in potential form. These archetypes are thus simultaneously the deepest pointers to organismic consciousness *and* the first corrupters of organismic consciousness. They point unerringly but, once seen and understood, must not be clung to. That is why, useful and even mandatory as they may be, they must eventually be by-passed, burned up destroyed in a sense. Savikalpa samadhi must give way to nirvikalpa samadhi, mythological experience to direct imageless awareness, the everlastingness of mythological time to the instantaneousness of the eternal present, seeing God to being the Godhead. That is why "The yogin is striving to ... 'burn-up' the *vasanas*."[10] In short, the archetypes are the ultimate pointers as well as the final barrier.

But, on the more positive and beneficial side, notice just what is involved when a person begins to consciously contact the vast store of archetypal experience lying at the very base of consciousness itself. Because these symbols are collective or transpersonal, to touch the archetype is actually to begin to transcend oneself, to find deeply within an intimation and pointer to the deeply beyond. So it might be said, from another angle, that the Transpersonal Bands represent a point where the individual *begins* to touch Mind. He does not yet directly realize that what he is, *is* Mind, but through insight and experience he understands indeed that there is within him that which goes beyond him. As such, it is not at all difficult to understand the immense therapeutic power of authentic Transpersonal Band therapies. As stated above, a general characteristic of the Transpersonal Bands is a suspension of all dualisms (except some form of the Primary Dualism). This necessarily includes the dualisms of persona vs. shadow as well as psyche vs. soma. In undercutting these dualisms, one simultaneously undercuts the support of individual neuroses, both egoic and existential. Is this not why a consistent practice of some form of transpersonal meditation can be so highly therapeutic for individual emotional dys-eases?

To say the same thing from a slightly different angle, in recognizing a depth of one's identity that goes beyond one's individual and separate being, a person can more easily go beyond his individual and separate neuroses. For example, by reflecting on one's life *through the eyes of the archetypes* and mythological images common to mankind, one's awareness necessarily begins to shift to a universal perspective—a transcendent, de-personal, transpersonal view. Once this process quickens, the individual is no longer *exclusively* identified with just his separate-self sense and hence is no longer exclusively tied to his purely personal problems. In a sense he can start to let go of his fears and anxieties, depressions and obsessions, and begin to view them with the same clarity and impartiality with which one might view clouds floating through the sky or waters rushing in a stream. The Transpersonal Band therapy discloses—probably for the first time—a *trans*-position from which he can comprehensively *look at* his individual emotional and ideational complexes. But the fact that he can comprehensively *look at* them means that he has ceased using them as something *with which to look at*, and thus distort, reality. For the fact that he can look at them means that he is no longer exclusively identified with them. His identity begins to touch that within which is beyond. In the words of Joseph Campbell, "the disturbed individual may learn to see himself depersonalized in the mirror of the human spirit and discover by analogy the way to his own larger fulfillment."[11]

But this leads us directly to a further aspect of the Transpersonal Bands, for, as the above suggests, the Transpersonal Bands are sometimes experienced as the *supra-individual Witness*: that which is capable of observing the flow of what is—without interfering with it, commenting on it, or in any way manipulating it. The Witness simply observes the stream of events both inside and outside the mind-body in a creatively detached fashion, since, in fact, the Witness is not exclusively identified with either. In other words, *when the individual realizes that his mind and his body can be perceived objectively, he spontaneously realizes that they cannot constitute a real subjective self*. As Huang Po put it, "Let me remind you, the perceived cannot perceive." This position of the Witness, or we might say, this state of Witnessing, is the foundation of all beginning Buddhist practice ("mindfulness"), of Psychosynthesis ("dis-identification and the transpersonal Self"), and of Hindu Jnana Yoga ("neti, neti"). Further, it seems to resemble very closely what Maslow called "plateau experiences," which "represent a witnessing of reality. It involves seeing the symbolic, or the mythic, the poetic, the transcendent, the miraculous. . . .It's the transcending of space and time which becomes quite normal, so to speak."[12] It is expressly through these types of experiences that one is fully initiated into the world of meta-motivations, B-values, transcendent values, mythological and supra-individual awareness—in short, the spiritual dimension of the Transpersonal Bands.

But I would like to remind the reader of the distinction between what I am calling—for lack of better terms—"lesser" mysticism and "true" mysticism, for it is again the distinction between the transpersonal Witness and the Level of Mind. The transpersonal Witness is a "position" of Witnessing reality. But notice at once that this state of the transpersonal Witness still contains a subtle form of the Primary Dualism, namely, the witness vs. what is witnessed. It is when this last trace of dualism is finally and completely shattered that one awakens to Mind, for at that moment (which is *this* moment), the witness and the witnessed are one and the same.

This, however, is not at all to denigrate the position of the transpersonal self or Witness, for—as we have seen—it can be highly therapeutic in itself, and further, in ways which we will explore in the final chapter, it can frequently act as a type of springboard to the Level of Mind. Nevertheless, it is not to be confused with Mind itself. This is why, in Zen, a student who remains in the peaceful bliss of the transpersonal self is called a "dead-void heretic," and the Tibetan Buddhists refer to it as being "stuck in the kun-gzhi." In general Mahayana terms, the tainted *alaya-vijnana* has to be smashed through, because it contains the subtle dualistic forms of the *vasanas,* which give rise to the subject-object dualism of the witness vs. the witnessed.

Such, then, is the major difference between the lesser mystical states of the transpersonal self, and the true mystical state which is Mind. In one, a person may witness reality; in the other he is reality. While one invariably retains some subtle form of the Primary Dualism, the other does not. It is this final dissolution of any form of the primary dualism that Zen refers to by the phrase, "the bottom of the bucket breaks," for there remains in one's awareness no bottom—that is to say, no sense of any inner subjectivity confronting any world of outer objectivity. The two worlds have radically coalesced, or rather, are understood to have never been separate. The individual goes right to the very bottom of his being to find who or what is doing the seeing, and he *ultimately* finds—instead of a transpersonal self—nothing other than what is seen, which Blyth called "the experience by the universe of the universe." The bottom of the bucket has broken.

With this, the Vedanta is in perfect agreement. Although Vedanta metaphorically speaks of the Atman-Brahman as the Seer, Knower, or Witness, it employs a very special connotation to distinguish the Seer from the transpersonal self, namely, the Seer is one with *all* worlds seen. In the words of Sri Ramana Maharshi, "The notion that the Seer is different from the seen abides in the mind. For those that ever abide in the Heart, the Seer is the same as the seen."

To bring this section to an end, we will briefly comment on the so-called paranormal occurrences: ESP, clairvoyance, other-world visions, astral travel, etc. The feature that they and all events of the Transpersonal Bands have in common is an incomplete breakdown or suspension of the Primary Dualism, so that although the self is still experienced as being more or less separate from the world, it nevertheless has greatly extended some portion of its boundary (representing the point where the primary dualism "breaks.") There seems to be a rapidly growing interest in parapsychology, especially in the scientific community, which has seized upon these events primarily because they can be "kicked," that is, subjected to the orthodox criteria of objectivity, measurement and verification. In ESP studies, for example, it is a fairly simple matter to set up laboratory controls, gather data and statistically evaluate it, and then draw a conclusion, which is usually that ESP does indeed exist. Inherently there is no reason that these experiments could or should not be performed, but it should be emphatically stressed that these areas have absolutely nothing to do with the Level of Mind or pure mysticism per se. Many scientists unfortunately slure over this distinction, and then feel that in "proving" the existence of ESP or psychokinesis or whatever, they have proved the existence of the Level of Mind, and so they document their experimental findings with the sayings of Eckhart, Rumi, Chung Tzu, or Shankara. Despite their unmistakably good intentions, this is really a rather elaborate hoax. The Level of Mind *cannot be externally proven,* for the simple reason that there is nowhere in the universe where one can go that is outside of Mind so as to be able to verify it, objectify it, or measure it. One cannot grasp it because it is in the very grasping itself. Scientific verification demands the Primary Dualism between the verifier and the verified, and that distinction is foreign to Mind. Mind can be "proven" experimentally by any individual who will consent to follow the Way, but this "proof" is not an external one. At best, these scientists are working on the Transpersonal Bands where they are showing that the primary dualism can be partially undercut.

But their zeal is perhaps understandable, for science is such a powerful tool on the upper levels of the spectrum that it is only natural to try to extend it to the lower levels, and certainly on some levels of the Transpersonal Bands this is perfectly legitimate. But to reach the Level of Mind one must eventually quit studying facts and instead become the facts. The light of science is here of no avail. This is the very old story of the drunk who lost his key and then looked for it under the lamp post—not because that is where he lost the key, but because that is where the light was.

Finally, we must recall the words of the enlightened Masters, who have universally claimed that paranormal powers, or *siddhi*, are always shunned by the sage, for behind the deliberate use of all paranormal phenomena lies the urge to power of the frightened ego, which is ever seeking to extend its capability to manipulate and control its environment. But when you are one with the environment, what possible meaning could manipulating the environment have? The urge to develop "psychotechnology" is at heart no different from the urge to develop typical technology, and the ego has so fouled the environment with regular technology, we can hardly guess to what ingenious uses it will put psychotechnology. The inescapable conclusion is that only a sage is qualified to use *siddhi*, but he will have nothing to do with it. Nevertheles, we are today seeing fools rush in where angels fear to tread. It is one thing to scientifically explore *siddhi*, but quite another to personally cultivate it. One can gain abundant personal benefits from the Transpersonal Bands by sticking to Jungian analysis through dream amplification, Tibetan or Hindu Tantra utilizing visualization techniques and *bijamantra* meditations, such as Transcendental Meditation, or Psychosynthesis, Progoff dialogue, or similar exercises.

With these concluding remarks on the Transpersonal Bands, we have finished our survey of the "therapies" that address themselves to the various levels, and so let us take this opportunity to make a few general comments on the levels of the spectrum and the various groups of therapy that address them. Our starting point, as always, is with Mind-only, the Void, Brahman, the non-dual, the Dharmadhatu. We have also called this non-dual awareness "Absolute Subjectivity" as a kind of signpost, for when you completely go "behind" the pseudo-subject, what you now call your "self," you will find only objects, which is the clearest demonstration that the real Self, the Absolute Subjectivity, is *one* with the universe it knows. It knows this page, for example, not by looking at it from afar but by being it. In other words, everything you observe *is* you who are observing it, and this is the fundamental condition of the real world prior to the illusory split between you and it.

Yet in a certain sense, you cannot *see* Mind or Absolute Subjectivity. As the Knower, it cannot be known; as the Seer, it cannot be seen; as the Investigator, it cannot be investigated. True, Absolute Subjectivity *is* everything of which you are now aware, but when you realize that, your sense of identity must likewise shift to *everything* of which you are aware—and when that occurs (it is occurring now), you will no longer feel yourself to be *separate* from that which you are now observing. Thus, as we have said many times, the subject vs. object dualism vanishes in Absolute Subjectivity, in Mind. The subject and the object don't vanish, but the *gap* between them does—or rather, it is understood to have never existed in the first place, so that the adjectives "subjective" and "objective" become quite nonsensical. There is simply a process of non-dual awareness wherein the observer is the observed. So in one sense you cannot see Mind, for it is the Seer; yet in another sense, you are never aware of anything but Mind, for it is *everything* that is seen!

Now "out of" this Absolute Subjectivity, *in this moment*, there evolves the spectrum of consciousness. We have described this evolution from several viewpoints, all somewhat different, but all pointing to the same process: The apparent splitting of a universe into a seer and a seen, and the numerous complexities and reverberations that follow inexorably from this initial complication.

First and foremost, we have described this evolution as resulting from the seeming superimposition of several major dualisms upon Mind, with each successive dualism generating a distinctly narrower sense of identity called a "level" or "band" of the spectrum. Simply stated, each dualism severs a "unitary" process, represses its non-duality, and projects it as two apparently antagonistic opposites—and we, to put it very figuratively, identify with only one of the opposites, or one of the poles of the duality, thereby restricting and narrowing our identity "by half." Each successive dualism-repression-projection thus drastically diminishes those phenomena with which we identify, and consequently our identity shifts successively from the universe to the organism to the ego to parts of the ego (i.e., from Mind to Existential to Ego to Shadow Levels). Since each dualism-repression-projection renders certain processes unconscious, it follows that each level of the spectrum is potentially productive of a specific class of dys-eases. At any rate, thus does the spectrum, with all its consequences, evolve.

We have also followed this evolution using the Tantric metaphor of Energy as Mind, and, from this point of view, we described each level of the spectrum as a certain stage of Energy disintegration, ranging from the originally pure, in-formal Energy (*prana, chi, ki, pneuma, ruh,* organismic consciousness) of Mind all the way "up" to its disintegrations that animate the symbolic and conceptual knowledge of the Ego Level. We have used this metaphor of Energy and its disintegrations because it furnishes a concrete way to relate the evolution of the spectrum to our very sensations at this moment, and also because this interpretation will prove most useful in the next chapter when we discuss ways to forestall the disintegration of Energy and so remember and discover Mind.

From yet another angle, we have described this evolution as the confusing of Absolute Subjectivity with a *particular* and *exclusive* group or complex of *objects:* This we have called the objectification of Absolute Subjectivity. And that means nothing more, nothing less, than that we mistakenly view the universe as a multiple of "objects out there" *separate* from and opposed to the "subject in here" that I call my "self."

Yet this separate and subjective "self," the "little man within" that supposedly looks out at the universe of objects, is obviously an illusion. It is an illusion because, although I imagine it to be the subject which sees, knows, and feels the universe, it is in fact simply another object of perception. That is to say, this "separate self" is actually something which I can see, know, or at least be aware of, for this I betray all the time by saying such things as, "I am aware of myself," or "I know who I am," or "Of course I am aware of myself reading this book!" Inescapably, I feel that I can look at myself, and yet anything at which I can look *must be an object of perception:* Thus my supposedly "subjective self" is not a true subject at all, it is a pseudo-subject, which, in actuality, is just another object! It is something which I can perceive and therefore it cannot be the real Perceiver!

As for the real Perceiver, the true Self, the Absolute Subjectivity—it cannot be seen because it is doing the seeing; it cannot be known for it is the Knower. My true Self can no more see itself as an object than fire can burn itself or a knife can cut itself. Yet, for some odd reason, I have identified my real Self with some peculiar complex of objects that I can look at, and this complex of objects I then mistake for my "subjective self." Thus my identify shifts from Absolute Subjectivity, which is one with its universe, to pseudo-subjectivity, which is supposedly separate from its objects of perception, even though a careful look will inescapably demonstrate this pseudo-subject to be nothing but one among other *objects* of perception. I have, in other words, *objectified* what I am, I have *tried* to see my real Self as an object, and *imagining* that I have succeeded, I have necessarily surrendered my original identity with the entire universe and have instead fastened onto a particular and exclusive set of objects. In short, I have confused the Seer with what, in fact, is something that can be seen. In this confusion, my identity shifts to a pseudo-subject which I now imagine confronts an alien world of objects.

But my case of mistaken identity does not end here, for, as we have seen, there are *levels of pseudo-subjectivity*. There follows, upon this, initial confusion, a progressive narrowing and restricting of my sense of personal identity, that is, a narrowing and restricting of my sense of *pseudo-subjectivity, of that which I feel to be the "separate subject" in me which confronts the world as object out there.* This sense of separate identity, of pseudo-subjectivity, ranges from my total organism to my ego to parts of my ego—each shift representing, of course, a level of the spectrum. We have called this viewpoint the "objectification of Mind," because each level represents just that—a particular and exclusive set of objects which I have mistaken for a real subjective self and with which I therefore inadvertently identify. In this sense, each level of the spectrum is a level of mistaken identity, of pseudo-subjectivity.

Such, then, are the three different ways we have described the evolution of the spectrum of consciousness. Of course, each is saying the same thing from a different angle; for to say that each level of the spectrum is a level of pseudo-subjectivity, or a progressively narrowed sense of personal identity, *is* to say that each level is marked by a particular dualism-repression-projection, inasmuch as this is precisely the mechanism which creates and supports each level, each sense of pseudo-subjectivity. Put rather figuratively, on each level our sense of pseudo-subjectivity is simply our mistaken identity with "one-half" of the dualism which creates that level. Thus a particular sense of pseudo-subjectivity is always supported by a particular dualism-repression-projection— for that dualism is simply the dividing line between the pseudo-subject "in here" and its "objects out there."

Now because the common thread running throughout each level is the process of dualism, then repression, then projection, the therapies of each level also share a common characteristic—*they reverse this process* (on their particular level) *by helping the individual contact the alienated and projected aspects, re-integrate them, and thus "heal," "make whole," and "unify" that level.* This process results in "cure," or "growth," or "healing," for the simple reason that the individual has, in effect, broadened or expanded his sense of self-identity. As a dualism is healed on any level, the elements of that level which once threatened the individual are seen to be nothing more than aspects of his own consciousness which he had split-off, repressed, and projected, a process which necessarily diminished his sense of identity and set the stage for a certain class of dys-eases. Reversing this process on any level simply yanks the support out from under that level's class of dys-eases.

Any time an individual completely reverses this process, heals and wholes the major dualism of any level, then it follows that he *automatically and quite spontaneously descends the spectrum to the next level,* to the level that "includes" both poles of the "old" duality, to the level of which the one above was merely a fragmentation. For example, when the tertiary split between psyche and soma is actually healed, the individual necessarily discovers the total organism: in other words, he has automatically descended to the Existential Level. The healing of any major dualism simply reveals the "underlying unitary process" or gestalt which was rendered unconscious by that dualism—and that in itself marks the descent of the spectrum to the new "underlying" level.

Once on the "new" level, whatever that level may be, the individual naturally becomes more sensitive to the major characteristics of that level: its particular "needs" or "instincts" or "drives," its potentials and values, its mode of knowing, its dream material (furnished by its unconscious processes), and of course its major dualism-repression-projection and the class of dys-eases potentially consequent upon it. We have spent the last four chapters very briefly outlining these characteristics of each level, and so, for convenience sake, we will summarize these in chart form only (see Table 1). Let us repeat, however, that these characteristics necessarily are rather general and abstract, leaving much room for individual elaboration. This is especially true of the concept of "need," "drive," or "instinct." Generally speaking, we understand the "needs" of any level to be a reflection of the potential for growth on that level as well as a type of compensation for what, on that level, seems lacking in the individual. Further, let us state here, without the embellishment that more space would allow, that we take the dreams of any level to be a symbolic intimation of that lack, i.e., a symbolic intimation of those aspects of the universe with which one is no longer identified. Wherever there is alienation of the universe from itself, there is the stuff of which dreams are made. At any rate, as the individual descends the spectrum, different characteristics of the "new" levels begin to more clearly emerge.

This phenomenon of spontaneous descent, which is potentially inherent in everyone, is an almost exact analogue of Maslow's hierarchical needs[13]—that is, neurotic needs (Shadow Level), basic needs (Ego and Existential Levels), and meta-needs (Transpersonal Bands. Mind has no needs for there is nothing outside it.) As soon as an individual clears up one set of needs, the next set spontaneously emerges, and failure to satisfy these emergent needs will result in a different set of problems ("grumbles and meta-grumbles").

Thus, on the Shadow Level, the basic needs are not satisfied. Through repression, alienation, or some other projective mechanism, the individual fails to recognize the nature of his basic needs. And since, as is well-known, one cannot get enough of what one does not really need, a whole battery of insatiable neurotic needs develop. If, on the other hand, these neurotic needs can be understood and displaced, so that the underlying basic needs can emerge (hierarchically), the individual can begin to act on them so as to find thereby his way to a larger fulfillment. He also finds—almost by definition—his way to a lower level of the Spectrum. And by the time the individual reaches the Existential Level, an entirely new set of needs, the meta-needs, begin to emerge, carrying with them a call, sometimes a demand, to transcendence. Acting upon these meta-needs initiates one into the world of the Transpersonal Bands; shunning them throws one into the grips of a meta-pathology. That these meta-needs correspond to a transpersonal reality is clearly announced by Maslow himself:

> Meta-motives are, therefore, no longer *only* intra-psychic [i.e., Egoic] or organismic [i.e., Existential]. They are equally inner and outer. . . .This means that the distinction between self and not-self has broken down (or has been transcended). There is now less differentiation between the world and the person. . . .He becomes an enlarged self, we could say. . . .To identify one's highest self with the highest values of the world out there means, to some extent at least, a fusion with the not-self.[14]

Keeping in mind that his partial fusion of organism and environment is a fusion without confusion, Maslow's quote may be taken as perfectly descriptive of the Transpersonal Bands.

At any rate, let us now continue with our basic discussion on the common thread running throughout the therapies which address the various levels of the Spectrum. Because each major dualism creates a corresponding sense of pseudo-subjectivity, we can also approach our topic from this angle. Since each level of the Spectrum is actually a *particular* set of objects mistaken for a real subject, that is, since each level is a progressively narrowed sense of personal identity or pseudo-subjectivity, *therapy consists, on each level, in bringing this particular pseudo-subject fully into consciousness.* For by bringing it completely into awareness and by seeing it *objectively*, the individual realizes that it is obviously not a real *subject,* a real self. Thereupon, he relinguishes his identity with that particular pseudo-subject and descends a level to a broader and firmer base of personal identity. Thus, it matters not whether we speak of healing a major dualism or of relinguishing the corresponding sense of pseudo-subjectivity. For to heal the major dualism of any level is to make that level fully conscious; to make it conscious is to see it as an object; to see it as an object is to cease confusing it with the Seer.

LEVEL	POTENTIALS	DYS-EASES
SHADOW	Overt compensations: pride, drive to success, righteous indignation, sensitivity, role playing, "neurotic creativity" Romantic love—heterosexual or homosexual (shadow-hugging)	Panic anxiety Guilt (Super-ego) Hatred (shadow-boxing) Depression (retroflected rage) Pressure (projected drive) Fear (projected aggression)
EGO	Intellectual-philosophical Character stability Civility Self-control, deliberate Verbal communication Linear illumination in general Crystallization of 1st mode of knowing Adjustment to Biosocial Band	Chronic low-grade emergency (Perls) Depression as dis-embodiment (Lowen) Lack of Prehension & Intentionality The world as banal (Watts) Lack of spontaneity and B-values World as linear-only
BIOSOCIAL	Civilization Culture Conventional stabilization Traditional perception Social membership Language, law, logic	Biosocialization of all existential and transpersonal awareness, needs, perceptions, etc. The Great Filter Breakdown of World Gloss and Conventional World View (one element common in "schizophrenia", but also, with different effects, in deep meditation—the latter rarely results in "dys-ease", however, because the World View can be easily resumed for all practical purposes)
EXISTENTIAL	Prehension Intentionality Emergence of B-values Authenticity (Perls) Centeredness Biological faith (Lowen) Exoteric religion Biological spontaneity	Angst—the cramp (Benoit) Existential despair Metaphysical distress Humanistic guilt (Fromm) Perinatal irruptions (Grof) of a negative nature Existential anxiety as the "inability to accept death" (Brown) Primordial hatred of Not-Self—a result of the primary dualism
TRANSPERSONAL	B-values Mythological awareness Plateau experience Detachment and the transpersonal Witness Paranormal phenomena Extra-terrestrial encounters Prana appears as higher Kundalini chakras (to Level of Mind, Chakras [Sefiroth] are symbolic only)	Archetype irruptions Transpersonal anxiety (Lilly) Dead void heresy (Zen) Negative out-of-the-body experiences Negative phylogenetic irruptions

JOHN LILLY (Gurdjieff) OTHER SIMILARITIES (Western Only)

	JOHN LILLY (Gurdjieff)	OTHER SIMILARITIES (Western Only)
SHADOW	−24 "Negative state; pain, guilt, fear."	Idealized self (Horney) Topdog/Underdog (Perls) Parent/Child (Berne) Lower unconscious (Assagioli) Remnants of infantile ego (Freud)
EGO	±48 "Neutral biocomputer state; absorption and transmission of new ideas; reception and transmission of new data and programs; teaching and learning with max. facilitation. Neutral state. On the earth."	Actual self (Horney) Self (Rogers) Ego (Freud) Eigenwelt Adult Ego State (Berne) Freudian level (Grof) Recollective Analytic Level (Houston/Masters)
BIOSOCIAL	+24 "All needed programs are in the unconscious of the biocomputer, operating smoothly. Ego is lost in pleasurable tasks one knows and likes."	Social Filter of: Social Character Langauge Logic (Fromm) Mitwelt Social gloss Consensual validation
EXISTENTIAL	+12 "Blissful state; cosmic love, reception of grace, heightened bodily awareness; highest function of bodily consciousness, being in love, etc." −12 "Extremely negative body state; one is still in the body, pain extreme."	Unwelt Real Self (Horney) Total organism (Rogers) Body-ego (Freud) Centered self (Perls) Biological self (Lowen) Ontogenetic layer (Ring) Basic Perinatal Birth Matrices (Grof) Rankian Level (Grof)
TRANSPERSONAL	+6 "Point source of consciousness. Astral travel, traveling clairaudience and clairvoyance; fusion with other entities in time." −6 "Purgatorial negativity."	Higher Self (Assagioli) Collective Unconscious (Jung) Trans-individual, Phylogenetic, and Extra-terrestrial layers (Ring) Supra-individual witnessing (Maslow) The Integral Level (Houston/Masters)

LEVEL	DREAMS	NEEDS
SHADOW	Nightmares Symbolic shadow Malevolent aspects Projected shadow	Neurotic needs, e.g.: manipulation power sexualization obsessive-compulsive
EGO	Hangover from the day Environmental unfinished gestalten Psychodynamic	Need for an accurate and acceptable self-image (Putneys) Basic needs (Maslow), which usually emerge hierarchically Linear stability Goal-oriented needs
BIOSOCIAL	As with most characteristics, the dreams above the Biosocial Bands reflect conventions of society; those below begin to be universal: existential or archetypal	Biosocialization of existential needs Demand (Lacan) Translation of reality accurately according to conventional paradigms (Reality principle is actually the Conventionality principle)
EXISTENTIAL	Nonconventional environmental background Angst, death dreams Perinatal factors Ontogenetic dreams	Emergence of meta-needs (Maslow) Need to endure (time) and to exist (space)—compensations of primary and secondary repressions Growth (as used by Perls) Intentionalities
TRANSPERSONAL	Hangovers from history Phylogenetic Incarnational Archetypal ESP dreams Translucent dreams (state of the transpersonal Witness)	Satisfaction of meta-needs Archetype elaboration Trans-individual relationship Avoidance of Mind (at this level, that is a true need, the last to be displaced)

UNCONSCIOUS

	PSU	POU
SHADOW	Ego Biosocial Band Centaur Transpersonal Bands Absolute Subjectivity (universe)	Shadow Body (biosocialized) Environment (biosocialized, archetypal)
EGO	Biosocial Band Centaur Transpersonal Bands Absolute Subjectivity (universe)	Body (biosocialized) Environment (biosocialized, archetypal)
BIOSOCIAL	Centaur Transpersonal Bands Absolute Subjectivity (universe)	Environment (biosocialized, archetypal)
EXISTENTIAL	Transpersonal Bands Absolute Subjectivity (universe)	Environment (archetypal)
TRANSPERSONAL	Absolute Subjectivity (universe)	Portions of environment (some archetypal, some "pure")

	TIME AND TENDENCIES	COMMON MODE OF LEVEL CONTACTING	OTHER ASPECTS
SHADOW	Distorted conventional time "Desparation" willpower; the frantic, demonic will	Active association—or "free association," discovering the linear or distorted linear "psychic enchainment" leading to shadow complex	On the Ego/Shadow level, a person is actively involved in conventional, linear *time structuring*, a phenomenon presently being studied by Transactional Analysis; this time structuring involves the manufacture of scripts, counterscripts, and egoic games.
EGO	Conventional time as linear past-present-future Will-power	Active reflection—if shadow complex is strong, active reflection, the mental grasp of one's self-image, can occur accurately only after active association or some other Shadow Level approach	Paternal mythology, incest, castration (Neumann) Deep-rooted inclination to time structuring

BIOSOCIAL	Socialization and serialization of the passing present Socialization as establishment of conventional "meaning" (spliting of prehensions)	No common mode here, but Lilly (see elsewhere on this table) suggests what amounts to *active dereflection*; Frankl, in fact, has long proposed active dereflection as a preliminary move to the Existential Level.	The distinctions of the BSB lead to rules which in turn structure games; these subtle games, however, which amount to something like a world gloss, are not to be confused with the more overt "games egos play," so admirably dealt with by Berne, although they are indeed their root source
EXISTENTIAL	Passing present (*nunc fluens*) Intentionalities (moving prehensions) The Will	Active prehension—the three-dimensional grasp of one's entire being; not to be confused with active reflection or association	Maternal mythology, incest, castration (Neumann) Breath as circulation of vital force (prana)
TRANSPERSONAL	Mythological everlastingness (Mind alone being strictly timeless) Vasanas—subtle, trans-individual tendencies, responsible for moment to moment "re-birth" of the separate-self sense	Active imagination, in the very special sense given it by Jung—a *radial* awareness Active detachment or dis-identification (For Level of Mind: *active attention*, factor 1 [See chap. XI])	Uroboric mythology, incest, castration (Neumann) Breath as circulation of vital force (prana) takes on supra-individual and spiritual dimensions (prana=-Holy Spirit)

This suggests that, in one sense, the descent of the spectrum of consciousness is a progressive process of *dis-identification* from a "narrower" sense of pseudo-subject to a "broader" one, a process which brings an expanded sense of freedom and control. In the words of Assagioli:

> We are dominated by everything with which our self becomes identified. We can dominate and control everything from which we dis-identify ourselves.[15]

That is quite true, but let us not forget it is only half the story. For if each successive shift down the spectrum is a process of dis-identifying with the "old" pseudo-subject, then it is also a process of discovering a "new" identity on the level beneath it. For when an individual ceases to identify with a pseudo-subject composing "one-half" of the major dualism of the particular level of the spectrum, he necessarily shifts down a level and discovers a new identity which includes "both halves" of the old duality, which harmonizes what were once thought to be antagonistic opposites. More correctly, he has simply discovered the particular gestalt of which the old level was a fragmentation. Dis-identifying with the "half," he spontaneously identifies with the "whole." At this broader level of pseudo-subjectivity, he is finally able to assume responsibility for what, on the level above, had appeared as involuntary, alien, outside.

Overall, then, the healing of a major dualism results in a shift of personal identity, for (again speaking very figuratively) the individual can no longer attach himself to "one-half" of the old dualism, such as, for example, his mind and not his body. The individual's "old" sense of pseudo-subject, which was confined to one pole of the dualism, is realized to be just another object of perception—as such, he is no longer using it as a pseudo-subject with which to see, and thus distort, the world. The collapse of a major dualism is simultaneously the collapse of the particular sense of pseudo-subjectivity supported by that dualism. Unconscious symbolic separation and its resultant dys-ease has been replaced by conscious authentic non-separation and its relative harmony. Because the "old" level was actually created by a splitting of the level beneath it, its "healing" automatically results in the restoration of that prior unity. This process occurs each time the individual descends a level. His identity has broadened to include aspects of the universe once thought alien; he now confronts the world from a broader and firmer base of pseudo-subjectivity. To be sure, this does not represent "final awakening"—the "new" level is still a pseudo-subject, but it is nevertheless a more comfortable one, a more dysease-less one. It is still a dream, but less of a nightmare. It is only in the final step that the dream of pseudo-subjectivity itself vanishes—and we are now ready to examine that step.

Finally, let us clarify one last technical but important point. And to do so, let us recall, as an illustration of what we will be discussing, the generation of the Ego Level. With the rise of the tertiary dualism, the centaur is rendered unconscious: it is split, repressed, and projected as the ego vs. the body. Correspondingly, the individual's sense of selfness, his pseudo-subjectivity, shifts from the centaur to the ego, with the body now felt to be an *object* out there.

So, we may ask, what becomes of the centaur? We know of course that its repression does not kill it, but merely buries it alive. Hence it continues to exist and to exert a profound, if sometimes subtle, influence upon the individual. For the centaur, although "unconscious", nevertheless acts—however indirectly—so as to color the individual's entire sense of being a separate self, the individual's entire sense of pseudo-subjectivity. Remember that the sense of being an ego rests upon the sense of being a centaur, although the latter is now more-or-less consciously forgotten. Because the centaur now lies in the direction of those factors that unconsciously but profoundly mold a person's conscious sense of pseudo-subjectivity, we can speak of the now buried centaur as an aspect of what might be called the "pseudo-subjectal unconscious", or PSU for short. In general, all of the levels and bands of the Spectrum that are *beneath* the one upon which an individual presently exists collectively contribute to that inwardly felt sense of pseudo-subjectivity, of which his present level is merely the conscious tip. And thus, all of these lower levels taken together constitute the pseudo-subjectal unconscious (Fig. 18 has been drawn to represent this PSU for an individual living as the persona). Because of this, a change in, for example, the Biosocial Band, or the activation of an archetype, can produce in the ego or persona significant alterations in its conscious sense of existence. Using Energy metaphor, we would say that the contents of the individual's consciousness have reached awareness only after transversing all of the levels of the PSU, the pseudo-subjectal unconscious. So just because a person is living on one particular level of the spectrum is no reason to disregard any of the lower levels—just the contrary: their influence is profound.

But, to finish with this illustration, what becomes of the "body" with the generation of the Ego Level? It is spoken of as a "content" of the unconscious, to be sure, yet the individual *does* perceive it, only in a very distorted and even illusory fashion, namely, as an object "out there." Yet remember that the same thing occurs with the Shadow: when the ego is rendered unconscious with the rise of the quaternary dualism, the Shadow is perceived as existing "objectively, out there." And so also with the environment itself: after the primary dualism, the environment appears as an "object out there." Now all of these—the environment, the body, the shadow—are indeed aspects of the unconscious, but through the major dualisms and projections, they are perceived in a distorted fashion: as false or illusory or pseudo objects. Thus, we may collectively speak of them as constituting the "pseudo-objectal unconscious", or POU for short. (See Fig. 18)

Thus, just as the contents of the PSU mold an individual's sense of existence from *within*, the contents of the POU mold it from *without*. And this molding action from without is always of one general type: the individual *reacts* to these "objects" instead of *acts,* he *avoids* instead of *witnesses,* he is *affected* instead of *informed.* This we have seen on every level of the Spectrum.

The different levels of the pseudo-subjectal and pseudo-objectal unconscious together constitute the entire unconscious. Needless to say, these two aspects of the total unconscious are actually just flip sides of one another. At any rate, in Fig. 18, which is representative of an individual on the Shadow Level, we have marked out the three major areas: the conscious pseudo-subject, the pseudo-subjectal unconscious, and the pseudo-objectal unconscious (as well as all of the levels and bands of the spectrum composing these areas.) These three areas together constitute the *entire* territory of consciousness/unconsciousness.

The import of what has been said thus far is that all of the lower levels, although unconscious in one sense, are in no sense dead or ineffectual. This is especially to be seen with such items as "symptoms", desires, or dreams. For although the individual is definitely more alive to the characteristics of his present level, to its dyseases and pains, its joys and potentials, its desires and needs, and its dreams, nevertheless all of the lower levels (the PSU and the POU) contribute, in one way or another, to the "contents" of consciousness. And the point is that—especially in any sort of "therapy"—it is most wise to determine where possible, the levels from which different dreams, symptoms, or desires originate, and respond accordingly.

For example, archetypal anxiety, existential anxiety, and shadow anxiety are different beasts indeed, and simply must not be treated as the same. The indiscriminate use of a single therapeutic technique for all symptoms may, on occassion, have the most unfortunate effects. Shadow anxiety, for instance, is that "hit the panic-button" feeling which usually arises from some projected bit of excitement and interest, or occasionally from some projected anger. This is handled—as we have seen—by integrating that

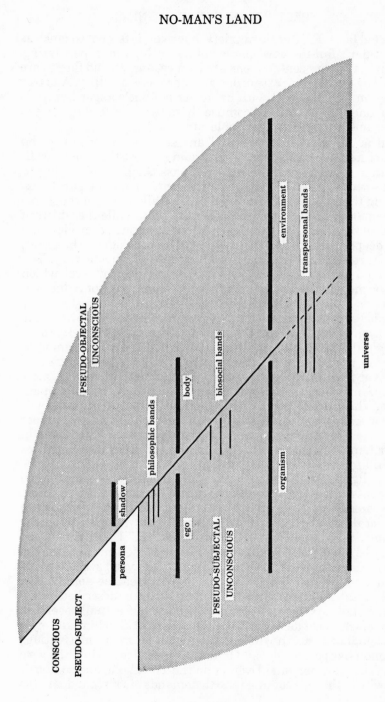

Figure 18

projected facet. Existential anxiety, however, is felt not so much as a "feet-don't-fail-me-now" panic but as a cold, almost paralyzing, cramp in the very center of one's existence, and its cold flames are fanned by the black debate of one's being vs. one's nullity. And this angst can only be dealt with by facing not one's anger but one's death, one's inner void. To confuse these two is indeed to run the risk of upsetting the entire apple cart.

And as for most transpersonal anxiety, we haven't even the foggiest notion of how to treat that, and so most therapists, well-intentioned to be sure, nevertheless pass the buck by trying to reduce it to shadow anxiety, thereby more or less elegantly extracting their own necks from the noose while so much the worse for the patients. (It is generally the case that, while therapists of one level recognize all of the levels *above* their own, they view any level deeper than their own as being of a pathological character, and so are quick to explain it away with a diagnostic fury. The same holds doubly for actual dys-eases of any "deeper" level, which must be met with dialogues on that level alone, and not reduced to the terms of an upper level.)

So also with dreams: we must recognize, where we are able, the level from which a dream originates. It is a nightmare dream, a terrifyingly direct message from the Shadow? Or is it simply a hangover from the day, originating from the Ego? Or deeper yet, a hangover from history, a "big dream" of archetypal import, messages from the Transpersonal Bands, hints from the gods themselves? The answer to this will determine which approach one will use: for example, Gestalt or Jungian (or perhaps both in proper sequence). Failure to recognize these differences will result in either impoverishment or inflation: archetype reduced to ego, or ego inflated to archetype.

Any slight appreciation of man's depth, of his pluridimensional awareness, of the spectrum-like nature of his consciousness, forces these considerations upon us—and they are extremely important considerations at that. It slowly begins to dawn on a person, for example, that he is leading a "life of despair." He might indeed simply be "madder 'n hell" and not know it, so that here on the Shadow Level "m-a-d" has become "s-a-d" (as most psychoanalytical thinkers would argue).[16] Yet he might instead be—on the Ego Level—totally out of direct touch with his body (as described by, for example, Lowen).[17] Or yet again, he might have actually seen the cramp of the secondary dualism, the spasm at Existential Level, the avoidance of death which is the root of all man's motivations (as Benoit has pointed out).[18] Or has he indeed looked into the very face of the transpersonal Dweller on the Threshold, and so knows deep within that his coming rebirth demands his instant death (as the mystics of all ages have told)? Can we be so callous and so insensitive as to dare throw them all into the same therapeutic bag?

Now I hope that this type of approach—recognizing Absolute Subjectivity as well as levels of conscious pseudo-subject, levels of pseudo-subjectal unconscious, and levels of pseudo-objectal unconsious—will also help to make sense of what *appears* to be some contradictory trends in humanistic, orthodox, and transpersonal psychologies. At one point we are told to "stop alienating, *identify* with your own actions and emotions and assume responsibility!" And yet other approaches will ask us to "*dis-identify* with your ego, your emotions, your body, etc." Are we to identify or dis-identify? The contradiction is resolved when we see, on the Shadow Level for example, that to identify with the Shadow (POU) *is* to dis-identify with the persona (conscious pseudo-subject) and thereby awaken to the Ego (heretofore PSU). Then going a step further, or deeper if you will, to identify with the body (POU) *is* to dis-identify with the ego (conscious pseudo-subject) and awaken to the centaur (heretofore PSU, now conscious pseudo-subject). And finally, to identify completely with the object of meditation (e.g., a koan) *is* to dis-identify with the last traces of the pseudo-subject in general and thus awaken as non-dual awareness. To be a consistent practice, most forms of therapy emphasize one of these approaches exclusively, and rightly so; it can otherwise be most confusing. But I don't think we need to conclude thereby that we have a contradiction here.

In other words, whether a therapy 1) "digs" for the PSU, like psychoanalysis on the Shadow Level or Jungian analysis on the Transpersonal Bands; or 2) identifies with the POU, like Gestalt on the Shadow Level and Bioenergetics on the Existential Level; or 3) dis-identifies with the pseudo-subject, like Transactional Analysis on the Shadow Level and Psycho-synthesis on the Transpersonal Bands—we see in every case the same basic process of "descent" at work: the remapping of a person's boundaries, the shift to the "next deepest" level of the Spectrum. The various schools of therapy simply aim at different levels, so that some therapies are geared to take this process to deeper and deeper realms.

And yet this is in no way to be taken as a denigration of therapies that work only with upper levels. The various levels of the Spectrum do apparently exist; they do have different characteristics, among which is different dys-eases; and thus we do need to recognize and utilize the therapies most appropriate for a particular level. Even if everybody in the world acknowledged Mind-only and were practicing shikan-taza or mahamudra or dzog-chen, we would still need upper level therapies, because a person characteristically avoids Mind-only by presently constructing boundaries (levels of the Spectrum); these different boundaries generate different dys-eases; and these dys-eases can best be dealt with by therapies which take them as their sole concern.

Let me give a small example of this. A woman who had been practicing a mantra meditation for about two years was one day violently interrupted during meditation by a startling vision of a dog about to attack her. This considerably disturbed this woman for some time, and the only advice her teacher had for her was to keep trying to meditate—which she did, for over two months without success. This is unfortunate, because I've seen a good Gestalt therapist permanently take care of *that* type of projection in 15 minutes. What had occurred was that some PSU hostility complex had surfaced, was resisted, and therefore projected as POU—a dog attacking her!

Now the PSU, if we may approach it from another angle, is that which, at this moment, unconsciously separates a person as "subject" from the world of objects "out there". The PSU, as a whole, is a type of unconscious wedge driven between subject and object, a wedge that separates you from this page, and thus distorts—*in different ways on different levels*—the real world of Suchness. Under the *special conditions* of any type of legitimate therapy, the PSU of the *corresponding level* is loosened, broken-up, dislodged, and rises to the surface, as it were. Every therapist recognizes that the essential aspect of the therapeutic process is an understanding, or witnessing, or working-through, or digesting, or giving awareness to, this "stuff which comes up." And the stuff which comes up is nothing other than the PSU. This is therapeutic not so much because it affords insight into a person's self, not so much because it is a working-through of infantile or birth trauma, not so much because it is a desensitization—although all these might be auxiliary reasons—but primarily because, in globally apprehending this uprising material, a person has made it an *object* of awareness and thus is no longer exclusively and *subjectively* identified with it. Because he can see it, he no longer confuses it with the Seer. Because he can look at it, he has ceased using it as something with which to *unconsciously* look at and thus distort reality. In short, the wedge between subject and object has been "thinned."

Every therapy—whether psychoanalysis, Rolfing, Gestalt, Jungian, rational-emotive, psychosynthesis, bioenergetics—deals with this "stuff which comes up" on its own level and with its own appropriate means. Furthermore, in a global fashion the therapy of any level ultimately cuts through the PSU of every level above it. Thus, transpersonal meditation, and especially Mind meditation, necessarily cuts through the PSU of all upper levels. What we see in meditation is thus a gradual surfacing of all of the PSU, until it is exhausted as object (emptied or cast out) and the person hence falls through his pseudo-subjectivity into Absolute Subjectivity. This exhausting of the PSU shows up as "makyo" (Zen), or "un-stressing thoughts" (TM), or "rising mind forms" (bhakti yoga), or the "casting up and out of demons" (contemplation)—the very same phenomenon seen in every other level therapy, except that meditation aimed at Mind takes this process to its ultimate conclu-sion, to the limit of the Spectrum, to the total dissolution of the PSU.

As the PSU comes up in an individual, it is made objective, no longer confused with the Real Subject until there is only the Real Subject. In some cases the PSU may come up in meditation so globally that it is almost unnoticed. But in a large number of cases the PSU comes up in a characteristic order, the same order fre-quently seen in LSD research, an order Grof sets out as Freudian, Rankian, Jungian, which we recognize easily as Ego, Existential, and Transpersonal, reflecting exactly the order of the boundaries of the Spectrum. It is not *necessary* that this order be passed through (since to directly contact one level is to undercut all levels above it), but it usually is.

We can conclude, therefore, that an upper level therapy can be beneficial for anyone pursuing the Transpersonal or Mind Levels. These therapies very rapidly loosen the PSU of their respective levels, so that meditation can more quickly proceed to deeper levels. At the same time, there is a danger, for someone pursuing Mind, in overdoing this shuffling of therapies, since a person might likely become enchanted with the games of an upper level instead of putting that level in order *so as to more easily drop it*. In general, then, we might say that until meditation becomes stabilized, ap-propriate upper level therapies might be most beneficial. Once stabilized, however, recourse to extended upper level therapy is indicated only in severe irruptions of the PSU which seriously disrupt further practice (as in the case of the woman and the dog vision.) Ultimately, a person in meditation must face having no recourse at all, and this is just what upper level therapies prevent. Having no recourse, no way out, no way forward or backward, he is reduced to the simplicity of the moment, with nothing ahead of him and nothing behind him. His boundaries collapse, and, as St. Augustine put it, "in one single flash he arrives at That Which Is." When Fa-ch'ang was dying, a squirrel screeched out from the roof-top. "It's just this," he said, "and nothing more."

With these concluding remarks, the only "therapies" remaining for us to consider are those that address themselves to the Level of

Mind. For those who wish to follow the mystics to this Level, it is the venture of all ventures, the quest for the Holy Grail, the search for the Philosopher's Stone, the Elixir of Immortality, the Master Game itself. It is not without risks, but then no voyage is. As a "therapy" this one is no different from any other—it, too, aims at healing a particular dualism, in this case, the Primary Dualism, the primordial dualism, the separation of the organism and environment, of subject and object, the separation of the Sun and the Moon, the splitting of Heaven and Earth, the very creation of Male and Female, the distinction between Inner Man and Outer Individuality, Sacredotium and Regnum, the primordial dismemberment of the endless Serpent—a dismemberment reenacted today exactly as it was performed in the most ancient of ancient times, long before the Gods descended from Mount Olympus and Meru and Tabor to counsel mortals, long before the Earth and Sun were separated out of a single mass of blazing fire in the remote darkness of space, a dismemberment that goes back to the very point where God emerged from the Void and divided the Light from the Dark, a point that is nevertheless everpresent, without date or duration, reenacting itself *Now*, not once, but thousands upon thousands of times in this single moment. And it is precisely here, in *this* moment, this never-fading Now, that the search ends, for it flashes clear that the Goal, the Sought, is nothing but the Seeker himself.

REFERENCES AND NOTES

1. C. G. Jung, *The Structure and Dynamics of the Psyche* (New York: Pantheon, 1960), pp. 310-311.

2. Joseph Campbell, ed., *The Portable Jung* (New York: Viking Press), p. 67.

3. Lama Govinda, *The Foundations of Tibetan Mysticism* (New York: Samuel Weiser, 1973), p. 91.

4. Ibid., p. 104.

5. P. W. Martin, *Experiment in Depth* (London: Routledge and Kegan Paul, 1967).

6. Govinda, *Foundations of Tibetan Mysticism*, p. 105.

7. C. G. Jung, *Modern Man in Search of a Soul* (New York: Harcourt Brace, 1936).

8. C. G. Jung, *Analytical Psychology: Its Theory and Practice* (New York: Vintage, 1968), p. 110.

9. Quoted in J. Campbell, *The Masks of God—Creative Mythology* (New York: Viking, 1968), p. 655.

10. M. Eliade, *Images and Symbols* (Sheed and Ward, 1969), p. 89.

11. Campbell, *Portable Jung,* p. xxii.

12. S.Krippner, ed., "The Plateau Experience: A. H. Maslow and others", *Journal of Transpersonel Psychology,* vol. 4, no. 2, 1972 pp. 107-120.

13. A. H. Maslow, *Toward a Psychology of Being* (New York: Van Nostrand, 1968).

14. A. H. Maslow, *The Farther Reaches of Human Nature* (New York: Viking, 1971).

15. R. Assagioli, *Psychosynthesis* (New York: Viking 1965).

16. O. Fenichel, *The Psychoanalytic Theory of Neurosis* (New York: Norton, 1972).

17. A. Lowen, *Depression and the Body* (Baltimore: Penguin, 1973).

18. H. Benoit, *The Supreme Doctrine* (New York: Viking,1955). For important works on some facets of the Transpersonal Bands, *See also Masters and Houston, Varieties of Psychedelic Experience.* (Dell); S. Groff, *Realms of the Human Unconscious* (Viking); and C. Tart, ed., *Transpersonal Psychologies* (Harper).

XI. *THAT WHICH IS ALWAYS ALREADY*

Misty rain on Mount Lu,
And waves surging on the river Che;
When you have not yet been there,
Many a regret surely you have;
But once there and homeward you wend,
How matter of fact things look!
Misty rain on Mount Lu,
And waves surging on the river Che.

Su Tung-Po

Although for convenience sake we have been speaking of Mind
as the "deepest level" of the spectrum, it is not actually a particular
level, let alone "deep." The "level" of Mind is in no way buried or
hidden in the obscure depths of our psyche—on the contrary, the
level of Mind is our present and ordinary state of consciousness,
for, being infinite and absolutely all-inclusive, it is compatible
with every imaginable level or state of consciousness. That is, the
"no-level" of Mind cannot be a particular level set apart from other
levels, for that would impose a spatial limitation on Mind. Mind is
rather the all-inclusive yet dimensionless reality of which each
level represents an illusory deviation. Now this must be emphasized—our present, everyday state of consciousness, whatever
it may be, sad, happy, depressed, ecstatic, agitated, calm, worried
or afraid—just that, just as it is, is the Level of Mind. Brahman is
not a particular experience, level of consciousness or state of
soul—rather it is precisely whatever level you happen to have now,
and realizing this confers upon one a profound center of peace that
underlies and persists throughout the worst depressions, anxieties, and fears. Even though our scholarship in the field of pure
mysticism, Eastern and Western alike, has dramatically improved
over the past few decades, there are those who continue to distort
its "doctrines" in all manner of idiotic ways, claiming mystics are
otherworldly, totally out of touch with everyday reality (whatever
that means), self-centered, constantly immersed in trance, and so
on. This tells us nothing about mysticism but quite a bit about the
ignorance of those who subscribe to such incredible views; and,
furthermore, it completely overlooks the sayings of the great masters of every tradition that "your everday and ordinary consciousness, that is the Tao."

To be sure, some mystics historically have led the secluded and
self-absorbing life of a hermit, but this is a matter of personal style
and not at all to be confused with mysticism per se, any more than
the life style of Rasputin is to be confused with Christianity per se.

For, in fact, the highest ideal of the mystic is that expressed by the Bodhisattva, who in Mahayana Buddhism is one who sees the Godhead everywhere and everywhen, in every person, place, and thing, and thus does not have to retire into solitude and trance in order to find his "god." The Bodhisattva's mystic vision is identical with whatever he happens to be doing at the moment, and whether that be dancing, working, crying, laughing, or intensely suffering, he knows that fundamentally "All shall be well, and all shall be well, and all manner of thing shall be well," for, as Hakuin put it, "This very earth is the Lotus Land of Purity; And this body is the body of Buddha."

Now precisely because Mind is everywhere and everywhen, because it is always already the case, there is no possibility or even meaning in "trying to find It" or in "trying to reach It," for that would imply a movement from a place where Mind is absent to a place where it is present—but there is no place where it is absent. Mind, being everywhere present, abides in no particular place where we can finally grab it. The no-level of Mind, therefore, we can never attain. But then, neither can we escape it.

> As [the Buddha] has no abiding place anywhere, none can take hold of him, nor can he be let go.
>
> Ma-tsu

> Real peace and eternal happiness, immortality and universal truth, the Way of heaven and earth, in other words the experience of the Absolute and infinite, or in religious terms the Buddha way—the great mistake is to think of getting it in some heaven or world on the other side. *We never leave the Way for a moment. What we can leave is not the Way.*[1]
>
> Amakuki Sessan

> Follow it and, behold, it escapes you; run from it and it follows you close. You can neither possess it nor have done with it. . . . Henceforth, there will be no need to grieve or to worry about such things.[2]
>
> Huang Po

> If you run away from the Void, you can never be free from it; if you search for the Void, you can never reach it.[3]
>
> Niu-tou Fa-yung

> Like the empty sky it has no boundaries,
> Yet it is right HERE, ever serene and clear.
> When you seek to attain it, you cannot see it.
> You cannot take hold of it,
> But neither can you lose it.[4]
>
> Yung-chia

If Mind or Tao or Godhead is the state that we are ardently

searching, and yet outside Mind there is absolutely nowhere to go, it follows that we are already there! That we are already one with the Godhead, that what we are Now is Mind. As Dame Julian of Norwich exclaimed:

> See! I am God; See I am in all things; see! I do all thing; see! I never lift mine hands off my works, nor ever shall, without end; see! I lead all thing to the end I ordained it to from without beginning, by the same Might, Wisdom, and Love whereby I made it. How should anything be amiss?

Or from Hakuin's *Zazen Wasan*:

> All beings are from the very beginning Buddhas:
> It is like ice and water,
> Apart from water, no ice can exist;
> Outside living beings, where do we find Buddhas?
> Not knowing how near Truth is,
> People seek it far away—what a pity!
> They are like him who, in the midst of water,
> Cries in thirst so imploringly.

And in the words of Eckhart:

> Simple people conceive that we are to see God as if He stood on that side and we on this. It is not so; God and I are one in the act of my perceiving Him.

Or the illustrious Sri Ramana Maharshi:

> You must get rid of the idea that you are an *ajnani* [ignorant one] and have yet to realize the Self. You *are* the Self. Was there ever a time when you were not aware of the Self?[5]

Thus, whether we realize it or not, want it or not, care about it or not, understand it or not, we *are* It—always have been and always will be. Says a Zenrin poem:

> If you understand, things are just as they are.
> If you do not understand, things are just as they are.

Now because we are It, we can never attain It, get It, reach It, grab It, or find It, any more than we can run after our own feet. In a sense, then, all search for Mind is ultimately in vain. In the words of Shankara:

> As Brahman constitutes a person's Self it is not something to be attained by that person. And even if Brahman were altogether different from a person's Self, still it would not be something to be obtained; for as it is omnipresent it is part of its nature that it is ever present to everyone.[6]

And Ramana Maharshi:

There is no reaching the Self. If Self were to be reached, it would mean that the Self is not here and now but that it is yet to be obtained. What is got afresh will also be lost. So it will be impermanent. What is not permanent is not worth striving for. So I say that the Self is not reached. You *are* the Self; you are already That.[7]

From the invincible Rinzai, King of Zen Masters:

O you mole-eyed, why are you wasting all the pious donations of the devout! Do you think you deserve the name of a monk, when you are still entertaining such a mistaken idea [of Zen]? I tell you, no Buddhas, no holy teachings, no disciplining, no testifying! What do you seek in a neighbor's house? O you, mole-eyed! You are putting another head upon your own! What do you lack in yourselves? O you, followers of the Truth, what you are making use of at this very moment is none other than what makes a Patriarch or Buddha. But you do not believe me, and seek it outwardly.[8]

And Rinzai's own teacher, Huang Po:

That there is nothing which can be attained is not idle talk; it is the truth. You have always been one with the Buddha, so do not pretend you can attain to this oneness by various practices. If, at this very moment, you could convince yourselves of its unattainability, being certain indeed that nothing at all can ever be attained, you would already be Bodhi-minded [enlightened]. Hard is the meaning of this saying! It is to teach you to refrain from seeking Buddhahood, since any search is doomed to failure.[9]

As a matter of fact, just because we are It, any search for It not only "is doomed to failure" but actually creates the impression that we lack It! By our very seeking, we apparently drive It away, just as if we misguidedly started looking for our head it would imply that we had lost it.

The One Mind alone is the Buddha, and there is no distinction between the Buddha and sentient beings, but that sentient beings are attached to forms and so seek externally for Buddhahood. By their very seeking they lose it, for that is using the Buddha to seek for the Buddha and using Mind to grasp Mind. Even though they do their utmost for a full aeon, they will not be able to attain to it.[10]

From the illustrious Bankei:

The Unborn [timeless Mind] is working in us. The Buddha-mind and our mind are not two. Those who strive after satori, or attempt to discover the self-mind, and exert themselves with this in view are committing a great mistake. . . . As soon

as an attempt is made to realize the way, to attain Buddhahood, you deviate from the Unborn and lose sight of what is
inborn in you.[11]

Hence seeking after Mind inevitably backfires, and for reasons
that should now be obvious—for one, seeking implies searching or
reaching out for an object, something "out there" that we can
grasp, be it a spiritual or material object, yet Mind is not an object.
Whatever you can think about, perceive, or grasp objectively is
never, was never, will never be that Absolute Subjectivity that is
the Thinker, Perceiver, and Grasper. For another, seeking implies
a present lack, yet—as the above quotations amply explain—right
now we lack nothing, and it is only our anxious and misguided
seeking that instills in us the apparent sense of lack, so that the
more we seek the more acutely we feel this supposed lack, and
because we will never never find It that way, after a while we
become chronically panic-striken, and so re-double our efforts,
pulling tighter on the knot around our own throat. And for yet
another, seeking is based on the implicit belief in some future
attainment, a belief that if we do not have salvation today we can
surely get it tomorrow, yet Mind knows no tomorrow, no time, no
past nor future, so that in running after It in some imagined future
we are only running away from It Now, for Mind exists nowhere
but in *this* timeless Moment. As always, those who seek to save
their souls will surely lose them.

The problem, then, is that the object of our search and the seeker
of that object are actually one and the same, so that each of us has
his head pursuing his own tail, as in the case of the beguiled snake
Ouroborous, prototype of all vicious circles.

> When the people of the world hear it said that the Buddhas
> transmit the Doctrine of Mind, they suppose that there is
> something to be attained or realized apart from Mind, and
> thereupon they use Mind to seek the Dharma [Truth], not
> knowing that Mind and the object of their search are one.
> Mind cannot be used to seek something from Mind; for then,
> after the passing of millions of aeons, the day of success will
> still not have dawned.[12]

Put simply, what we are looking for is none other than the
Looker. And just because of that, It can never be known as an
object, searched for as an object, seen as an object. It is the Knower,
the Searcher, the Seer.

> Thou couldst not see the seer of sight, thou couldst not hear the
> hearer of hearing, nor perceive the perceiver of perception, nor
> know the knower of knowledge.
>
> (*Brihadaranyaka Upanishad*, III.4.2)

As the *Zenrin* puts it:

> Like a sword that cuts, but cannot cut itself;
> Like an eye that sees, but cannot see itself.

In short, we cannot perceive our Self. And yet exactly here is the problem, the genesis of the Primary Dualism, for we *imagine* that we do see and know our Self, not realizing that whatever we see and know is a complex of perceived objects and thus could not be our Self—as Huang Po put it, "the perceived cannot perceive." Wei Wu Wei so forcefully explains:

> To know that oneself has no objective quality whatever, has absolutely nothing objective about it, is devoid of any trace-element of objectivity, is surely to know what one is, which, in metaphysical terms, is just the absence itself, the very absence, *of the absence*, the total lack of any objective character, nature, or quality.[13]

Thus any "self" of which you are conscious is absolutely, unequivocally, and most definitely not your Self! Declares Ramana Maharshi:

> The gross body which is composed of the seven humors (*dhatus*), I am not; the five cognitive sense-organs, viz. the senses of hearing, touch, sight, taste, and smell, which apprehend their respective objects, viz. sound, touch, color, taste, and odour, *I am not*; the five cognitive sense-organs, viz. the organs of speech, locomotion, grasping, excretion, and procreation, which have as their respective functions speaking, moving, grasping, excreting, and enjoying, *I am not*; the five vital airs, *prana*, etc. which perform respectively the five functions of in-breathing, etc. *I am not*; even the mind which thinks, *I am not*; the nescience too . . . *I am not*.[14]

So that Wei Wu Wei asks,

> Has one not realized that a "self" is only one's object, perceptual and conceptual, that it could not be what we are?

But we do not realize this, although it is so obvious—or perhaps *because* it is so obvious. We cannot hear the hearer, smell the smeller, feel the feeler, touch the toucher, taste the taster— similarly, we cannot see the seer. But we *think* we can—just that is the problem, and just that is the genesis of the Primary Dualism.

This is what happens: the Seer, the THAT IN YOU WHICH KNOWS, in actuality is not separate from what it sees—it *is* what it sees, for the Knower sees a thing by being that thing, as St. Thomas Aquinas stated, "Knowledge comes about in so far as the object known is within the knower."[15] This page, for instance, is identical to that in you which is reading it, or as William James expressed it, "the paper seen and the seeing of it are only two names for one indivisible fact."[16] This is not to say that the page, the supposed object of our perception, doesn't exist in some sense (so that if I close my eyes the page actually vanishes off the face of the earth), only that *it does not exist as an object "out there."* Between Seer and page, subject and object: no gap, no distance, no space!

Because we suppose, however, that we can see the Seer, as when we say "I know who I am!" or "I am perfectly aware of myself!" — just because of this supposition that I now can see and know the Seer, we consequently and very naturally feel that this "seer" of which we are supposedly aware must reside "within" us, as Wittgenstein bluntly put it, "What is troubling us is the tendency to believe that the mind is a little man within." Thus it appears that this "seer," my "self," is separate from what it sees, and that is the Primary Dualism

To put it another way, in imagining that we really do see the Seer, or know our Self as an object, we apparently (i.e., illusorily) turn our Subjectivity into an object, called "self," which is a complex of (objective) ideas, feelings, identities, valuations, and so on. We mistake that complex of objects for Subjectivity, *we mistake what we can see for that which is doing the seeing*, not realizing that Subjectivity is never an object except in illusion, as when you see your eye you have cataracts. Our "self," our "ego," is not even a real subject. Because we can see and know it objectively, this "subject" is a pseudo-subject and this self is a pseudo-self, a pure case of mistaken identity. Identified with this pseudo-subject, all other objects seem separate from me—thus, the Primary Dualism.

This state of affairs is *samsara*, the wheel of birth and death, bondage, the Hell of fire and brimestone, the agony of *dukha*.

> Ye suffer from yourselves, none else compels,
> None other holds you that ye live and die
> And whir upon the wheel, and hug and
>   kiss its spokes of agony,
> Its tire of tears, its nave of nothingness.

Wei Wu Wei summarizes the state of bondage, of identity with objects, as follows:

> Our state of apparent bondage is due to identification with an imaginary objectivisation of "I" [i.e., Mind, Witness]. I become identified with my selves, and my selves are all sentient beings. Whenever we think or speak as from the object with which we are illusorily identified we are thereby making an object of Subject.
> As long as we are identified with an object: that is bondage.

As long as we think, act, live via an object, or as an object: that is bondage.

As long as we feel ourselves to be an object, or think we are such (and a "self" is an object): that is bondage.

Working on or through the phenomenal concept known as our "self" is working on or through the very false identification from which we are seeking to escape. Surely that is the way *in*, not the way *out*?[17]

Put simply, that in you right now which knows, which sees, which reads this page—that is the Godhead, Mind, Brahman, and it cannot be seen or known as an object, just as an eye cannot see itself. Whatever you know about your "self" is an object; whatever you see, think, and feel about your "self"—that is a complex of perceived objects, the "ego." What is seen is the ego; what is doing the seeing is Mind. We have inadvertently identified with the former, with what can be seen, with the ego, or centaur, or persona, etc., and hence we are no longer identified with all phenomenal manifestation, we are separated from all that appears to be not-self. Hence, again, the Primary Dualism.

Thus separated from the environment, that environment becomes a threat. We have already seen that this Primary Dualism initiates the being-nullity debate which in turn results in man's repression of death and his life-long battle with the universe, trying desperately to put as much distance (called "security") between himself and the environment as possible, a project driven by fear and trembling. The sad thing is not that this is a tough and violent battle, but that the cause of the battle is an illusion. The separate self just isn't there to protect, prolong, or save, so that we spend our lives in the futile attempt to salvage what doesn't exist.

> Why are you unhappy?
> Because 99.9 per cent
> Of everything you think
> And of everything you do,
> Is for yourself —
> And there isn't one.[18]

Now if, while reading this, you decide to go "behind" the "self" to find what is really doing the looking, to find the Perceiver, the Seer, you will find only—this page! "Whether someone sees waves or particles, cyclones or poached-eggs . . . all are objects and, whatever he thinks he is seeing— that is ultimately what is looking. . . ."[19] But when this occurs (and it is occurring now), there won't be any you *as subject* nor any page *as object*, for both subject and object alike will have vanished into non-dual Subjectivity, a state we inadequately try to express by saying that at this moment you are the page reading itself. For here, beyond all duality, *all objects are their own subjects*, subject and object being nothing but two different ways of approaching this reality called Mind.

This split, this gap between subject and object, this Primary Dualism, is the initiator of the spectrum of consciousness, and it continues to operate throughout all levels, forming that irreducible but illusory severance between thinker and thought, knower and known, feeler and feelings, I and me, psyche and soma, voluntary and involuntary, what is and what ought. In short, it marks off the persistent feeling of a separate "I," and each level of the spectrum is simply a variation of this primordially basic dualism, a variation marked by an ever-increasing restriction of the sense of identity, or pseudo-subjectivity, from the universe to the organism to the ego to parts of the ego.

Now this *space*, this gap between subject and object, necessarily has a *time* component, for space and time are not separate Newtonian absolutes but rather a continuum. The time component of the Primary Dualism is none other than the *Secondary Dualism*, the dualism of life vs. death. We have been discussing the primary and secondary dualisms as if they were separate from one another, but this is merely an exegetical convenience, a device to make the complex story of the generation of the spectrum of consciousness a little easier to tell. In actuality, however, as soon as man lives in space (the primary dualism), he lives in time (the secondary dualism).

Recall that the secondary dualism propels man out of the timeless Now, where life and death are one, into the imaginary world of time where he battles to escape an illusory death by securing himself a fantasy future. That is, to live in the timeless moment is to have no future, and to have no future is to die—but man cannot accept death, and so he cannot live in the Now above time. The secondary dualism which separates life from death is thus the progenitor of time. But man's life in time (secondary dualism) is just the flip-side of man's life in space (primary dualism), for as soon as man severs his organism from his environment (primary dualism), the problem of being vs. nullity, existence vs. nonexistence, life vs. death—in short, the problem of time—simultaneously arises. Stated differently, when man is one with the universe (no primary dualism), then there is absolutely nothing outside of him to threaten his existence, and thus no being vs. nullity debate (no secondary dualism). Conversely, when life and death are seen to be one (no secondary dualism), then there is absolutely nothing that can threaten man's existence, and therefore nothing outside of him in a position to do this—hence no gap between man and the universe (no primary dualism).

Put bluntly, *the gap between you and this page is the same gap as that between you and the Now moment.* If you could live totally in the Now, you and this page (and all your other "objects") would be one, and conversely if you and this page were one, you would be living in the Now. The Primary Dualism and the Secondary Dualism are only two ways of describing this single space-time gap.

Naturally, then, since there is no way to find Mind through space by searching for It as an object "out there," there is no way to find Mind through time by searching for It as a future occurrence. That is, just as there is no path to HERE, there is no path to NOW. In fact, any Mind, God, or Brahman that we find in time would be a strictly temporal being, and not the Godhead at all. Most of us imagine that we lack Mind at this time, but that we can find It some tomorrow if we work hard enough. But any Mind that we find tomorrow will necessarily have a beginning in time, for it seems absent today but present tomorrow. Strictly speaking, we cannot enter Eternity since Eternity is ever-present, and any state we can *enter* is a purely temporal state. We will find It Now, or we will find It not at all.

> Hsuan-tse heard of a meditation master named Chih-huany, and when he went to visit him, Chih-huang was meditating.
>
> "What are you doing there?" inquired Hsuan-tse.
>
> "I am entering into a samadhi [timeless union with the universe]," replied Chih-huang.
>
> "You speak of *entering*, but how do you *enter* into a samadhi—with a thoughtful mind or with a thoughtless mind? If you say with a thoughtless mind, all non-sentient beings such as plants or bricks could attain samadhi. If you say with a thoughtful mind, all sentient beings could attain it."
>
> "Well," replied Chih-huang, "I am not conscious of either being thoughtful or being thoughtless."
>
> Hsuan-tse's verdict was swift-coming. "If you are conscious of neither, you are actually in samadhi all the time; why do you even talk at all of *entering into* or *coming out of* it? If, however, there is any *entering* or *coming out*, it is not the Great Samadhi."[20]

The masterful Shankara was equally adamant on this point:

> If Brahman were represented as supplementary to certain actions, and release [liberation, *moksha*] were assumed to be the effect of those actions, it would be temporal, and would have to be considered merely as something holding a pre-eminent position among the described temporal fruits of actions with their various degrees. But . . . release is eternal. . . . Release is shown to be of the nature of the eternally free Self,

(and) it cannot be charged with the imperfections of temporality.[21]

In other words, any release or "discovery" of Mind that has a beginning in time is no release at all. Release is not a future hope but a present fact. All dualism being illusory, there is nothing that really binds us, no chains to break, no freedom to attain.

> Monk: How are we released from [the agony of] the triple world?
> Tien-lung: Where are you this very moment?
>
> Tao-hsin: Pray show me the way to release!
> Seng-tsan: Who binds you?
> Tao-hsin: Nobody.
> Seng-tsang: Then why ask for release?

Perhaps Alan Watts summarized this best when he stated, "All that needs to be experienced for cosmic consciousness is already present, and anything in excess of this is obstructive and redundant."[22] Any "how," any "way," any "path," if it leads anywhere, leads *away* from Now. This reflects the fact that, in Nagarajuna's phrase, "There is no difference whatsoever between *nirvana* and *samsara*; there is no difference whatsoever between *samsara* and *nirvana*," and Dogen's statement that "the goal and the path are one," and similar statements by the Masters of every tradition that enlightenment and ignorance, reality and illusion, heaven and hell, liberation and bondage—all are non-dual and not to be separated. Thus, "you are already where any path can take you."

Most of us, however, are in the position of the man in the example who believes that the earth is flat and doesn't realize his mistake until he travels completely around the world and ends up—exactly where he started! We are convinced that we lack Mind, and so we are led to pursue "spiritual exercises" of one form or another, until, finally, we will end up—exactly where we started! Right here, right now. In the words of Huang Po:

> Even if you go through all the stages of a Bodhisattva's progress towards Buddhahood, one by one; when at last, in a single flash, you attain to full realization, you will only be realizing the Buddha-Nature which has been with you all the time; and by all the foregoing stages you will have added to it nothing at all. You will come to look upon those aeons of work and achievement as no better than unreal actions performed in a dream.[23]

But if we do believe that the earth is flat, that we lack Buddha-nature, our only real choice is to start traveling. The means whereby we travel "towards" Mind are technically called *upaya*, "skillful means," a word that is often translated as "trick" because we are tricking ourselves into looking for what we have never lost. *Upaya*, skillful means, constitute precisely that experiment which, if conducted in the personal laboratory, will allow the individual to decide for himself whether or not Mind exists. This experiment, like all scientific experiments, consists of a set of injunctions or instructions which the individual is free to follow or reject—but should he reject them, then he, in the spirit of scientific honesty, must withhold his judgments on the experience of Mind-only. If a scientist denies Mind-only as so much mystical pap without himself performing the experiment, then he is behaving as blatantly unscientific as if he denounced the experimental data of one of his colleagues without himself repeating that experiment. These *upaya*, which we will hereafter translate as Skillful Experiments, are perfectly intelligible, reasonable, and scientific, and any logical positivist or scientist who dismisses them must do so on purely unscientific and emotional grounds.

Now the number of Skillful Experiments that have developed over the centuries is considerable, but we contend that the "active ingredients," the essential factors, are very similar in all of them.[24] To document this contention, we will now present a rather detailed survey of some of the more prevalent forms of the Skillful Experiment, pointing out the essential similarities among them.

Let us begin with Dr. Hubert Benoit, whose Skillful Experiment embodies a particular "inner gesture," which, when faithfully and repeatedly carried out, will allow us to realize that "each one of us lives in the state of satori and could not live otherwise. . . . [Because] it is our eternal state, independent of our birth and of our death."[25] Benoit's study of this "inner gesture" is devoted primarily

> to analysing the inner processes which now condition our illusion of not living in the state of satori. We will see that they are our imaginative-emotive processes—in which our vital Energy is disintegrated—and we will try to define clearly what incomplete functioning of our attention conditions in its turn these imaginative-emotive processes.[26]

Throughout this volume we have been describing these "processes which now condition our illusion of not living in the state of satori," and, in short, we pointed out that they are our tendencies of conceptualization, objectification, and dualism, which Benoit simply calls our "imaginative-emotive processes," and these tendencies result in "identifying myself only with my organism and not the rest of Manifestation." Thus, to perceive our fundamental cosmic identity we must surrender—at least *temporarily*—all of our concepts, mental images, and mental objects. Now to do this effectively—and this is the Experiment, the inner gesture—we must first understand the psychological process which conditions us to go on forming thoughts, concepts, and images, all that "mental chatter" and "talking to oneself" that seems to ramble on continuously in our heads. As a matter of experimental fact, you can stop reading for a moment and watch how you continue thinking and chattering to yourself. Further, you cannot, without the greatest difficulty, stop this mental chatter and kaleidoscope of ideas and thoughts through your mind, because the idea to stop chattering is itself nothing but more chatter! This is the old trap of "for the next 10 seconds, don't think of the word 'monkey.' " *That* approach will never work, for we will spend all of our time thinking about not thinking.

Instead, we need to understand the process which gives rise to conceptualization so that we can cut it off at its root-source, and Benoit has pinpointed this process. To understand his explanation of it, we need only recall that Benoit is working within the framework of "Energy mobilization" — that is, each instant our Energy is constantly rising from "below," from the Level of Mind, where it is pure, informal, non-objective, timeless and spaceless Energy that operates Now "in a moment without duration." This Energy, as it mobilizes, seems to "well-up" from within, and then, as it passes the Existential-Biosocial Level, it starts to take on *form* as *thoughts* and direction as *emotions*, and these "imaginative-emotive processes" act to disintegrate and disperse our Energy.

Now it is very important to understand this as clearly and concretely as possible, or we shall miss the sense of Benoit altogether. This "mobilization of Energy" and its subsequent "disintegration into forms" of thought and emotion is happening to us right now, at each and every moment, but it can most easily be seen in certain situations. For instance, if I come up behind you and yell "Boo!" there will be a few seconds wherein you remain still, even though you have heard me yell, and during this very brief time you might feel a type of passive or quiet alertness, but this feeling shortly explodes into a sensation of mild shock (or something similar) accompanied with an onrush of thoughts and emotions (imaginative-emotive processes). In those few seconds of passive awareness, your Energy was beginning to mobilze but it was not yet experienced as shock or mild terror—it was pure and without form, and only later did it disintegrate into thoughts and emotions of shock and fright.

As another simple example, a piece of very fragile crystal accidentally falls off the top shelf of the cabinet—your Energy mobilizes instantly and with a swift and completely spontaneous movement, you race over and catch it, without any thought, idea, or intention crossing your mind. Only after you catch it do you start to think about what has happened, do you realize what you have done, and then your heart starts pounding, thoughts race through your mind, and only then does your Energy start to disintegrate into thoughts and emotions. These are two extreme cases of what is happening all the time, for our Energy is constantly being snapped up by ideas, concepts, thoughts, emotions,and mental objects, and thus do we introduce a screen between self and Reality. This screen must be lifted, and to do that, we must understand the process that builds it. What process conditions the disintegration of our Energy into imaginative-emotive forms? Benoit supplies the answer:

> This intimate process is the passive mode according to which my attention functions. *It is because my attention is passive that it is alerted by a mobilisation of energy already produced,* at a late stage at which there is no longer anything else to be done but to disintegrate this Energy. My [ordinary] attention is not, actually, in a state of autonomous, unconditioned vigilance; it is only awakened by mobilisations of energy which are produced in my organism, and its awakening is conditioned by these mobilisations. Thus I am always faced with a *fait accompli*. As soon as the moment-without-duration is passed in which my Energy wells up, still informal, from non-manifestation, this Energy is as though snapped up by the formal world [of thought and concepts]; the chance has been missed of [contacting Reality]. The disintegration into imaginative-emotive forms is inevitable. My Energy is now in the domain in which my egotistical identification reigns [the Ego Level].[27]

And, of course, once our Energy is on the Ego Level, it bears about as much relation to Reality as a square circle, for here our Energy is so wrapped in thoughts, symbols, and maps, that we have great difficulty in seeing the territory directly. After these thoughts arise, it does no good to try to get rid of them or to suppress them or to disown them—this only results in the quaternary dualism, and we do not succeed in suppressing these thoughts, but only in suppressing *ownership* of these thoughts, and hence we project them. As Hui Neng put it, "To suppress the working of the mind . . . is a disease and not Zen." Once thought-forms have appeared, it is too late to do anything about them, although most of us try—which is like saying don't get mad at the tiger until he bites your head off.

What Benoit would have us do, therefore, is not to suppress

thinking, but to evoke the "inner gesture" which forestalls thought-forms from rising by cutting them off at their source:

> My attention ought not to be awakened by the mobilisation of my Energy, but before that; and this is realised when instead of seeing the imaginative-emotive processes which are being produced, I regard the processes which are about to be produced. *This is realised when, instead of being passively attentive to my mobilised Energy and its disintegrating future, I tend actively to perceive the very birth of my energy. A new vigilance now superintends the mobilisation of Energy.* To put it more simply, an active attention lies in wait for the advent of my inner movements. It is no longer my emotions which interest me, but their coming to birth; it is no longer their movement that interests me, but this other informal movement which is the birth of their formal movement.[28]

It is the genius of Benoit to point out that when our attention operates in the passive mode, this conditions the rising of thought-concepts, while, on the contrary, when our attention operates in an active and vigilant fashion, *then thought-concepts do not arise,* for this active attention prevents the disintegration of our Energy into the imaginative-emotive forms. We will presently elaborate upon this so that the reader will firmly understand just what this entails, but for the moment, we must forewarn the reader: when our attention is operating in the active mode that Benoit describes, there is *absolutely nothing objective to perceive.* In the active mode of attention, mental objects (thoughts) do not arise, and—since it is this screen of conceptualization that appears to separate me from the world—when these mental concept-objects no longer arise, then "I" and "the world" are no longer separate, "I" and "the world" become one in the act of this pure non-conceptual seeing. Hence there remains no *objective* world "out there" to perceive—the "world looks at itself" in a non-dual fashion. There is *seeing*, but nothing *objective* seen! Benoit explains it thus:

> Our attention, when it functions in the active mode, is pure attention, without manifested object. My mobilised Energy is not perceptible in itself, but only in the effects of its disintegration, the images [thoughts, concepts, mental objects, etc.]. But this disintegration only occurs when my attention operates in the passive mode; active attention forestalls this disintegration. And so, when my attention operates in the active mode there is nothing to perceive. . . .[29]

Benoit then gives an example of this, and in so doing, he describes just what this "active attention" entails:

> It is easy for me to verify concretely that active attention to my

inner world is without an object. If I take up, in the face of my inner monologue [the incessant chattering to ourselves], the attitude of an active auditor who authorises this monologue to say whatever it wishes and however it wishes, if I take up the attitude which can be defined by the formula "Speak, I am listening," I observe that my monologue stops [without my forcing or suppressing it]. It does not start up again until my attitude of vigilant expectation ceases.[30]

It is this "attitude of vigilant expectation" that constitutes the "inner gesture," the inner gesture that forestalls thought-concepts and therefore puts us directly in touch with Reality. Benoit describes this inner gesture of active attention in several fashions, one of which we have just given, another of which follows:

It is clearly impossible to describe this presence within oneself which is the immediate and in-formal [active] perception ... precisely on account of the informal character of this perception. Let us suppose that I ask you: "How are you feeling at this moment?" You will ask in reply: "From what point of view? Physically or morally?" I answer: "From all points of view together, how do you feel?" You are silent for a couple of seconds, then you say, for example: "Not so bad," or "So-so," or "Very well," or something else. ... Of the two seconds during which you were silent the latter does not interest us for you were using it in order to put into a form [thought] of expression your perception. . . ; *you had then already slipped away from that inner presence which interests us*. It is during the first second that you perceived what is really in question for you all the time, and of which you are habitually unconscious, being conscious only of forms [thought-objects] which derive from this unconscious perception. . . . If someone, after having read this, tries to obtain the in-formal perception of which we are speaking, let him beware; there are a thousand ways of believing that one has it, whereas one has it not; in any case the mistake is the same and consists in one complication or another which comprises forms; one is not simple-minded enough.[31]

Elsewhere, Benoit describes this inner gesture of vigilant awareness in yet another way:

This gesture . . . is like a look which, cast on the full center of my inner world, transpierces the plane of this world towards that which is unknown to me. This look, because it does not prefer any object, because it is sent, without preconception, towards no matter what, meets nothing [objective] and so results, without my having wished it, in the suspension of my imaginative film. It is a total interrogation without particular formal expression, which remains without answer since it does not carry any. It is a challenge which neither aims at nor meets anybody; it is *an attention to everything, which has no object*. The suspension of my imaginative film, thus obtained without having been sought, is instantaneous; it is without duration, an intemporal flash of lightning in the heart of time. . . .[32]

All three of these descriptions by Benoit refer to the same inner gesture, an inner gesture that results in the suspension of dualistic seeing, of "I" seeing "objects" or "concepts" — in a phrase, *it suspends thought without suppressing it*—and that is the key. When I give total and active awareness to my thought processes, when I say "Speak, I am listening," when I authorize any thought to arise that wants to, and then actively *listen* and *watch* for it to arise, then none arises! As Benoit pointed out, my thinking process will start up again only when I cease the "Speak-I-am-listening" attitude. He summarizes this inner gesture by stating that it *"is realized when I authorize the totality of my tendencies before the conscious appearance of any one of them; and then none of them appears."*[33] And when none of these imaginative-emotive tendencies appear as conscious objects, then I am grounded in pure nondual organic consciousness, "thanks to which I am virtually already free."

Let us now analyze Benoit's inner gesture of vigilant attention without object and point out the essential factors that, as we shall see, all Skillful Experiments have in common. Basically, these factors are three in number:

Factor 1: Active Attention—a special type of intense yet relaxed alertness, which can be described as a "Speak-I-am-listening" attitude, as a *total* authorization or *total* acceptance of my tendencies, as an active vigilance and watchfulness directed at the very birth of thought and emotions. It is a burning attention-authorization to what is Now, watching inside and outside with equal eye. When this active attention is carried out correctly, it results in:

Factor 2: Stopping—the suspension of thought, of conceptualization, of objectification, of mental chatter. This "stopping" is, in fact, the suspension of the first mode of knowing, of the dualistic and symbolic-map knowledge that ultimately distorts Reality. In short, this is a *stopping of the Primary Dualism*. It is a suspension of space, time, form, and dualism, and in this condition an utter mental Silence prevails. *This is remaining with what is*. The condition of "remaining" in this "isness," this Silence, this Stillness, we will call (after Huang Po) "sitting in a Bodhimandala," that is, sitting in a place where enlightenment can errupt at any instant.[34] If this "stopping" is clean and complete, it will result in:

Factor 3: Passive Awareness—a special seeing that is *seeing into nothing*. "Seeing into nothingness—this is true seeing and eternal seeing."[35] Again, this awareness, this seeing, is not a looking into a mere blank or vacuum, but a looking into nothing *objective*—it is pure timeless awareness without the primary dualism of subject vs. object, and thus it is complete in itself, with nothing external or objective to it. Because nothing is outside it, it operates without any effort whatsoever, in a completely spontaneous fashion, without reference to past or future. It operates above space-time in the absolute Now, pointing to nothing beyond itself and seeing nothing beyond itself. In other words, it is the second mode of knowing, knowing all without separation from any. And one instant of this pure awareness *is* itself Mind. Whether we realize it or not, it *is always already the case*.[36]

These three factors are the essentials in any Skillful Experiment, and although they assume a startling variety of forms, they are clearly discernible in almost every major *upaya*. To document this, let us continue our survey by turning to Krishnamurti.

Perhaps nobody has described what we mean by Passive Awareness (Factor 3) with such clarity, perception, and profundity as has Krishnamurti. For over half a century this incredible man, whose discourses Aldous Huxley compared to those of the Buddha himself, has traveled the world speaking to people about the necessity of passive, choiceless, yet intensely alert awareness not contaminated with thought, symbols, or duality, an awareness of *Now*, of *what is*, not of what was, will be, should be, ought to be, or might be. *What is* is real, and it is only by knowing *this* reality that we are set free:

> The real is near, you do not have to search for it; and a man who seeks truth will never find it. Truth is in what *is*— and that is the beauty of it. But the moment you conceive it, the moment you seek it, you begin to struggle; and a man who struggles cannot understand. That is why we have to be still, observant, passively aware.[37]

But Krishnamurti's listeners invariably ask, "*How* can I get this awareness that will free me?" Yet, Krishnamurti replies, the very search for a *how* leads *away* from *what is* now, and thus the very desire for awareness prevents it. There can be no preparation for that which always is.

> Can one realize truth immediately, without preparation? I say yes—not out of some fancy of mine, not out of some illusion; but psychologically experiment with it and you will see. Take any challenge, any small incident—don't wait for some great crisis—and see how you respond to it. Be aware of it, of your

responses, of your intentions, of your attitudes and you will understand them, you will understand your background. I assure you, you can do it immediately if you give your whole attention to it. If you are seeking the full meaning of your background, it yields its significance and then you discover in one stroke the truth, the understanding of your problem. Understanding comes into being from the now, the present, which is always timeless. . . . Merely to postpone, to prepare to receive that which is tomorrow, is to prevent yourself from understanding what is *now*. . . . You will prepare to understand tomorrow what can only be understood in the "now." Therefore you will never understand. To perceive truth needs no preparation; preparation implies time and time is not the means of understanding truth. Time is continuous and truth is timeless. . . .[38]

Furthermore, Krishnamurti maintains, as do all true metaphysicians, that "God or truth cannot be thought about. If you think about it, it is not truth." We do not understand the truth of what is because we avoid it, obscure it with thought and symbols that divide and slash the heart of reality, leaving us clutching at fragmentary ghosts, confused, frustrated, distraught. And then we seek a way out of this confusion, trying again to avoid what is!

How eager we are to solve our problems! How insistently we search for an answer, a way out, a remedy! We never consider the problem itself, but with agitation and anxiety we grope for an answer. . . . To look for an answer is to avoid the problem—which is just what most of us want to do. . . . The solution is not separate from the problem; the answer is *in* the problem [since that is *what is now*], not away from it. If the answer is separate from the main issue, then we create other problems: the problem of how to realize the answer, how to carry it out, how to put it into practice, and so on.[39]

For example, let us say that at this moment I am experiencing intense fear. Now most of us don't want to be *aware* of fear, we want to get *away* from fear. We don't want to watch it, we want to deny it. This, however, can be done only if "I" and "fear" are two different things, only if there is the primary dualism of knower vs. known, experiencer vs. experiences, subject vs. object. Yet just here is the problem, for if in actuality this primary dualism is illusory, if in reality I *am* my present experience instead of *having* my present experience, then "I" and "fear" are, at this moment, one and the same process, so that I can no more separate myself from fear than I can from my head. If I see that I *am* fear, then fear ceases to threaten and push me, for there is now no "I" separate from "fear" to be pushed or threatened. Fear ceases to be frightening. On the other hand, if I seek to get away from fear, this is really nothing but being *afraid* of fear, and fear is trying to cut itself in two in order to escape from itself. This is, of course, the primary dualism, and in this vicious circle of thinker vs. thought, experiencer vs. experienced, observer vs. observed, fear can divide and multiply itself into terrifying proportions in a vain effort to get away from itself. In short, trying to escape fear is itself fear.

Krishnamurti brings this point home again and again, whether talking of fear, anger, jealousy, or suffering—we cannot handle pain or fear by avoiding it, but by realizing that we *are* it.

> Now, you are fully aware of the suffering. Is that suffering apart from you and therefore you are merely the observer who perceives the suffering, or is that suffering *you*?
>
> When there is no *observer* [pseudo-subject] who is suffering, is the suffering different from you? You *are* the suffering, are you not? You are not apart from the pain—you *are* the pain. What happens? There is no labeling, there is no giving it a name and thereby brushing it aside—you are merely that pain, that feeling, that sense of agony. When you are that, what happens? When you do not name it, when there is no fear with regard to it, is the centre [pseudo-self] related to it? If the centre is related to it [i.e., different from it], then it is afraid of it, then it must act and do something about it. But if the centre *is* that, then what do you do? There is nothing to be done, is there? If you *are* that and you are not accepting it, not labeling it, not pushing it aside—if you *are* that thing, what happens? Do you say you suffer then? Surely, a fundamental transformation has taken place. Then there is no longer "I suffer," because,there is no centre to suffer. . . . As long as I have no relationship to [or, no separation from] the thing as outside me, the problem is not; the moment I establish a relationship *with it outside me*, the problem is. As long as I treat suffering as something *outside*. . . . I establish a relationship to it and that relationship [the primary dualism] is fictitious. But if I *am* that thing, if I see the fact, then the whole thing is transformed, it all has a different meaning. Then there is *full* attention, *integrated* attention and that which is completely regarded is understood and dissolved, and so there is no fear and therefore the word 'sorrow' is non-existent.[40]

One might say that Krishnamurti's entire message is that we must disperse (or rather see through) the fictitious primary dualism and thus awaken the second mode of knowing, our non-dual and non-conceptual awareness, for that and that alone will reveal Reality, which is always already the case:

> If we can experience a feeling directly, without naming it, I think we shall find a great deal in it; then there is no longer a battle with it, because the experiencer and the thing ex-

perienced are one, and that is essential. So long as the experiencer verbalizes the feeling, the experience, he separates himself from it and acts upon it; such action is an artificial, illusory action. But if there is no verbalization, then the experiencer and the thing experienced are one. *That integration* [of the primary dualism] *is necessary and has to be radically faced.*[41]

Now that integration results in passive awareness (Factor 3), but if there remains the slightest trace of the primary dualism, of the split between thinker and thought, knower and known, seer and seen, then there is no awareness.

First we have to understand what awareness is: to be aware, aware outwardly, the colours, the proportions of this hall, aware of the various colours that you have on, aware without any choice, just to watch. And also to be inwardly aware of all the movement of thought, the movement of your gestures, the way you walk, the things you eat, the habits you have formed, again without choice—merely to observe attentively. *You cannot be aware if there is a division between the observer and the observed....*[42]

We have already seen that this split between the observer and the observed, this primary dualism, is perpetuated by thought and conceptualization, and in this regard, Krishnamurti agrees:

You know one of the most difficult things is to observe, to look: to look at anything without the image of that thing, to look at a cloud without the previous associations with regard to that cloud, to see a flower without the image, the memories, the associations, concerning that flower. *Because these associations, these images and memories, create distance between the observer and the observed.* And in that distance, the division between the seer and the thing seen, in that division the whole conflict of man exists. It is necessary to see without the image, so that the space between the observer and the thing observed is simply not there.[43]

To "see without the image" is thus the crucial issue, and so Krishnamurti naturally asks, "Now the question is, can that image come to an end, not through time, not gradually, but instantly? To answer that question, *one has to go into what the machinery is that builds images*." And then he proceeds to describe this "machinery that builds images," and in this description we can clearly see the three factors (attention-stopping-awareness) starting to emerge.

Now what is that machinery? Please, we are sharing the problem together. I am not instructing you. We are asking each other. What is this image, how is this image produced and what is it that sustains this image? *Now the machinery that builds the image is inattention.* You understand, Sir?[44]

Here Krishnamurti is agreeing completely with Benoit that *the machinery of image production is inattention*, or as Benoit called it, passive attention. Krishnamurti continues:

> You insult or flatter me. When you insult me, I react and that reaction builds the image. The reaction comes about when there is no attention. You follow? When I am not attending completely [or as Benoit would say, *actively*] to your insult, this inattention breeds the image. When you call me an idiot, I react, which is, I am not fully attentive to what you are saying, and therefore the image is formed. *But when I am completely attentive to what you are saying, there is no image forming.*[45]

Thus, according to Krishnamurti, full and complete attention (Factor 1) results in suspension or stopping of image formation (Factor 2). Krishnamurti further agrees that as long as we are completely and actively attentive, as long as we maintain the "Speak-I-am-listening" attitude, no mental images arise:

> At the moment of attention all the conditioning disappears, all the image-building comes to an end; it is only when you are not attentive that the whole thing begins. . . .[46]

And—as we pointed out earlier—when there is no image, no thought, then there is no duality, and this results, according to Krishnamurti, in passive awareness (Factor 3) wherein Reality is revealed. Thus we lucidly see in Krishnamurti the three factors of 1) active attention, 2) stopping, and 3) passive, non-dual awareness. In Krishnamurti's own words, at the moment images arise,

> give complete attention at that moment [Factor 1], then you will see that there is no image [Factor 2], and having no image there is then no division between the observer and the observed [Factor 3].[47]

And in *that* moment, which is *this* moment, "it is finished."

Moving to Vedanta Hinduism, we find the same three factors, but they assume a slightly different outer form, predominantly because the Vedanta is working with the metaphor of Absolute Subjectivity (Brahman-Atman) instead of Absolute Energy (as are Krishnamurti and Benoit). Nevertheless, the three factors of attention-stopping-awareness are present, as the following quotations from the Vedanta's greatest modern sage, Sri Ramana Maharshi, will demonstrate.

To begin with, Sri Ramana Maharshi maintains that thought—as the root cause of dualism—is the source of all illusion and bondage. Again, this in no way means that we are to forever surrender conceptualization and return to the purely animalistic level of evolution. Symbolic thought is mandatory, provided we don't so confuse it with Reality as to be unable to tell the difference between a map and the actual territory. The trouble is, we have hopelessly confused the two, and thus, for practical purposes only, it is usually necessary to completely suspend thought and throw away our maps (Factor 2) for short periods, so that we can actually see the territory for a change. *Then* we will be able to take up and possess our maps again without them possessing us. Thus does Ramana declare that "thought alone is bondage."[48]

But the Maharshi's unique contribution to the ways of liberation is his insistence that the "I-thought" is the source of all other thoughts. That is, every time you think of your "self" that is the I-thought, and Ramana declares it to lie behind every other thought:

> The first and foremost of all the thoughts that arise in the mind is the primal "I"-thought. It is only after the rise or origin of the "I"-thought that innumerable other thoughts arise.[49]

Thus the suspension of the I-thought marks the suspension of all other thoughts and mental objects. Now Sri Ramana Maharshi realizes that the I-thought cannot be suppressed—for who would suppress "I" except another "I"? Spiritual altruism is spiritual hypocrisy. The I-thought, like any other thought, is to be suspended, not suppressed, and for this suspension, Ramana recommends what he calls "Self-Inquiry (*nan yar*)," which is the intensively active inquiry "Who am I?" This attentive inquiry, which we recognize as Factor 1, leads—according to Ramana—to a suspension of images, which we recognize as Factor 2. Thus:

> Since every other thought can occur only after the rise of the I-thought and since the mind is nothing but a bundle of thoughts, it is only through the inquiry "Who am I?" that the mind subsides. Moreover, the integral I-thought, implicit in such inquiry, having destroyed all other thoughts, gets itself finally destroyed or consumed, just as the stick used for stirring the burning funeral pyre gets consumed.
>
> Even when extraneous thoughts sprout up during such inquiry, do not seek to complete the rising thought, but instead, deeply inquire within, "To whom has this thought occurred?" No matter how many thoughts thus occur to you, if you would with *acute vigilance inquire immediately* [Factor 1] as and when each individual thought arises to whom it has occurred, you would find it is to "me." If then you inquire "Who am I?" the mind gets introverted and the rising thought also subsides

[and] the perception of the world as an *objective* reality ceases [Factor 2].[50]

How does this self-inquiry work? Let us suppose, for example, that I ask you, "Who are you?" and you reply, "Well, I am so-and-so, I work at this particular job, I'm married, and I am of such-and-such religion. Is that what you mean?" "No," I would answer, "Those are all objects of perception, they are mere ideas. Who are you that sees these objects, these ideas?" "Well, I am a human being, an individual organism endowed with certain biological faculties. Is that closer?" "Not really," I would have to counter, "for those are still ideas and thoughts. Now deeply, *who are you?*" As your mind keeps turning back in on itself in search of the answer, it gets quieter and quieter. If I kept asking "Who are you? Who are you?" you would quickly enter a mental silence, and that mental silence would be identical to the one produced by Benoit's question, "How do you feel from all possible views at once?" That *object-less silence* produced by active attention, by vigilant watchfulness, by intense inquiry, is a Bodhimandala, for right at the point where no mental answer, image, or object is forthcoming, you are open to seeing the Real in a flash. This silence, or stopping, which is Factor 2, opens the door to infinite awareness, or Factor 3, as Ramana explains:

> By inquiring into the nature of the I, the I perishes. With it you and he [objects] also perish. The resultant state, which shines as Absolute Being, is one's own natural state, the Self. . . . The only inquiry leading to Self-realization is seeking the source of the "I" with in-turned mind and without uttering the word "I". . . . If one inquires "Who am I?" within the mind, the individual "I" falls down abashed . . . and immediately Reality manifests itself spontaneously as "I-I" [Absolute Subjectivity, non-dual awareness, Factor 3].[51]

Thus we see that the Skillful Experiment of the Vedanta, as expounded by its most enlightened sage, also comprises the three factors of attention-stopping-awareness. The following statement of Ramana completely summarizes his *upaya*, and the three factors are again clearly present:

> Whence does this 'I' arise? Seek for it within [Factor 1]; it then vanishes [Factor 2]. This is the pursuit of Wisdom.
> Where the "I" vanished, there appears "I-I" by itself [Factor 3]. This is the Infinite.[52]

Let us now move from Vedanta Hinduism to some of the "higher" forms of Buddhism. We have already seen how the Madhyamika Buddhism uses critical inquiry (Factor 1) to abolish all concepts

(Factor 2) so that *prajna* can shine forth (Factor 3), and so we will not repeat these observations here. Instead, we will examine the Ch'an (Zen) and Tien Tai (Tendai) schools of Buddhism in an effort to uncover the same three factors in their forms of the Skillful Experiment.

The Supreme Vehicle of Ch'an (Zen) Buddhism began as a "direct pointing to Mind" and a "seeing into one's Self-Nature," without apparently emphasizing any spiritual means or exercises, such as concentration or meditation. In the words of the Sixth Patriarch of Ch'an, Hui Neng:

> It is a mistake to think that sitting quietly in contemplation is essential to deliverance. The truth of Ch'an opens by itself from within and it has nothing to do with the practice of dhyana [meditation]. For we read in the *Vajracchedika* that those who try to see the Tathagata in one of his special attitudes, as sitting or lying, do not understand his spirit, and that the Tathagata is designated as Tathagata because he comes from nowhere and departs nowhere, and for that reason he is the Tathagata. His appearance has no whence, and his disappearance no whither, and this is Ch'an. In Ch'an, therefore, there is nothing to gain, nothing to understand; what shall we then do with sitting cross-legged and practising dhyana? Some may think that understanding is needed to enlighten the darkness of ignorance, but the truth of Ch'an is absolute in which there is no dualism, no conditionality. To speak of ignorance and enlightenment, or of Bodhi and Klesa [Enlightenment and passions], as if they were two separate objects which cannot be merged in one, is not Mahayanistic. In the Mahayana every possible form of dualism is condemned as not expressing the ultimate truth.[53]

Few people, however, were awake and aware enough to see THIS directly, and so over the centuries that Ch'an grew and developed in China, with its popularity and number of followers ever-increasing, it began to create ingenious *upaya* to help persons of all mentalities awaken to Mind, such as the shouting of Ma-tsu, Lin Chi, and Yun-men, the striking of Ma-tsu and Te-shan, the *koan* (*hua tou*) of Yuan-wu and Ta-hui, and the "silent illumination" associated with Tien-tung. Much has been made of the slappings, shakings, and shoutings dealt out by these early Ch'an masters by modern day interpreters who altogether miss the point of these actions, but what would you do if someone were sleeping and you wanted to awaken him, especially if he were having a nightmare? You would shake, slap, or shout at him—and that's exactly what these Masters did to awaken their students.

Our present concern, however, is with the widely used exercises of the *koan* on the one hand and silent illumination on the other.

The *koan* exercise—which in China is referred to as a *hua tou* exercise[54]— uses as a "theme" for meditation a riddle, usually based on the conversations between the old Ch'an Masters and their students, such as "What is the sound of one hand clapping?" or "Stop that ship on the distant shore!" or "A goose is trapped in a bottle—without breaking the bottle or hurting the goose, get the goose out." These riddles—"like life itself"— cannot be solved by any form of intellection at all, and thus the *koan* meditation consists not in analyzing the *koan* but in completely merging with it—whereupon it solves itself. The *koan* exercise thus has one major aim—to merge the subject and object, break the primary dualism, and awaken us to Mind.

The *koan* (or *hua tou*), however, is not just an exercise in concentration— on the contrary, mere concentration on a *koan* is condemned as mechanical and mind-dulling. Instead, the student is to actively and intensively inquire, search, and look into the *koan*, raising in himself a fiery and attentive attitude, known technically as the *i-ching*, the Great Doubt, Great Attention, or Great Inquiry. Thus:

> To exercise yourself properly in Zen you ought to cherish a spirit of inquiry (i-ching); for according to the strength of your inquiring spirit will be the depth of your enlightenment.[55]
>
> Zen-work does not consist in merely reciting a koan. What is the use of repeating a sentence again and again? The primary thing is arouse the "doubt-sensation" [Great Inquiry], no matter what koan you are working on.[56]
>
> When working on Zen, the important thing is to generate the I-ching. . . . The Masters of old said:
> The greater the Inquiry, the greater the awakening;
> The smaller the Inquiry, the smaller the awakening,
> No Inquiry, no awakening.[57]

The Great Inquiry is thus the crucial key to this type of Zen meditation. This inquiring spirit is a total, complete, and active attention, a pure presence of mind, directed to no special object whatsoever; but as a type of aid, especially in the beginning phases of meditation, the mind might be directed towards a particular object or place, which is usually the *koan* itself, but might also be the inquirer himself, as when Ku-yin Ching-chin says, "reflect within yourself who it is that is pursuing the koan so untiringly and asking you this question so unremittingly," or perhaps the actual source of thought, as when Han Shan exhorts us to "search out the point where your thoughts arise and disappear." But the important point is that the mental state thus evoked is the same—one of intense yet relaxed inquiry and attention, which Suzuki calls "one great question-mark with no special object." This we recognize as Factor 1—active attention— and it is greatly emphasized in Zen.

Zen maintains that the efficacy of the Great Inquiry lies in its ability to suspend all thought processes, resulting in a state of no-image, no-thought, or stopping, which is Factor 2:

> Just lay down old thoughts ... [and] then, slowly, call: "Amitabha!" and without loosening your grip on this word, *look into* where this thought arises.... Repeat this 5 or 7 times and your thoughts will cease to arise.[58]

> This feeling of doubt [or inquiry], which the masters likened to an indestructible sword, cuts down all thoughts and mental states during the training.[59]

> Tai-hui never advises us just to hold up a koan before the mind; he tells us, on the contrary, to make it occupy the very centre of attention by the sheer strength of an inquiring spirit. When a koan is backed up by such a spirit, it is, he says, "like a great consuming fire which burns up every insect of idle speculation that approaches it."[60]

There is thus a world of difference between mere concentration and suppression of thought, on the one hand, and Zen meditation on the other, for the latter uses the Great Inquiry to suspend thought at its source before it disintegrates our Engergy. As we have seen, *inattention is the machinery of image-production*, and the Great Inquiry temporarily suspends the machine without suppressing or destroying it. Zen is most emphatic on this point:

> When working on Zen, some people, owing to their incapability [or just reluctance] of raising the "doubt-sensation," begin to suppress the arising of thoughts. When all thoughts have been suppressed, these people experience a lucid and pure serentiy, thoroughly clear, without the slightest taint. This, however, constitutes the very root source of the consciousness which they cannot break through. This is the consciousness within the realm of life and death. It is not Zen. Their fault is that at the start of their Zen practice they did not work penetratingly enough on the Hua Tou: thus, the doubt-sensation did not arise. As a result they either suppress thought and become dead-void heretics, or plunging into self-indulgent conceit, they mislead and cheat the ignorant, diverting people's faith and hindering their progress on the *Bodhi* Path.[61]

The Great Inquiry, therefore, when it is clean and complete, results in a suspension of the image-weaving film that normally lies between ourselves and Reality. When this suspension is total, it results in a state that Hakuin called Great Fixation (*daigi*), wherein all thought is suspended and the subject and object become completely identified, marking the destruction of the primary dualism. This, of course, is Factor 2:

> It is by means of this i-ching, "spirit of inquiry," that we finally attain Hukuin's *daigi* (tai-i), "great fixation," or "a state of oneness."[62]

The Great Fixation (Factor 2) is thus a Bodhimandala, from which *prajna* (Factor 3) can burst forth at any time. In the words of Kao-feng Yuan-miao:

> Do not give yourself up to a state of doing nothing; do not exercise your fantastic imagination, but try to bring about a state of perfect identification [Factor 2] by pressing your spirit of inquiry forward [Factor 1], steadily and uninterruptedly. . . . When your searching spirit comes to this stage, the time has come for your mental flower to burst out [Factor 3].[63]

Ku-yin puts it thus:

> As you thus go on, intensely in earnest, inquiring after the inquirer himself [Factor 1], the time will most assuredly come to you when it is absolutely impossible for you to go on with your inquiry, as if you had come to the very foundation of a stream and were blocked by the mountains all around. This is the time when the tree together with the entwining wistaria breaks down, that is, when the distinction of subject and object is utterly obliterated, when the inquiring and the inquired are fused into one perfect identity [Factor 2]. Awakening from this identification, there takes place a great satori that brings peace to all your inquires and searchings [Factor 3].[64]

Of this satori, Suzuki states that "we may say that here a perception takes place in its purest and simplest form, where it is not at all tainted by intellectual analysis or conceptual reflection."[65] So whether called enlightenment, awakening, *wu, satori,* or whatever, we recognize it as the emergence of Factor 3: *prajna,* passive and non-dual awareness. Thus this form of the Ch'an-Zen tradition emphatically utilizes the three factors of active attention (Great Inquiry), stopping (Great Fixation), and passive awareness (*prajna*). As Shen Hui put it:

> If there are among you some who are still in the stage of learners, let them turn their illumination (inwards) whenever thoughts are awakened in their minds [Factor 1]. When the awakened mind is dead, the conscious illumination vanishes by itself [Factor 2]—this is the unconscious [Factor 3].[66]

And perhaps Mumon put it most succinctly:

> To realize this wondrous thing called enlightenment [Factor

3], you must look into the source of your thoughts [Factor 1], thereby annihilating them [Factor 2].[67]

The second major form of Zen meditation practiced today is that of "silent illumination (*mo chao*)," which is known in Japan as *shikan-taza,* sitting in meditation "just to sit." The famous Ch'an Master Hung Chih describes it thus:

> Silently and serenely one forgets all words;
> Clearly and vividly *That* appears. . . .
> When one realizes it, it is vast and without limit;
> In its Essence, it is pure awareness.
> Singularly reflecting in this bright awareness,
> Full of wonder in this pure reflection. . . .
> Infinite wonder permeates this serenity;
> In this Illumination all intentional efforts vanish.
> Silence is the final word.
> Reflection is the response to all [manifestation].
> Devoid of any effort,
> This response is natural and spontaneous. . . .
> The Truth of silent illumination
> Is perfect and complete.[68]

This silent illumination, devoid of any effort or conceptualization, is easily recognized as Factor 3, passive awareness. But then we are moved to ask just how does one reach this stage? Not surprisingly, the answer is that one begins *shikan-taza* by bringing the mind to a state of crystal, vigilant alertness, of intense but relaxed attention. Yasutani Roshi explains:

> Now, in shikan-taza the mind must be unhurried yet at the same time firmly planted or massively composed, like Mount Fuji let us say. But it must also be alert, stretched, like a taut bowstring. So shikan-taza is a heightened state of concentrated awareness wherein one is neither tense nor hurried, and certainly never slack. It is the mind of somebody facing death. Let us imagine that you are engaged in a duel of swordsmanship of the kind that used to take place in ancient Japan. As you face your opponent you are unceasingly watchful, set, ready. Were you to relax your vigilance even momentarily, you would be cut down instantly. A crowd gathers to see the fight. Since you are not blind you see them from the corner of your eye, and since you are not deaf you hear them. But not for an instant is your mind captured by these sense impressions.[69]

There is no question of what one should think about while doing *shikan-taza,* for in active and vigilant attention thoughts themselves do not arise, since the machinery of thought-production is *inattention.* If thoughts do arise, they are simply to be noted and then let go, and one then gently returns to the active attention of "Speak-I-am-listening." As one becomes proficient in this active attention (Factor 1), thoughts will gradually subside (Factor 2), and "silent illumination" will begin to energy (Factor 3).

We can now touch briefly on the Tien Tai school of Buddhism, and we do not have to search very far for the three factors of attention-stopping-awareness, since the two main pillars of the Tien Tai Skillful Experiment are *chih* and *kuan,* translated as "stopping" and "awareness," which are exactly our Factors 2 and 3. *Chih* (stopping) and *kuan* (awareness) are actually not peculiar to Tien Tai, for the equivalent of these two terms are found in the earliest Buddhist scriptures, and in a certain sense they form the backbone of every system of Buddhist meditation. *chih* is the Chinese equivalent of the Sanskrit and Pali *samatha* and is considered synonymous with *samadhi,* so that all in all *chih* refers to a state of image-cessation and disappearance of the subject-object dualism (i.e., the primary dualism). This is clearly Factor 2. *Kuan* is the equivalent of the Sanskrit *vipasyana* (Pali, *vipasanna*), and is synonymous with *prajna* (Pali, *panna*), so that its general sense is that of the non-dual awareness which results with the suspension of the primary dualism, and so we recognize this as Factor 3. Every school of Buddhism treats these two factors somewhat differently, and each varies slightly the emphasis it gives to each (such as which comes "first" in meditation, which is more "important," etc.—the "purer" schools of Buddhism acknowledge that both are indispensible and are to be present in equal proportions). The Tien Tai contains the most elaborate descriptions of *chih* and *kuan,* and it is for this reason that we briefly examine this school.

According to the Tien Tai, there are numerous means of reaching the state of stopping or cessation (*chih,* Factor 2), from mere concentration to a type of intellectual analysis designed to halt thought-formation. But the supposedly purest way to reach *chih,* called "embodying the real (*ti chen chih*)," entails the understanding that thoughts are devoid of reality and thus not to be followed or clung to. But the real core of "embodying the real" consists in turning inward one's attention (Factor 1), thereby cutting-off the "false-mind" of image-production (Factor 2), as the venerable Chiang Wei Chiao explains:

> The training according to the method of embodying the real consists, while sitting in meditation, in closing the eyes and in turning backward the contemplation.... The practiser should *turn inwards the contemplation to look into the thoughts that arise* [Factor 1] in his mind...; he will find that past thoughts have gone, that present ones do not stay and that future ones have not yet come.... Thus he will realize

that his false mind which so rises and falls is also unreal and devoid of reality. Gradually, he will become familiar (with this unreality) and *his false mind will then come to an end by itself* [Factor 2].[70]

Thus "embodying the real" is an efficacious method to reach the state of *chih*; it is also very similar to another Tien Tai method that is referred to the "most subtle" of the ways to reach cessation of thought. This "subtle" practice

means that we should *look into* [*the mind*] *to find out where a thought arises* [Factor 1], *thereby stopping it* [Factor 2]. . . . This method is much more subtle than fixing the mind on an object: this is a shift from a coarse to a subtle exercise.[71]

Thus, although Tien Tai uses mere concentration as a preliminary exercise, it views it as rather "coarse" compared with the more refined and efficient means of active inquiry into the very source of the imaginative-emotive processes. This active inward attention (which we recognize as Factor 1) itself leads to *chih*, to the cessation of conceptualization (Factor 2), and this in turn allows the emergence of *kuan* (Factor 3). Such are the three factors in the Tien Tai Skillful Experiment.

As for the Taoists, we have already mentioned that they lay great emphasis on "mind-fasting" or the "forgetting" of conventional and dualistic knowledge as a way to "enter" the Tao (as if one could deviate from it!) In the words of Chung Tzu:

Make your will one! Hear not with your ears, but with your mind; rather, not with your mind, but with your spirit. Let your hearing stop with the ears, and let your mind stop with its images. Let your spirit, however, be like a blank, passively responsive to externals. In such open *receptivity* only can Tao abide. And that open receptivity is the fasting of the mind.[72]

The Taoists emphasize that the fasting of the mind, which we recognize as Ffactor 2, places one in a state of open receptivity, of "blank" and passive awareness, which we recognize as Factor 3. This state of open receptivity Chung-tzu likened to using the mind as a mirror:

The perfect man employs his mind as a mirror. It grasps nothing; it refuses nothing; it receives, but does not keep.

This passive awareness, or total reflection, is not, however, a dualistic affair wherein the subject passively watches its objects, for the subject and object become one in pure awareness, as Chung-Tzu explained:

Only the truly intelligent understand this principle of identity. They do not view things as apprehended by themselves, subjectively, but transfer themselves into the position of the things viewed.[73]

This reminds one of Schroedinger's remark that "the original and the mirror-image are identical," for passive awareness is one with what it knows—no primary dualism here! Chung Tzu tells the following story:

> Yen Huei said, "I'm improving!"
> Confucius said, "How so?"
> "I've forgotten benevolence and righteousness!"
> "That's good. But you still haven't got it."
> Another day, the two met again, and
> Yen Huei said, "I'm improving!"
> "How so?"
> "I've forgotten rites and music!"
> "That's good, but you still haven't got it."
> Another day, the two met again, and Yen Huei said,
> "I'm improving!"
> "How so?"
> "I can forget myself while sitting," replied Yen Huei.
> Confucius looked startled and said,
> "What do you mean by that?"
> "I have freed myself from my body, answered Yen Huei. "I have discarded my reasoning powers. And by thus getting rid of my body and mind, I have become One with the Infinite. That is what I mean by forgetting myself while sitting."
>   "If you have become One," said Confucius, "there can be no room for bias. If you have lost yourself, there can be no more hindrance. So you really are a wise man! I trust to be allowed to follow in your steps."[74]

The actual way to reach image-less mind-fasting or self-forgetting was never really spelled out in detail by the early Taoists, for a systematic, forced, and ritual meditation practice was considered most un-Taoistic. Actually trying to forget or get rid of the "self" was considered no better than following its egotistical dictates, for, as Chung-Tzu asked, "Is not the desire to get rid of self a positive manifestation of self?" Nevertheless, it could be paradoxically said that the course to mind-fasting was to follow no special course, for at the heart of all Taoist "non-discipline" is *wu-wei,* which means no volitional activity, no intentional or forced activity, non-interference—*wu-wei* thus represents the art of letting the mind alone, of letting it move as it will, of not forcing it or restraining it, of *totally authorizing all of the mind's tendencies in a moment of perfect impartiality,* of allowing thoughts to flow just as we let the clouds drift through the sky. As we have seen, it is exactly this type of mental attitude (Factor 1) that can result in "mind-fasting" (Factor 2), and there is evidence that this is just what happened. The undisputed master of this mental *wu-wei* was Lieh Tzu, and his story shows clearly how this mental "letting-go" led to a state of mind-fasting that was above the primary dualism:

> Sit down, and I will tell you what I learned from my Master. After I had served him . . . for the space of three years, my mind did not venture to reflect on right and wrong, my lips did not venture to speak of profit and loss. Then, for the first time, my Master bestowed one glance upon me—and that was all.
>
> At the end of five years a change had taken place; my mind was reflecting on right and wrong, and my lips were speaking of profit and loss. Then, for the first time, my Master relaxed his countenance and smiled.
>
> At the end of seven years, there was another change. I let my mind reflect on what it would, but it no longer occupied itself with right and wrong. I let my lips utter whatsoever they pleased, but they no longer spoke of profit and loss. Then, at last, my Master led me in to sit on the mat beside him.
>
> At the end of nine years my mind gave free rein to its reflections, my mouth free passage to its speech. Of right and wrong, profit and loss, I had no knowledge, either as touching myself or others. I knew neither that the Master was my instructor, nor that the other man was my friend. Internal and External were blended into Unity [no primary dualism].[75]

In this state of mind-fasting (Factor 2), temporarily free of conventional and dualistic knowledge, Lieh Tzu was sitting in a Bodhimandala, which eventually revealed him to be one with Tao (Factor 3), so that "I was born this way and that on the wind, like dry chaff or leaves falling from a tree. In fact, I knew not whether the wind was riding on me or I on the wind." Lieh Tzu and his environment were non-dual, and his "riding the wind" does not imply a moronic mushy-mindedness but rather the sense of ease, spontaneity, and elation that usually accompanies "awakening," as when Suzuki was asked what *satori* felt like, he replied, "Just like ordinary experience, except about two inches off the ground!"

Chang Chan's comment on this passage from Lieh Tzu is important, because it clearly announces that the aim of this mental *wu-wei* is indeed mind-fasting:

> The question is, how to bring the mind into a state of calm, in which there is no thinking or mental activity [Factor 2]. . . . If you give yourself up to mental perfection, right and wrong will cease to exist; if the lips follow their natural law they know not profit or loss. Their ways agreeing, Master and friend sat side

by side with him on the same seat. That was only as it should be.[76]

Thus, it was by letting mind and speech alone (wu-wei), by letting them follow their own natural way, by giving a total authorization to all mental tendencies (Factor 1), that mind-fasting (Factor 2), "in which there is no thinking or mental activity," could be attained. Shen Hui would later explicitly note this connection, for—in a most profound statement—he says: "One without a purposeful intention [wu-wei] is free from conceptualization [wu-nien]."[77] In other words, the authorization of all mental tendencies without interfering with any of them (wu-wei) would itself result in no-thought (wu-nien). In sum, the "authorization of all mental tendencies" we recognize as Factor 1, which itself leads to mind-fasting, or Factor 2, and this in turn reveals the passive awareness called Tao, Factor 3.

Let us finish this survey with Wei Wu Wei, who, since he draws from the essentials of Vedanta-Ch'an-Taoism, will serve as a convenient yet most authoritative resumé. Now to understand Wei Wu Wei, we need only recall that what I am—Reality itself!—is nothing objective, nothing that can be seen, felt, touched, heard, or thought about. What I imagine to be my "perceiving self," that "little man" in my head who is supposedly reading this, who is supposedly "a subject," is actually a perceived object, for I can look at it, think about it, respect it, loathe it, improve it, etc. It thus cannot be what I am, the Perceiver, for the "perceived cannot perceive." Thus my thoughts, my mind, my body, my wishes, my hopes, my fears—those are exactly what I am not—they are all objects of perception and therefore could never be the Perceiver. As a matter of fact, it is precisely in identifying my Self exclusively with some such objects that I throw my Self into apparent bondage—this is the beginning of the spectrum of consciousness, and with each new dualism and consequent level of the spectrum, my identification becomes ever narrower and more exclusive, and thus my "bondage" becomes ever more painful, for there are more and more things that I see as belonging outside of my Self and hence as being potentially threatening. What Wei Wu Wei would have us do, therefore, is dis-identify[78] ourselves from all phenomenal, perceptible, particular and exclusive objects, therein to discover our original and timeless unity with all manifestation:

Although [Mind] is all that they [we] are—and despite the fact that in it, therefore, they have nothing to attain, grasp or possess—in order that they may "live" it in any sense apart from having objective understanding of what it is, that is, of what they are, they must de-phenomenalise themselves, dis-

> *objectify themselves, disidentify their Subjectivity from its pro-*
> *jected phenomenal* [i.e., conceptual object] *selfhood,* which is
> dominated by a concept of "I". . . . This displacement of subjec-
> tivity is from apparent object to ultimate subject in which it
> inheres, from phenomenon to noumenon. . . , from supposed
> individual to universal absolute.[79]

This dis-identification does not entail any particular action, but
rather the *understanding* that whatever I can know, see, feel, or
think about my self is precisely *not* my Self, for all those perceptions are objects and thus never Subject. It is as if my eye
identified with some of the things it saw, and to "find itself" it
would have to dis-identify with all of its objective perceptions. To
firmly understand that as the Seer I cannot be seen—*that* is the
beginning of the essential insight.

Then all we have to do is to look within and thus find the Seer?
Not quite, for if I look within and see *anything,* it will necessarily
be an *object* of perception! I am so close to It now that I cannot see It!
It is what is doing the looking, and that I can never see. As Wei Wu
Wei puts it, "No amount of looking in any direction could help you
to see what is looking." We are always already *directly in touch*
with It, but we cannot see It, name It, or think of It, for in so doing
we turn It into an illusory object! Even saying it is Absolute
Subjectivity misses the point, for then we start *thinking* about
"Absolute Subjectivity"; thus making an object out of it, imagining
what it is and where it can be found and what steps will be
necessary to get it—and those mental picture-objects parade by in
our consciousness, while the "actual" Absolute Subjectivity is that
which is watching the parade!

> How obvious the answer is! But how frustrating!—since we
> cannot think it, much less give it a name, make a word of it,
> without thereby turning it back into the object which it is not!
> The supposed mystery, so incomprehensible, is only due to
> seeking the truth as an object.

Let us take it one step further. If I do look for my Self, for
Subjectivity, for the Seer, which is no object whatsoever, then what
will I find? If my eye tries to see itself, what will it see? Totally,
completely, absolutely, it will see nothing!

> When Subject looks at itself, it no longer sees anything, for
> there cannot be anything to see, since Subject, not being an
> object as subject, cannot be seen.
>   That is the "mirror-void"—the absence of anything seen, of
> anything seeable, which Subject is.

Or again:

What is the use of looking outside? All you will see is objects!
Turn round and look within.
  Shall I then see Subject instead?
  If you did you would be looking at an object. An object is such
in whatever direction you look.
  Shall I not see myself?
  You cannot see what is not there!
  What, then, shall I see?
  Perhaps you may see the absence of yourself, which is what
is looking. It has been called "the void". . . . "The Void" is what
you can't see when you are looking for a self that isn't there.
Why is that? Because it is what is looking.

Understanding this, we are in a Bodhimandala—and It can
happen any time. We postpone our awakening, we postpone seeing
what is always already the case because we insist on retaining the
primary dualism, on seeing It as an object, as something we can
grasp or perceive, while It actually is that in us right now which is
trying to grasp and perceive!

The fact of endeavoring to conceive [It] as objects is itself
simply looking in the wrong direction, for until the habitual
mechanism of seeking to objectify every perception, to turn
every percept into an objective concept, is abandoned, or laid
aside in such contexts as these, the essential understanding
cannot begin to develop.
  We can see immediately that these so familiar emptinesses,
variously described as "the non-existent, the void, non-being,
etc." are not objects at all, can never be anything as objects, *for
they are what the perceiver of them is,* and they can neither be
seen to exist, to be, not to exist, or not to be—*for they cannot be
seen at all.*

And here is the point:

The perceiver in fact has arrived at a point in his investigation
at which he is looking at what he is himself; he has reached a
dead-end in his analysis and finds himself face to face with his
own nature, but, instead of recognizing it as such and realising
that *his void is what an eye sees when it looks at itself,* he goes
on trying to objectify what he does not see, what he can never
see, by turning it into an objective concept, like the good and
well-trained philosopher he usually is.

Thus, when I reach the point where I realize that I cannot be
perceived, where I look within and *see nothing objective whatsoever,* then I, as Perceiver, have been returned to my "original
abode." The Perceiver, the Brahman-Atman, which is nothing
objective, is exactly what I don't see when I look for myself—and
that is It! As Wei Wu Wei puts it, "It was Mind that was looking for

Mind and not finding itself as an object! And not-finding was finding!" Or "Looking for me, looking for looking, is *finding* my absence [the Void Mind]."

If you now say, "Yes, I almost understand, but I just can't quite see it," that is exactly the point! You can't see It as an object, so give up! Your very not-seeing is exactly It, and if you remain in this Bodhimandala of "not-seeing," of mind-fasting, then and there it can happen, for you are face to face with your nothingness-objective which is precisely what you are searching for. The Void that you are looking for is identical to the Void that you don't see when you look within for the Looker, so that the *sought* is the *seeker*, the *seeker* is the *sought*.

> THAT WHICH you seek and cannot find—is the Seeker.
>
> The reason why the "Dharmakaya" [Mind] cannot be found or described is that ultimately IT is the Seeker, the Describer, which is seeking—and so would be the Subject making an object of Itself.
>
> Everytime you try to name [or see or think of] THIS-HERE-NOW you are an eye trying to see itself. You cannot objectify THIS-WHICH-YOU-ARE, and that which you can objectify is THAT-WHICH-YOU-ARE-NOT.
>
> THIS which is seeking is THAT which is sought, and THAT which is sought is THIS which is seeking.

And Wei Wu Wei then quotes Padma Sambhava, the "Lotus-Born," that incredible sage who brought Buddhism to Tibet around the eighth century:

> Padma Sambhava, the supreme Master, said "There are no two such things as sought and seeker...; when fully comprehended, the sought is found to be one with the seeker. *If the seeker himself, when sought, cannot be found, thereupon is attained the goal of the seeking and also the end of the search itself.* Then nothing more is there to be sought, nor is there any need to seek anything."
>
> And the only practice is seeing this, which is Awareness, which is this which an eye cannot see when it looks for itself.

If you come away from reading Wei Wu Wei, saying "I just don't see it," then I can't tell you how very close you are! And should you continue to try to see the Seer, you are a hand trying to grab itself or lips trying to kiss themselves. "Words like this will be labeled the Supreme Swindle."

And what of the so-called objective universe—what becomes of it in this moment of pure non-objective awareness? People imagine the Void as a pure blank, where everything in the universe evaporates, leaving a monoform, featureless mush, whereas actually the

universe only ceases to be objective. The Perceiver is one with the
universe that it perceives, so that the *objective* universe as well as
my "*subjective*" self disappear into the act of pure non-dual seeing.
In Wei Wu Wei's words:

> The sought is the seeker,
> The observed is the observer thereof,
> That which is heard is the hearer of what is heard,
> The odour is who inhales it,
> The tasted is who savours what he tastes,
> That which is touched is the feeler of it,
> The thought is the thinker of the thought,
> In brief, the sensorially perceived is the perceiver whose
> senses perceive.

Seeing this, one's sense of identity explodes into *everything* that
is experienced—but then there is no separate experiencer nor
separate objects experienced, but just one encompassing and non-
dual *experiencing*. Thus, as one looks within to find the Perceiver,
he finds nothing *objective*—what he will find, however, is the
entire universe which has now ceased to appear as "an object out
there" and is instead completely felt to be identical with the Seer.
Thus is healed the Primary Dualism.[80]

It should now be rather obvious that Wei Wu Wei's skillful
Experiment is a masterful embodiment of the three factors, and so
we will simply point them out without embellishment: Active
looking within (Factor 1) results in seeing nothing (Factor 2), and
out of this Bodhimandala can emerge pure non-objective awareness (Factor 3).

We conclude, then, that the three factors are at the very heart of
every major Skillful Experiment, from Mahayana Buddhism to
Krishnamurti, from Vedanta to Taoism, and these are the factors
that we can incorporate into our lives if we desire to "reach" Mind.
To be sure, the outward forms of the three factors vary, and we in
no way wish to reduce these great *upaya* to their lowest and
therefore featureless common denominator. We only contend that,
despite these outward differences—which are not to be casually
dismissed—the psychological states induced by all are essentially
identical. Thus Benoit's active attention of "Speak-I-am-
listening," which was "a look cast on the full center of my inner
world meeting *nothing*;" Krishnamurti's complete and total attention; the complete mental authorization of the Taoist's *wu wei*; the
Self-Inquiry of Ramana and the Great Inquiry of the Zen Buddhists; as well as Wei Wu Wei's "look within to see nothing"—all
point to a state of complete attention and openness, as if one were
listening and watching for an answer from the center of one's

being, as if one were looking within to the very Source of one's consciousness. This is Factor 1, "active attention," but just because there *is no answer* in terms of mental images and objects, the mind of itself becomes quiet. The silence of Benoit and Krishnamurti, the *samadhi* and *chih* of the Mahayana Buddhists, the "mind-fasting" of the Taoists, the "disappearance of the I-thought" of Ramana, the Great Fixation of the Zen Buddhists, the "void that you don't see" of Wei Wu Wei—all point to a state of object-less silence, of the temporary suspension of the image-weaving screen of the mind, of the disruption of the primary dualism, of a profound quiet in which Reality can be received in its most nakedly direct and untranslated fashion. This is Factor 2, "Stopping," the suspension of subject vs. object, the sitting in a Bodhimandala. Out of this state, at any moment, without apparent cause or reason, it can happen: the emergence of that which has always been, of *prajna,* of Tao-awareness, of *kuan,* of non-objective seeing, of Brahman, of Mind itself. This is Factor 3, and with its emergence, the search is over.[81]

Now just as on each previous level the healing (or whole-ing) of a major dualism resulted in our assuming responsibility for facets of ourselves that we had disowned, so on the Level of Mind. Healing the quaternary dualism, we accepted responsibility for our depressions, for our anxieties, for our pressures, because we realized that these were things we were doing to ourselves. Thus identifying with these alienated aspects, they no longer stood "outside" of us to push us and threaten us, and so they ceased to be problems. Healing the tertiary dualism, we accepted responsibility for our entire organism, for our bodily feelings and our organismic actions, as well as our entire being-in-the-world, realizing that if we could not choose the fate of our being-in-the-world, we could *accept* and assume responsibility for our attitude towards that fate. Thus accepting our fate, it no longer stood "outside" of us to worry, bother, or terrify us.

And finally, healing the primary dualism, we assume responsibility for *everything* that happens to us, because now what happens to us is our own doing. This is so because my actions are the actions of the universe, and vice versa, so that when I and the universe are no longer separate, what "it" does to "me" and what "I" do to "it" are one and the same action. If a rock falls on my head, I did it. If a man shoots me in the back, I did it. If I get lung disease and painfully suffocate to death, I did it. Thus, on each level, things and events seemed to happen to me against my will, while in actuality it was I who was doing it to myself, but pretending with utmost sincerity that these things were "outside" of me. Finally, on the Level of Mind, nothing lies outside of me, so that the final word is that "there is but one will: Mine and God's." This is the inner meaning of karma, that "what happens to you is your own doing, your own *karma*,"[82] and the statement of G. S. Brown that "At this stage the universe cannot be distinguished from how we act upon it. . . ."[83]

Here, then, problems cease to be problems. It is not that they are answered by God or solved by ourselves, but that the problem itself just doesn't arise. In the words of Wittgenstein:

> When the answer cannot be put into words, neither can the question be put into words. *The riddle* does not exist. If a question can be framed at all, it is also *possible* to answer it. . . . For doubt can exist only where a question exists, a question only where an answer exists, and an answer only where something *can be said.*
>
> We feel that even when *all possible* scientific questions have been answered, the problems of life remain completely untouched. Of course there are then no questions left, and this itself is the answer.
>
> The solution of the problem of life is seen in the vanishing of the problem.[84]

Compare this with the following from G. S. Brown:

> It seems hard to find an acceptable answer to the question of how or why the world conceives a desire, and discovers an ability, to see itself, and appears to suffer in the process. That it does so is sometimes called the original mystery. Perhaps, in view of *the form* in which *we* presently *take* ourselves *to exist*, the mystery *arises from* our insistence on *framing* a question where there is, in reality, *nothing* to question.[85]

And Suzuki succinctly put it:

> That is to say, the question is answered only when it is no more asked. . . . The real answer lies where the question has not yet been asked.[86]

And the point where the "question has not yet been asked" is none other than the dimensionless point called Now, for in the Now-moment past and/future fall away, and with them, thought—since thought is based on the past and oriented towards the future. It is thus in *this Now-moment of active attention that the question—any question—ceases to arise—and just that is its ultimate solution.*

Acute and active attention to what is Now (Factor 1) results in the suspension of thought (Factor 2), because thought looks to the past for its substance and the future for its consequence. Thought is time, and hence the time-less Now is the thought-less Now—

thus silent awareness (Factor 3) emerges as I become present to the Present. This entails vigilant attention to whatever is at this moment, watching the "inner" stream of thought just as one would watch the "outer" stream of, say, a river; for ultimately the inner and outer streams are not two. "This is really all there is to contemplative mysticism—to be aware without judgement or comment of what is actually happening at this moment, both outside ourselves and within, listening even to our involuntary thoughts as if they were no more than the sound of rain. This is possible only when it is clear that there is nothing else to do, and no way on or back."[87] There is nothing else to do because there is no time to do it; there is no way on or back for there is no past or future. The answer is close, and tomorrow it will be no closer. And precisely at the point where we realize this, we cease using the present to get "somewhere else," and thus we awaken to what Coomaraswamy called "a perpetual uncalculated life in the present."

A moment's awareness is sufficient to reveal to us the fact that this "perpetual uncalculated life in the present" is exactly the type of life that we are always leading anyway, whether we realize it or not. Mystical and eternal awareness of the Now-moment is in no way other than what you are already experiencing now. We "miss" realizing this because we imagine that we should in some way try to get in touch with the Now-moment, as if it were something different from what we are already doing at THIS moment. "Now if I say that to you, what does it do to you? It may puzzle you, or it may make you say, 'Am I experiencing this moment properly? Somehow I don't seem to understand this. Therefore let me look a little more carefully at this moment to find out if that's so.' Already you've made a mistake, you see? You've tried to get away from this moment into a new moment in which you see this moment more clearly. I wasn't talking about the next moment in which you see this moment more clearly, I was talking about THIS moment before you have done anything at all to alter the situation." Of course, hearing this we try not to alter the situation, and so again we have "missed" it, for to try *not* to alter this moment also requires the next moment in which you try not to alter this moment, and yet it is still WITH THIS MOMENT that we are concerned. And hearing this we are simply confused, but only because we are always trying to use this moment to get to the next moment, to use this moment as a point of departure toward Mind. And yet in this moment, right now, we are nevertheless always arriving at Mind, we are always arriving at WHAT IS NOW, whether that be suffering, seeking, pain, joy, or simple confusion. The journey does not start Now, it ends Now, with whatever state of consciousness is present at this moment. That is the mystical state, and that we are: we do not receive the Now nor watch it nor escape it—the receiving, the watching, the escaping—all are equally it, equally a movement of the Eternal Now which we are.

But, of course, to completely awaken to the Now, to awaken from the nightmare of history, is to suffer the death of the future-less Present. "Now wonder that man is terrified," says Kierkegaard, "for between man and Truth lies mortification." Nevertheless, in the words of St. Gregory, "No one gets so much of God as the man who is thoroughly dead." And likewise Eckhart, "The Kingdom of God is for none but the thoroughly dead." Thus Ramana Maharshi declares that "You will know in due course that your glory lies where you cease to exist."

Yet this mortification, this Great Death, this total dying to the future by seeing Now-only, is not, in the words of Coomaraswamy, "sudden death" at the end of one's life, but "instant death" all through it. "The time of death," remarks T. S. Eliot, "is every moment." Yet every moment is this moment, for there is no other, and hence in this moment we are always already suffering "instant death" and thus we are always already awakening to that which has no future: To that which has no future and therefore to that which has no past; to that which has no beginning in time, and therefore to that which has no end in time; and hence to that which is Unborn, and therefore to that which is Undying.

> In this moment there is nothing which comes to be. In this moment there is nothing which ceases to be. Thus there is no birth-and-death to be brought to an end. Wherefore the absolute tranquility in this present moment. Though it is at this moment, there is no limit to this moment, and herein is eternal delight.
>
> Hui-Neng

Always already suffering death Now, we are always already living eternally. The search is always already over.

> Misty rain on Mount Lu,
> And waves surging on the river Che;
> When you have not yet been there,
> Many a regret surely you have;
> But once there and homeward you wend,
> How matter of fact things look!
> Misty rain on Mount Lu,
> And waves surging on the river Che.

REFERENCES AND NOTES

1. Trevor Legget, trans., *A First Zen Reader* (Vermont: Tuttle, 1971), p. 85.

2. J. Blofeld, trans., *The Zen Teaching of Huang Po* (New York: Grove Press, 1958), p. 107.

3. C. Chung-yuan, trans., *The Original Teachings of Ch'an Buddhism* (New York: Pantheon, 1969), p. 21.

4. From his *Cheng-tao Ke.*

5. *Spiritual Teachings of Ramana Maharshi* (Berkeley: Shambhala, 1972), p. 53.

6. Shankara's Commentary On *The Vedanta Sutras of Badarayana,* George Thibaut, trans. (New York: Dover), pp. 32-33.

7. *Spiritual Teachings,* pp. 72-73.

8. D. T. Suzuki, *Essays in Zen Buddhism,* First Series (London: Rider, 1970), p. 348.

9. Bloefeld, *Zen Teaching of Huang Po,* pp. 34, 79, 83, 112.

10. Ibid, pp. 29-30.

11. D. T. Suzuki, *Living by Zen* (London: Rider, 1972), p. 177.

12. Blofeld, *Zen Teaching of Huang Po,* p. 37.

13. Wei Wu Wei, *Open Secret* (Hong Kong: Hong Kong University Press, 1970), p. 57.

14. *Spiritual Teachings,* pp. 1-2.

15. *Summa Theologia.* I., Q. 59, A. 2.

16. J. McDermott, *The Writings of William James* (New York: Modern Library, 1968), p. 156.

17. Wei Wu Wei, *All Else Is Bondage* (Hong Kong: Hong Kong University Press, 1970), p. 19, 27.

18. Wei Wu Wei, *Ask the Awakened* (London: Routledge and Kegan Paul,1963), p. 1.

19. Wei, *Open Secret,* p. 157.

20. Suzuki, *Zen Buddhism,* First Series p. 224. Samadhi is a state of non-dual awareness.

21. Thibaut, *Shankara's Commentary,* pp. 28-32.

22. Alan Watts, *Cloud-Hidden, Whereabouts Unknown* (Pantheon, 1973), p. 159. Cf. Eckhart: "Thou shalt know him [God] without *image*, without *semblance*, and without *means*. . . . So long as this he and this I, to wit, God and the soul, are not one single here, one single now, the I cannot work with nor be one with that he." Also Ramana Maharshi: "There is neither creation nor destruction, neither destiny nor free-will; Neither path nor achievement; this is the final truth."

23. Blofeld, *Zen Teaching of Huang Po,* p. 35.

24. Since approach to Mind is usually from the Existential Level through the Primary Dualism of self vs. other, mystics of all ages have generally fallen into one of two classes, reflecting the Primary Dualism itself. The first is "jiriki," self-power, while the second is "tariki," other-power, or salvation by works vs. faith, etc. The fact is, however, that "there is nothing you can do or not do," jiriki or tariki, to "get" what always is.

25. H. Benoit, H., *The Supreme Doctrine* (New York: Viking, 1955), p. 177.

26. Ibid., pp. . 178-179.

27. Ibid., pp. 186-187. For emphasis, I have capitalized "Energy." (My italics).

28. Ibid., p. 190. (My italics).

29. Ibid., pp. 190.

30. Ibid., pp. 190-191.

31. Ibid., p. 55. (My italics).

32. Ibid., p. 196.

33. Ibid., p. 206. (My italics).

34. We are now in a position where we can finally point out that prajna is not really separate from vijnana. The two appear separate only so long as the Primary Dualism is taken for real. Thus Suzuki, who so carefully explained the difference between the two (*see* Chap. II), could nevertheless state that "prajna is vijnana and vijnana is prajna." *Studies in Zen,* p. 95. We might make this statement more palatable to rationalists by saying that vijnana is the mode of knowing characterized by dualism, and prajna is non-dual. Since, however, all dualism is illusory, what vijnana is, is actually prajna. Unity is diversity, diversity is unity.

Thus, it is not necessary to stop thought processes to awaken prajna. Rather, when we *see* through the Primary Dualism, then thought is prajna. We might say that prajna is directly experienced even while there is thinking as long as there is no thinker (or as long as the thinker is the thought, i.e., as long as the Primary Dualism is not taken for real). Thus does Wei Wu Wei define *wu-nien* as "What thinking is when there is no thinker." The distinction between vijnana and prajna is "real", however, as long as we take the Primary Dualism as "real."

For practical purposes, however, about the only way to see through the Primary Dualism is to suspend thought, whereupon it becomes obvious that there is no thinker left. Thus, Factor 2, "stopping," is in actuality the stopping of the Primary Dualism, but pragmatically it involves the stopping of thought, of symbolic-map knowledge.

Does this invalidate our equating conceptualization with objectification? That is, once the Primary Dualism is seen through, and the world is no longer perceived as objects, then shouldn't concepts also cease to arise in the Mind? No; concepts will still arise, as will "objects," but just as "objects" no longer appear "objective" (i.e., "out there"), then concepts no longer are "conceptive," (i.e., "objects of thought," as the dictionary defines it). Just as "objects" still exist, but no longer have a "separate subject," so concepts still arise, but they no longer have a "separate conceiver." The subject = object, the conceiver = the concept. Where formerly concepts seemed about the universe, they are now simply movements of the universe.

At this point we must also comment on the current interest in the two hemispheres of the brain and their connection with two complementary modes of knowing. The right hemisphere (R-H) is the seat of intuitive, holistic, arational knowledge, while the left hemisphere (L-H) is the seat of logical, rational, and analytic knowledge. See, for example, Ornstein, *Psychology of Consciousness,* which is a superb introduction to the field, even if it occasionally confuses prajna with R-H knowledge. Important as this research is, we must emphasize that the "intuition" knowledge of the R-H is not to be confused with prajna, with what we have called our second and non-dual mode of knowing. R-H knowledge is holistic, it sees "patterned wholes." In one sense, we might say prajna is holistic, but in another sense, when a Zen Master holds up a blade of grass and sees the entire universe therein, that could hardly be called a patterned whole—prajna doesn't see unity, it sees unity-diversity. R-H knowledge is also arational, but as we just explained, prajna is not arational or anti-logical; it is, perhaps, ante-logical, but never anti-logical; prajna is logic when there is no thinker. Rather, R-H knowledge and L-H knowledge both belong to dualistic knowledge, to what we have called our first mode of knowing. To be sure, they represent widely separated poles of dualistic knowledge, but they both are nevertheless dualistic. We agree with Ornstein that R-H and L-H knowledge are like the Yin and Yang, light and dark, complementary opposites, but we must never forget that "underlying" the Yin and Yang is the conciliating principle itself, namely the Tao, which is itself prajna. Thus, we must not confuse R-H knowledge with prajna, just as we would not confuse the Tao with the principle of Yin. Besides, prajna certainly cannot be located in the R-H, for as Schroedinger so rightly

pointed out, "the localization of the . . . conscious mind inside the body
is only symbolic, just an aid for practical use."

35. Shen hui, quoted in D. T. Suzuki, *The Zen Doctrine of No Mind* (London: Rider, 1970), p. 30.

36. "It is always already the case" is a phrase used extensively by Franklin Jones. *See* for example, *The Knee of Listening*, (Los Angeles; Dawn Horse, 1973).

37. J. Krishnamurti, *The First and Last Freedom* (Wheaton: Quest 1954), p. 24.

38. Ibid., p. 268-269.

39. J. Krishnamurti, *Commentaries on Living,* 1st Series (Wheaton: Quest, 1956), p. 98-99.

40. Krishnamurti, *First and Last Freedom,* pp. 170-171.

41. Ibid., p. 196. (My italics).

42. J. Krishnamurti, *Talks and Dialogues, Sydney, Australia, 1970* (Sydney: Krishnamurti Books, 1970), p. 75.

43. J. Krishnamurti, *Talks In Europe 1968* (Netherlands: Service/ Wassenaar, 1969), p. 50. (My italics).
The whole drift of Krishnamurti's non-message is admirably summed up in the Mahayana doctrine of non-abiding mind (apratistha or "no-abode" of the Vimalakirti Sutra; Mujushin or kokoro tomuna of Zen, etc.) The mind of no-abode is the fluid mind, the non-blocked mind, the un-obstructed mind, the mind without "attachments," "blocks," "stops" (tomaru). "Zen is concerned with a movement of instantaneity. . . . Whenever or wherever it [i.e., the mind] "stops"—this is the sign of being moved by something external, which is a delusion. . . ." (Takuan) "What might be called a 'psychical stoppage' comes out of a very much deeper source. When there is the slightest feeling of fear of death or attachment to life, the mind looses its 'fluidity.' The fluidity is nonhindrance. Have the mind devoid of all fear, free from all forms of attachment, and it is master of itself, it knows no hindrances, no inhibitions, no stoppages, no cloggings. It then follows its own course like water. It is like the wind that bloweth where it listeth." (Suzuki) The main "blockage" is the Primary Dualism, as Takuan notes. When there is "no subject here" (no ego) there is "no object there" (external things)—this is non-abiding, total awareness (Factor 3). "No subject here" means no ego, no Primary Dualism, no center around which this Moment is organized, and since it is by thought-memory wrongly interpreted that the Primary Dualism comes into existence, much emphasis is placed on seeing without the image, without memory. (Cf. St. John of the Cross, Eckhart, etc.) In the words of Eshin Nishimura, "If some memory remains of the mirror, the next object cannot be reflected as it really is. . . . The

ordinary self tends to keep the memory of the object once it is printed on its consciousness and to judge the next object in relation to that memory. . . . But the real self, which is a formless self, is understood always to be empty ["no subject here"] like a mirror. To live one's life at each moment with full awareness is to live in the past and future at this moment. On the other hand, to live without full awareness of this present moment, with only memory and expectation, is not one's life at all; it is death." Thought is time; awareness is eternity.

Paradoxically, the non-abiding mind is fluid yet unmoved. All objects are in a state of total flux (anicca), incessant change, while Subjectivity (prajna) is the eternally unmoved—further, they are identical. Thus the non-abiding mind moves unmoved.

44. J. Krishnamurti, *Krishnamurti in India 1970-71* (India: Krishnamurti Foundation, 1971, p. 13. (My italics).

45. Ibid. (My italics).

46. Ibid., p. 69.

47. Ibid., p. 13.

48. A. Osborne, ed., *The Collected Works of Ramana Maharshi* (London: Rider, 195)9, p. 20.

49. Ibid., p. 41.

50. Ibid., pp. 40-1. (My italics).

51. Ibid., pp. 73-75.

52. Ibid., p. 85.

53. Suzuki, *Zen Buddhism, Second Series,* p. 213.

54. There are technical differences between koan and hua tou, but in essence they are similar.

55. Suzuki, *Zen Buddhism, Second Series,* p. 117.

56. Garma C. C. Chang, *The Practice of Zen* (New York: Harper and Row Perennial, 1970), pp. 95-99.

57. Ibid.

58. Lu K'uan Yu (Charles Luk), *The Secrets of Chinese Meditation* (New York: Samuel Weiser, 1971), p. 57.

59. Lu K'uan Yu (Charles Luk), *Practical Buddhism* (London: Rider, 1972), p. 23.

60. Suzuki, *Zen Buddhism, Second Series,* p. 130.

61. Chang, *Practice of Zen,* p. 101.

62. Suzuki, *Zen Buddhism, Second Series,* p. 143.

63. Ibid., p. 131.

64. Ibid., p. 131.

65. Ibid., p. 62.

66. Suzuki, *Zen Doctrine,* p. 30.

67. *Mu-mon-kan,* case 1, translated in Philip Kapleau, *The Three Pillars of Zen* (Boston: Beacon, 1970).

68. Chang, *Practice of Zen,* p. 68. Cf. Eckhart, "God is a light shining itself in silent stillness."

69. Kapleau, *Three Pillars of Zen,* p. 54.

70. Lu, *Chinese Meditation,* p. 158. (My italics)

71. Ibid., p. 158. (My italics)

72. *Chuang Tzu,* Chap. 4. After Yutang.

73. Ibid., Chap. 2. After Giles.

74. Ibid., Chap. 6. After Watson, Yutang.

75. Lionel Giles, *Taoist Teachings* (London: John Murray, 1959), p. 38-39.

76. Ibid.

77. Cf. Eckhart, "If I were perpetually doing God's will, (wu-wei), then I would be a virgin in reality, as exempt from idea-handicaps (wu-nien) as I was before I was born."

78. Thus the strong emphasis in the orthodox tradition on detachment from all objects. Cf. Eckhart: "I have read many writings both of heathen philosophers and sages, of the Old and New Testaments, and I have earnestly and with diligence sought the best and highest virtue whereby one may come most closely to God and wherein he may once more become like the original image as he was in God when there was yet no distinction between God and himself before God produced creatures [objects]. And having dived into the basis of things to the best of my ability I find that it is no other than absolute detachment from everything that is created. . . . He who would be untouched and pure needs just one thing, detachment." (after Blakney).

This "detachment" is equally emphasized in Buddhism (detachment: anabhinivesa, Sanskrit mushujaku, Japanese wu chih chu, Chinese). Cf. also Ramana Maharshi: "Therefore complete non-attachment is the only path for him who aspires to the bliss of union with the bride Liberation." Oddly enough, true detachment obtains only when one becomes the object from which one seeks detachment. At any rate, detachment means only that, "It is not objects that one should seek to understand, but the Seer of objects." (Kausitaki Upanishad 3.8) Mind is "above" objects, "above" form: it is trans-form so that we may be transformed. This does not exclude form or objects, however, for void is form; it is in the visible yet invisible, in the divisible yet indivisible.

79. This and the following quotations from Wei Wu Wei are taken at random from his most profound books—*Open Secret, The Tenth Man, Posthumous Pieces, Ask the Awakened,* and especially, *All Else Is Bondage.* Unfortunately these books are rather hard to come by, although they can be ordered from the Buddhist Society, London. Sometimes Wei Wu Wei capitalizes "Subject, Mind," etc., whereas other times he doesn't. I have taken the liberty of capitalizing "Subject" and "Subjectivity" in certain places.

80. Let us note that the Supreme Vehicle in all traditions maintains that the Primary Dualism is healed abruptly. I Corinthians 15:51-2, "Behold, I show you a mystery; We shall not all sleep, but we shall all be changed. In a moment, in the twinkling of an eye, at the last trump . . . we shall be changed." This abrupt change is called by the Lankavatara Sutra an "asraya-paravritti" (a sudden turning-about at the very base of consciousness). With this "flip," the spectrum continues to evolve, but now it does so out of Karuna-upaya, the lila of Sambhogakaya, and not out of avidya and trishna, as previously. Tanha (trishna) becomes Karuna. Rupan na prithak sunyata sunyataya na prithag rupam. The individual levels are trans-formed into perfect expressions of prajna. Said Asanga: "When the eighth vijnana is inverted, the Mirror Wisdom is attained. When the 7th vijnana is inverted, the Universal Wisdom is attained; when the 6th vijnana is inverted, the Observing Wisdom is attained; when the remaining 5 vijnanas are inverted, the Perfecting-of-Action Wisdom is attained."

81. Mythologically, Sun and Moon, Eros and Psyche, Male and Female, Death and the Lady (who is frequently Life), enter into the Hrdaya, the cave of the heart; there they unite, they are "married," (become one). But as "to marry" also means "to die," and all death being to the future, the couple—now as one—enjoy life eternal. As for the Hrdaya, "the Heart is the same as Prajapati, it is Brahman, it is all." Brhadaranyaka Upanishad 5.3.

82. A frequent saying of A. Watts.

83. G. S. Brown, *Laws of Form* (New York: Julian Press), p. v.

84. L. Wittgenstein, *Tractatus Logico-Philosophicus* (London: Routledge and Kegan Paul, 1969), p. 149.

85. Brown, *Laws of Form,* p. 105.

86. Suzuki, *Zen Buddhism,* Third Series, p. 157.

87. Alan Watts, *Behold the Spirit* (Vintage, 1971) p. xxiii.

BIBLIOGRAPHY

Alexander, F. G., and Selesnich, S. T. *The History of Psychiatry*. New York: The New American Library (A Mentor Book), 1966.

Allport, G. *The Nature of Personality*. Addison-Wesley, 1950.

_____*Pattern and Growth in Personality*. New York: Holt, Rinehart and Winston, New York, 1961.

Alpert, R. (Baba Ram Das). *Be Here Now*. New Mexico: Lama Foundation, San Cristobal, 1971.

Andrade, E. N. da C. *An Approach to Modern Physics*. New York: Doubleday Anchor Books, 1957.

Angyal, A. *Neurosis and Treatment: A Holistic Theory*. New York: John Wiley and Sons, 1965.

Aquinas, T. *Summa Theologiae, Volume 1: The Existence of God; Volume 2: The Mind and Power of God. New York:* Doubleday and Company (Image Books), Garden City, 1969.

Arlow, J. A., and Brenner, C. *Psychoanalytic Concepts and the Structural Theory*. New York: International Universities Press, 1964.

Aronson, E. *The Social Animal*. New York: The Viking Press, 1972.

Assagioli, R. *Psychosynthesis*. New York: A Viking Compass Book, 1965.

Bahm, A. J. *Philosophy of the Buddha*. London: Rider and Company, 1958.

Bateson, G. *Steps to an Ecology of Mind*. New York: Ballantine Books, 1972.

Benedictine of Stanbrook. *Mediaeval Mystical Tradition and St. John of the Cross*. London: Burns and Oates, 1954.

Benoit, H. *The Supreme Doctrine*. New York: The Viking Press, 1955.

_____*Let Go!* London: George Allen and Unwin Ltd., 1962.

Berdyaev, N. *Spirit and Reality*. New York: 1939.

_____*Freedom and Spirit*. London.

_____*The Destiny of Man*. New York: Harper and Row (Harper Torchbook), 1966.

Bergson, H. *Time and Free Will*. New York: Harper and Row (Harper Torchbooks), 1960.

Berne, E. *Games People Play*. New York: Grove Press, 1967.

_____ *What Do You Say After You Say Hello.* New York: Bantam Book, 1974.

Bharati, A. *The Tantric Tradition.* New York: Anchor Books, Garden City, 1965.

Blake, W. *The Portable Blake.* Edited by A. Kazin. New York: The Viking Press, 1971.

Blakney, R. B., trans. *Meister Eckhart.* New York: Harper and Row (Harper Torchbooks), 1941.

Blanck, G., and Blanck, R. *Ego Psychology: Theory and Practice.* New York: Columbia University Press, 1974.

Blavatsky, H. P. *The Secret Doctrine* (An Abridgement). London: Theosophical Publishing House, 1966.

Blofeld, J. *The Tantric Mysticism of Tibet.* New York: E. P. Dutton and Company, 1970.

_____ trans. *The Zen Teaching of Huang Po.* New York: Grove Press, 1958.

_____ trans. *The Zen Teaching of Hui Hai on Sudden Illumination.* London: Rider and Company, 1969.

Bloom, A. *Shinran's Gospel of Pure Grace.* Arizona: University of Arizona Press, Tuscon, 1968.

Blum, G. S. *Psychoanalytic Theories of Personality.* New York: McGraw-Hill Book Company, 1953.

Blyth, R. H. *Zen in English Literature and Oriental Classics.* New York: E. P. Dutton and Company, Inc. 1960.

_____ *Zen and Zen Classics,* Volumes 1 - 5 Tokyo: Hokuseido Press, 1960, 1964, 1970, 1966, 1962.

Boehme, J. *Six Theosophic Points And Other Writings.* Ann Arbor: University of Michigan Press, (Ann Arbor Paperbacks), 1970.

Broad, C. D. *The Mind and its Place in Nature.* New Jersey: Littlefield, Adams and Company, Paterson, 1960.

Bronowski, J. *The Common Sense of Science.* Cambridge: Harvard University Press, 1955.

Brooks, C. *Sensory Awareness.* New York: Viking Press, 1974.

Brown, G. S. *Laws of Form.* New York: The Julian Press, 1972.

Brown, N. O. *Life Against Death–The Psychoanalytic Meaning of History.* Connecticut: Wesleyan University Press, Middletown, 1959.

_____ *Love's Body.* New York: Vintage Book, 1966.

Buber, M. *I and Thou*. New York: Charles Scribner's Son, 1958.

Bucke, R. *Cosmic Consciousness*. New York: E. P. Dutton, 1923.

Burrow, T. *Science and Man's Behavior*. New York: Greenwood Press, 1968.

Campbell, A. *Seven States of Consciousness*. New York: Perennial Library, 1974.

Campbell, J. *The Hero with a Thousand Faces*. New York: Meridian Books, 1956.

_____*The Masks of God: Primitive Mythology*. New York: Viking Compass Book, 1971.

_____*The Masks of God: Occidental Mythology*. New York: Viking Compass Book, 1971.

_____*The Masks of God: Oriental Mythology*. New York: Viking Compass Book, 1972.

_____*The Masks of God: Creative Mythology*. New York: Viking Compass Book, 1971.

Casper, Marvin. "Space Therapy and the Maitri Project", *The Journal of Transpersonal Psychology*, volume 6, no. 1, 1974.

Casteneda, C. *Journey to Ixtlan*. New York: Simon and Schuster, 1972.

Chan, W. *The Way of Lao Tzu*. New York: Bobbs-Merrill Company, 1963.

Chang, G. C. C. *The Hundred Thousand Songs of Milarepa*. New York: Harper Colophon Books, 1970.

_____*The Practice of Zen*. New York: Harper and Row (Perennial Library), 1970.

_____*The Buddhist Teaching of Totality*. Pennsylvania: The Pennsylvania State University Press, University Park, 1971.

_____trans. *Teachings of Tibetan Yoga*. New Jersey: Citadel Press, Secaucus, 1974.

Chaudhuri, H. *Philosophy of Meditation*. New York: Philosophical Library, 1965.

Ch'en, K. *Buddhism in China*. New Jersey: Princeton University Press, Princeton, 1964.

Chung-Yuan, C., trans. *Original Teachings of Ch'an Buddhism*. New York: Pantheon Books, 1969.

_____*Creativity and Taoism*. New York: Harper Colophon Books, 1970.

Commins, A., and Linscott, R. N., ed. *Man and The Universe, The Philosophers of Science*. New York: Washington Square Press, 1969.

Conze, E. *Buddhism: Its Essence and Development.* New York: Harper Torchbooks, 1959.

——*Buddhist Meditation.* New York: Harper Torchbooks, 1969.

——*Buddhist Wisdom Books.* London: Ruskin House, George Allen and Unwin Ltd., 1970.

—— *Buddhist Texts Through the Ages,*(Horner, J. B., Snellgrove, D., and Waley, A., ed.) New York: Harper Torchbooks,1964.

Cooper, D. *Psychiatry and Anti-Psychiatry,* New York: Ballatine Books, 1971.

Coomaraswamy, A. K. *Hinduism and Buddhism.* New York: Philosophical Library, 1943.

——*Time and Eternity.* Switzerland: Artibus Asial, Ascona, 1947.

——*The Bugbear of Literacy.* London: Dennis Dobson Ltd., 1949.

——*Christian and Oriental Philosophy of Art.* New York: Dover Publications, Inc., 1956.

——*The Transformation of Nature in Art.* New York: Dover Publications, Inc., 1956.

——*The Dance of Shiva.* New York: The Noonday Press, 1957.

——*Buddha and The Gospel of Buddhism.* New York: Harper Torchbooks, 1964.

——*History of Indian and Indonesian Art.* New York: Dover Publications, Inc., 1965.

——*The Mirror of Gesture.* New Delhi: Munshiram Manoharlai, 1970.

——*Elements of Buddhist Iconography.* New Delhi: Munshiram Manoharlai, 1972.

——*The Origin of the Buddha Image.* New Delhi: Munshiram Manoharlai, 1972.

——and Sister Nivedita. *Myths of the Hindus and Buddhists.* New York: Dover Publications, 1967.

Copleston, Frederick A., *History of Philosophy:* Vols.1 – 8. New York: Doubleday and Company, (Image Books), Garden City, 1962.

Coville, W. J., Costello, T. W., and Rouke, F. L. *Abnormal Psychology.* New York: Barnes and Noble, 1971.

Cowell, E. B., ed. *Buddhist Mahayana Texts.* New York: Dover Publications, Inc., 1969.

Dasgupta, Shashi B. *An Introduction to Tantric Buddhism.* California: Shambhala, Berkeley, 1974.

deBary, T., ed. *The Buddhist Tradition*. New York: Modern Library, 1969.

de Broglie, L. *The Revolution in Physics*. New York: Noonday Press, 1953.

de Chardin, T. *The Future of Man*. New York: Harper Torchbooks, 1964.

_____ *The Phenomenon of Man*. New York: Harper Torchbooks, 1965.

DeLubac, H. *Teilhard de Chardin–The Man and His Meaning*. New York: New American Library (Mentor Omega Book), 1965.

De Ropp, R. *The Master Game*. New York: Delacorte Press, 1968.

Deutsch, E. *Advaita Vedanta: A Philosophical Reconstruction*. Honolulu: East-West Center Press, 1969.

Dewey, J., and Bentley, A. F. *Knowing and the Known*. Boston: Beacon, Press, 1949.

Dostoyevsky, F. *Notes from the Underground*. New York: New American Library (Signet), 1961.

Dumoulin, H. *A History of Zen Buddhism*. Boston: Beacon Press, 1963.

Edgerton, F., trans. *The Bhagavad Gita*. New York: Harper Torchbooks, 1964.

Eisendrath, C. R. *The Unifying Moment*. Cambridge: Harvard University Press, 1971.

Eliade, M. *The Sacred and the Profane*. New York: Harvest Book, 1959.

_____ *From Primitives to Zen*. New York: Harper and Row, 1967.

_____ *Images and Symbols*. New York: Sheed and Ward (A Search Book), 1969.

Eliot, C. *Hinduism and Buddhism: An Historical Sketch,* Vols. 1-3. New York: Barnes and Noble, 1968.

Enomiya-La Salle, H. M. *Zen–Way to Enlightenment*. New York: Taplinger Publishing House, 1966.

Erikson, E. H. *Childhood and Society*. New York: W. W. Norton and Company, 1963.

_____ *Insight and Responsibility*. New York: Norton, 1964.

Evans-Wentz, W. Y. *The Tibetan Book of the Dead*. London: Oxford University Press, 1968.

_____ *The Tibetan Book of the Great Liberation*. London: Oxford University Press, 1968.

_____ *Tibetan Yoga and Secret Doctrines*. London: Oxford Universtiy Press, 1971.

Fadiman, J., and Kewman, D., ed. *Exploring Madness*. California: Brooks/Cole Publishing Company, Monerey, 1973.

Fagan, J., and Sheperd, I. L., ed. *Gestalt Therapy*. New York: Harper Colphon Books, 1970.

Feng, G-F, and English, J., trans. *Lao Tsu-Tao Te Ching*. New York: Vintage Books, 1972.

_____*Chuang Tsu-Inner Chapters*. New York: Vintage Books, 1974.

Ferenczi, S. "Stages in the Development of the Sense of Reality". In *Sex in Psychoanalysis*. Boston: Gorham Press, 1916.

Fernichel, O. *The Psychoanalytic Theory of Neurosis*. New York: W. W. Norton and Company, 1972.

Festinger, L. A. *Theory of Congnitive Dissonance*. New York: Peterson, 1957.

Feuerstein, G. *Textbook of Yoga*. London: Rider and Company, 1975.

Frank, P. *Philosophy of Science*. New Jersey: Prentice-Hall, (A Spectrum Book), Englewood Cliffs, 1957.

Frankl, V. E. *The Unconscious God*. New York: Simon and Schuster, 1975.

Fremantle, A., ed. *The Protestant Mystics*. New York: New American Library (A Mentor Book), 1965.

Frey-Rohn, L. *From Freud to Jung*. New York: A Delta Book, 1974.

Freud, A. *The Ego and the Mechanisms of Defense*. New York: International Universities Press, 1946.

Freud, S. *Three Essays on the Theory of Sexuality: Standard Edition*, Volume 7. London: Hogarth Press, 1953.

_____*Beyond the Pleasure Principle: Standard Edition*, Volume 18. London: Hogarth Press, 1955.

_____*Totem and Taboo: Standard Edition*, Volume 13. London: Hogarth Press, 1955.

_____"Instincts and Their Vicissitudes", *Standard Edition*, Volume 14. London: Hogarth Press, 1957.

_____"On Narcissism: An Introduction", *Standard Edition*, Volume 14. London: Hogarth Press, 1957.

_____*Dictionary of Psychoanalysis*. Connecticut: Fawcett Premier Book, Greenwich, 1958.

_____*Civilization and Its Discontents: Standard Edition*, Volume 20. London: Hogarth Press, 1961.

_____*The Ego and the Id: Standard Edition*, Volume 19. London: Hogarth Press, 1961.

_____*The Future of an Illusion*. New York: Doubleday Anchor Book, Garden City, 1964.

_____*The Interpretation of Dreams*. New York: Discus Book, 1965.

_____*A General Introduction to Psychoanalysis*. New York: Pocket Books, 1971.

Fromm, E. *The Sane Society*. New York: Rinehart, 1955.

_____*Psychoanalysis and Religion*. New York: Bantam Books, 1967.

_____*Suzuki, D. T., and De Martino, R. Zen Buddhism and Psychoanalysis*. New York: Harper Colophon Books, 1970.

Gardener, H. *The Quest For Mind*. New York: Vintage Books, 1972.

Giles, H. A. *Chuang Tzu*. Shanghai: Kelly and Walch, 1926.

Giles, L. *Taoist Teachings*. London: John Jurry, 1959.

Gilson, E. et al. *Saint Augustine*. Cleveland: World Publishing Company (Meridan Books), 1964.

Glasser, W. *Reality Therapy*. New York: Harper and Row, 1965.

Goble, F. G. *The Third Force*. New York: Pocket Books, 1974.

Goddard, D., ed. *A Buddhist Bible*. Boston: Beacon Press, 1966.

Goldstein, D. *The Organism*. New York: American Book, 1939.

Goleman, D. "The Buddha on Meditation and States of Consciousness, Part 1: The Teachings," *The Journal of Transpersonal Psychology*, Volume 4, No. 1, 1972.

_____"The Buddha on Meditation and States of Consciousness, Part 2: A Typology of Meditation Techniques," *The Journal of Transpersonal Psychology*, Volume 4, No. 2, 1972.

Gooch, S. *Total Man*. New York: Ballantine Books, 1974.

Gopi Krishna. *Kundalini: The Evolutionary Energy in Man*. California: Shambala Publicaitons, Berkeley, 1970.

Govinda, Lama A. *Foundations of Tibetan Mysticism*. New York: Samuel Weiser, 1973.

Graham, A. C. *The Book of Lieh-tzu*. London: John Murray, 1960.

Graham, Dom A. *Zen Catholicism*. New York: Harvest Book, 1963.

_____*Conversations: Christian and Buddhist*. New York: Harvest Book, 1968.

Groddeck, G. *The Book of It*. New York: Vintage Book, 1961.

Grof, S. "Varieties of Transpersonal Experiences: Observations from LSD Psychotherapy," *The Journal of Transpersonal Psychology,* Volume 4, No. 1, 1972.

———"Theoretical and Empirical Basis of Transpersonal Psychology and Psychotherapy: Observations from LSD Research," *The Journal Transpersonal Psychology, Volume 5, No. 1 1973.*

———*Realms of the Human Unconscious.* New York: Viking Press, 1975.

Guénon, R. *Introduction to the Study of the Hindu Doctrines.* London: Luzac and Company, 1945.

———*Man and His Becoming–According to the Vedanta.* London: Luzac and Company, 1945.

Guenther. H. V. *Buddhist Philosophy In Theory and Practice.* Maryland: Penguin Books Baltimore, 1971.

———*Treasures on the Tibetan Middle Way.* California: Shambala Publication, Berkeley, 1971.

———*Philosophy and Psychology in the Abhidharma.* California: Shambala Publications, Berkeley, 1974.

———trans. *The Life and Teaching of Naropa.* London: Oxford University Press, 1963.

———, and Kawamura, L. S., trans. *Mind in Buddhist Psychology.* California: Dharma Publishing, Emeryville, 1975.

———, and Trungpa, C. *The Dawn of Tantra.* California: Shambala, Berkeley, 1975.

Guillaumont, Puech, and Quispel, Tilland, trans. *The Gospel According to Thomas.* New York: Harper, 1959.

Hakeda, Y. S., trans. *The Awakening of Faith.* New York: Columbia University Press, 1967.

Hammond, G. B. *The Power of Self-Transcendence.* St. Louis: Bethany Press, 1966.

Harper, R. A. *Psychoanalysis and Psychotherapy.* Englewood Cliffs: Spectrum Book, 1959.

Harris, T. A. *I'm O.K.–You're O.K.* New York: Avon Books, 1969.

Hartmann, H. *Ego Psychology and the Problem of Adaptation.* New York: International Universities Press, 1958.

Hartshorne, C. *The Logic of Perfection.* Illinois: Open Court Publishing Company, 1973.

Heidegger, M. *Being and Time.* New York: Harper, 1962.

Heisenberg, W. *The Physicist's Conception of Nature*. New York: Harcourt, Brace, 1958.

_____*Physics and Philosophy: The Revolution in Modern Science*. New York: Harper, 1958.

Henry, J. *Culture Against Man*. New York: Random House, 1963.

Herberg, W., ed. *The Writings of Martin Buber*. Cleveland: World Publishing Company (Meridan Books), 1968.

Hook, S., ed. *Dimensions of Mind*. New York: Collior Books, 1973.

Horney, K. *The Neurotic Personality of Our Time*. New York: Norton Library, 1968.

_____*Self-Analysis*. New York: Norton Library, 1968.

Howe, E. G. *Cure or Heal?* London: George Allen and Unwin, 1965.

_____, and Le Mesurier, L. *The Open Way*. London: John M. Watkins, 1958.

Huang, A. C. *Embrace Tiger, Return to Mountain*. Utah: Real People Press, Moab, 1973.

Hume, R. E., trans. *The Thirteen Principal Upanishads*. London: Oxford University Press, 1974.

Humphreys, C. *A Western Approach to Zen*. London: George Allen and Unwin, 1971.

Huxley, A. *The Perennial Philosophy*. New York: Harper and Row (Harper Colophon Books), 1970.

Hyers, M. C. *Zen and the Comic Spirit*. London: Rider and Company, 1974.

Jacobi, J. *The Psychology of C. G. Jung*. London: Routledge and Kegan Paul, 1968.

James, M. R. *The Apocryphal New Testament*. London: Oxford, 1924.

James, W. *The Principles of Psychology*, Vol. 1-2. New York: Kover Publications, 1950.

_____*The Varieties of Religious Experience*. New York: Collier Books, 1961.

Johnson, H. A., and Thustrup, N., ed. *A Kierkegaard Critique*. Chicago: Henry Regnery Company (First Gateway Edition), 1967.

Johnson, R. C. *Watcher on the Hills*. New York: Harper and Row, 1959.

Johnston, W. *The Still Point*. New York: Perennial Library, 1971.

Jones, F. (Bubba Free John) *The Knee of Listening*. Los Angeles: Dawn Horse Press, 1973.

————*The Method of the Siddhas.* Los Angeles: Dawn Horse Press, 1973.

————*Garbage and the Goddess,* Edited by S. Bonder, and T. Patten. California: Dawn Horse Press, Lower Lake, 1974.

Jung, C. G. *Modern Man in Search of a Soul.* New York: Harcourt Brace, 1936.

————*Analytical Psychology: Its Theory and Practice.* New York: Vintage Book, 1968.

————*Psychology and Religion.* New Haven: Yale University, 1971.

————*Man and His Symbols.* New York: Dell Publishing Company, 1972.

————*The Portable Jung,* Edited by J. Campbell. New York: Viking Press, 1972.

————(Adler, G., Fordhamand, M., and Read, H., ed.; Hull, R.F.C., trans.) *The Collected Works of C.G. Jung,* Bolligen series XX, Princeton, Princeton University Press.
Symbols of Transformation, Collected Works 5.
Psychological Types, Collected Works 6.
Two Essays on Analytical Psychology, Collected Works 7.
The Structure and Dynamics of the Psyche, Collected Works 8.
The Archetypes and the Collective Unconscious, Collected Works 9, Part 1.
Aion—Researches into the Phenomenology of the Self, Collected Works 9, Part II.
Mysterium Coniuntionis, Collected Works 14.

Kapleau, P., ed. *The Three Pillars of Zen.* Boston: Beacon Press, 1965.

————*The Wheel of Death.* New York: Harper and Row, 1971.

Kato, B., Tamura, Y., and Meyasaka, K., trans. *The Three Fold Lotus Sutra.* New York: Weatherhill/Kosei, 1975.

Keleman, S. *Your Body Speaks Its Mind.* New York: Simon and Schuster, 1975.

Kennett, J. *Selling Water by the River.* New York: Vintage Books, 1972.

Kent, J., and Nicholls, W. *I AMness.* New York: Bobbs-Merril Company, 1972.

Kern, H., trans. *Saddharma Pundarika or the Lotus of the True Law.* New York: Dover Publications, 1963.

Kierkegaard, S. *The Concept of the Dread,* Translated by W. Lowrie. Princeton: Princeton University Press, 1944.

Koestler, A. *The Lotus and the Robot.* New York: Harper Colophon Books, 1966.

Korzybski, A. *Science and Sanity.* Connecticut: International Non-Aristotelian Library Publishing Company, Lakeville, 1948.

Krippner, S., ed. "The Plateau Experience: A. H. Maslow and Others." *The Journal of Transpersonal Psychology*, Volume 4, No., 1972.

Krishnamurti, J. *The First and Last Freedom*. Wheaton: Quest Book, 1954.

———*Commentaries on Living*, 1st, 2nd, and 3rd series. Wheaton: Quest Book, 1968.

———*Freedom from the Known*. New York: Harper and Row, 1969.

———*Talks In Europe, 1968*. Netherlands: Servire/Wassenaar, 1969.

———*Krishnamurti Talks and Dialogues*. South Australia: Griffin Press, Netley, 1970.

———*Talks and Dialogues, Sydney, Australia, 1970*. Sydney: Krishnamurti Books, 1970.

———*Krishnamurti in India, 1970-71*. India: Krishnamurti Foundation, 1971.

———*Tradition and Revolution*. India: Krishnamurti Foundation, 1972.

Kuhn, T. *The Structure of Scientific Revolutions*. Chicago: University of Chicago Press, 1962.

La Barre, W. *The Human Animal*. Chicago: University of Chicago Press, 1954.

Lacan, J. "The insistence of the letter in the unconscious," *Structuralism.*, Ehrmann, J. ed., New York: Doubleday Anchor, 1970.

Laing, R. D. *Interpersonal Perception*. New York: Perennial Library, 1966.

———*The Politics of Experience*. New York: Ballantine Books, 1967.

———*Knots*. New York: Pantheon Books, 1970.

———*The Politics of the Family*. New York: Pantheon Books, 1971.

———, and Cooper, D. G. *Reason and Violence*. New York: Vintage Book, 1971.

Legge, J., trans. *The Texts of Taoism*. New York: Julian Press, 1959.

Leggett, T., trans. *A First Zen Reader*. Vermont: Charles E. Tuttle Company, Rutland, 1971.

Leonard, G. G. *The Transformation*. New York: Delta Book, 1973.

Lévi-Strauss, C. *Structural Anthropology*. New York: Basic, 1963.

Lilly, J. C. *The Center of the Cyclone, An Autobiography of Inner Space*. New York: Julian Press, 1972.

Linssen, R. *Living Zen*. New York: Grove Press, 1960.

Loevinger, J. *Ego Development*. San Francisco: Jossey-Bass, 1976.

Lonergan, B. *Insight, A Study of Human Understanding*. New York: Philosophical Library, 1970.

Longchenpa. *Kindly Bent to Ease Us* Vols. 1 -2, (Guenther, H. V., trans.) California: Dharma Publishing, Emeryville, 1975.

Lowen, A. *The Betrayal of the Body*. New York: Macmillan, 1967.

———*The Language of the Body*. New York: Macmillan, 1967

———*Depression and the Body*. Maryland: Penguin Books Baltimore, 1973.

Luk, C. *Chán and Zen Teaching,* Series 1-3 London: Rider and Company, 1960, 1961, 1962.

———*The Secrets of Chinese Meditation*. New York, Samuel Weiser, 1971

———*Practical Buddhism*. London: Rider and Company, 1972.

———, trans. *The Surangama Sutra*. London: Rider and Company, 1969.

———, trans. *The Vimalakirti Nirdesa Sutra*. California: Shambala, Berkeley, 1972.

———*The Transmission of the Mind Outside The Teaching*. New York: Grove Press, 1975.

Maddi, S. R. *Personality Theories: A Comparative Analysis*. Illinois: Dorsey Press, Homewood, and Ontario: Irwin-Dorsey Limited, Georgetown, 1968.

Malinowski, B. *Magic, Science and Religion*. New York: Doubleday Anchor Books, Garden City, 1954.

Marcel, G. *Philosophy of Existence*. New York: Philosophical Library, 1949.

Marcuse, H. *Eros and Civilization*. Boston: Beacon, 1955.

Martin, P. W. *Experiment in Depth*. London: Routledge and Kegan Paul, 1967.

Maslow, A. H. *Toward a Psychology of Being*. New York: Van Nostrand Reinhold Company, 1968.

———*Religions, Values and Peak-Experiences*. New York: Viking Compass Book, 1970.

———*The Farther Reaches of Human Nature*. New York: Viking Compass Book, 1971.

Masters, R., and Houston, J. *The Varieties of Psychedelic Experience*. New York: Dell (Delta), 1967.

Masunaga, R., trans. *A Primer of Soto Zen.* Honolulu: East-West Center Press, 1971.

Matics, M. L., trans. *Entering the Path of Enlightenment.* London: Mac-Millan Company, 1970.

Matson, F. W. *The Broken Image.* New York: Doubleday and Company (Anchor Books), Garden City, 1966.

May, R. *Love and Will.* New York: W. W. Norton and Company, 1969.

_____*Paulus.* New York: Harper and Row, 1973.

_____ed. *Existential Psychology.* New York: Random House, 1969.

McDermott, J. J., ed. *The Writings of William James.* New York: Random House (The Modern Library), 1968.

McGovern, W. M. *An Introduction to Mahayan Buddhism.* Nagar: Sahityaratan Malakaryalaya, 1968.

McLuhan, M. *The Gutenberg Galaxy.* New York: Signet Book, 1969.

Merrell-Wolff, F. *Pathways Through to Space: A Personal Record of Transformation in Consciousness.* New York: Richard R. Smith

Merton, T. *Mystics and Zen Masters.* New York: Delta Book, 1967.

_____, comp. *The Way of Chuang Tzu.* New York: New Directions, 1969.

Mitchell, E. D. *Psychic Exploration.* New York: Capricorn Books, 1976.

Miura, I,. and Sasaki, R. F. *Zen Dust* New York: Harcourt, Brace and World, 1966.

Monroe, R. *Journeys Out of the Body.* New York: Doubleday, 1972.

Murphy, G. *Psychological Thought from Pythagoras to Freud.* New York: Original Harbinger Book, 1968.

_____, and Murphy, L. B. *Asian Psychology.* New York, Basic Books, 1968.

Murti, T. R. V. *The Central Philosophy of Buddhism.* London: George Allen and Unwin 1960.

Musès, C., and Young, A.M., ed. *Consciousness and Reality.* New York: Discus Books, 1974.

Naranjo, C., and Ornstein, R. E. *On the Psychology of Meditation.* New York: Viking Press, 1973.

Needham J. *Science and Civilization in China,* Volume 2. London: Cambridge University Press, 1956.

Needleman, J. *The New Religions*. New York:Pocket Books, 1972.

Neumann, E. *The Origins and History of Consciousness*. Princeton: Princeton University Press, 1973.

Nicholas of Cusa (Salter, E. G.), trans. *The Vision of God*. New York: Frederick Ungar Publishing Company, 1969.

Nishada, K. *Intelligibility and the Philosophy of Nothingness*. Honolulu: East-West Center Press, 1958.

Northrop, F.S.C. *The Meeting of East and West*. New York: Collier Books, 1968.

Novak, M. *The Experience of Nothingness*. New York: Harper and Row (Harper Colophon Books), 1971.

Ornstein, R. E. *The Psychology of Consciousness*. San Francisco: W. H. Freeman and Company, 1972.

Otto, R. *Mysticism East and West*. Translated by B. L. Bracey, and R. C. Payne, New York: MacMillan Company, 1960.

Ouspensky, P. D. *The Fourth Way*. New York:Knopf,

Pearce, J. C. *The Crack in the Cosmic Egg*. New York:Julian,

Pears, D. *Ludwig Wittgenstein*. New York: Viking Press, 1971.

Perls, F. S. *Ego, Hunger and Aggression*. New York: Vintage Book, 1969.

_____*Gestalt Therapy Verbatim*. California: Rea People Press, Lafayette, 1969.

_____, Hefferline, R. F., and Goodman, P. *Gestalt Therapy*. New York: Dell (Delta Book), 1951.

Peterson, S. *A Catalog of the Ways People Grow*. New York: Ballantine Books, 1971.

Piaget, J. *The Child's Conception of the World* London: Humanities Press, 1951.

_____*The Construction of Reality in the Child*. New York: Basic Books, 1954.

_____*Structuralism*. New York: Basic Books, 1970.

Polster, E., and Poster, M. *Gestalt Therapy Integrated*. New York: Vintage Books, 1974.

Prabhavandada, and Isherwood, C,. trans. *Shanhara's Crest-Jewel of Discrimination*. New York: Metor Book, 1970.

Price, A. F., and Mou-Lam, W., trans. *The Diamond Sutra and The Sutra of Hui Neng*. California: Shambala Publications, Berkeley, 1969.

Pursglove, P. D. ed. *Recognitions in Gestalt Therapy*. New York: Harper Colophon Books, 1968.

Putney, S., and Putney, G. J. *The Adjusted American: Normal Neurosis in the Individual and Society*. New York: Harper Colophon Books, 1966.

Ramana Maharshi. *The Spiritual Teaching of Ramana Maharshi*. California: Shambala, Berkeley, 1972.

_____*The Collected Works of Ramana Maharshi*. Edited by A. Osborne. London: Rider and Company, 1959.

_____*The Teachings of Bhagavan Sri Ramana Maharshi in His Own Words*. Edited by A. Osborne. London: Rider and Company, 1962.

Rank, O. *The Myth of the Birth of the Hero*. New York: Nervous and Mental Disease Publishing Company, 1914.

Reck, A. J. *The New American Philosophers*. New York: Delta Book, 1970.

Reich, W. *The Function of the Orgasm*. New York: Orgone Institute Press, 1942.

_____*Character Analysis*. New York: Farrar, Straus and Giroux, 1949.

Richardson, H. W., and Cutler, D. R., ed. *Transcendence*. Boston: Beacon Press, 1969.

Ricoeur, P. *Freud and Philosophy: An Essay on Interpretation*. New Haven: Yale University Press, 1970.

Ring, K., "A transpersonal view of consciousness," *Journal of Transpersonal Psychology*, Vol. 6, No. 2, 1974.

Rogers, C. R. *On Becoming a Person*. Boston: Houghton Mifflin, 1961.

Rossi, I., ed. *The Unconscious In Culture*. New York: E.P. Dutton and Company, 1974.

Roszak, T., ed. *Sources*. New York: Harper and Row (Harper Colophon Books), 1972.

Ruesch, J., and Bateson, G. *Communication*. New York: Norton Library, 1968.

Ruitenbeck, H. M. *Psychoanalysis and Existential Philosophy*. New York: Dutton Paperback, 1962.

Russell, B. *A History of Western Philosophy*. New York: Simon and Schuster, 1945.

Rycroft, C. *A Critical Dictionary of Psychoanalysis*. New Jersey: Littlefield, Adams and Company, Totowa, 1973.

Saint John of the Cross. *Dark Night of the Soul*. New York: Doubleday and Company (Image Books), Garden City, 1959.

———*Ascent of Mount Carmel*. Trans. and ed. E. A. Peers. New York:, Doubleday and Company (Image Books), Garden City, 1958.

Sanford, J. H., and Wrightsman, L. S., Jr. *Psychology A Scientific Study of Man*. California: Brooks/Cole Publishing Company, Belmont, 1970.

Sartre, J.P. *Existential Psychoanalysis*. Chicago: Gateway Edition, 1966.

Schaff, A. *Language and Cognition*. New York: McGraw-Hill Book Company, 1973.

Schapero, S. A. "A Classification Scheme for Out-of-Body Phenomena." In *Journal of Altered States of Consciousness*, Vol. 2, No. 3, 1975-76.

Schaya, L. *The Universal Meaning of the Kabbalah*. Maryland: Penguin Books, Baltimore, 1973.

Schroedinger, E. *My View of the World*. London: Cambridge University Press, 1964.

———*What is Life? and Mind and Matter*. London: Cambridge University Press, 1969.

Schumann, H. W. *Buddhism, An Outline of its Teaching and Schools*. London: Rider and Company, 1973.

Schuon, F. *In the Tracks of Buddhism*. London: George Allen and Unwin 1968.

———*The Transcendent Unity of Religions*. New York: Harper Torchbooks, 1975.

———*Logic and Transcendence,* trans. P. N. Townsend.

Senzaki, N., and McCandless, R. S. *Buddhism and Zen*. New York: Philosophical Library, 1953.

Sgam. Po. Pa (Guenther, H. V.), trans. *The Jewel Ornament of Liberation*. London: Rider and Company, 1970.

Shah, I. *The Way of the Sufi*. New York: Dutton Paperback, 1970.

Sharma, C. *Indian Philosophy: A Critical Survey*. London: Barner and Noble, 1962.

Shibayama, Zenkei. *A Flower Does Not Talk*. Vermont: Charles E. Tuttle Company, Rutland, 1970.

———*Zen Comments on the Mumonkan*. New York: Harper and Row, 1974.

Siu, G. H. *The Tao Science*. New York: Technology Press and John Wiley and Sons, 1957.

Skinner, B. F. *Walden Two*. New York: Macmillan, 1948.

Smith, H. "The Relation Between Religious". In *Main Currents,* Vol. 30, No. 2.

Soloman, P., and Patch, V. D. *Handbook of Psychiatry*. Canada: Lange Medical Publications, 1969.

Stcherbatsky, T. *Buddhist Logic,* Vols. 1-2. New York: Dover Publications, 1962.

_____*The Central Conception of Buddhism and the Meaning of the Word "Dharma."* India: Motilal Banarsidass, Delhi, 1970.

Strauss, A., ed. *George Herbert Mead on Social Psychology*. Chicago: University of Chicago Press, 1964.

Streng, F. J. *Emptiness—A Study in Religious Meaning*. Nashville: Abingdon Press, 1967.

Stryk, L., ed. *World of the Buddha: A Reader from the 'Three Baskets' to Modern Zen*. New York: Doubleday Anchor Book, 1969.

_____, and Ikemoto, T., ed. and trans. *Zen: Poems, Prayers, Sermons, Anecdotes Interviews*. New York: Doubleday and Company, (Anchor Books), Garden City, 1963.

Sullivan, H. S. *The Interpersonal Theory of Psychiatry*. New York: Norton, 1953.

Sullivan, J. W. N. *The Limitations of Science*. New York: Mentor Books, 1949.

Suzuki, B. L. *Mahayana Buddhism*. Toronto: MacMillan Company, 1969.

Suzuki, D. T. *Studies in Zen*. New York: Dell Publishing (A Delta Book), 1955.

_____*Manual of Zen Buddhism*. New York: Grove Press, 1960.

_____*Outlines of Mahayana Buddhism*. New York: Schocken Books, 1963.

_____*Studies in the Lankavatara Sutra*. London: Routledge and Kegan Paul, 1968.

_____*Mysticism: Christian and Buddhist*. New York: MacMillan Company, 1969.

_____*Essays in Zen Buddhism,* 1st, 2nd and 3rd Series. London: Rider and Company, 1970.

_____*Shin Buddhism*. New York: Harper and Row, 1970.

_____*The Zen Doctrine of No Mind*. London: Rider and Company, 1970.

———Zen and Japanese Culture. Princeton: Princeton University Press, 1970.

———Living by Zen. London: Rider and Company, 1972.

———, trans. The Lankavatara Sutra. London: Routledge and Kegan Paul, 1968.

Suzuki, S. Zen Mind, Beginner's Mind. New York: Walker, Weatherhill, 1970.

Swearer, D. K. Secrets of the Lotus. New York: MacMillan Company, 1971.

Takakusu, J. The Essentials of Buddhist Philosophy. Honolulu: University of Hawaii, 1956.

Tart, C. T. Altered States of Consciousness. New York: Anchor Books, Garden City, 1969.

———, ed. Transpersonal Psychologies. New York: Harper and Row, 1975.

Thera, N. The Heart of Buddhist Meditation. London: Rider and Company, 1972.

Thibaut, G. trans. The Vedànta Sutras of Bàdaryana, Parts 1 and 2. New York: Dover Publications, 1962.

Tillich, P. The Courage To Be. New Haven: Yale University Press, Connecticut, 1952.

Tohei, K. Akido in Daily Life. Tokyo: Rikugei Publishing House, 1966.

Trevor, M. H., trans. The Ox and His Herdsman. Tokyo: Hokuseido Press, Chiyoda-ku, 1969.

Trungpa, C. Cutting Through Spritual Materialism. California: Shambhala, Berkeley, 1973.

———The Myth of Freedom Shambhala, Berkeley, California, 1976.

Tsunoda, R., DeBary, W. T., and Keene, D., comp. Sources of Indian Tradition, Vol, 1. New York:, Columbia University Press, 1958.

———Sources of Chinese Tradition, Vol.1. New York: Columbia University Press, 1969.

———Sources of Japanese Tradition, Vol.1. New York: Columbia University Press, 1969.

Tulku, T., ed. Reflections of Mind. California: Dharma Publishing, Emeryville, 1975.

Underhill, E., ed. The Cloud of Unknowing. London: Stuart and Watkins, 1970.

Vivekananda, S. Raja Yoga, 2nd edition. New York: Ramadrishna-Vivekananda Center, 1956.

Van der Leeuw, J. J. *The Conquest of Illusion.* Wheaton: Quest Book, 1968.

von Bertalanffy, L. *General System Theory.* New York: George Braziller, 1968.

_____*Robots, Men and Minds.* New York: George Braziller, 1969.

von Durckheim, K. G. *The Way of Transformation.* London: George Allen and Unwin, 1971.

Waley, A. *The Way and Its Power.* New York: Grove Press, 1958.

Warren, H. C., trans. *Buddhism In Translation.* New York: Atheneum, 1970.

Wartofsky, M. W. *Conceptual Foundations of Scientific Thought.* New York: MacMillan Company, 1968.

Watson, B., trans. *The Complete Works of Chuang Tzu.* New York: Columbia University Press, 1968.

Watts, A. W. *The Way of Zen.* New York: Vintage Books, 1957.

_____*The Wisdom of Insecurity.* New York: Vintage Books, 1968.

_____*Psychotherapy East and West.* New York: Ballantine Books, 1969.

_____*The Two Hands of God.* New York: Collier Books, 1969.

_____*The Book: On the Taboo Against Knowing Who You Are.* New York: Collier Books, 1970.

_____*Myth and Ritual in Christianity.* Boston: Beacon Press, 1970.

_____*Behold the Spirit.* New York: Vintage, 1971.

_____*The Supreme Identity.* New York: Vintage Books, 1972.

Wayman, A. *The Buddhist Tantras.* New York: Samuel Weiser, 1973.

Wei Wu Wei. *Ask the Awakened.* London: Routledge and Kegan Paul, 1963.

_____*The Tenth Man.* Hong Kong: Hong Kong University Press, 1966.

_____*Posthumous Pieces.* Hong Kong University Press, Hong Kong, 1968.

_____*All Else is Bondage.* Hong Kong: Hong Kong University Press, 1970

_____*Open Secret.* Hong Kong: Hong Kong University Press, 1970.

Weil, A. *The Natural Mind.* Boston: Houghton Mifflin Company, 1972.

Weiner, H. *9½ Mystics—The Kabbala Today.* New York: Collier Books, 1973.

Weiner, N. *The Human Use of Human Beings*. New York: Doubleday (Anchor), 1956.

Welch, H. *Taoism (The Parting of the Way)*. Boston: Beacon Press, 1970.

White, J. *Everything You Want to Know About TM Including How to Do It*. New York: Pocket Books, 1976.

————, ed. *The Highest State of Consciousness*. New York: Anchor Books, Garden City, 1972.

————, ed. *What Is Meditation?* New York: Anchor Books, Garden City, 1972.

————, and Fadiman, J., ed. *Relax*. New York: Confucian Press, 1976.

White, M. *Social Thought in America*. Boston: Beacon Press, 1961.

Whitehead, A. N. *Modes of Thought*. New York: Macmillan Company (A Free Press Paperback), 1966.

————*Adventures of Ideas*. New York: Macmillan Company (The Free Press), 1967.

————*Science and the Modern World*. New York: Macmillan Company (The Free Press), 1967.

————*Process and Reality*. New York: Macmillan Company (The Free Press), 1969.

————, and Russel, B. *Principia Mathematica*. London: Cambridge University Press, 1967,

Whorf, B. L. *Collected Paper on Metalinguistics*. Washington, D. C.: Department of State, Foreign Service Institute, 1952.

————, and Carroll, J. B. ed. *Language Thought and Reality*. Cambridge: M.I.T. Press, 1956.

Whyte, L. L. *The Next Development in Man*. New York: New American Library (Mentor Books), 1950.

Wilber, K. "The Spectrum of Consciousness". In *Main Currents,* Vol. 31, No. 2, November-December, 1974.

————"Psychologia Perennis: The Spectrum of Consciousness". In *Journal of Transpersonal Psychology,* Vol 7, No. 2, 1975.

————"The Ultimate States of Consciousness". In *Journal of Altered States of Consciouness,* Vol. 2 ,No. 3, 1975-76.

Wilde, J. T., and Kimmel, W., trans. and ed. *The Search for Being*. New York: Farrar, Straus and Giroux (The Noonday Press), 1962.

Wilden, A. *Language of the Self*. New York: John Hopkins, 1968.

Wilhelm, R., trans. *The Secret of the Golden Flower*. New York: Harvest Book, 1962.

Wilson, C. *The Outsider*. New York: Houghton Mifflin, 1967.

Wing-Tsit Chan, trans. *A Source Book in Chinese Philosophy*. Princeton: Princeton University Press, 1972.

Wittgenstein, L. *Philosophical Investigations*. Oxford: B. Blackwell, 1953.

_____*Tractatus Logico Philosophicus*. London: Routledge and Kegan Paul, 1969.

Wolman, B. B. *Handbook of General Psychology*. Englewood Cliffs: Prentice-Hall, 1973.

Woodroffe, J. *The Serpent Power*. Madras: Ganesh, 1964.

Wu, J.C.H. *The Golden Age of Zen*. National War College, 1967.

Yampolsky, P. B., trans. *The Platform Sutra of the Sixth Patriarch*. New York: Columbia University Press, 1967.

_____, trans. *The Zen Master Hakuin: Selected Writings*. New York: Columbia University Press, 1971.

Yankelovich, K., and Varrett, W. *Ego and Instinct*. New York: Vintage Books, 1971.

Yu-Lan, F. *A History of Chinese Philosophy*, Vols. 1-2. Princeton: Princeton University Press, 1952, 1953.

Yutang, L. *The Wisdom of China and India*. New York: Modern Library, 1942.

Zaehner, R. C. *Zen, Drugs and Mysticism*. New York: Pantheon Books, 1972.

Zimmer, H. *Myths and Symbols in Indian Art and Civilization*. New York: Harper Torchbooks, 1962.

_____*Philosophies of India*. London: Routledge and Kegan Paul, 1969.

_____*The King and the Corpse*. Princeton: Princeton University Press, 1973.

INDEX

A

Absolute, 58, 107; *see also* Mind
Absolute Subjectivity, 82-89, 91, 100-103, 106-107, 120, 127, 148, 164, 190, 276, 293, 305, 319, 331; *see also* Mind
Abstraction, 45; *see also* knowing, first mode of
Acts of Peter, 62
Adam, and creation, 114-115
Admiration, 211
Aggression, 210
Alaya-Vijnana, 169, 268, 274
Alexander, F., 17
Ambrose, St., 262
Amphi-Existentialism, 256-257
Anandamayakosa, 166-168, 270, 271
Annamayakosa, 166-168
Anxiety, existential, 124, 258-259, 290; shadow, 204-205; transpersonal, 290-291
Aparavidya, 44
Apophatic, 56
Aquinas, St. Thomas, 56, 92, 114, 303
Archetype-Elaboration, 268-269
Archetypes, 267-273
Arieti, 153
Aristotle, 94
Asanga, 74, 169
Assagioli, 19, 193, 288
Astral-Projection, 120, 270, 275
Asvaghosha, 110, 116
Atman, 87-88, 164-168
Augustine, St., 79, 89, 92, 97-98, 100, 113
Aurobindo, 152
Avidya, 110, 162, 164
Awakening of Faith, 60, 87, 93, 110-111, 169

B

B Values, 273
Bankei, 301
Bassui, 84
Bateson, G., 25, 95, 136, 141
Being-In-The-World, 257

Benoit, H., 18, 125, 131, 183-188, 309-314
Berdyaev, N., 44, 82, 86, 208
Bergson, 45, 71
Bhagavad Gita, 24
Bija, 169, 268, 271, 272
Bijamantra, 276
Bioenergetics, 244
Biofeedback, 250
Biosocial Bands, 18, 133-136, 148-149, 225ff, 253
Biosocial Unconscious, 146, 148-149, 231-234, 241
Birth, as condition of no-past, 122-124
Blake, 72, 138
Blyth, R. H., 78, 96
Bodhimandala, 314
Bodhisattva, 299
Body, 124-125, 130-131, 250-251; *see also* Tertiary Dualism
Boethius, 99
Bohr, N., 34, 39
Brahma-Sutras, 24
Brahman, 56-57, 62-63, 72, 82, 87, 164-168, 185, 271, 276, 298; *saguna,* 56, 77, 271; *nirguna,* 57, 77, 271
Brown, G. S., 29, 40, 57, 86, 108-109, 337
Brown, N. O., 45, 124, 156, 158-159
Bucke, 19, 152
Burrow, T., 45

C

Campbell, J., 273
Castaneda, C., 133, 230
Causal-Body, 166-168, 169
Centaur, 130-131, 136, 149, 244; blocked and unblocked, 254-255; *see also* Existential Level
Chardin, T. de, 51, 152
Chih, 327-328
Christ-Only, 62, 63, 78
Chung Tzu, 62, 79, 180, 208, 328-329

369

QUEST BOOKS

are published by
The Theosophical Society in America,
a branch of a world organization
dedicated to the promotion of brotherhood and
the encouragement of the study of religion,
philosophy, and science, to the end that man may
better understand himself and his place in
the universe. The Society stands for complete
freedom of individual search and belief.
In the Theosophical Classics Series
well-known occult works are made
available in popular editions.

The subject is consciousness

QUEST BOOKS has other titles on different aspects of this fascinating topic. May we recommend:

Integral Yoga
by Haridas Chaudhuri

**Commentaries on Living,
Series I, II, and III**
by J. Krishnamurti

**Creative Meditation and
Multi-Dimensional
Consciousness**
by Lama Anagarika Govinda

An Approach to Reality
by N. Sri Ram

Available from

QUEST BOOKS
306 W. Geneva Road
Wheaton, Illinois 60187